Modern America

Modern America

———————★———————

A Documentary History of the Nation Since 1945

Gary Donaldson

EDITOR

M.E.Sharpe
Armonk, New York
London, England

Library of Congress Cataloging-in-Publication Data

Modern America : a documentary history of the nation since 1945 / Gary
Donaldson, editor.
    p. cm.
  Includes bibliographical references.
  ISBN: 978-0-7656-1537-4 (cloth: alk. paper)

  1. United States—History—1945– Sources. I. Donaldson, Gary.

E740.5.M63 2006
973.92--dc22   2006022275

Printed in the United States of America

The paper used in this publication meets the minimum requirements of
American National Standard for Information Sciences
Permanence of Paper for Printed Library Materials,
ANSI Z 39.48-1984.

BM (c)   10   9   8   7   6   5   4   3   2   1

Contents

Preface

In a well-known (and perhaps apocryphal) story, Chinese premier Zhou Enlai was once asked what he thought was the historical significance of the French Revolution. Zhou was a well-educated man and an astute student of history. His response still rings in the ears of most modern historians: "It's too soon to tell." Whether or not the story is true, it is useful. It begs a very important question: Can we study and understand modern history when we are so close to it? Is it possible to study, objectively, events that we ourselves may have experienced—events that may even have changed our own lives? The answer is, of course, yes. If history is past events, then modern history fills that bill. It is simply more difficult—but not impossible—to keep personal opinions and bias in check. It is an intellectual challenge. It is, in fact, the best of all exercises in historical detachment.

It can be argued that it is the most recent events that have most affected our lives; we are who we are (as a nation, as a people, as individuals) because of the events of the last fifty years or so. Those events, then, should be studied with the greatest of care. Otherwise, how will we know ourselves well?

In some ways, perhaps old Zhou Enlai was correct. The total impact of the French Revolution may not yet be known. However, he would certainly have agreed that we should study the events anyway, because it is modern history that has built upon the groundwork of the past and made us who we are today.

This collection of documents is designed as a supplemental reading text for courses in post–World War II American history. It should not be considered a comprehensive text. That is, not all topics (or even relevant topics) are discussed here. The documents have been chosen to give a good representation of events, to spark interest and discussion, and to establish a strong foundation for the use of primary material in the classroom. They might best be used selectively.

Each of the twenty chapters includes an introduction designed to explain the general events covered in the chapter. Each chapter contains three or four documents, and each document is introduced with a brief statement explaining its historical significance. In every case possible, the entire document is included. But, for obvious reasons, some documents have had to be abridged and edited for space considerations. In each case, great care has been taken to include as much of the document as possible, and to avoid the all-too-common "snippet," the document piece that is only a shadow of the entire thing. Three or four long documents that develop a broad-based idea or an opinion on a topic are much more useful than many snippets.

Each chapter also includes a biographical sketch of a figure germane to the events or topic covered. Most of those chosen were major players in history—the Henry Kissingers, the Barry Goldwaters. But occasionally a figure is included who was on the ground—a nurse in Vietnam, a civil rights worker. One criterion was that they all be interesting.

A series of questions follows each chapter. These are designed to stimulate thought and discussion. It is intended that not all questions can be answered only from the documents. Some answers will require further reading outside the chapter, a personal opinion from the reader in some cases, or even a broader understanding of certain historical events or ideas. Not unlike the documents themselves, the questions might best be used selectively.

At the end of each chapter is a bibliography. These recommendations for further reading are not intended to be comprehensive, but rather a starting point for further research in the area.

Modern history may not explain our origins or even our development over time, but it does tell us most about ourselves today, and about those events that most changed our lives.

Modern America

1 • Origins of the Cold War

INTRODUCTION

The end of World War II was hailed as a total American victory over the forces of evil—over the horrors of Nazism and the brutality of Japanese imperialism. All wartime goals had been realized in a complete military and moral victory. The sacrifices had been tremendous, but the war's end left the United States astride the world, free of any serious enemies, free to carry on as it wished, and free to convert its huge military-industrial complex to peaceful production that would bring jobs, products, and, all hoped, prosperity to the American people.

But it quickly became apparent that World War II, like most other wars, caused as many problems as it solved: turning victory into a stable peace would not be easy. One problem was the huge and dangerous power vacuums left by the retreating German and Japanese armies in Europe and Asia. In Eastern Europe, Soviet troops occupied every capital city except Athens. In Asia, the Red Army was in northern Iran, Manchuria, and northern Korea. Communists were trying to topple governments in China, Vietnam, Greece, Turkey, and even Italy. For most Americans, communism became the new fear, and soon became a haunting enemy.

In the aftermath of the war, misunderstandings, disagreements, provocations, and outright belligerence pitted the U.S. and the Soviets against each other. The result was a cold war, a diplomatic battleground that, in the United States, gave rise to the policy of military containment and a revulsion for appeasement. Over the next forty years, the country would become involved in hundreds of incidents and situations, large and small, across the globe for the expressed purpose of containing the spread of communism. Americans were often frustrated by these events, but through the entire era they maintained the belief that the United States had the power and the will to keep up a vigil against Soviet expansion. Between 1945 and 1948 both President Harry S. Truman and Soviet leader Josef Stalin put the mechanisms in place that would fuel and govern the cold war.

U.S. involvement in the Korean War began in June 1950, just five years after World War II ended, when North Korean troops invaded the South. Most Americans saw entry into this conflict, with a United Nations force under U.S. command, as the proper response to what seemed to be the onward march of world communism—and the impending decline of American influence abroad if the United States did not intervene and stop the communist expansion. Strictly speaking, it was not even a war. President Truman called it a "police action," and often referred to the situation in Korea as a "conflict."

However it became apparent very quickly that the Korean conflict was, in fact, a war in which the U.S. military was having a great deal of difficulty with the combined armies of North Korea and Communist China. Possibly for the first time in the nation's history, the American people began to question the abilities of their soldiers in the field. They blamed their lack of success on everything from a soft upbringing of the new generation, to the influence of "progressive" thinking. If there was blame to be laid, however, it should have been placed at the feet of decision makers who had drastically downsized the nation's conventional forces in the years after World War II in favor of air power and atomic weapons. The war pushed the Truman administration to increase military spending dramatically, with a renewed focus on conventional forces.

The Korean War raised a whole series of questions about the nature of war and warfare in the context of a "cold" war. Truman had gone to war in Korea without the formal consent of Congress. To his critics, calling it a "police action" rather than a war made little difference. That issue would have to be resolved. There was also the question of limited versus total war. Truman was determined to keep the hostilities from spreading beyond the Korean peninsula; that is, he did not want the war to escalate into a global conflict between the United States and the communist world. His commander, General Douglas MacArthur, would have none of the idea of limited warfare. Following a successful UN counteroffensive in the spring of 1951, Truman began to move toward ending the war through a negotiated peace. While Truman prepared to hold out an olive branch, MacArthur held out a sword. He spoke to the press of the need to attack China directly. On April 9, Truman fired MacArthur. The question of limited versus total war was decided.

Today, Korea is the last outpost of the cold war—just as it was the first major cold war flare-up. The war ended with the signing of a truce, not a peace treaty. And today, in what has become an almost anachronistic play, the armies of South Korea look across the cease-fire line at the armies of North Korea. South Korea has become one of the five Asian "Tigers" in the world of economic competition, while the North periodically threatens the world with nuclear war and continues to languish under socialist stagnation.

DOCUMENT 1.1
President Harry Truman's Decision to Drop the Bomb (1945)

*The dropping of the two atomic bombs on Japan in August 1945 contrib-
uted to the American image of the "Good War," a war in which the forces
of "good" surmounted an obvious "evil," with decisive and uncomplicated
results. Since Americans, generally, did not see the awful death and destruction caused by the bombs, the events appeared to be little more than a
decisive strike that ended the war and saved the lives of American soldiers.
It was also, to many Americans, payback for the horror and deception of
the Pearl Harbor attack.*

*But the bomb was more than that. Whether Truman intended it or not, the
events surrounding the development and use of the bomb caused the relationship
between Washington and Moscow to become strained. Stalin, who was, of course,
an ally of the United States and Great Britain during the war, had been left out
of the loop in the bomb's development. However, his spy network in the United
States had kept him fairly well abreast of the program (known as the Manhattan
Project) almost from the beginning. All this added to Stalin's legendary fear that
the capitalist West was conspiring to destroy the Soviet Union. Some historians
have referred to the atomic blasts as the first salvo of the cold war. To be sure, the
events surrounding the development of the bomb added to the growing distrust
between the United States and the Soviets in late 1945.*

*President Truman's decision to drop the bomb is interesting. Truman was
an intelligent man; if nothing else, he was well read in the history of the world.
But he was also a simple man. In the document below, Truman recounts his
fateful decision. For him, it was not a difficult one, as he describes it here in
his memoirs, written some ten years after the events. Years later, he said he
did not lose a wink of sleep over the decision.*

*The Hiroshima bomb killed close to 100,000 people; the Nagasaki bomb
killed about 36,000. Many more died in the following days and years from
radiation sickness and cancer. On August 9, three days after the Hiroshima
bomb was dropped and just a few hours before the Nagasaki bomb, the Soviets
entered the war against Japan by attacking Japanese troops in Manchuria.
Japan accepted surrender terms on August 14, 1945.*

SOURCE: Harry S. Truman, *1945, Year of Decisions: Memoirs by Harry S. Truman*
(New York, 1955). Reprinted by arrangement.

The historic message of the first explosion of an atomic bomb was flashed
to me in a message from Secretary of War [Henry] Stimson on the morning
of July 16. The most secret and the most daring enterprise of the war had

succeeded. We were now in the possession of a weapon that would not only revolutionize war but could alter the course of history and civilization. This news reached me at Potsdam the day after I had arrived for the conference of the Big Three.*

Stimson flew to Potsdam the next day to see me and brought with him the full details of the test. I received him at once and called in Secretary of State [James] Byrnes, Admiral [William] Leahy, General [George] Marshall, General [H.H.] Arnold, and Admiral [Ernest] King to join us at my office at the Little White House. We reviewed our military strategy in the light of this revolutionary development. We were not ready to make use of this weapon against the Japanese, although we did not know as yet what effect the new weapon might have, physically or psychologically, when used against the enemy. For that reason the military advised that we go ahead with the existing military plans for the invasion of the Japanese home islands.

At Potsdam, as elsewhere, the secret of the atomic bomb was kept closely guarded. We did not extend the very small circle of Americans who knew about it. Churchill naturally knew about the atomic bomb project from its very beginning, because it had involved the pooling of British and American technical skill.

On July 24 I casually mentioned to Stalin that we had a new weapon of unusual destructive force. The Russian Premier showed no special interest. All he said was that he was glad to hear it and hoped we would make "good use of it against the Japanese."

A month before the test explosion of the atomic bomb the service Secretaries of the Joint Chiefs of Staff had laid their detailed plans for the defeat of Japan before me for approval. . . . The Army plan envisaged an amphibious landing in the fall of 1945 on the island of Kyushu, the southernmost of the Japanese home islands. This would be accompanied by our Sixth Army, under the command of General Walter Krueger. The first landing would then be followed approximately four months later by a second great invasion, which would be carried out by our Eighth and Tenth Armies, followed by the First Army transferred from Europe, all of which would go ashore in the Kanto plains area near Tokyo. In all, it had been estimated that it would require until the late fall of 1946 to bring Japan to her knees.

This was a formidable conception, and all of us realized fully that the fighting would be fierce and the losses heavy. But it was hoped that some

---

*The "Big Three" were Truman, Soviet leader Josef Stalin, and British prime minister Winston Churchill. On July 28, in the middle of the conference, Churchill was defeated in a national election and replaced by a new prime minister, Clement Attlee, leader of the British Labour Party.

of Japan's forces would continue to be preoccupied in China and others would be prevented from reinforcing the home islands if Russia were to enter the war. . . .

The entire development of the atomic bomb had been dictated by military considerations. The idea of the atomic bomb had been suggested to President Roosevelt by the famous and brilliant Dr. Albert Einstein, and its development turned out to be a vast undertaking. It was the achievement of the combined efforts of science, industry, labor, and the military, and it had no parallel in history. The men in charge and their staffs worked under extremely high pressure, and the whole enormous task required the services of more than one hundred thousand men and immense quantities of material. It required over two and a half years and necessitated the expenditure of two and a half billions of dollars.

Only a handful of the thousands of men who worked in these plants knew what they were producing. So strict was the secrecy imposed that even some of the highest-ranking officials in Washington had not the slightest idea of what was going on. I did not. Before 1939 it had been generally agreed among scientists that it was theoretically possible to release energy from the atom. In 1940 we had begun to pool with Great Britain all scientific knowledge useful to war, although Britain was at war at the time and we were not. Following this—in 1942—we learned that the Germans were at work on a method to harness atomic energy for use as a weapon of war. This, we understood, was to be added to the V-1 and V-2 rockets with which they hoped to conquer the world. They failed, of course, and for this we can thank Providence. But now a race was on to make the atomic bomb—a race that became "the battle of the laboratories. . . ."

My own knowledge of these developments had come about only after I became President, when Secretary Stimson had given me the full story. He had told me at that time that the project was nearing completion and that a bomb could be expected within another four months. It was at his suggestion, too, that I had then set up a committee of top men and had asked them to study with great care the implications the new weapon might have for us. . . .

It was their recommendation that the bomb be used against the enemy as soon as it could be done. They recommended further that it should be used without specific warning and against a target that would clearly show its devastating strength. I had realized, of course, that an atomic bomb explosion would inflict damage and casualties beyond imagination. On the other hand, the scientific advisors of the committee reported, "We can propose no technical demonstration likely to bring an end to the war; we see no acceptable alternative to direct military use." It was their conclusion that no technical demonstration they might propose, such as over a deserted island, would be likely to bring the war to an end. It had to be used against an enemy target.

The final decision of where and when to use the atomic bomb was up to me. Let there be no mistake about it. I regarded the bomb as a military weapon and never had any doubt that it should be used. The top military advisers to the President recommended its use, and when I talked to Churchill he unhesitatingly told me he favored the use of the atomic bomb if it might aid to end the war.

In deciding to use this bomb I wanted to make sure that it would be used as a weapon of war in the manner prescribed by the laws of war. That meant that I wanted it dropped on a military target. I had told Stimson that the bomb should be dropped as nearly as possible upon a war production center of prime military importance. . . .

On July 28 Radio Tokyo announced that the Japanese government would continue to fight. There was no formal reply to the joint ultimatum to the United States, the United Kingdom, and China. There was no alternative now. The bomb was scheduled to be dropped after August 3 unless Japan surrendered before that day.

On August 6, the fourth day of the journey home from Potsdam, came the historic news that shook the world. I was eating lunch with members of the *Augusta*'s crew when Captain Frank Graham, White House Map Room watch officer, handed me the following message:

TO THE PRESIDENT
FROM THE SECRETARY OF WAR
    Big bomb dropped on Hiroshima August 5 at 7:15 p.m. Washington time. First reports indicate complete success which was even more conspicuous than earlier test.

I was greatly moved. I telephoned Byrnes aboard ship to give him the news, and then said to the group of sailors around me, "This is the greatest thing in history. It's time for us to get home. . . ."

On August 9 the second atom bomb was dropped, this time on Nagasaki. We gave the Japanese three days in which to make up their minds to surrender, and the bombing would have been held off another two days had weather permitted. During those three days we indicated that we meant business. On August 7 the 20th Air Force sent out a bomber force of some one hundred and thirty B-29's, and on the eighth it reported four hundred and twenty B-29's in day and night attacks. The choice of targets for the second atom bomb was first Kokura, with Nagasaki second. The third city on the list was Niigata, had been ruled out as too distant. By the time Kokura was reached the weather had closed in, and after three runs over the spot without a glimpse of the target, with gas running short, a try was made for the second choice, Nagasaki.

There, too, the weather had closed in, but an opening in the clouds gave the bombardier his chance, and Nagasaki was successfully bombed.

The second demonstration of the power of the atomic bomb apparently threw Tokyo into a panic, for the next morning brought the first indication that the Japanese Empire was ready to surrender.

DOCUMENT 1.2
George Kennan and the Strategy of "Containment" (1946–47)

In February 1946 George Kennan, a low-level counselor at the U.S. embassy in Moscow and an expert on Soviet affairs, sent an 8,000-word telegram to the State Department outlining what he believed to be the nature and objectives of the Soviet Union. He focused mostly on the historical antecedents of a totalitarian Soviet leadership with a history of expansionist tendencies and driven to act by ideology as well as impulses of paranoia. In this "Long Telegram," Kennan hinted at the idea that the United States should adopt a foreign policy of containment, an aggressive strategy that would contain an expansionist Soviet Union. About eighteen months later, Kennan, writing under the pseudonym "X," explained this containment strategy in an article in Foreign Affairs. *The "Long Telegram" and the "X" article are usually identified as the source of the containment strategy that remained a pillar of U.S. foreign policy throughout the cold war. However, it might also be argued that the Truman administration was already implementing a containment policy against the Soviets in several regions of the world.*

Kennan went on to head the State Department's Policy Planning Staff until 1950. In 1952 he served for a short time as ambassador to the Soviet Union. In the Kennedy administration, he was named ambassador to Yugoslavia after being passed over for a cabinet post because of his opposition to the nuclear arms race ("stop the madness," he proclaimed), and for his belief that the United States should recognize the Chinese government of Mao Zedong, a move that Kennedy believed was politically impossible.

SOURCE: X, "The Sources of Soviet Conduct." Reprinted by permission of *Foreign Affairs* XXV (July 1947), 566–82. Copyright (1946) by the Council on Foreign Relations, Inc.

Marxian ideology, in its Russian-Communist projection, has always been in process of subtle evolution. The materials on which it bases itself are extensive and complex. But the outstanding features of Communist thought as it existed in 1916 may perhaps be summarized as follows: (a) that the central factor in the life of man, the factor which determines the character of public life and the "physiognomy of society," is the system by which material goods are produced and exchanged; (b) that the capitalist system of production is a nefarious one which inevitably leads to the exploitations of the working class by the capital-owning class and is incapable of developing adequately the economic resources of society or of distributing fairly the material goods produced by human labor; (c) that capitalism contains the seeds of its own destruction and must, in view of the inability of the capital-owning class to adjust itself to economic change, result eventually and inescapably in a revolutionary transfer of power to the working class; and (d) that imperialism, the final phase of capitalism, leads directly to war and revolution.

The rest may be outlined in Lenin's own words: "Unevenness of economic and political development is the inflexible law of capitalism. It is from this that the victory of Socialism may come originally in a few capitalist countries or even in a single capitalist country. The victorious proletariat of that country, having expropriated the capitalists and having organized Socialist production at home, would rise against the remaining capitalist world, drawing to itself in the process the oppressed classes of other countries." It must be noted that there is no assumption that capitalism would perish without proletarian revolution. A final push was needed from a revolutionary proletariat movement in order to tip over the tottering structure. . . .

Now the outstanding circumstance concerning the Soviet regime is that down to the present day this process of political consolidation has never been completed and the men in the Kremlin have continued to be predominately absorbed with the struggle to secure and make absolute [the] power which they seized in 1917. They have endeavored to secure it primarily against forces at home, within Soviet society itself. But they have also endeavored to secure it against the outside world. For ideology, as we have seen, taught them that the outside world was hostile and that it was their duty eventually to overthrow the political forces beyond their borders. . . . It is an undeniable privilege of every man to prove himself right in the thesis that the world is his enemy; for if he reiterates it frequently enough and makes it the background of his conduct he is bound eventually to be right. . . .

Now the maintenance of this pattern of Soviet power, namely, the pursuit of unlimited authority domestically, accompanied by the cultivation of the semi-myth of implacable foreign hostility, has gone far to shape the actual machinery of Soviet power as we know it today. Internal organs of administration which did not serve this purpose became vastly swollen. The security of Soviet power came to rest on the iron discipline of the party, on the severity and ubiquity of the secret police, and on the uncompromising economic monopolism of the state. The "organs of suppression," in which the Soviet leaders had sought security from rival forces, became in large measure the masters of those whom they were designed to serve. Today the major part of the structure of Soviet power is committed to the perfection of the dictatorship and to the maintenance of the concept of Russia as in a state of siege, with the enemy lowering beyond the walls. And the millions of human beings who form that part of the structure of power must defend at all costs this concept of Russia's position, for without it they are themselves superfluous.

As things stand today, the rulers can no longer dream of parting with these organs of suppression. The quest for absolute power, pursued now for nearly three decades with a ruthlessness unparalleled (in scope at least) in modern times, has again produced internally, as it did externally, its own reaction. The excesses of the police apparatus have fanned the potential opposition to the regime into something far greater and more dangerous than it could have been before those excesses began. . . .

So much for the historical background. What does it spell in terms of the political personality of Soviet power as we know it today?

Of the original ideology, nothing has been officially junked. Belief is maintained in the basic badness of capitalism, in the inevitability of its destruction, in the obligation of the proletariat to assist in that destruction and to take power into its own hands. But stress has come to be laid primarily on those concepts which relate most specifically to the Soviet regime itself: to its position as the sole truly Socialist regime in a dark and misguided world, and to the relationships of power within it.

The first of these concepts is that of the innate antagonism between capitalism and Socialism. We have seen how deeply that concept has become imbedded in foundations of Soviet power. It has profound implications for Russia's conduct as a member of international society. It means that there can never be on Moscow's side . . . any powers which are regarded as capitalist. It must invariably be assumed in Moscow that the aims of the capitalist world are antagonistic to the Soviet regime, and therefore to the interests of the peoples it controls. If the Soviet government occasionally sets its signature to documents which would indicate the contrary, this is to be regarded as tactical maneuver permissible in dealing with the enemy (who is regarded without honor) and should be taken in the spirit of *caveat emptor.* Basically, the antagonism remains. It is postulated. And from it flow many of the phenomena which we would find disturbing in the Kremlin's conduct of foreign policy: the secretiveness, the lack of frankness, the duplicity, the wary suspiciousness and the basic unfriendliness of purpose. These phenomena are there to stay, for the foreseeable future. There can be variations of degree and of emphasis. When there is something the Russians want from us, one or the other of these features of their policy may be thrust temporarily into the background; and when that happens with gleeful announcements that "the Russians have changed," and some who will even try to take credit for having brought about such "changes." But we should not be misled by tactical maneuvers. These characteristics of Soviet policy, like the postulate from which they flow, are basic to the internal nature of Soviet power, and will be with us, whether in the foreground or in the background, until the internal nature of Soviet power is changed.

This means that we are going to continue for a long time to find the Russians difficult to deal with. It does not mean that they should be considered as embarked upon a do-or-die program to overthrow our society by a given date. The theory of the inevitability of the eventual fall of capitalism has the fortunate connotation that there is no hurry about it. The forces of progress can take their time in preparing the final *coup de grace*. Meanwhile, what is vital is that the "Socialist fatherland"—that oasis of power which has already been won for Socialism in the person of the Soviet Union—should be cherished and defended by all good Communists at home and abroad, its fortunes promoted, its enemies badgered and confounded. The promotion of premature, "adventuristic" revolutionary projects abroad which might embarrass Soviet power in any way would be an inexcusable, even a counterrevolutionary act. . . .

This brings us to the second of the concepts important to the contemporary Soviet outlook. That is the infallibility of the Kremlin. The Soviet concept of power, which permits no focal points of organization outside the Party itself, requites that the Party leadership remain in theory the sole repository of truth. For if truth were to be found elsewhere, there would be justification for its expression in organized activity. But it is precisely what the Kremlin cannot and will not permit.

The leadership of the Communist Party is therefore always right, and has always been right since in 1929 Stalin formalized his personal power by announcing that decisions of the Politburo were being taken unanimously. . . .

But we have seen that the Kremlin is under no ideological compulsion to accomplish its purposes in a hurry. Like the Church, it is dealing in ideological concepts which are of long-term validity, and it can afford to be patient. It has no right to risk the existing achievements of the revolution for the sake of vain baubles of the future. The very teachings of Lenin himself require great caution and flexibility in the pursuit of Communist purposes. . . .

In these circumstances it is clear that the main element of any United States policy toward the Soviet Union must be that of a long-term, patient but firm and vigilant containment of extensive tendencies. It is important to note, however, that such a policy has nothing to do with outward histrionics: with threats or blustering or superfluous gestures of outward "toughness." While the Kremlin is basically flexible in its reaction to political realities, it is by no means unamenable to considerations of prestige. Like almost any other government, it can be placed by tactless and threatening gestures in a position where it cannot afford to yield even though this might be dictated by its sense of realism. The Russian leaders are keen judges of human psychology, and as such they are highly conscious that loss of temper and of self-control is never a source of strength in political affairs. They are quick to exploit such evidences of weakness. For these reasons, it is a *sine qua non* of successful dealing with Russia that the foreign government in question should remain at all times cool and collected and that its demands on Russian policy should be put forward in such a manner as to leave the way open for a compliance not too detrimental to Russian prestige.

In the light of the above, it will be clearly seen that the Soviet pressure against the free institutions of the Western world is something that can be contained by adroit and vigilant application of counterforce at a series of constantly shifting geographical and political points, corresponding to the shifts and maneuvers of Soviet policy, but which cannot be charmed or talked out of existence. The Russians look forward to a duel of infinite duration, and they see that already they have scored great successes. It must be borne in mind that there was a time where the Communist Party represented far more of a minority in the sphere of Russian national life than Soviet power today represents in the world community. . . .

Thus the future of Soviet power may not be by any means more secure as Russian capacity for self-delusion would make it appear to the men in the Kremlin. That they can keep power themselves, they have demonstrated. That they can quietly and easily turn it over to others remains to be proved. Meanwhile, the hardships of their rule and the vicissitudes of international life have taken a heavy toll of the strength and hopes of the great people on whom their power rests. It is curious to note that the ideological power of Soviet authority is strongest today in areas beyond the frontiers of Russia, beyond the reach of its police power. . . . And who can say with assurance that the strong light still cast by the Kremlin on the dissatisfied peoples of the Western world is not the powerful afterglow of a constellation which is in actuality on the wane? This cannot be proved. And it cannot be disproved. But the possibility remains (and in the opinion of this writer it is a strong one) that Soviet power, like the capitalist world of its conception, bears within it the seeds of its own decay, and that the sprouting of these seeds is well advanced.

It is clear that the United States cannot expect in the foreseeable future to enjoy political intimacy with the Soviet regime. It must continue to regard the Soviet Union as a rival, not a partner, in the political arena. It must continue to expect that Soviet politics will reflect no abstract love of peace and stability, no real faith in the possibility of a permanent happy coexistence of the Socialist and capitalist worlds, but rather a cautious, persistent pressure toward the disruption and weakening of all rival influence and rival power. . . .

But in actuality the possibilities for American policy are by no means limited to holding the line and hoping for the best. It is entirely possible for the United States to influence by its actions the internal developments, both within Russia and throughout the international Communist movement, by which Russian policy is largely determined. This is not only a question of the modest measure of informational activity which this government can conduct in the Soviet Union and elsewhere, although that too is important. It is rather a question of the degree to which the United States can create among the peoples of the world generally the impression of a country which knows what it wants, which is coping successfully with the problems of internal life and with the responsibilities of a world power, and which has a spiritual vitality capable of holding its own among the major ideological currents of the time. To the extent that such an impression can be created and maintained, the aims of the Russian Communism must appear sterile and quixotic, the hopes and enthusiasm of Moscow's supporters must wane, and added strain must be imposed on the Kremlin's foreign policies. For the palsied decrepitude of the capitalist world is the keystone of Communist philosophy. Even the failure of the United States to experience the early economic depression which the ravens of Red Square have been predicting with such complacent confidence since hostilities ceased would have such deep and important repercussions throughout the Communist world.

By the same token, exhibitions of indecision, disunity and internal disintegration within this country have an exhilarating effect on the whole Communist movement. At each evidence of these tendencies, a thrill of hope and excitement goes through the Communist world; a new jauntiness can be noted in the Moscow tread; new groups of foreign supporters cling onto what they can only view as the bandwagon of international politics; and Russian pressure increases all along the line in international affairs.

It would be an exaggeration to say that American behavior unassisted and alone could exercise a power of life and death over the Communist movement and bring about the early fall of Soviet power in Russia. But the United States has it in its power to increase enormously the strains under which Soviet policy must operate, to force upon the Kremlin a far greater degree of moderation and circumspection than it has had to observe in recent years, and in this way to promote tendencies which must eventually find their outlet in either the breakup or the mellowing of Soviet power. For no mystical, messianic movement—particularly not that of the Kremlin—can face frustration indefinitely without eventually adjusting itself in one way or another to the logic of that state of affairs.

Thus the decision will fall in large measure on this country itself. The issue of Soviet-American relations is in essence a test of the overall worth of the United States as a nation among nations. To avoid destruction the United States need only measure up to its own best traditions and prove itself worthy of preservation as a great nation.

DOCUMENT 1.3
General Omar Bradley on the Risks of a Global War
(May 1951)

The question of limited versus total war finally came to a head when President Truman fired General Douglas MacArthur. But to many Americans (and not a few members of Congress) the question had not been resolved. Just one month after MacArthur's celebrated speech before Congress on the virtues of total war, Joint Chiefs chairman General Omar Bradley in May 1951 testified before the Senate Foreign Relations Committee on the need to contain the limited war in Korea. To Bradley, there were no advantages to expanding the war to China or to the Soviet Union. That would be, in his famous phrase, "the wrong war, at the wrong place, at the wrong time, and with the wrong enemy."

SOURCE: Statement of General of the Army Omar Bradley before the Senate Committee on Armed Services and the Senate Committee on Foreign Relations, 82d Cong., 1st sess., pt. 2, USGPO, 1951, 729–35.

Mr. Chairman and members of the committees, at the very outset, I want to make it clear that I would not say anything to discredit the long and illustrious career of General Douglas MacArthur. We may have different views on certain aspects of our government's military policy, but that is not unusual. . . .

The fundamental military issue that has arisen is whether to increase the risk of a global war by taking additional measures that are open to the United States and its allies. We now have a localized conflict in Korea. Some of the military measures under discussion might well place the United States in the position of responsibility for broadening the war and at the same time losing most if not all of our allies.

General MacArthur has stated that there are certain additional measures which can and should be taken, and that by so doing no unacceptable increased risk of global war will result. . . .

One of the great power potentials of this world is the United States of America and her allies. The other great power in this world is Soviet Russia and her satellites. As much as we desire peace, we must realize that we have two centers of power supporting opposing ideologies.

From a global viewpoint—and with the security of our nation of prime importance—our military mission is to support a policy of preventing communism from gaining the manpower, the resources, the raw materials, and the industrial capacity essential to world domination. If Soviet Russia ever controls the entire Eurasian land mass, then the Soviet-satellite imperialism may have the broad base upon which to build the military power to rule the world.

Three times in the past five years the Kremlin-inspired imperialism has been thwarted by direct action. In Berlin, Greece, and Korea, the free nations have opposed Communist aggression with a different type of action. But each time the power of the United States has been called upon and we have become involved. Each incident has cost us money, resources, and some lives.

But in each instance we have prevented the domination of one more area, and the absorption of another source of manpower, raw materials, and resources.

Korea, in spite of the importance of the engagement, must be looked upon with proper perspective. It is just one engagement, just one phase of this battle that we are having with the other power center in the world which opposes us and all we stand for. For five years this "guerrilla diplomacy" has been going on. In each of the actions in which we have participated to oppose this gangster conduct, we have risked world war III. But each time we have used methods short of total war. As costly as Berlin and Greece and Korea may be, they are less expensive than the vast destruction which would be inflicted upon all sides if a total war were to be precipitated.

I am under no illusion that our present strategy of using means short of total war to achieve our ends and oppose communism is a guarantee that a world war will not be thrust upon us. But a policy of patience and determination without provoking a world war, while we improve our military power, is one which we believe we must continue to follow.

As long as we keep the conflict within its present scope, we are holding to a minimum the forces we must commit and tie down.

The strategic alternative, enlargement of the war in Korea to include Red China, would probably delight the Kremlin more than anything else we could do. It would necessarily tie down additional forces, especially our sea power and our air power, while the Soviet Union would not be obliged to put a single man into the conflict.

Under present circumstances, we have recommended against enlarging the war. The course of action often described as a "limited war" with Red China would increase the risk we are taking by engaging too much of our power in an area that is not the critical strategic prize.

Red China is not the powerful nation seeking to dominate the world. Frankly, in the opinion of the Joint Chiefs of Staff, this strategy would involve us in the wrong war, at the wrong place, at the wrong time, and with the wrong enemy. . . .

There are many critics who have become impatient with this strategy and who would like to call for a showdown. From a purely military viewpoint, this is not desirable. We are not in the best military position to seek a showdown, even if it were the nation's desire to forfeit the chances for peace by precipitating a total war. . . .

I would not be a proponent of any policy which would ignore the military facts and rush us headlong into a showdown before we are ready. It is true that this policy of armed resistance to aggression which we pursue while we are getting stronger, often risks a world war. But so far we have taken these risks without disastrous results. . . .

There are also those who deplore the present military situation in Korea and urge us to engage Red China in a larger war to solve this problem. Taking on Red China is not a decisive move, does not guarantee the end of the war in Korea, and may not bring China to her knees. . . . I would say that from past history one would only jump from a smaller conflict to a larger deadlock at greater expense. My own feeling is to avoid such an engagement if possible because victory in Korea would not be assured and victory over Red China would be many years away. We believe that every effort should be made to settle the present conflict without extending it outside Korea. If this proves to be impossible, other measures may have to be taken.

In my consideration of this viewpoint, I am going back to the basic objective of the American people—as much peace as we can gain without appeasement.

Some critics of our strategy say if we do not immediately bomb troop concentration points and airfields in Manchuria, it is "appeasement." If we do not immediately set up a blockade of Chinese ports—which to be successful would have to include British and Russian ports in Asia—it is "appeasement." These same critics would say that if we do not provide the logistical support and air and naval assistance to launch Chinese Nationalist troops into China it is "appeasement."

These critics ignore the vital questions:

Will these actions, if taken, actually assure victory in Korea?

Do these actions mean prolongation of the war by bringing Russia into the fight?

Will these actions strip us of our allies in Korea and in other parts of the world?

From a military viewpoint, appeasement occurs when you give up something, which is rightfully free, to an aggressor without putting up a struggle, or making him pay a price. Forsaking Korea—withdrawing from the fight unless we are forced out—would be an appeasement to aggression. Refusing to enlarge the quarrel to the point where our global capabilities are diminished, is certainly not appeasement but is a militarily sound course of action under the present circumstances.

It is my sincere hope that these hearings will encourage us as a nation to follow a steadfast and determined course of action in this world, which would deny any free nation to Soviet imperialism, and at the same time preserve the peace for which so many men died in World War I, World War II, and in Greece, Indochina, Malaya, and Korea.

DOCUMENT 1.4
From Korea: Love Letters Home

Soldiers in the cold of Korea had to deal with the fear of Chinese attacks, often at night. For many soldiers, anticipating the worst, the only thing they had to grasp was the memory of a loved one. And letters home became an outlet, a touch with the life they once had and hoped they would have again when the war ended. Below is a series of three letters from soldier-in-the-field Bob Spiroff to Cassie Spiroff, his wife back in Maryland. The two had been married only a short time before Bob went off to Korea. The letters show his fears of war, but mostly they describe his anxiety of being away from his wife—and his desire to be with her again.

The fear of death in combat often caused solders to keep on their bodies a last letter home—to be sent only in the case of their deaths. Bob Spiroff carried such a letter. It is the last of the three letters below. Spiroff survived the war and the letter was never sent.

SOURCE: Bob Spiroff, and the Korean War Educator Foundation. Reprinted by permission.

December 11, 1950
My Dearest Darling,

I don't know how to start this. I don't even know if you will receive it. This is the first chance I've had to write in over a week. I can't explain everything now. All I want to do at this time [is] to let you know that I am O.K., and for you not to worry. I will try to write you a longer letter tomorrow. I've got to hurry this off, darling. The past two weeks have been nightmares—simply hell. I could never begin to explain just what happened. I'll try to in my next letter. I only hope this gets to you. I know you must be worried. Please don't dear—don't worry. Just keep loving me and praying for me. It's so cold now I can't hardly write. . . .

I hope you are O.K., Cassie. Please take care of yourself and please stay strong. All my thoughts are of you, darling, and you're the only reason that I've made it through so far.

I love you more than ever, Cassie, and more so each day.

Forever yours, Love Bob

***

January 3, 1951, 9:30 a.m.
My Dearest Darling Wife,

Honey, I don't know when I'll be able to mail this letter. I won't hardly have time to write it. I'll have to hurry. I just thought I'd let you know that so far I'm O.K., and that I still love you more than ever. Right now, darling, I'm in an old shack trying to get warmed up a little. On the hills around me I have my men all dug-in in their fox holes. We have been here two days and nights now. The Chinese are on their way. We are the outpost line. That is, we are about two miles in front of our regiment. I have fifty men with me. The enemy will hit us first—or else we will fire on them as soon as we see them, then pull back to our regiment. I hope everything works out all right. It will if they don't cut us off. (If you get this letter, then you will know that we made it O.K.) This is a very dangerous and important job for us. I just hope they don't attack us at night—for we have only one trail to use to get back to our lines. Everything else is mined and barb wired. But we will make it, darling—for we have God on our side and I have your love to guide me.

Well, dearest, I hope this finds you well. Please see my aunt and tell her this. I'll write you both the very first chance I get. 'Till then, darling, please don't worry, and remember that I love you. I will forever.

With all my love, Bob

***

In case of accident: Please deliver to Mrs. Bob Spiroff,
405 Hammonds Ferry Road, Linthicum Heights, Maryland

October 3, 1950

My darling wife,

I hope you never receive this letter—unless I show it to you myself. As I am writing this we are out on patrol. Right now we have stopped for a rest. I've had these few sheets in my pocket so I thought I'd write you this letter. I hope I get it finished in time.

My platoon has the mission of clearing out the surrounding villages of all enemy snipers who are hiding and shooting our troops one by one. Most of them are wearing civilian clothing. At the present time we have just cleared one village and are now taking a short rest before starting on the next one. This is a dangerous job, dear. Anything may happen. I hope it all goes O.K. With God's help, it will. However, darling, if anything should happen to me today—or before this war ends—and I do not return to you, please do this one thing for me. I don't want you to break down and lose all hope. I don't want you to pine your life away. Please don't, dear, for it won't help you any. I want you to get accustomed to your new life and make your mind up that you will remain strong and face the future with a strong will. You still have a lot to live for, darling. You are still young and beautiful and have a long life ahead. I know it will be awful hard for you at first, but that is the way life is. For a while you will be well set as far as money goes. You will continue receiving my pay for six months, and besides that you will collect my life insurance.

Darling Cassie, I want you to try to find someone else, for you can't go on alone—and shouldn't! Only please be careful who you choose, Cassie. Make sure it's the right one—for you deserve the best. I only hope whoever you choose will be worthy of you and appreciates you—for there is no one else like you, dear. God made only one like you, and He made you mine. . . .

So, if this is my last letter to you, my darling, I want you to know that I left this world loving you—and only you. I didn't die here on the battlefield, dear. I think I died that night in the station when I said goodbye to you.

I want to thank you over again, sweetheart, for making me the happiest man in the world by marrying me. The days we spent together, dearest, were so happy, and, Oh! So few. But those few days were a whole lifetime to me, Cassie, for right now they are the only days I remember.

My only regret, dear, is that you had to bear through all this heartache. For if you love me, as I love you, and I'm sure you do, then I know just how you must have felt all these lonesome days. I'm sorry darling for causing you all this misery. For in marrying me, dear, that is all you've had, misery and heartache. Rather, I should say, Cassie, that since we've been married, we have both had at least a month of misery for each happy day.

However, I'm asking you again to try to put that aside and start life anew.

Life is what you make it, darling, so please, for my sake, make it as bright for yourself as possible. So, in saying goodbye, my darling, I want you to remember that I love you and have loved you 'till the end. May you have a happier life in the future than you've had with me. And if there is a life "hereafter," as they say, I hope someday to see you again.

'Till then, beloved wife, I'll keep on loving you—even from afar. You're the only one.

With all my heart and soul, your husband, Bob.

BIOGRAPHICAL SKETCH
J. Robert Oppenheimer

The development of the atomic bomb was a massive undertaking that involved several thousand people. Only one man, however, is credited with being "the father of the atomic bomb," J. Robert Oppenheimer. Considering the efforts of so many talented scientists involved in the production of the bomb, it might seem unreasonable to place so much credit on the shoulders of one man. Nevertheless, to most Americans, Oppenheimer still gets top billing in that endeavor.

Oppenheimer was born in 1904 in New York City to a wealthy Jewish family. At age seventeen he entered Harvard where, a classmate said, he "intellectually looted the place." After Harvard he attended Cambridge University in England where he studied under Ernest Rutherford, and then received a Ph.D. from Göttingen University in Germany. He studied and published in quantum theory and theoretical physics, but throughout his life he maintained his interests in the classics and Eastern philosophy; he constantly contemplated the conflict between science and ethics, and national interest and personal conscience.

In 1929, Oppenheimer took positions at the University of California and then at California Institute of Technology. He was absorbed in his teaching and research, and found little time for the world beyond his university life. But in the 1930s, the rise of Nazism in Germany, and the anti-Semitism that grew with it, pushed Oppenheimer to take a strong stand against the European fascist movement. These events drew Oppenheimer into the flow of left-wing politics of the period, and he became involved with a number of left-leaning organizations, several of which had associations with the Communist Party.

By 1939, Niels Bohr and other European scientists had brought the news to the United States that a group of scientists at the Kaiser Wilhelm Institute in Germany had split the atom. The prospect that the Nazis might use this new technology to produce an atomic bomb prompted President Roosevelt to set up the Manhattan Project in 1941. The next year, Oppenheimer was named the project's scientific director, and at Oppenheimer's suggestion the project was housed at Los Alamos in New Mexico. There, Oppenheimer brought together the best minds in physics to work through the countless problems of developing an atomic bomb.

The first bomb was exploded at Alamogordo Air Force Base in southern New Mexico on July 16, 1945, with the force of something near 18,000 tons of TNT. Oppenheimer supposedly commented on the event by quoting Krishna from the Bhagavad-Gita: "I am become death, shatterer of worlds." A colleague standing next to Oppenheimer recounted the event with a more earthy tone: "Now Oppie, we're all sons-a-bitches." In August, two atomic bombs were dropped on Japan, ending the war.

After the war, Oppenheimer chaired the U.S. Atomic Energy Commission. Many close to Oppenheimer recognized that he carried with him the ethical burden of aiding in the development of a weapon that was capable of such mass destruction—a weapon that had changed the course of world events. This burden, apparently, pushed Oppenheimer to oppose the development of the hydrogen bomb—the Truman administration's answer to the Soviet acquisition of the atomic bomb in the fall of 1949. Edward Teller, Oppenheimer's colleague at Los Alamos, was named director of the new project.

Oppenheimer's refusal to be a part of the H-bomb development, and his continued criticism of it, caused some to question his patriotism—and finally to probe his past. In 1953 Oppenheimer was accused of communist sympathies because of his past associations with communist (and communist-front) organizations, and his security clearance was revoked. Through the remainder of his life he was the director of the Institute of Advanced Study at Princeton and never again influenced national policy. He died of cancer in 1967.

Oppenheimer remains a symbol of the ethical dilemma of using scientific knowledge to produce weapons of mass destruction.

STUDY QUESTIONS

1. What issues did Truman consider in making his decision to drop the bomb? Were there other things he should have (or might have) considered?

2. It was writer Studs Terkel who popularized the phrase "The Good War," in reference to World War II. How did the bomb contribute to that belief? And how might this attitude have caused the postwar years to be a time of anxiety and disappointment?

3. What is General Omar Bradley's argument for limited war in Korea? In his statement, Bradley does not mention victory. Why might that be so? Can a limited war be won? How might General Douglas MacArthur have responded?
4. Why is the Korean War often called the Forgotten War? What about it has been "forgotten?"

FURTHER READINGS

John Lewis Gaddis, *We Now Know: Rethinking Cold War History* (1998).
Walter LaFeber, *America, Russia, and the Cold War* (1991).
Melvyn P. Lefler, *A Preponderance of Power: National Security, the Truman Administration, and the Cold War* (1992).
Thomas McCormick, *America's Half-Century: United States Foreign Policy in the Cold War* (1995).
James L. Stokesbury, *A Short History of the Korean War* (1988).
William Whitney Stueck, *The Korean War: An International History* (1997).

2 • Postwar Political Trends

INTRODUCTION

The national political landscape changed dramatically in the years following World War II. Although President Harry Truman guided the nation through the last months of the war following Franklin Roosevelt's death in April 1945, his immediate postwar decisions, particularly as they related to the peacetime reconversion of the economy and the handling of labor unions and strikes, were considered by many to be harsh and too restricting. By 1946, the Republicans had retaken Congress (for the first time since 1928) and showed up on opening day with brooms, ready, it seemed, to sweep out the New Deal.

But as the 1948 campaign approached, the wily Truman took a dramatic left turn and began building a coalition of traditional liberals, African Americans in the northern cities, farmers, and organized labor. It was his overtures to a burgeoning civil rights movement that caused the greatest uproar. At the Democratic National Convention in Philadelphia, liberal Democrats forced a strong civil rights plank into the party's platform, and the Democrats took a giant step toward being the party of civil rights.

But southern whites in the party objected, and delegates from Mississippi and Alabama bolted the convention and formed the States' Rights Party—better known as the "Dixiecrats." They nominated South Carolina governor Strom Thurmond as their candidate for president. Thurmond mostly took the high road, pounding home the states' rights message that the federal government did not have the right to interfere in state affairs, while his running mate, Mississippi governor Fielding Wright, hit hard at the race issue. In November, northern African Americans voted for Truman, while most of the South stayed with the Democratic Party. Truman won reelection, but new lines were being drawn. If African Americans were going to join the Democrats, the white South might be open to cultivation by the Republicans.

Four years later, America liked retired general Dwight David Eisenhower. And Ike would be hard to beat if he decided to run. By the summer of the campaign year he returned from Europe, where he was serving as the head of NATO, and entered the campaign. Truman considered another run, but the lagging Korean War and a corruption scandal in his administration pushed him to the sidelines. The Democrats found a candidate in Illinois governor Adlai Stevenson.

Ike's choice for vice president was an ambitious anti-communist crusader, California senator Richard M. Nixon. Nixon was a leader of the effort by conservative lawmakers to find communists in the federal government, particularly in the State Department. Eisenhower, a moderate, saw Nixon as a counterbalance, making them a perfect political match for a party that was divided between moderates and conservatives.

Ike also saw the 1948 Democratic Party split as an opportunity for the Republicans to make big advances in the South. He plunged into Dixie in search of conservative votes. His overtures were successful. He carried Texas, Florida, Tennessee, Virginia, and Maryland, along with Oklahoma and Truman's own Missouri. The white South was beginning its long trek from the Reconstruction-era Democratic Solid South to the heartland of new-age Republican conservatism.

Fear of communism had become a hot political issue in the late 1940s and early 1950s. The entire era is often painted with the same brush of "McCarthyism," named after the Republican senator from Wisconsin, the man who made the pursuit of domestic communists and communist sympathizers his political cause. McCarthy deserves top billing as the primary figure of the era, but he did not organize the Red Scare, nor was he the first postwar communist hunter.

One mechanism for the postwar Red Scare was first put in place in 1938 with the establishment of the House Committee on Un-American Activities (known universally by the inaccurate acronym HUAC). The committee was designed to investigate "subversives," or radicals from both the left and the right. In 1940 the Smith Act (the Alien Registration Act) made it illegal to advocate the overthrow of the U.S. government by force. Throughout the 1940s, 1950s, and even well into the 1960s, HUAC held hearings to identify communist involvement within various national institutions. Its examination of the film industry in the late 1940s was by far the most dramatic HUAC investigation.

It is ironic that just as anti-communism was hitting its peak, membership in the American Communist Party was the lowest it had been since the 1920s. As the fear of domestic communist subversion ripped at the heart and soul of the nation, the threat itself was actually diminishing.

Eisenhower's middle-of-the-road conservatism (Modern Republicanism, he called it) remained popular through the rest of the 1950s—although the Democrats regained control of both houses of Congress after 1954. As the 1960 campaign approached, the Republican Party front-runner was naturally the vice president, Richard Nixon. Although support from Ike was not as strong as it might have been, Nixon won the nomination and the support of his party with little difficulty. The Democrats pinned their hopes on Massachusetts senator John F. Kennedy, a young war hero and the son of a large and wealthy Boston Irish Catholic family, a candidate with all the attributes necessary to beat Nixon and put the Democrats back in the White House.

Television by 1960 had finally become a universal medium, and for the first time it would play an important part in a presidential campaign. The two candidates agreed to engage in a series of televised debates. Journalist Theodore White observed these debates and wrote about them in his Pulitzer Prize–winning book on the campaign, *The Making of the President, 1960*. Kennedy's November margin of victory was one of the narrowest in the nation's history. At the same time, the new administration offered hope to many Americans for a new era.

DOCUMENT 2.1
Hubert Humphrey Calls on the Democratic Party to Champion Civil Rights (July 14, 1948)

At age thirty-seven, Hubert Humphrey was a fresh young face in the Democratic Party. The popular mayor of Minneapolis, Humphrey was preparing for a Senate run, and for a future in the party and the nation. He was a strong supporter of civil rights for African Americans. When the Republicans adopted a fairly progressive civil rights plank in their 1948 political platform, Humphrey concluded that it was time for the Democrats to step forward and give the full weight of the party to the cause of civil rights. The problem for the Democrats (as it had always been a problem for the Democrats) was sectionalism; the white South would not stand for a strong civil rights plank in the 1948 Democratic Party platform.

As Humphrey explained in his memoirs, the Democratic Party strategy on race had been, for many years, to "make a gesture toward what was right in terms of civil rights, but not so tough a gesture that the South would leave the Democratic coalition." But, he added, in 1948, "For me personally, and for the party, the time had come to suffer whatever the consequences."

At the Philadelphia convention, the strong civil rights plank supported by Humphrey and other liberals was soundly defeated in the Platform Committee by the southern delegations. But Humphrey was persuaded to take the fight to the convention floor. His speech before the convention, reprinted below, is often listed as one of the great political speeches of the postwar era. It carried the day, and the plank became a part of the 1948 platform. It also provoked the walkout of the Alabama and Mississippi delegates and finally the formation of the Dixiecrats.

Interestingly, Humphrey, later in his life, came to consider his actions at the 1948 convention a mistake. In his two runs for the presidency (in the 1960 primaries against John Kennedy and again as the party's nominee in 1968) the 1948 speech was used against him to undermine any possibility of southern support.

SOURCE: Democratic National Committee, *Official Proceedings of the Democratic National Convention* (1948), 192.

Fellow Democrats, fellow Americans:

I realize that in speaking on behalf of the minority report on civil rights . . . I am dealing with a charged issue—with an issue which has been confused by emotionalism on all sides of the fence. I realize that there are here today friends and colleagues of mine, many of them, who feel just as deeply and keenly as I do about this issue and who are yet in complete disagreement with me. . . .

Now let me say at the outset that this proposal is made with no single region [in mind]; our proposal is made for no single class, for no single racial or religious groups. . . . All of the regions of this country, all of the states have shared in the precious heritage of American freedom. All the states and all the regions have seen at least some infringements of that freedom. All people, white and black, all groups, all racial groups, have been the victims at times in this nation of . . . vicious discrimination.

The masterly statement of our keynote speaker, the distinguished United States Senator from Kentucky, Alben Barkley,* made that point with great force. Speaking of the founder of our party, Thomas Jefferson, he said this, and I quote from Alben Barkley:

"He did not proclaim that all the white, or the black, or the red, or the yellow men are equal; that all Christian or Jewish men are equal; that all Protestant and all Catholic men are equal; that all rich or poor men are equal; that all good and bad men are equal. What he declared was that all men are equal; and the equality which he proclaimed was the equality in the right to enjoy the blessings of free government in which they may participate and to which they have given their support."

Now these words of Senator Barkley's are appropriate to this conven-

---

*Alben Barkley became Harry Truman's vice president in his second term.

tion—appropriate to this convention of the oldest, the most truly progressive political party in America. From the time of Thomas Jefferson, the time of that immortal American doctrine of individual rights, under just and fairly administered laws, the Democratic Party has tried hard to secure expanding freedoms for all citizens. Oh, yes, I know, other political parties may have talked more about civil rights, but the Democratic Party has surely done more about civil rights.

We have made progress; we have made great progress in every part of this country. We've made great progress in the South; we've made it in the West, in the North, and in the East, but we must now focus the direction of that progress toward the realization of a full program of civil rights for all. This convention must set out more specifically the direction in which our party efforts are to go.

We can be proud that we can be guided by the courageous trail blazing of two great Democratic presidents. We can be proud of the fact that our great and beloved immortal leader Franklin Roosevelt gave us guidance. And we can be proud of the fact that Harry Truman has had the courage to give to the people of America the new emancipation proclamation.

It seems to me that the Democratic Party needs to make definite pledges of the kinds suggested in the confidence placed in it by the people of all races and all sections of this country. . . .

We can't use a double standard—there is no room for double standards in American politics—for measuring our own and other people's policies. Our demands for democratic practices in other lands will be no more effective than the guarantees of those practiced in our own country.

Friends, delegates, I do not believe that there can be any compromise on the guarantee of civil rights which I have mentioned in the minority report.

In spite of my desire for unanimous agreement on the entire platform, in spite of my desire to see everybody here in honest and unanimous agreement, there are some matters which I think must be stated clearly and without qualification. There can be no hedging—the newspaper headlines are wrong. There will be no hedging, and there will be no watering down—if you please—of the instruments and the principles of the civil rights program.

To those who say, my friends, that we are rushing this issue of civil rights, I say to them we are 172 years late. To those who say [that] this civil-rights program is an infringement on states' rights, I say this: the time has arrived in America for the Democratic Party to get out of the shadow of states' rights and walk forthrightly into the bright sunshine of human rights. . . .

Let us not forget the evil passions, the blindness of the past. In these times of world economic, political, and spiritual crisis, we cannot—we must not—turn from the path so plainly before us. That path has already led us through many valleys of the shadow of death. Now is the time to recall those who were left on that path of American freedom. . . .

My good friends, I ask . . . the Democratic Party, to march down the high road of progressive democracy. I ask this convention, to say in unmistakable terms that we proudly hail, and we courageously support, our President and leader Harry Truman in his great fight for civil rights in America.

DOCUMENT 2.2
House Committee on Un-American Activities Investigates Hollywood (1947)

In 1947 Ronald Reagan had still not made his celebrated transition from liberal to right-wing conservative. In fact, in the 1948 election he voted for Harry Truman. That may make Reagan's comments in the HUAC testimony below seem contradictory. But in the late-1940s, liberalism and anti-communism often went hand in hand. The Americans for Democratic Action (ADA) was organized after the war by New Deal–type liberals who opposed communism. Reagan was a founding member of that organization, along with Arthur Schlesinger, Jr., Reinhold Niebuhr, Walter Reuther, David Dubinsky, and Eleanor Roosevelt. Only in the early 1950s, as an Eisenhower supporter, did Reagan move into the Republican Party. Then, through the 1950s, he shifted to the right on economic and social issues and emerged as the leader of his party's right wing following Barry Goldwater's defeat in 1964.

The members of HUAC undoubtedly considered it their duty to rid the nation of communist influence and activity. The 1947 HUAC investigation in Hollywood was designed to uncover communist activity in the film industry under the assumption that film, in the hands of a few "subversives," might have some destructive or corrupting influence on the nation. HUAC investigated numerous industries, but because of Hollywood's high profile, it became the best-known target of the committee. The Hollywood interviews began with several "friendly" witnesses. Reagan fit that category, along with Walt Disney, Robert Montgomery, Gary Cooper (who said he didn't think communism was "on the level"), Robert Taylor, and Louis B. Mayer. Nineteen "unfriendly" witnesses were then subpoenaed. The committee undoubtedly had predetermined that these witnesses were communists, had been communists, or knew something incriminating about communists. The big question, the one that rang in the ears of many witnesses for years to come, was "Are you now, or have you ever been, a member of the Communist Party?"

Of the nineteen, only eleven were called to testify. Ten refused to answer questions. German playwright Bertolt Brecht claimed never to have been a communist and then immediately returned to East Berlin. The remaining witnesses became the celebrated Hollywood Ten. One director (Edward Dmytryk) and nine screenwriters (John Howard Lawson, Dalton Trumbo, Albert Maltz, Alvah Bessie, Samuel Ornitz, Herbert Biberman, Adrian Scott, Ring Lardner, Jr., and Lester Cole) were held in contempt for choosing the Fifth Amendment as their defense and served between six and twelve months in jail. The committee's sentences were upheld by the courts upon appeal. Dmytryk agreed to cooperate with the committee and did not serve his entire sentence. The other nine were blacklisted. Trumbo (and possibly others) continued their careers by writing screenplays under pseudonyms.

SOURCE: House Committee on Un-American Activities, *Hearings Regarding the Communist Infiltration of the Motion Picture Industry*, 80th Congress, 1st Sess., 1947.

Testimony of Actor Ronald Reagan

[Chief Counsel] **Mr.** [Robert] **Stripling:** Are you the president of the [Screen Actors] Guild at the present time?

Mr. Reagan: Yes, sir. . . .

Mr. Stripling: As a member of the board of directors, as president of the Screen Actors Guild, and as an active member, have you at any time observed or noted within the organization a clique of either Communists or fascists who were attempting to exert influence or pressure on the guild?

Mr. Reagan: Well, sir, my testimony must be very similar to that of Mr. [George] Murphy and Mr. [Robert] Montgomery. There has been a small group within the Screen Actors Guild which has consistently opposed the policy of the guild board and officers of the guild, as evidenced by the vote on various issues. The small clique referred to has been suspected of more or less following the tactics that we associated with the Communist Party. . . .

Mr. Stripling: Would you say that this clique has attempted to dominate the guild?

Mr. Reagan: Well, sir, by attempting to put over their own particular views on various issues, I guess you would have to say that our side was attempting to dominate, too, because we were fighting just as hard to put over our views, and I think we were proven correct by the figures—Mr. Murphy gave the figures—and those figures were always approximately the same, an average of ninety percent or better of the Screen Actors Guild voted in favor of those matters [that are] now guild policy.

Mr. Stripling: Mr. Reagan, there has been testimony to the effect here that numerous Communist-front organizations have been set up in Hollywood. Have you ever been solicited to join any of those organizations or any organization which you considered to be a Communist-front organization?

Mr. Reagan: Well, sir, I have received literature from an organization called the Committee for a Far-Eastern Democratic Policy. I don't know whether it is Communist or not. I only know that I didn't like their views and as a result I didn't want to have anything to do with them. . . .

Mr. Stripling: Mr. Reagan, what is your feeling about what steps should be taken to rid the motion picture industry of any Communist influence?

Mr. Reagan: Well, sir, 99 percent of us are pretty well aware of what is going on, and I think, within the bounds of our democratic rights and never once stepping over the rights given us by democracy, we have done a pretty good job in our business of keeping those people's activities curtailed. After all, we must recognize them at present as a political party. On that basis we have exposed their lies when we came across them, we have opposed their propaganda, and I can certainly testify that in the case of the Screen Actors Guild we have been eminently successful in preventing them from, and with their usual tactics, trying to run a majority of an organization with a well-organized minority. In opposing those people, the best thing to do is make democracy work. In the Screen Actors Guild we make it work by insuring everyone a vote and by keeping everyone informed. I believe that, as Thomas Jefferson put it, if all the American people know all of the facts they will never make a mistake. Whether the [Communist] Party should be outlawed, that is a matter for the government to decide. As a citizen, I would hesitate to see any political part outlawed on the basis of its political ideology. We have spent a hundred and seventy years in this country on the basis that democracy is strong enough to stand up and fight against the inroads of any ideology. However, if it is proven that an organization is an agent of a foreign power, or in any way not a legitimate political party—and I think the government is capable of proving that—then that is another matter. I happen to be very proud of the way in which we conducted the fight. I do not believe the Communists have ever at any time been able to use the motion picture screen as a sounding board for their philosophy or ideology.

Chairman [Congressman J. Parnell Thomas]: There is one thing that you said that interested me very much. That was the quotation from Jefferson. That is just why this committee was created by the House of Representatives, to acquaint the American people with the facts. Once the American people are acquainted with the facts there is no question but what the American people will do a job, the kind of job that they want done; this is, to make

America just as pure as we can possibly make it. We want to thank you very much for coming here today.

Mr. Reagan: Sir, if I might, in regard to that, say that what I was trying to express, and didn't do very well, was this other fear. I detest, I abhor their philosophy, but I detest more than that their tactics, which are those of the fifth column, and are dishonest, but at the same time I never as a citizen want to see our country become urged, by either fear or resentment of this group, that we ever compromise with any of our democratic principles through that fear or resentment. I still think that democracy can do it.

Testimony of Screenwriter Albert Maltz

Chairman [Congressman J. Parnell Thomas]: Mr. Maltz, the committee is unanimous in permitting you to read the statement.

Mr. Maltz: Thank you.

I am an American and I believe there is no more proud word in the vocabulary of man. I am a novelist and screenwriter and I have produced a certain body of work in the past fifteen years. As with any other writer, what I have written has come from the total fabric of my life—my birth in this land, our schools and games, our atmosphere of freedom, our tradition of inquiry, criticism, discussion, tolerance. Whatever I am, America has made me. And I, in turn, possess no loyalty as great as the one I have in this land, to the economic and social welfare of its people, to the perpetuation and development of its democratic way of life.

Now at the age of thirty-nine, I am commanded to appear before the House Committee on Un-American Activities. For a full week this committee has encouraged an assortment of well-rehearsed witnesses to testify that I and others are subversive and un-American. It has refused us the opportunity that any pickpocket receives in a magistrate's court—the right to cross-examine these witnesses, to refute their testimony, to reveal their motives, their history, and who, exactly, they are. Furthermore, it grants these witnesses congressional immunity so that we may not sue them for libel for their slanders.

I maintain that this is an evil and vicious procedure; that it is legally unjust and morally indecent—and that it places in danger every other American, since if the right of any one citizen can be invaded, then the constitutional guaranties of every other American have been subverted and no one is any longer protected from official tyranny.

What is it about me that this committee wishes to destroy? My writing? Very well, let us refer to them.

My novel, *The Cross and the Arrow*, was issued in a special edition of 140,000 copies by a wartime government agency, the armed services edition, for American servicemen abroad.

My short stories have been reprinted in over thirty anthologies, by as many American publishers—all subversive, no doubt.

My film, *The Pride of the Marines*, was premiered in twenty-eight cities at Guadalcanal Day banquets under the auspices of the United States Marine Corps.

Another film, *Destination Tokyo*, was premiered aboard a United States submarine and was adopted by the Navy as an official training film.

My short film, *The House I Live In*, was given a special award by the Academy of Motion Picture Arts and Sciences for its contribution to racial tolerance.

My short story, *The Happiest Man on Earth*, won the 1938 O. Henry Memorial Award for the best American short story.

This, then, is the body of work for which this committee urges I be blacklisted in the film industry—and tomorrow, if it has its way in the publishing and magazine fields also.

By cold censorship, if not legislation, I must not be allowed to write. Will this censorship stop with me? Or with the others now singled out for attack? If it requires acceptance of the ideas of this committee to remain immune from the brand of un-Americanism, then who is ultimately safe from this committee except members of the Ku Klux Klan?

Why else does this committee now seek to destroy me and others? Because of our ideas, unquestionably. In 1801, when he was President of the United States, Thomas Jefferson wrote: "Opinion and the just maintenance of it, shall never be a crime in my view; nor bring injury to the individual."

But a few years ago, in the course of one of the hearings of this committee, Congressman J. Parnell Thomas said, and I quote from the official transcript: "I just want to say this now, that it seems that the New Deal is working along hand-in-glove with the Communist Party. The New Deal is either for the Communist Party or it is playing into the hands of the Communist Party."

Very well, then, here is the other reason why I and others have been commanded to appear before this committee—our ideas. In common with many Americans, I supported the New Deal. In common with many Americans, I supported, against Mr. Thomas and Mr. Rankin,* the anti-lynching bill.

---

*Rep. John Rankin was a Mississippi Democrat, a notorious racist, and a member of HUAC.

I opposed them in my support of the [Office of Price Administration] controls and emergency veteran housing and a fair employment practices law. I signed petitions for these measures, joined organizations that advocated them, contributed money, sometimes spoke from public platforms, and I will continue to do so. I will take my philosophy from Thomas Paine, Thomas Jefferson, Abraham Lincoln, and I will not be dictated to or intimidated by men to whom the Ku Klux Klan, as a matter of committee record, is an acceptable American institution.

I state further that on many questions of public interest my opinions as a citizen have not always been in accord with the opinions of the majority. They are not now nor have my opinions ever been fixed and unchanging, nor are they now fixed and unchanging; but, right or wrong, I claim and I insist upon my right to think freely and to speak freely; to join the Republican Party or the Communist Party, the Democratic or the Prohibitionist Party; to publish whatever I please; to fix my mind or change my mind, without dictation from anyone; to offer any criticism I think fitting of any public official or policy; to join whatever organizations I please, no matter what certain legislators may think of them. Above all, I challenge the right of the committee to inquire into my political or religious beliefs, in any manner or degree, and I assert that the conduct of this committee by its very existence [is] a subversion of the Bill of Rights.

If I were a spokesman for [Spanish dictator and fascist] General [Francisco] Franco, I would not be here today. . . . I would rather die than be a shabby American, groveling before men [like you] who now carry out activities in America like those carried out in Germany by Goebbels and Himmler.

The American people are going to have to choose between the Bill of Rights and [this] committee. They cannot have both. One or the other must be abolished in the immediate future.

Chairman (pounding gavel) Mr. Stripling. Mr. Stripling. . . .

Mr. Stripling: Are you a member of the Screen Writers Guild. . . . ?

Mr. Maltz: Next you are going to ask me what religious group I belong to.

Mr. Stripling: No, no, we are not.

Mr. Maltz: And any such question as that . . . is an obvious attempt to invade my rights under Constitution.

Mr. Stripling: Do you object to answering whether or not you are a member of the Screen Writers Guild?

Mr. Maltz: I have not objected to answering that question. On the contrary, I point out that next you are going to ask me whether or not I am a member of a certain religious group and suggest that I be blacklisted from an industry because I am a member of a group you don't like.

(Chairman Thomas pounding gavel)

Mr. Stripling: Mr. Maltz, so you decline to answer the question?

Mr. Maltz: I certainly do not decline to answer the question. I have answered the question.

Mr. Stripling: I repeat. Are you a member of the Screen Writers Guild?

Mr. Maltz: And I repeat my answer, sir, that any such question is an obvious attempt to invade my list of organizations as an American citizen and I would be a shabby American if I didn't answer as I have.

Mr. Stripling: Mr. Maltz, are you a member of the Communist Party?

Mr. Maltz: Next you are going to ask what my religious beliefs are.

[Rep.] Mr. [John] McDowell: That is not answering the question.

Mr. Maltz: And you are going to insist before various members of the industry that since you do not like my religious beliefs I should not work in such industry. Any such question is quite irrelevant.

Mr. Stripling: I repeat the question. Are you now or have you ever been a member of the Communist Party?

Mr. Maltz: I have answered the question, Mr. Stripling. I am sorry. I want you to know—

Mr. McDowell: I object to that statement.

Chairman: Excuse the witness. No more questions. Typical Communist line.

DOCUMENT 2.3
Senator Joseph McCarthy Attacks the State Department
(February 1950)

Wisconsin Republican Joseph McCarthy first won a seat in the Senate in the 1946 mid-term elections, which brought Republicans to Washington in the majority for the first time since Hoover's administration. By 1950, however, McCarthy had established little or no record in the Senate. Under advice from some party leaders, he took on the mantle of anti-communism. In a speech before a Republican women's organization in Wheeling, West Virginia, in February, McCarthy went on the attack, charging that the State Department and its secretary, Dean Acheson, harbored "traitorous" communists in their midst. He claimed to have 205 names (later he claimed to have said he had fifty-seven names) of communists then employed by the State Department. In fact, he had none.

This was the beginning of McCarthy's anti-communist career. Below is McCarthy's Wheeling speech.

SOURCE: Senator Joseph McCarthy, Speech at Wheeling, West Virginia, February 9, 1950. *Congressional Record*, 81st Cong., 2d sess. (February 20, 1950), 1956.

Five years after a world war has been won, men's hearts should anticipate a long peace, and men's minds should be free from the heavy weight that comes with war. But this is not such a period—for this is not a period of peace. This is a time of the cold war. This is a time when all the world is split into two vast, increasingly hostile armed camps—a time of a great armament race.

Today we can almost physically hear the mutterings and rumblings of an invigorated god of war. You can see it, feel it, and hear it all the way from the hills of Indochina, from the shores of Formosa, right over into the very heart of Europe itself.

The one encouraging thing is that the "mad moment" has not yet arrived for the firing of the gun or the exploding of the bomb which will set civilization about the final task of destroying itself. There is still a hope for peace if we finally decide that no longer can we safely blind our eyes and close our ears to those facts which are shaping up more and more clearly. And that is that we are now engaged in a showdown fight—not the usual war between nations for land areas or other material gains, but a war between two diametrically opposed ideologies.

The great difference between our western Christian world and the atheistic Communist world is not political, ladies and gentlemen, it is moral. There are other differences, of course, but those could be reconciled. For instance, the Marxian idea of confiscating the land and factories and running the entire economy as a single enterprise is momentous. Likewise, Lenin's invention of the one-party police state as a way to make Marx's idea work is hardly less momentous.

Stalin's resolute putting across of these two ideas, of course, did much to divide the world. With only those differences, however, the East and the West could most certainly still live in peace.

The real, basic difference, however, lies in the religion of immoralism—invented by Marx, preached feverishly by Lenin, and carried to unimaginable extremes by Stalin. This religion of immoralism, if the Red half of the world triumphs—and well it may, gentlemen—this religion of immoralism will more deeply wound and damage mankind than any conceivable economic or political system.

Karl Marx dismissed God as a hoax, and Lenin and Stalin have added in clear-cut, unmistakable language their resolve that no nation, no people who believe in a god, can exist side by side with the communistic state.

Karl Marx, for example, expelled people from his Communist Party for mentioning such things as love, justice, humanity or morality. He called this "soulful ravings" and "sloppy sentimentality."

Today we are engaged in a final, all-out battle between communistic atheism and Christianity. The modern champions of communism have selected this as the time, and ladies and gentlemen, the chips are down—they are truly down. . . .

Six years ago . . . there was within the Soviet orbit 180 million people. Lined up on the anti-totalitarian side there were in the world, at that time, roughly 1,625,000,000 people. Today, only six years later, there are 800 million people under the absolute domination of Soviet Russia—an increase of over 400 percent. On our side, the figure has shrunk to around 500 million. In other words, in less than six years the odds have changed from nine-to-one in our favor to eight-to-five against us. This indicates the swiftness of the tempo of Communist victories and American defeats in the cold war. As one of our outstanding historical figures once said, "When a great democracy is destroyed, it will not be from enemies from without, but rather because of enemies from within."

The truth of this statement is becoming terrifyingly clear as we see this country each day losing on every front.

At war's end we were physically the strongest nation on earth and, at least potentially, the most powerful intellectually and morally. Ours could have been the honor of being a beacon in the desert of destruction, a shining living proof that civilization was not yet ready to destroy itself. Unfortunately, we have failed miserably and tragically to arise to the opportunity.

The reason why we find ourselves in a position of impotency is not because our only powerful potential enemy has sent men to invade our shores, but rather because of the traitorous actions of those who have been treated so well by this nation. It has not been the less fortunate, or members of minority groups who have been traitorous to this nation, but rather those who have had all the benefits that the wealthiest nation on earth has had to offer—the finest homes, the finest college education, and the finest jobs in government we can give.

This is glaringly true in the State Department. There the bright young men who are born with silver spoons in their mouths are the ones who have been most traitorous. . . .

I have here in my hand a list of 205—a list of names that were made known to the Secretary of State as being members of the Communist Party, and who nevertheless are still working and shaping policy in the State Department.

When this pompous diplomat in striped pants, with a phony British accent,* proclaimed to the American people that Christ on the Mount endorsed communism, high treason, and betrayal of a sacred trust, the blasphemy was so great that it awakened the dormant indignation of the American people.

He has lighted the spark which is resulting in a moral uprising and will

---

*Secretary of State Dean Acheson

end only when the whole mess of twisted, warped thinkers are swept from the national scene so that we may have a new birth of national honesty and decency in government.

DOCUMENT 2.4
The Kennedy-Nixon Debates (1960)

One of the best examples of reportage in the twentieth century is Theodore H. White's The Making of the President, 1960. *Winner of the Pulitzer Prize and a bestseller for nearly a year, White's fascinating book took the American reader inside the workings of a modern political campaign—really for the first time in the nation's history.*

White had many insights into the political process, but among his most useful observations was his colorful look at image in politics. White recognized that the political campaign of 1960 would be the first national election that would ultimately be decided by image, mainly because of the influence of television.

In the excerpt below, White describes the first-ever nationally televised political debate between two presidential candidates, Vice President Richard M. Nixon and Senator John F. Kennedy. Image is foremost in White's attention as he recounts the events as they unfolded in Chicago in late September 1960. It should be apparent that after these debates American politics would never be the same again.

White refers several times to Nixon's hospital stay just prior to the debate. At the end of August, Nixon had cracked his knee on his car door while campaigning in Greensboro, North Carolina. The knee finally had to be drained and then became badly infected. The candidate spent two weeks out of action and flat on his back at Walter Reed Hospital. But in late September, as the first debate approached, the knee still hurt badly.

SOURCE: Theodore White, *The Making of the President, 1960* (New York, 1961).

[O]n Sunday, September 25th, 1960, John F. Kennedy arrived in Chicago from Cleveland, Ohio, to stay at the Ambassador East Hotel, and Richard M. Nixon came from Washington, D.C., to stop at the Pick-Congress Hotel, to prepare, each in his own way, for their confrontation.

Kennedy's preparation was marked by his typical attention to organization and his air of casual self-possession; the man behaves, in any crisis, as if it consisted only of a sequence of necessary things to be done that will become complicated if emotions intrude. His personal Brain Trust of three had arrived and assembled at the Knickerbocker Hotel in Chicago on Sunday, the day before. The chief of these three was, of course, Ted Sorensen; with Sorensen was Richard Goodwin, a twenty-eight-year-old lawyer, an elongated elfin man with a capacity for fact and reasoning that had made him Number One man only two years before at the Harvard Law School; and Mike Feldman, a burly and impressive man, a one-time instructor of law at the University of Pennsylvania, later a highly successful businessman, who had abandoned business to follow Kennedy's star as chief of the Senator's Legislative Research. With them they had brought the portable Kennedy campaign research library—a Sears Roebuck foot locker of documents—and now, for twenty-four-hour sessions at the Knickerbocker Hotel, stretching around the clock, they operated like young men at college cramming for an exam. When they had finished, they had prepared fifteen pages of copy boiling down into twelve or fifteen subject areas the relevant facts and probable questions they thought the correspondents on the panel, or Mr. Nixon might raise. All three had worked with Kennedy closely for years. They knew that as a member of the House and the Senate Committees on Labor he was fully familiar with all the issues that might arise on domestic policy (the subject of the first debate) and that it was necessary to fix in his mind, not the issues or understanding, but only the latest data. . . .

The candidate lay on his bed in a white, open-necked T shirt and army suntan pants, and fired questions at his intimates. He held in his hand the fact cards that Goodwin and Feldman had prepared for him during the afternoon, and as he finished each, he sent it spinning off the bed to the floor. Finally, at about 6:30, he rose from his bed and decided to have dinner. He ate what is called "a splendid dinner" all by himself in his room, then emerged in a white shirt and dark-gray suit, called for a stop watch and proceeded to the old converted sports arena that is now CBS Station WBBM at McClurg Court in Chicago, to face his rival for the Presidency of the United States.

Richard M. Nixon had preceded him to the studio. Nixon had spent the day in solitude without companions in the loneliness of his room at the Pick-Congress. The Vice-President was tired; the drive of campaigning in the previous two weeks had caused him to lose another five pounds since he had left the hospital; his TV advisors had urged that he arrive in Chicago on Saturday and have a full day of rest before he went on the air on Monday, but they had been unable to get through to him. . . . Mr. Nixon thus arrived in Chicago late on Sunday evening, unbriefed on the magnitude of the trial he was approaching; on Monday he spoke during the morning to the United Brotherhood of Carpenters and Joiners, an appearance his TV advisors considered a misfortune—the Brotherhood was a hostile union audience, whose negative reaction, they knew, would psychologically disturb their contender.

When Nixon returned to his hotel from the Brotherhood appearance at 12:30, he became incommunicado while his frantic TV technicians tried to reach him or brief him on the setting of the debate, the staging, the problems he might encounter. The Vice-President received one visitor for five minutes that afternoon in his suite, and he received one long telephone call—from Henry Cabot Lodge, who, reportedly, urged him to be careful to erase the "assassin image" when he went on the air. For the rest, the Vice-President was alone, in consultation with no one. Finally, as he emerged from the hotel to drive through Chicago traffic to the studio, one TV adviser was permitted to ride with him and hastily brief him in the ten-minute drive. . . . Thus they arrived at the studio; as Nixon got out [of the car], he stuck his knee again—a nasty crack—on the edge of the automobile door, just as he had on his first accident to the knee at Greensboro, North Carolina. An observer reports that his face went "all white and pasty" but that he quickly recovered and entered the studio.

Both candidates had had representatives in the CBS studio from 8:30 in the morning of the day of the debates.

Mr. Nixon's advisors and representatives, understandably nervous since they could not communicate with their principal, had made the best preparation they could. They had earlier requested that both candidates talk from a lectern, standing—and Kennedy had agreed. They had asked several days earlier that the two candidates be seated farther apart from each other than originally planned—and that had been agreed on too. Now, on the day of the debate, they paid meticulous attention to each detail. They were worried about the deep eye shadows in Nixon's face and they requested and adjusted two tiny spotlights ("inkies" in television parlance) to shine directly into his eye wells and illuminate the darkness there; they asked that a table be placed in front of the moderator, and this was agreed to also; they requested that no shots be taken of Nixon's left profile during the debate, and this was also agreed to.

The Kennedy advisors had no requests; they seemed as cocky and confident as their chief.

Nixon entered the studio about an hour before air time and inspected the setting, let himself be televised on an interior camera briefly for the inspection of his advisers, then paced moodily about in the back of the studio. He beckoned the producer to him at one point as he paced and asked as a personal favor that he not be on cameras if he happened to be mopping sweat from his face. (That night, contrary to most reports, Nixon was wearing no theatrical make-up. In order to tone down his dark beard stubble on the screen, an adviser had applied only a light coating of "Lazy Shave," a pancake make-up with which a man who has heavy afternoon beard growth may powder his face to conceal the growth.)

Senator Kennedy arrived about fifteen minutes after the Vice-President; he inspected the set; sat for the camera; and his advisers inspected him, then declared they were satisfied. The producer made a remark about the glare of the Senator's white shirt, and Kennedy sent an aide back to his hotel to bring back a blue one, into which he changed just before air time. The men took their seats, the tally lights on the cameras blinked red to show they were on live now. . . .

The defensive quality of Mr. Nixon's performance . . . can still be reconstructed from the texts. What cannot be reconstructed is the visual impact of the first debate. For it was the sight of the two men side by side that carried the punch.

There was, first and above all, the crude, overwhelming impression that side by side the two seemed evenly matched—and this even matching in the popular imagination was for Kennedy a major victory. Until the cameras opened on the Senator and the Vice-President, Kennedy had been the boy under assault and attack by the Vice-President as immature, young, inexperienced. Now, obviously, in flesh and behavior he was the Vice-President's equal.

Not only that, but the contrast of the two faces was astounding. Normally and in private, Kennedy under tension flutters his hands—he adjusts his necktie, slaps his knee, strokes his face. Tonight he was calm and nerveless in appearance. The Vice-President, by contrast, was tense, almost frightened, at turns glowering and, occasionally, haggard-looking to the point of sickness. Probably no picture in American politics tells a better story of crisis and episode than that famous shot of the camera on the Vice-President as he half slouched, his "Lazy Shave" powder faintly streaked with sweat, his eyes exaggerated hollows of blackness, his jaw, jowls, and face drooping with strain.

It is impossible to look at the still photographs of Nixon in his ordeal and to recollect the circumstances without utmost sympathy. For everything that could have gone wrong that night went wrong. The Vice-President, to begin with, suffers from a handicap that is serious only in television—his is a light, naturally transparent skin. On a visual camera that takes pictures by optical projection this transparent skin photographs cleanly and well. But a television camera projects electronically, by an image-orthicon tube, which is a cousin of the x-ray tube; it seems to go beneath the skin, almost as the x-ray photograph does. On television, the camera on Nixon is usually held away from him, for in close-up his transparent skin shows the tiniest hair growing in the skin follicles beneath the surface, even after he has just shaved. And for the night of the first debate, CBS, understandably zealous, had equipped its cameras with brand-new tubes for the most perfect projection possible—a perfection of projection that could only be harmful to the Vice-President. (In the later debates, Nixon was persuaded to wear theatrical make-up to repair the ravage TV's electronic tube makes of his countenance; but for this first debate he wore only "Lazy Shave.")

The scene of the debate, the studio of WBBM, had, further, been tense all day long, as furniture, desks, lecterns, background, had been rearranged and then rearranged again for best effect. Nixon's TV advisors had been told that the background would be gray-scale five, a relatively dark tone; therefore they had urged their principal to dress in a light-gray suit for contrast. Yet the backdrop when they saw it, was so markedly lighter than they had anticipated that they insisted, rightly, it be repainted. Several times that day it was repainted—but each time the gray tone dried light. (The background indeed was still tacky to the touch when the two candidates went on the air.) Against this light background Nixon, in his light suit, faded into a fuzzed outline, while Kennedy in his dark suit had the crisp picture edge of contrast. The Nixon advisors had, further, adjusted all lighting to a master lighting scheme for their candidate before he went on the air; but in the last few minutes before the debate a horde of still photographers from newspapers and magazines were permitted on the set, and as they milled for their still pictures, they kicked over wires and displaced lights and television cameras from their marked positions.

There was, lastly, the fact that the Vice-President had still not recovered from his illness, and was unrested from the exertions of his first two weeks of intense campaigning. His normal shirt hung loosely about his neck, and his recent weight loss made him appear scrawny. And, most of all, psychologically, his advisers now insist, he lacked the energy to project—for Nixon does best on television when he projects, when he can distract the attention of the viewer from his passive countenance to the theme or the message he wants to give forth, as in his famous "Checkers" appearance on television in 1952.

All this, however, was unknown then to the national audience. Those who heard the debates on radio, according to sample surveys, believed that the two candidates came off almost equal. Yet every survey of those who watched the debates on television indicated that the Vice-President had come off poorly and, in the opinion of many, very poorly. It was the picture image that had done it—and in 1960 television had won the nation away from sound to image, and that was that.

BIOGRAPHICAL SKETCH
Strom Thurmond

Strom Thurmond's life spanned the twentieth century. His public life in politics occupied the last five decades of that time. For the first half of his adult life Thurmond was a Democrat; for the second half he was a Republican. While he was in transition between the two parties, many called him a Dixiecrat. Thurmond would have insisted that it was the parties that had changed. He was always a conservative.

Born in 1902 in Edgefield, South Carolina, in the heart of the Old South, James Strom Thurmond lived in comfortable circumstances. He attended Clemson University, received a degree in horticulture and became a farmer, then a teacher and athletic coach. In 1929 he became Edgefield County Superintendent of Education. He passed the bar the next year, and in 1933 he was elected to the South Carolina Senate. During the war, as a member of the 82d Airborne Division, he was part of the D-Day invasion at Normandy. After the war, in 1946, he ran for governor and won.

In 1948 Thurmond was pressed by southern segregationists and states' righters to run for president on the States' Rights Democratic Party ticket—the Dixiecrats—against President Harry Truman. In a February 1948 speech, Truman had picked up the gauntlet of civil rights and asked Congress for several bills to deal with the nation's civil rights problems. Although Thurmond did not, at first, lead the southern opposition to this stand, he was quickly thrust into that position, and accepted the Dixiecrat nomination in Houston in the late summer of 1948. In the election he received thirty-nine electoral votes from four southern states (Alabama, Louisiana, Mississippi, and South Carolina).

It is often pointed out that the 1948 Dixiecrat revolt was led by southern governors who were limited to one term in office, and, at the same time, unable to run for Congress because the incumbents were too powerful and entrenched to unseat. Certainly, Thurmond and his running mate, Mississippi governor Fielding Wright, were in exactly that position. As the Dixiecrat candidate for president—and thus an outspoken defender of southern interests—Thurmond placed himself in a favorable situation to run for the Senate against Olin D. Johnson in 1950. But he lost. Four years later, following the death of the other South Carolina Senator, Burnet Rhett Maybank, Thurmond ran a successful write-in campaign and won the seat. He served until 2003, when he retired at age 100, having served in the Senate forty-eight years.

Thurmond's tenure in the Senate was marked by a number of notable events, such as his record for the longest one-man filibuster in Senate history (in opposition to the 1957 Civil Rights Act). But Thurmond is best known for what he stood for through the last half of the twentieth century. More than any other figure, he personified traditional southern values and beliefs. Even as Alabama governor George Wallace became the leader of another southern revolt against liberalism and integration in the late 1960s, Thurmond remained the guardian of southern conservativism.

It has been argued that Thurmond pulled the South out of the Democratic Party in 1948, and then led the region into the Republican Party in 1964. That may be something of an overstatement, but in 1964 Thurmond did make the fateful jump from the Democratic Party to the Republican Party.

Thurmond's shift in affiliation came in response to Republican candidate Barry Goldwater's attacks on the Johnson administration's civil rights bill, which passed Congress that year.

In 1968, Thurmond was instrumental in putting Richard Nixon in the White House, first by holding the South for Nixon against Ronald Reagan at the Republican Party convention, and then in the general election by keeping southern conservatives in line for Nixon in the face of a third-party challenge from George Wallace. By 1980, the South was solidly Republican. And then, during the 1980s and 1990s, Thurmond, to the surprise of many, moved with the changing tide, even to the point of reaching out to South Carolina's African American population, and receiving their votes.

Even after Thurmond had died in 2003, he continued in the news. An African American woman, Essie Mae Washington-Williams, revealed to the press that she was the daughter of Strom Thurmond. Her mother, Carrie Butler, was a maid in the Thurmond household in the mid-1920s. For southern whites who understood southern ways of the past, that news was hardly a revelation, but others saw a tragic contradiction in the fact that an avowed racist like Thurmond had been involved in an interracial relationship in his youth.

STUDY QUESTIONS

1. Why was Hubert Humphrey's speech before the 1948 Democratic National Convention considered so radical? Why was it such a departure from the party's past?
2. Republicans had been warning against communism in the U.S. government for some time. What had happened in the world to make McCarthy's 1950 speech so significant?
3. What was the fear of domestic communism in the postwar years? Was the fear genuine or political—or both? Explain.
4. Theodore White's writings are usually referred to as "reportage." Do you see any differences between White's reportage and the writings of history?

FURTHER READINGS

Nadine Cohadis, *Strom Thurmond and the Politics of Southern Change* (1993).
Gary Donaldson, *Truman Defeats Dewey* (1999).
Robert Griffith, *The Politics of Fear: Joseph R. McCarthy and the Senate* (1970).
David M. Oshinsky, *A Conspiracy So Immense: The World of Joe McCarthy* (1983).
Carl Solberg, *Hubert Humphrey* (1984).
Theodore White, *The Making of the President, 1960* (1961).

3 • Origins of the Modern Civil Rights Movement

INTRODUCTION

The American civil rights movement took on a new intensity following World War II, fueled by a general national optimism along with postwar economic growth and opportunity. It became a mass movement, organized on a national level, with leaders who focused on specific objectives and goals. With the assistance of television and the sporadic (but significant) aid of the federal government, the movement, by the mid-1960s, achieved the objective of ending de jure segregation in the South.

It is important to understand that the effort to secure civil rights for African Americans had been an active process from the very beginnings of the African American experience in the New World. And there were significant successes, particularly during the period of Reconstruction after the Civil War. At the beginning of the twentieth century, the Great Migration to the cities of the rapidly industrializing North created an important African American voting base. In 1941 A. Philip Randolph launched a new era of direct action by threatening a march on Washington if President Franklin Roosevelt failed to establish a Federal Employment Practices Commission that would end racial discrimination in war industries.

These advances were significant, and they certainly laid the groundwork for the postwar successes. One important aspect of the postwar movement was the willingness of the federal government to support civil rights. Often that support was insincere, sporadic, and politically self-serving, but it also helped advance the movement.

The second catalyst for the postwar civil rights movement came from the National Association for the Advancement of Colored People. The NAACP had been in existence since the beginning of the twentieth century, mostly as a legal aid society working to demand equality for blacks under the separate-but-equal system established by the 1896 Supreme Court case *Plessy v. Ferguson*.

During the 1930s the NAACP scored a number of successes in the courts. After the war, Thurgood Marshall and his associates began to argue before the Court that separate was inherently unequal—that a segregated system denied blacks equal rights under the law. That initiative culminated in the *Brown v. Board of Education of Topeka, Kansas* decision of 1954. Enforcement of the *Brown* decision brought on significant resistance, but it also marked the beginning of the end of de jure segregation in the South, a system that was grounded in the southern educational system, but was pervasive throughout southern society.

The third apparatus for success in the postwar period came from direct action, possibly the oldest form of civil rights protest. During the war years, the Congress for Racial Equality (CORE) organized several small protest marches and demonstrations in Chicago. Direct action grew into a mass movement in the 1960s and into the 1970s: sit-ins, stand-ins, wade-ins, pray-ins, marches, protests, freedom rides, all designed to confront the system and draw attention to its inequities and brutality.

Thus the modern civil rights movement advanced on three fronts: in the courts, led by the NAACP legal team; in the streets, led by Dr. Martin Luther King and his strategy of nonviolence; and in Washington, led by politicians who saw the importance of both equal opportunity and African American voter strength. The early civil rights movement changed the nation's attitude toward race, while spurring on other movements for equality of opportunity and freedoms.

DOCUMENT 3.1
To Secure These Rights. The Report of the President's Commission on Civil Rights (1947)

President Harry Truman created the President's Commission on Civil Rights (PCCR) in December 1946. The commission was established at least partly in response to a series of violent acts against African Americans in the South— including attacks on several soldiers who had recently returned from the war. The commission was instructed to recommend ways in which the federal government might be strengthened to bring an end to racial discrimination. The result was the commission's report, To Secure These Rights, *issued in October 1947 and excerpted here. Many of the commission's recommendations were incorporated into Truman's civil rights message to Congress in February 1948—the first major address by a president on civil rights.*

SOURCE: *To Secure These Rights: The Report of the President's Commission on Civil Rights* (New York, 1947).

The Condition of Our Rights

The crime of lynching. In 1946 at least six persons in the United States were lynched by mobs. Three of them had not been charged, either by the police or anyone else, with an offense. . . .

While available statistics show that, decade by decade, lynchings have decreased, this Committee has found that in the year 1947 lynching remains one of the most serious threats to the civil rights of Americans. It is still possible for a mob to abduct and murder a person in some sections of the country with almost certain assurance of escaping punishment for the crime. The decade from 1936 through 1946 saw at least 43 lynchings. No person received the death penalty, and the majority of the guilty persons were not even prosecuted.

The communities in which lynchings occur tend to condone the crime. Punishment of lynchers is not accepted as the responsibility of state or local governments in these communities. Frequently, state officials participate in the crime, actively or passively. Federal efforts to punish the crime are resisted. Condonation of lynching is indicated by the failure of some local law enforcement officials to make adequate efforts to break up a mob. It is further shown by failure in most cases to make any real effort to apprehend or try those guilty. If the federal government enters a case, local officials sometimes actively resist the federal investigation. . . .

Police brutality. We have reported the failure of some public officials to fulfill their most elementary duty—the protection of persons against mob violence. We must also report more widespread and varied forms of official misconduct. These include violent physical attacks by police officers on members of minority groups, and use of third degree methods to extort confessions, and brutality against prisoners. Civil rights violations of this kind are by no means universal and many law enforcement agencies have gone far in recent years toward stamping out these evils. . . .

The total picture—adding the connivance of some police officials in lynchings to their record of brutality against Negroes in other situations—is, in the opinion of this Committee, a serious reflection on American justice. We know that Americans everywhere deplore this violence. We recognize further that there are many law enforcement officers in the South and the North who do not commit violent acts against Negroes or other friendless culprits. We are convinced, however, that the incidence of police brutality against Negroes is disturbingly high. . . .

The right to vote. The right of all qualified citizens to vote is today considered axiomatic by most Americans. To achieve universal adult suffrage we have carried on vigorous political crusades since the earliest days of the Republic. In theory the aim has been achieved, but in fact there are many backwaters in our political life where the right to vote is not assured to every qualified citizen. The franchise is barred to some citizens because of race; to others by institutions or procedures which impede free access to the polls. Still other Americans are in substance disfranchised whenever electoral irregularities or corrupt practices dissipate their votes or distort their intended purpose. . . .

The denial of the suffrage on account of race is the most serious present interference with the right to vote. Until very recently, American Negro citizens in most southern states found it difficult to vote. Some Negroes have voted in parts of the upper South for the last twenty years. In recent years the situation in the deep South has changed to the point where it can be said that Negroes are beginning to exercise the political rights of free Americans. In the light of history, this represents progress, limited and precarious, but nevertheless progress. . . .

Discriminatory hiring practices. Discrimination is most acutely felt by minority group members in their inability to get a job suited to their qualifications. Exclusions of Negroes, Jews, or Mexicans in the process of hiring is effected in various ways—by newspaper advertisements requesting only whites or gentiles to apply, by registration or application blanks on which a space is reserved for "race" or "religion," by discriminatory job orders placed with employment agencies, or by the arbitrary policy of a company official in charge of hiring. . . .

On-the-job discrimination. If he can get himself hired, the minority worker often finds that he is being paid less than other workers. This wage discrimination is sharply evident in studies made of individual cities and is especially exaggerated in the South. A survey conducted by the Research and Information Department of the American Federation of Labor shows that the average weekly income of white veterans ranges from 30 to 78 percent above the average income of Negro veterans in 26 communities, 25 of them in the South. In Houston, for example, 36,000 white veterans had a weekly income of $49 and 4,000 Negro veterans had average incomes of $30—a difference of 63 percent. These differences are not caused solely by the relegation of the Negroes to lower types of work, but reflect wage discriminations between whites and Negroes for the same type of work. The Final Report of the FEPC states that the hourly wage rates for Negro common laborers averaged 47.4 cents in July, 1942, as compared with 65.3 cents for white laborers. . . .

Government's Responsibility: Securing The Rights

The National Government of the United States must take the lead in safeguarding the civil rights of all Americans. We believe that this is one of the most important observations that can be made about the civil rights problem in our country today. . . .

Leadership by the federal government in safeguarding civil rights does not mean exclusive action by that government. There is much that the states and local communities can do in this field, and much that they alone can do. The Committee believes that Justice Holmes' view of the states as 48 laboratories for social and economic experimentation is still valid. The very complexity of the civil rights problem calls for much experimental, remedial action which may be better undertaken by the states than by the national government. Parallel state and local action supporting the national program is highly desirable. It is obvious that even though the federal government should take steps to stamp out the crime of lynching, the states cannot escape the responsibility to employ all the powers and resources available to them for the same end. Or again, the enactment of a federal fair employment practice act will not render similar state legislation unnecessary.

Furthermore, government action alone, whether federal, state, local, or all combined, cannot provide complete protection of civil rights. Everything that government does stems from and is conditioned by the state of public opinion. Civil rights in this country will never be adequately protected until the intelligent will of the American people approves and demands that protection. Great responsibilities, therefore, will always rest upon private organizations and private individuals who are in a position to educate and shape public opinion. The argument is sometimes made that because prejudice and intolerance cannot be eliminated through legislation and government control we should abandon that action in favor of the long, slow, evolutionary effects of education and voluntary private efforts. We believe that this argument misses the point and that the choice it poses between legislation and education as to the means of improving civil rights is an unnecessary one. In our opinion, both approaches to the goal are valid, and are, moreover, essential to each other.

DOCUMENT 3.2
Brown v. Board of Education of Topeka, Kansas (1954)

The Brown *decision was the catalyst that pushed the civil rights movement forward into the 1960s and the movement's greatest successes since Emancipation. It also marked the end of the old strategy, the court battles that were orchestrated by the NAACP to overturn* Plessy v. Ferguson *and the Jim Crow doctrine of separate but equal.*

The Brown *ruling applied only to the desegregation of public schools, but it carried with it much wider implications. The old doctrine of separate but equal no longer had the legitimacy of the courts, and this enabled African Americans to pursue their full rights as citizens of their nation armed with the full weight of the law.*

The Supreme Court justices, however, left implementation of the decision up to federal judges in the South, and, a year later, instructed them to impose school desegregation "with all deliberate speed." What the Court meant by this phrase has been a point of contention since it was handed down, but it was perceived by southerners (and the southern courts) as leeway, a reason to avoid compliance for as long as possible.

This Brown *decision, excerpted below, was, in its original form, footnoted heavily. Those notes have been removed here. Many of those deleted citations were to works from the relatively new field of social psychology that contained convincing arguments that African American children, living in the segregated world of the South, had a low self-esteem. The findings had significant influence over the justices.*

SOURCE: 347 U.S., 483, 1954.

Mr. Chief Justice Warren delivered the opinion of the Court

These cases come to us from the States of Kansas, South Carolina, Virginia, and Delaware. They are premised on different facts and different local conditions, but a common legal question justifies their consideration together in this consolidated opinion.

In each of the cases, minors of the Negro race, through their legal representatives, seek the aid of the courts in obtaining admission to the public schools of their community on a nonsegregated basis. In each instance, they have been denied admission to schools attended by white children under laws requiring or permitting segregation according to race. This segregation was alleged to deprive the plaintiffs of the equal protection of the laws under the Fourteenth Amendment. In each of the cases other than the Delaware case, a three-judge federal district court denied relief to the plaintiffs on the so-called "separate but equal" doctrine announced by this court in *Plessy v. Ferguson*, 163 U.S. 537. Under the doctrine, equality of treatment is accorded when the races are provided substantially equal facilities, even though these facilities be separate. In the Delaware case, the Supreme Court of Delaware adhered to that doctrine, but ordered that the plaintiffs be admitted to the white schools because of their superiority to the Negro schools.

The plaintiffs contend that segregated public schools are not "equal" and cannot be made "equal," and that hence they are deprived of the equal protection of the laws. Because of the obvious importance of the question presented, the Court took jurisdiction. Argument was heard in the 1952 Term, and reargument was heard this Term on certain questions propounded by the Court.

Reargument was largely devoted to the circumstances surrounding the adoption of the Fourteenth Amendment in 1868. It covered exhaustively consideration of the Amendment in Congress, ratification by the states, then existing practices in racial segregation, and the views of proponents and opponents of the Amendment. This discussion and our own investigations convince us that, although these sources cast some light, it is not enough to resolve the problem with which we are faced. At best, they are inconclusive. The most avid proponents of the post-War Amendments undoubtedly intended them to remove all legal distinctions among "all persons born or naturalized in the United States." Their opponents, just as certainly, were antagonistic to both the letter and the spirit of the Amendments and wished them to have the most limited effect. What others in Congress and the state legislatures had in mind cannot be determined with any degree of certainty.

An additional reason for the inconclusive nature of the Amendment's history, with respect to segregated schools, is the status of public education at that time. In the South, the movement toward free common schools, supported by general taxation, had not yet taken hold. Education of white children was largely in the hands of private groups. Education of Negroes was almost non-existent, and practically all [members] of the race were illiterate. In fact, any education of Negroes was forbidden by law in some states. Today, in contrast, many Negroes have achieved outstanding success in the arts and sciences as well as in the business and professional world. It is true that public school education at the time of the Amendment had advanced further in the North, but the effect of the Amendment on Northern States was generally ignored in the congressional debates. Even in the North, the conditions of public education did not approximate those existing today. The curriculum was usually rudimentary; ungraded schools were common in rural areas; the school term was but three months a year in many states; and compulsory school attendance was virtually unknown. As a consequence, it is not surprising that there should be so little in the history of the Fourteenth Amendment relating to its intended effect on public education. . . .

In approaching this problem, we cannot turn the clock back to 1868 when the Amendment was adopted, or even to 1896 when *Plessy* v. *Ferguson* was written. We must consider public education in the light of its full development and its present place in American life throughout the nation. Only in this way can it be determined if segregation in public schools deprives these plaintiffs of equal protection of the laws.

Today, education is perhaps the most important function of state and local governments. Compulsory school attendance laws and the great expenditures for education both demonstrate our recognition of the importance of education to our democratic society. It is required in the performance of our most basic public responsibilities, even service in the armed forces. It is the very foundation of good citizenship. Today it is a principal instrument in awakening the child to cultural values, in preparing him for later professional training, and in helping him to adjust normally to his environment. In these days, it is doubtful that any child may reasonably be expected to succeed in life if he is denied the opportunity of an education. Such an opportunity, where the state has undertaken to provide it, is a right which must be made available to all on equal terms.

We come then to the question presented: Does segregation of children in public schools solely on the basis of race, even though the physical facilities and other "tangible" factors may be equal, deprive the children of the minority group of equal educational opportunities? We believe that it does.

In *Sweatt* v. *Painter, supra,* in finding that the segregated law school for Negroes could not provide them equal educational opportunities, this Court relied in large part on "those qualities which are incapable of objective measurement but which make for greatness in a law school." In *McLaurin* v. *Oklahoma State Regents, supra,* the Court, in requiring that a Negro admitted to a white graduate school be treated like all other students, again resorted to intangible considerations: ". . . his ability to study, to engage in discussions and exchange views with other students, and, in general, to learn his profession." Such considerations apply with added force to children in grade and high schools. To separate them from others of similar age and qualifications solely because of their race generates a feeling of inferiority as to their status in the community that may affect their hearts and minds in a way unlikely ever to be undone. The effect of this separation on their educational opportunities was well stated by a finding in the Kansas case by a court which nevertheless felt compelled to rule against the Negro plaintiffs:

> Segregation of the white and colored children in public schools has a detrimental effect upon the colored children. The impact is greater when it has the sanction of the law; for the policy of separating the races is usually interpreted as denoting the inferiority of the negro group. A sense of inferiority affects the motivation of the child to learn. Segregation with the sanction of law, therefore, has a tendency to [retard] the educational and mental development of negro children and to deprive them of some of the benefits they would receive in a racially integrated school system.

Whatever may have been the extent of psychological knowledge at the time of *Plessy* v. *Ferguson*, this finding is amply supported by modern authority. Any language in *Plessy* v. *Ferguson* contrary to this finding is rejected.

We conclude that in the field of public education the doctrine of "separate but equal" has no place. Separate educational facilities are inherently unequal. Therefore, we hold that the plaintiffs and others similarly situated for whom the actions have been brought are, by reason of the segregation complained of, deprived of the equal protection of the laws guaranteed by the Fourteenth Amendment. This disposition makes unnecessary any discussion whether such segregation also violates the Due Process Clause of the Fourteenth Amendment.

Because these are class actions, because of the wide applicability of this decision, and because of the great variety of local conditions, the formulation of decrees in these cases presents problems of considerable complexity. On reargument, the consideration of appropriate relief was necessarily subordinated to the primary question—the constitutionality of segregation in public education. We have now announced that such segregation is a denial of the equal protection of the laws. In order that we may have the full assistance of the parties in formulation decrees, the cases will be resorted to the docket, and the parties are requested to present further argument on Questions 4 and 5 previously propounded by the Court for the reargument this Term. The Attorney General of the United States is again invited to participate. The Attorney General of the states requiring or permitting segregation in public education will also be permitted to appear as *amici curiae* upon request to do so by September 15, 1954, and submission of briefs by October 1, 1954.

It is so ordered.

DOCUMENT 3.3
The "Southern Manifesto" (March 1956)

"The Declaration of Constitutional Principles," or as it is most commonly known, the "Southern Manifesto," is often counted as the opening salvo of resistance to the Brown v. Board of Education *decision. Actually, well before the Manifesto was written, the South had already begun significant mobilization against the* Brown *decision and school desegregation. This was, however, the first notification to the nation that southern legislators in Washington would be working to resist the court's decision.*

The Calhounesque statement of states' rights originated with senators Harry F. Byrd of Virginia and Richard Russell of Georgia, two great lions of national politics and southern history. The Manifesto was signed by 101 senators and representatives, including the entire congressional delegations of Alabama, Arkansas, Louisiana, Mississippi, Georgia, South Carolina, and Virginia. It might be just as important to note who did not sign the document.

Lyndon Johnson, a senator from Texas with national political aspirations, refused to sign.

SOURCE: *Congressional Record,* 84th Cong., 2d sess. (March 12, 1956), 4460–61.

DECLARATION OF CONSTITUTIONAL PRINCIPLES

The unwarranted decision of the Supreme Court in the public school cases is now bearing the fruit always produced when men substitute naked power for established law.

The Founding Fathers gave us a Constitution of checks and balances because they realized the inescapable lesson of history that no man or group of men can be safely entrusted with unlimited power. They framed this Constitution with its provisions for change by amendment in order to secure the fundamentals of government against the dangers of temporary popular passion or the personal predilections of public officeholders.

We regard the decisions of the Supreme Court in the school cases as a clear abuse of judicial power. It climaxes a trend in the Federal Judiciary undertaking to legislate, in derogation of the authority of Congress, and to encroach upon the reserved rights of the States and the people.

The original Constitution does not mention education. Neither does the 14th Amendment nor any other amendment. The debates preceding the submission of the 14th Amendment clearly show that there was no intent that it should affect the system of education maintained by the States. . . .

In the case of *Plessy* v. *Ferguson* in 1896 the Supreme Court expressly declared that under the 14th Amendment no person was denied any of his rights if the States provided separate but equal facilities. This decision has been followed in many other cases. It is notable that the Supreme Court, speaking through Chief Justice Taft, a former President of the United States, unanimously declared in 1927 in *Lum* v. *Rice* that the "separate but equal" principle is "within the discretion of the State in regulating its public schools and does not conflict with the 14th Amendment."

This interpretation, restated time and again, became a part of the life of the people of many of the States and confirmed their habits, traditions, and way of life. It is founded on elemental humanity and commonsense, for parents should not be deprived by Government of the right to direct the lives and education of their own children.

Though there has been no constitutional amendment or act of Congress changing this established legal principle almost a century old, the Supreme Court of the United States, with no legal basis for such action, undertook to exercise their naked judicial power and substituted their personal political and social ideas for the established law of the land.

This unwarranted exercise of power by the Court, contrary to the Constitution, is creating chaos and confusion in the States principally affected. It is destroying the amicable relations between the white and Negro races that have been created through 90 years of patient effort by the good people of both races. It has planted hatred and suspicion where there has been heretofore friendship and understanding.

Without regard to the consent of the governed, outside mediators are threatening immediate and revolutionary changes in our public school systems. If done, this is certain to destroy the system of public education in some of the States.

With the gravest concern for the explosive and dangerous condition created by this decision and inflamed by outside meddlers:

We reaffirm our reliance on the Constitution as the fundamental law of the land.

We decry the Supreme Court's encroachment on the rights reserved to the States and to the people, contrary to established law, and to the Constitution.

We commend the motives of those States which have declared the intention to resist forced integration by any lawful means.

We appeal to the States and people who are not directly affected by these decisions to consider the constitutional principles involved against the time when they too, on issues vital to them may be the victims of judicial encroachment.

Even though we constitute a minority in the present Congress, we have full faith that a majority of the American people believe in the dual system of government which has enabled us to achieve our greatness and will in time demand that the reserved rights of the States and of the people be made secure against judicial usurpation.

We pledge ourselves to use all lawful means to bring about a reversal of this decision which is contrary to the Constitution and to prevent the use of force in its implementation.

In this trying period, as we all seek to right this wrong, we appeal to our people not to be provoked by the agitators and troublemakers invading our States and to scrupulously refrain from disorder and lawless acts.

DOCUMENT 3.4
John Lewis Remembers the Nashville Sit-ins (1960)

Of all the events of the early civil rights movement, possibly none was more satisfying for African Americans than the sit-in movement. Sit-ins, mostly at drugstore lunch counters, had taken place as early as 1943 in Chicago and Baltimore, but in 1959 a group of students from Nashville's African American universities planned to use the strategy to desegregate Nashville's downtown, including department stores, lunch counters, bus terminals, and finally movie theaters. On February 1, 1960, students in Greensboro, North Carolina, conducted a sit-in at a Woolworth's store. Twelve days later, the sit-ins in Nashville began. The action continued through the spring, until May 10, when Nashville's mayor, Ben West, asked the city to desegregate.

The sit-ins regenerated a sagging civil rights movement that had had few victories since the Montgomery bus boycott, which had ended four years earlier. The events in Greensboro and Nashville sparked similar sit-ins in some sixty cities throughout the South in just a few weeks, involving thousands of high school and college students. By the end of the year, sit-ins had shaken over two hundred southern communities. The sit-ins spawned kneel-ins, wade-ins (at segregated swimming pools), stand-ins, and then finally freedom rides to bring attention to the segregation of interstate bus travel in the South.

Possibly the most important aspect of the sit-ins was that they gave the press something new to write about and photograph. That coverage made it increasingly clear to the nation that segregation was brutal and oppressive, something many northern whites did not understand in 1960.

John Lewis was a student at the American Baptist Theological Seminary in Nashville and one of several leaders of the movement. A devout follower of nonviolence, a student of Gandhi's philosophy of satyagraha, *and an admirer of Martin Luther King, Jr., Lewis saw the events in Nashville in the spring of 1960 as more than a victory over segregation. For Lewis, nonviolence had become an ideal, an exhilarating event, even an end in itself, but it was also the dividing line between his generation and the generation of black leaders who had gone before him. Below is Lewis's account of the Nashville sit-in movement through the spring of 1960.*

SOURCE: From *Walking with the Wind: A Memoir of the Movement* by John Lewis, with Michael D'Orso. Copyright © 1998 by John Lewis. Abridged by permission of Simon & Schuster Adult Publishing Group.

This is what we had prepared for. That night Bernard [Lafayette] and I let ourselves into the [American Baptist Theological Seminary] administration building . . . and "liberated" a ream of mimeograph paper. Though many of the students who would be sitting in the next day had been trained, our numbers were swelling so fast that there were hundreds who had not. So I wrote up a basic list of dos and don'ts to be distributed the next day:

DO NOT:

1. Strike back nor curse if abused.
2. Laugh out.
3. Hold conversations with floor walker.
4. Leave your seat until your leader has given you permission to do so.
5. Block entrances to stores outside nor the aisles inside.

DO:

1. Show yourself friendly and courteous at all times.
2. Sit straight; always face the counter.
3. Report all serious incidents to your leader.
4. Refer information seekers to your leader in a polite manner.
5. Remember the teachings of Jesus Christ, Mahatma Gandhi and Martin Luther King.

Love and nonviolence is the way.

MAY GOD BLESS EACH OF YOU

Bernard and I, with the help of a young administrative secretary, made five hundred copies of the leaflet that night. Then we locked up and left. . . .

There was no question we would continue, no debate, no protest from any of the adults. We knew that sooner or later the stakes would be raised. It was a natural step in the process, a step we had practiced and prepared for. Our workshops had been like little laboratories in human behavior and response to nonviolent protest. Now we were seeing real humans respond in almost exactly the same ways Jim Lawson had taught us they would. The danger waiting for us this day was to be expected, which didn't mean I wasn't a little bit nervous. But by now I was so committed deep inside to the sureness and sanctity of the nonviolent way, and I was so calmed by the sense that the Spirit of History was with us, that the butterflies were gone by the time we left the church and headed downtown. . . .

As soon as my group entered our target store, Woolworth's, we were confronted with a group of young white men shouting, "Go home, nigger!" and "Get back to Africa!" They jabbed us as we passed and chided us for not fighting back. "What's the matter? You *chicken?*" they teased, trying to force the situation onto terms they were comfortable with—fists and fighting.

We weren't playing by those rules, of course, and that infuriated them even further. No sooner did we take our seats at the upstairs counter than some of these young men began pushing the group at the downstairs restaurant off their stools, shoving them against the counter, punching them.

We immediately went down to join our brothers and sisters, taking seats of our own. I was hit in the ribs, not too hard, but enough to knock me over. Down the way I could see one of the white men stubbing a lit cigarette against the back of a guy in our group, though I couldn't tell who it was in the swirl of the action.

I got back on my stool and sat there, not saying a word. The others did the same. Violence does beget violence, but the opposite is just as true. Hitting someone who does not hit back can last only so long. Fury spends itself pretty quickly when there's no fury facing it. We could see in the mirror on the wall in front of us the crowd gathered at our backs. They continued trying to egg us on, but the beating subsided. . . .

At the same time, we would learn later, the same thing was happening in the other stores. Yellow mustard was squeezed onto the head of one black male student in Kress's while the crowd hooted and laughed. Ketchup was poured down the shirt of another. Paul LaPrad, being white, attracted particularly brutal attention over at McClellan's. He was pulled off his stool, beaten and kicked by a group of young whites with the word "Chattanooga" written on their jackets—a reference to recent white-on-black attacks in that city that had followed a series of sit-ins there.

A television camera crew was at McClellan's, recording the scene as LaPrad's attackers spent themselves. It filmed Paul—bloody and bruised and silent—pulling himself back on to his chair. When the footage aired that night on national television, it marked one of the earliest instances where Americans were shown firsthand the kind of anger and ugliness that the peaceful movement for civil rights was prompting in the South. Many viewers were sickened by what they saw. They would see more in the years to come.

We didn't sit there long before the police, conspicuous by their absence during the attacks, arrived. I didn't imagine they had come to arrest anyone for assault, and I was right. As the young men who had beaten us looked on and cheered, we were told that we were under arrest for "disorderly conduct.". . .

But I felt no shame or disgrace. I didn't feel fear, either. As we were led out of the store single file, singing "We Shall Overcome," I felt exhilarated. As we passed through a cheering crowd gathered on the sidewalk outside, I felt high, almost giddy with joy. As we approached the open rear doors of a paddy wagon, I felt elated.

It was really happening, what I'd imagined for so long, the drama of good and evil playing itself out on the stage of the living, breathing world. It felt holy, and noble, and good.

That paddy wagon—crowded, cramped, dirty, with wire cage windows and doors—seemed like a chariot to me, a freedom vehicle carrying me across a threshold. I had wondered all along, as anyone would, how I would handle the reality of what I had studied and trained and prepared for for so long, what it would be like to actually face pain and rage and the power of uniformed authority.

Now I knew. Now I had crossed over, I had stepped through the door into total, unquestioning commitment. This wasn't just about that moment or that day. This was about forever. It was like deliverance. I had, as they say in Christian circles when a person accepts Jesus Christ into his heart, come home. But this was not Jesus I had come home to. It was the purity and utter certainty of the nonviolent path.

When we got to the city jail, the place was awash with a sense of jubilation. With all these friends, these familiar faces piling out of those wagons, it felt like a crusade, as if we were prisoners in a holy war. We sang as we were led into cells much too small for our numbers, which would total eighty-two by the end of the day. Cubicles built for three or four prisoners were jammed with fifteen to twenty of us each. The police could hardly keep up with the waves of students who were replacing one another back at those lunch counters. No sooner would one group be arrested than another would take its place. Once word would spread back to the campuses what was happening downtown, students arrived at First Baptist literally by the hundreds, angry, outraged, and ready to put their own bodies on the line. Even the adults stood ready to join. C.T. Vivian, an ABT graduate who was now pastor of a small church near Fisk [University], urged his fellow NCLC members to join him on the sit-in line. "We'll let our vacant pulpits be our testimony tomorrow morning," he proclaimed.

But by then word had come that the police had stopped the arrests. They couldn't deal with the numbers they were facing. And there was no more room at the jail. . . .

It didn't take Nashville's powers-that-be long to realize it was fruitless to try forcing us to pay our way out. At eleven that night, after about six hours behind bars, we were released into the custody of the president of Fisk, Dr. Stephen J. Wright. With him were reporters and about two hundred cheering students. We were exultant. Those six hours had been an act of baptism for all involved. . . .

The next day we went to court—the eighty-two who had been arrested, along with more than two thousand supporters. . . . The judge then found us all guilty. He gave us the option of paying a $50 fine each or serving thirty days in the county workhouse. . . . [W]hen the city followed through with its workhouse routine, sending these students out into the streets to shovel snow and pick up trash, it prompted outrage from all over the country. Telegrams of support arrived from Ralph Bunche, Eleanor Roosevelt and Harry Belafonte. . . .

The following day, March 3, the mayor of Nashville, Ben West, ordered our release. . . . What West did was name a biracial committee to study the situation of segregation in the city. He asked us to halt the sit-ins while the committee looked into the problem, and we agreed. . . .

It had begun quietly, almost invisibly, in late March. No one knew quite where it started, but it became organized and communicated through the churches. "Don't buy Downtown" was the simple slogan, and it was amazingly effective. Estimates were that black Nashville spent as much as $60 million a year in the city, a figure which meant even more to downtown merchants who had seen many of their white customers move to the suburbs in recent years and were depending increasingly on the black buyers who remained.

By the beginning of April, those stores stood virtually empty. One leader at a local black Baptist church asked every person in the congregation who had not spent a penny downtown in the previous two weeks to stand. Everyone in the room rose.

White people, too, were staying away. Some were wary of the violence and disturbances caused by the sit-ins. Others joined the boycott as a sign of support for our cause. A few white women went down to their favorite Nashville stores and made a visible show of turning in their credit cards as their own act of protest. . . .

[T]he next night . . . Thurgood Marshall, who was seven years away from becoming the nation's first black U.S. Supreme Court justice, arrived at the Fisk gymnasium to address an audience of more than four thousand. The atmosphere was intense as Marshall began by praising what we had accomplished with our sit-ins. But then he told us we were making a mistake by staying in jail and refusing bail. The way to change America, Marshall maintained, was the way the country's black power structure had been doing it since the 1940s—through the courts. . . . It was clear to me that evening that Thurgood Marshall, along with so many of his generation, just did not understand the essence of what we, the younger blacks of America, were doing. . . . Thurgood Marshall was a good man, a historic figure, but watching him speak on that April evening in Nashville convinced me more than ever that our revolt was as much against this nation's traditional black leadership structure as it was against racial segregation and discrimination. Five days after Marshall's speech we resumed our sit-ins. . . .

By noon, nearly two thousand students, faculty and townspeople had gathered at Tennessee State to march on city hall. We . . . had decided that morning to march and had sent the mayor a telegram telling him we were on our way.

I had never seen anything like the scene as we moved toward city hall that day.

The nation had never seen anything like it. This was the first such mass march in the history of America, the first civil rights assault on such a scale. People kept coming and coming. The newspapers said there were three thousand of us, but I think that figure is low. I'm certain the number was closer to five thousand.

We walked three and four abreast in complete silence, blacks and whites, ten miles through the heart of Nashville. People came out of their homes to join us. Cars drove beside us, moving slowly, at the speed of our footsteps. The line looked as if it went on forever. Everyone was very intense, but very disciplined and very orderly. It was a stupendous scene. There was some singing at first, but as we neared city hall it stopped. The last mile or so, the only sound was the sound of our footsteps, all those feet.

Diane [Nash] and C.T. Vivian were at the very front. I was a row or two back from them. When we reached city hall, Mayor West, in his bow tie and hat, came down the steps out front to meet us.

Vivian spoke first, saying how outraged we were that such a thing could happen in this city. The crowd exploded with applause at that. When West began to respond, Vivian cut him off and the two argued for a minute or two. Then West made a plea with us to be peaceful.

"You all have the power to destroy this city," he said. "So let's not have any mobs."

He went on to say he would enforce the laws without prejudice, but that he had no power to force restaurant owners to serve anyone they did not want to. Then he said, "We are all Christians together. Let us pray together."

To which one student shouted, "How about *eating* together?"

Then Diane stepped forward. She held a typed list of questions, which we'd come up with that morning. When she asked West if he would use "the prestige of your office to appeal to the citizens to stop racial discrimination," his answer was succinct.

"I appeal to all citizens," said the mayor, "to end discrimination, to have no bigotry, no bias, no hatred."

Then Diane asked the million-dollar question, pushing the mayor to be specific.

"Do you mean that to include lunch counters?". . .

"Yes," said West.

The crowd exploded, cheering and applauding.

"That's up to the store managers, of course," West added, a little awkwardly. But those words were drowned out. All anyone had heard was the word "Yes." That's the word that rang out in the next morning's *Tennessean,* which ran a front-page banner headline:

INTEGRATE COUNTERS—MAYOR

BIOGRAPHICAL SKETCH
Rosa Parks

The first real hero of the modern civil rights movement was Rosa Parks, the woman who "stood up and sat down," as children today learn in grade school. Her small protest set off the direct action side of the modern movement, and that changed the nature of dissent in the nation. Certainly, she did not know the significance of her actions. She was, she later recalled, "just tired." But her small protest against inequality launched a mass movement.

On December 1, 1955, Rosa Parks refused to give up her seat on a Montgomery city bus to a white passenger, precipitating the Montgomery bus boycott, which lasted nearly a year and succeeded in desegregating the busses of the Alabama capital. Her action elevated Martin Luther King, Jr., to a leadership role in the movement, and her defiance of the system, followed by the success of the boycott itself, inspired the sit-ins, the freedom rides, and other acts of direct action. Today, she is often called the mother of the movement, a symbol of its success, and an inspiration to all African Americans.

Rosa Parks worked in Montgomery as a seamstress in 1955. She had been the secretary for the local branch of the NAACP, and had recently attended an interracial workshop at the Highlander Folk School in Monteagle, Tennessee. The incident that took place on December 1 was spontaneous, but Rosa Parks was an activist who had been involved in the civil rights movement in one way or another for most of her life. She had worked to mobilize a voter registration drive in the 1940s, and as the secretary to the Montgomery branch of the NAACP she had worked closely with Edgar Nixon, the organization's state president. It was Nixon who paid Parks's bail on the night of December 1.

The incident itself was fairly simple. Parks was riding the city bus home from work. She refused to surrender her seat to a white male passenger, and was arrested. Although three black women had been arrested earlier that year for similar acts of defiance (and Parks herself had been thrown off a Montgomery bus by the same bus driver twelve years before), this time the Montgomery NAACP was prepared to mount a counterattack against the system. They had been looking for someone to represent in a test case, someone with impeccable character, and Rosa Parks filled that bill. In response to the incident, Nixon and other Montgomery NAACP leaders launched a boycott of the buses that finally succeeded in November 1956 when the Supreme Court ruled that the buses must be integrated.

One of the most significant aspects of the event was that once the boycott was underway, the NAACP brought in local black ministers (including King) to lead the boycott. These ministers used their pulpits to preach the message of the movement, and then provided their churches as bases to organize the boycott. This approach was so successful that it became the prevailing strategy of the civil rights movement in the South. It was a church-based, nonviolent movement—until it changed its character completely in the mid-1960s. King, the minister at the Dexter Street Baptist Church in Montgomery, was the leader of the movement.

In the final analysis, however, desegregation was mandated by a Supreme Court decision, and leaders like King would work hard to convince the nation's political establishment to use their powers to bring down the old system.

STUDY QUESTIONS

1. Why was press coverage so important to direct action movements like the Nashville sit-ins? How do you think the advent of television news coverage of the civil rights movement changed the national opinion of the movement itself?

2. Texas Senator Lyndon Johnson refused to sign the Southern Manifesto. Georgia Senator Richard Russell, one of the instigators of the document and a good friend of Johnson's, always understood Johnson's decision. Why do you think Johnson would not sign? And why would Russell have understood his decision?

3. Prior to Rosa Parks's refusal to give up her seat to a white man in Montgomery in December 1955, there had been successful bus boycotts in Baton Rouge, Louisiana, and other southern cities. Parks herself had been subjected to almost the same situation twelve years before by the same bus driver. Why do you think the 1955 incident was more significant than those that went before?

FURTHER READINGS

Douglas Brinkley, *Rosa Parks* (2000).

Clayborne Carson, Myrlie Evers-Williams, et al., *Civil Rights Chronicle: The African American Struggle for Freedom* (2003).

Michael Klarman, *From Jim Crow to Civil Rights: The Supreme Court and the Struggle for Racial Equality* (2004).

John Lewis, *Walking with the Wind: A Memoir of the Movement* (1998).

James T. Patterson, *Brown v. Board of Education: A Civil Rights Milestone and Its Troubled Legacy* (2001).

4 • The Eisenhower Administration's "New Look" Foreign Policy

INTRODUCTION

Dwight Eisenhower's election in 1952 brought a new foreign policy initiative to Washington; the new administration called it "New Look." The architect of New Look was Eisenhower's secretary of state, John Foster Dulles, an ardent anti-communist who believed with a religious zeal that the United States was the world's moral leader and that the forces of communism represented a clear moral evil that must be contained at all costs.

The administration's New Look foreign policy reflected the Republican Party's 1952 campaign promise to keep spending under control and balance the budget. The initiative was intended to be aggressive and engaging, but also frugal. The cornerstone of the policy was what the administration called "massive retaliation." This strategy rejected U.S. military reliance on the expensive ground forces and conventional weapons that had been so inconclusive in Korea, in favor of an aggressive (and considerably less expensive) nuclear strategy. The policy was designed as a threat to the Soviets—a threat that Washington might respond with nuclear weapons against Soviet-sponsored aggression. "We have adopted a new principle," Vice President Richard Nixon told the nation. "Rather than let the Communists nibble us to death all over the world in little wars, we will rely [in] the future on [our] massive mobile retaliatory powers."

The key to nuclear retaliation was, of course, weapons delivery, and in the early 1950s that meant jet aircraft with the capability of delivering the nuclear weapons, presumably, to targets in the Soviet Union. Under New Look, the Eisenhower administration expanded the air force from 115 to 137 wings and added 300,000 troops. Delivery capability became the left arm of massive retaliation. Although air power was expensive, it still cost considerably less than ground forces (and the considerable expenditures, materiel, and manpower necessary to support those troops), and that kept costs down and budgets manageable.

Another aspect of the administration's New Look policy was use of what were called "proxy armies," a plan designed to keep American boys out of combat in Korean-style local wars. In the case of an outbreak of conventional warfare, particularly in Asia, Eisenhower and Dulles intended to rely on friendly indigenous forces or traditional allies to fight the communists and support America's interests. This strategy, too, was inexpensive. By keeping American boys out of harm's way, it held anti-war sentiment at home to a minimum. This strategy of using proxy armies would establish precedents for future policies and actions—particularly in Vietnam before the mid-1960s

Also in the arsenal of New Look was Dulles's strategy of "brinkmanship." This was a reflection of Dulles's personality as much as it was an approach to foreign policy. Simply, it was an aggressive foreign policy designed to convince the Soviets that Washington was willing to go to war. The term came from an interview Dulles gave to *Life* magazine in early 1956—an interview he probably wished he had not given. "The ability to get to the verge," he said, "without getting into a war is the necessary art. If you cannot master it, you inevitably get into the war. If you try to run away from it, if you are scared to go to the brink, you are lost."

The last aspect of New Look was the nasty business of covert operations—a feature of the administration's foreign policy that was not shared with the American people. The primary operations force here was the CIA (Central Intelligence Agency), a mostly secret organization set up by President Truman in the National Security Act of 1947 for the purpose of consolidating all the various intelligence services that had grown up in Washington and inside each of the military services during the war. During Eisenhower's administration, the CIA grew enormously in size, scope, and importance. In holding with the basic philosophy of Eisenhower's foreign policy, CIA actions were almost always inexpensive—and the results were immediately effective. Unfortunately, CIA operations in Iran, Guatemala, and in Southeast Asia during this period caused much of the world to distrust U.S. intentions, and several Eisenhower-era CIA operations would return to plague the United States in later years.

New Look was inexpensive and generally decisive; it achieved an economy of scale in military defense. Eisenhower was able to keep military spending at roughly $40 billion per year, below what even many Democrats in Congress believed was necessary. Ike's secretary of defense called it "more bang for the buck."

DOCUMENT 4.1
Secretary of State John Foster Dulles and the Strategy of Massive Retaliation (January 1954)

When Eisenhower came to office in January 1953 he was under great pressure from his party's right wing to cut spending and balance the budget. In April 1953, when he presented his first budget to Republican congressional leaders, with a deficit of some $5.5 billion, Senator Robert Taft barked at him, "You're taking us down the same road Truman traveled." Although Eisenhower had cut Truman's spending nearly in half, Taft and his party's right wing refused to accept that the first Republican budget submitted in twenty years would not be balanced.

At least in part to keep Taft and his faction in line, Eisenhower set out to cut spending; and with the Korean War ended, he made his greatest cuts in national defense. That required a radical change in the nation's defense strategy. The New Look, then, was to focus on the use of atomic weapons as a war deterrent and on air power for delivery and defense. The country's military-industrial complex held supremacy in both of these areas.

In the document below, Secretary of State John Foster Dulles explains massive retaliation as a military deterrent to war. It is easy to see how the Soviets might have viewed this statement as a threat, and how such statements (from both sides) might well have contributed to an escalation in the arms race and a hardening of the cold war.

Here Dulles also explains the administration's internationalist foreign policy, a policy that Eisenhower had come to appreciate as the Allied Commander of the anti-Nazi coalition in Europe during the war. However, his internationalism was directly opposed to Taft's neo-isolationism—often called unilateralism, or, disparagingly, go-it-alone-ism. Ike and Dulles believed in the UN and its collective security.

SOURCE: *Department of State Bulletin,* Vol. XXX, 017–110.

It is now nearly a year since the Eisenhower administration took office. During that year I have often spoken of various parts of our foreign policies. Tonight I should like to present an overall view of those policies which relate to our security.

First of all, let us recognize that many of the preceding foreign policies were good. Aid to Greece and Turkey had checked the Communist drive to the Mediterranean. The European Recovery Program had helped the peoples of Western Europe to pull out of the postwar morass. The Western powers were steadfast in Berlin and overcame the blockade with their airlift. As a loyal member of the United Nations, we had reacted with force to repel the Communist attack in Korea. When that effort exposed our military weakness, we rebuilt rapidly our military establishment. We also sought a quick buildup of armed strength in Western Europe.

These were the acts of a nation which saw the danger of Soviet communism; which realized that its own safety was tied up with that of others; which was capable of responding boldly and promptly to emergencies. These are precious values to be acclaimed. Also, we can pay tribute to congressional bipartisanship which puts the nation above politics.

But we need to recall that what we did was in the main emergency action, imposed on us by our enemies. . . .

We live in a world where emergencies are always possible and our survival may depend upon our capacity to meet emergencies. Let us pray that we shall always have that capacity. But, having said that, it is necessary also to say that emergency measures—however good for the emergency—do not necessarily make good permanent policies. Emergency measures are costly; they are superficial; and they imply that the enemy has the initiative. They cannot be depended on to serve our long-time interests.

This "long time" factor is of critical importance. The Soviet Communists are planning for what they call "an entire historical era," and we should do the same. They seek, through many types of maneuvers, gradually to divide and weaken the free nations by overextending them in efforts which, as Lenin put it, are "beyond their strength, so that they come to practical bankruptcy." Then, said Lenin, "our victory is assured." Then, said Stalin, will be "the moment for the decisive blow."

In the face of this strategy, measures cannot be judged adequately merely because they ward off an immediate danger. It is essential to do this, but it is also essential to do so without exhausting ourselves.

When the Eisenhower administration applied this test, we felt that some transformations were needed. It is not sound military strategy permanently to commit U.S. land forces to Asia to a degree that leaves us no strategic reserves. It is not sound economics, or good foreign policy, to support permanently other countries; for in the long run, that creates as much ill will as good will. Also, it is not sound to become permanently committed to military expenditures so vast that they lead to "practical bankruptcy."

Change was imperative to assure the stamina needed for permanent security. But it was equally imperative that change should be accompanied by understanding of our true purposes. Sudden and spectacular change had to be avoided. Otherwise, there might have been a panic among our friends and miscalculated aggression by our enemies. We can, I believe, make a good report in these respects.

We need allies and collective security. Our purpose is to make these relations more effective, less costly. This can be done by placing more reliance on deterrent power and less dependence on local defensive power. This is accepted practice so far as local communities are concerned.

We keep locks on our doors, but we do not have an armed guard in every home. We rely principally on a community security system so well equipped to punish any who break in and steal that, in fact, would-be aggressors are generally deterred. That is the modern way of getting maximum protection at a bearable cost. What the Eisenhower administration seeks is a similar international security system. We want, for ourselves and other free nations, a maximum deterrent at a bearable cost.

Local defense will always be important. But there is no local defense which alone will contain the mighty land power of the Communist world. Local defenses must be reinforced by the further deterrent of massive retaliatory power. A potential aggressor must know that he cannot always prescribe battle conditions that suit him. Otherwise, for example, a potential aggressor might be tempted to attack in confidence that resistance would be confined to manpower. He might be tempted to attack in places where his superiority was decisive.

The way to deter aggression is for the free community to be willing and able to respond vigorously at places and with means of its own choosing. So long as our basic policy concepts were unclear, our military leaders could not be selective in building our military powers. If an enemy could pick his time and place and method of warfare—and if our policy was to remain the traditional one of meeting aggression by direct and local opposition—then we needed to be ready to fight in the Artic and in the Tropics; in Asia, the Near East, and in Europe; by sea, by land, and by air; with old weapons and with new weapons. . . .

But before military planning could be changed, the President and his advisers, as represented by the National Security Council, had to take some basic policy decisions. This has been done. The basic decision was to depend primarily upon a great capacity to retaliate, instantly, by means and at places of our choosing. Now the Department of Defense and the Joint Chiefs of Staff can shape our military establishment to fit what is *our* policy, instead of having to try to be ready to meet the enemy's many choices. That permits a selection of military means instead of a multiplication of means. As a result, it is now possible to get, and share, more basic security at less cost.

Let us now see how this concept has been applied to foreign policy, taking first the Far East.

In Korea this administration effected a major transformation. The fighting has been stopped on honorable terms. That was possible because the aggressor, already thrown back to and behind his place of beginning, was faced with the possibility that the fighting might, to his own great peril, soon spread beyond the limits and methods which he had selected.

The cruel toll of American youth and the nonproductive expenditure of many billions have been stopped. Also our armed forces are no longer largely committed to the Asian mainland. We can begin to create a strategic reserve which greatly improves our defensive posture.

This change gives added authority to the warning of the members of the United Nations which fought in Korea that, if the Communists renew their aggression, the United Nations response would not necessarily be confined to Korea. I have said in relation to Indochina that, if there were open Red Chinese army aggression there, that would have "grave consequences which might not be confined to Indochina." . . .

We do not, of course, claim to have found some magic formula that insures against all forms of Communist successes. It is normal that at some times and at some places there may be setbacks to the cause of freedom. What we expect to insure is that any setbacks will have only temporary and local significance, because they will leave unimpaired those free world assets which in the long run will prevail.

If we can deter such aggression as would mean general war, and that is our confident resolve, then we can let time and fundamentals work for us. We do not need self-imposed policies which sap our strength. . . .

If we persist in the courses I outline we shall confront dictatorship with a task that is, in the long run, beyond its strength. For unless it changes, it must suppress the human desires that freedom satisfies—as we shall be demonstrating.

If the dictators persist in their present course then it is they who will be limited to superficial successes, while their foundation crumbles under the tread of their iron boots. . . .

We can be sure that there is going on, even within Russia, a silent test of strength between the powerful rulers and the multitudes of human beings. Each individual no doubt seems by himself to be helpless in this struggle. But their aspirations in the aggregate make up a mighty force. There are promises of more food, more household goods, more economic freedom. That does not prove that the Soviet rulers have themselves been converted. It is rather that they may be dimly perceiving a basic fact, that is that there are limits to the power of any ruler indefinitely to suppress the human spirit.

In that God-given fact lies our greatest hope. It is a hope that can sustain us. For even if the path ahead be long and hard, it need not be a warlike path; and we can know that at the end may be found the blessedness of peace.

DOCUMENT 4.2
National Security Council Briefing on the "Implications of the Soviet Earth Satellite" (October 10, 1957)

In the first week of October 1957 the Soviet Union announced the successful launch of a satellite into space. It was something of a technological wake-up call to the United States, and an embarrassment for the Eisenhower administration—although Ike continued to insist that the event was of no significance.

To many observers both at home and around the world, the Soviet Sputnik (as the satellite came to be known) represented an American failure in the race for technological superiority. To make matters worse, just a week earlier, an Atlas rocket had blown up off Cape Canaveral in Florida and the explosion had been shown on national television. Now it was clear that the Soviets had pushed ahead. If the Soviets could not yet hit the United States with missiles carrying nuclear weapons, they were coming close.

The event also caused a great deal of consternation in Washington. Clare Boothe Luce called the launch "an intercontinental outer-space raspberry to a decade of American pretensions that the American way of life was a gilt-edged guarantee of our material superiority." And Edward Teller, the "father" of the hydrogen bomb, said the Soviet launch was a worse defeat for the United States than Pearl Harbor. The event also opened the door to Democratic accusations that the Eisenhower administration had allowed a gap to develop between U.S. and Soviet military power.

Some of the problems facing the Eisenhower administration are discussed below in a National Security Council briefing on the topic.

SOURCE: National Security Council, "Discussion at the 339th Meeting of the National Security Council, October 10, 1957" (October 11, 1957), NSC Series, Eisenhower Papers, 1953–1961 (Ann Whitman File), Dwight D. Eisenhower Library, Abilene, Kansas.

[CIA Director Allen] Dulles* stated that at 1930 hours on October 4 the Soviets had fired their earth satellite from the Tyura Tam range.

Its initial path followed the range, crossing approximately over the range's other end at Klyuchi. Two hours after the successful orbiting of the earth satellite and after the second circuit of the earth by the satellite, the Soviets announced their achievement. This delay in the announcement was in line

---

*CIA Director Allen Dulles was the brother of Secretary of State John Foster Dulles.

with the previous statements of the Soviet Union that they would not announce an attempt to orbit their satellite until they had been assured that the orbiting had been successful. Moreover, all the indications available to the intelligence community prior to the actual launching of the satellite pointed to the fact that the Soviets were preparing to launch either an earth satellite or an intercontinental ballistic missile.

Mr. Dulles then stated that the actual launching of the earth satellite had not come as a surprise. Indeed as early as last November the intelligence community had estimated that the Soviets would be capable of launching an earth satellite any time after November 1956.

Information on the earth satellite itself remains rather sparse, but it is believed to weigh between 165 and 185 pounds. . . .

Mr. Dulles continued by pointing out that the Soviets had joined together their ICBM and earth satellite programs, which fact helps to explain the speed of the Soviet launching of its earth satellite. We do not as yet know if the satellite is sending out encoded messages. Furthermore, we must expect additional launchings of Soviet earth satellites [this year.] The Soviets have said that they would launch between six and thirteen such satellites.

Mr. Dulles then turned to the world reaction to the Soviet achievement. He first pointed out that [Soviet Premier Nikita] Khrushchev had moved all his propaganda guns into place. The launching of an earth satellite was one of a trilogy of propaganda moves, the other two being the announcement of the successful testing of an ICBM and the recent test of a large-scale hydrogen bomb at Novaya Zemlya.

Larded in with Khrushchev's propaganda statements had been a number of interesting remarks, such as the one in which Khrushchev consigned military aircraft to museums in the future. With respect to this remark, Mr. Dulles pointed out that U.S. intelligence had not observed as many Soviet heavy bombers on airfields as had been expected. This raised the question as to whether the Soviets are in the process of de-emphasizing the role of the heavy bomber. There had been no clear verdict yet by the intelligence community on this question.

Mr. Dulles thought that there was no doubt that in gearing up all this propaganda of recent days and weeks, the Soviets had had an eye to the situation in the Middle East, and wished to exert the maximum influence they could summon on that situation. Much of the Soviet propaganda comment is following closely the original Soviet boast relating their scientific accomplishments of the effectiveness of the Communist social system. The target for this particular trust, thought Mr. Dulles, was evidently the underdeveloped nations in the world. . . .

The Chinese Communist reaction was to declare quickly that the launching of the earth satellite was proof of Soviet military and scientific supremacy over the United States. Maximum play on this theme was being provided in all Soviet satellites.*

Thereafter, Mr. Dulles touched on the reactions in Western Europe, in Asia, and in Africa. He concluded his remarks by emphasizing that the Soviet Union was making a major propaganda effort which was exerting a very wide and deep impact.

At the conclusion of Mr. Allen Dulles' briefing, [Special Assistant to the President, Robert] Cutler asked [the Deputy] Secretary [of Defense] to speak. [Deputy Defense] Secretary [Donald] Quarles began by stating that much of what he was going to say would be familiar to the President and other members of the Council. The President quipped that this was indeed the case, and he was beginning to feel somewhat numb on the subject of the earth satellite. Thereafter, Secretary Quarles outlined briefly the development of satellite programs beginning with the period of World War II. The possibilities of a satellite had been picked up first in this country by the Air Force, because of its interest in the possibilities of a reconnaissance satellite. The birth of the earth satellite program occurred in Rome, at the IGY [International Geophysical Year] meeting of 1954. The President had announced in 1955 the nature of the U.S. earth satellite program, in which he had stressed the supremacy of scientific objectives. . . .

DOCUMENT 4.3
President Dwight Eisenhower's Farewell Address
(January 17, 1961)

World War II had brought together the forces of the U.S. military and the nation's industrial might. The cold war and then the Korean War pushed them even closer. Military leaders wanted newer and better weaponry, while private industry was eager to produce that equipment under lucrative government contracts. In the immediate postwar years, Truman seemed to see this cooperative endeavor as an opportunity for sustained economic growth. But by the late 1950s, Eisenhower had come to believe that the massive amounts being spent by this combination threatened the health of the nation's economy. This "military-industrial complex," he warned, might also facilitate the rise of "misplaced power," or a scientific-technological elite. In his farewell address to the nation, Eisenhower, like George Washington before him, wished to warn the American people against harmful

---

*"Soviet satellites" refers here both to the extraterrestrial objects orbiting the Earth and to Soviet-dominated states, particularly those in Eastern Europe.

trends that he believed could weaken the nation in the future. It was, he later said, "the most challenging message I could leave the people of this country."

SOURCE: *Public Papers of the Presidents: Dwight D. Eisenhower, 1960–1961,* 1035–40.

My fellow Americans, three days from now, after half a century in the service of our country, I shall lay down the responsibilities of office as, in traditional and solemn ceremony, the authority of the Presidency is vested in my successor.

This evening I come to you with a message of leavetaking and farewell, and to share a few final thoughts with you, my countrymen. . . .

Throughout America's adventure in free government our basic purposes have been to keep the peace; to foster progress in human achievement; and to enhance liberty, dignity, and integrity among people and among nations. To strive for less would be unworthy of a free and religious people. Any future traceable to arrogance, or our lack of comprehension or readiness to sacrifice would inflict upon us grievous hurt both at home and abroad.

Progress toward these noble goals is persistently threatened by the conflict now engulfing the world. It commands our whole attention, absorbs our very beings. We face a hostile ideology—global in scope, atheistic in character, ruthless in purpose, and insidious in method. Unhappily, the danger it poses promises to be of indefinite duration. To meet it successfully, there is called for, not so much the emotional and transitory sacrifices of crisis, but rather those which enable us to carry forward steadily, surely, and without complaint the burdens of a prolonged and complex struggle—with liberty the stake. . . .

Crises there will continue to be. In meeting them, whether foreign or domestic, great or small, there is a recurring temptation to feel [that] costly action could become the miraculous solution to all current difficulties. A huge increase in newer elements of our defense; development of unrealistic programs to cure every ill in agriculture; a dramatic expansion in basic and applied research—these and many other possibilities, each possibly promising in itself, may be suggested as the only way to the road we wish to travel.

But each proposal must be weighed in the light of a broader consideration: The need to maintain balance in and among national programs—balance between the private and the public economy, balance between cost and hoped for advantage—balance between the clearly necessary and the comfortably desirable; balance between our essential requirements as a nation and the duties imposed by the Nation upon the individual; balance between actions of the moment and the national welfare of the future. Good judgment seeks balance and progress; lack of it eventually finds imbalance and frustration.

The record of many decades stands as proof that our people and their Government have in the main, understood these truths and have responded to them well, in the face of stress and threat. But threats, new in kind or degree, constantly arise. I mention two only.

A vital element in keeping the peace is our military establishment. Our arms must be mighty, ready for instant actions, so that no potential aggressor may be tempted to risk his own destruction.

Our military organization today bears little relation to that known by any of my predecessors in peacetime, or indeed by the fighting men of World War II or Korea. Until the latest of our world conflicts, the United States had no armaments industry. American makers of plowshares could, with time and as required, make swords as well. But now we can no longer risk emergency improvisation of national defense; we have been compelled to create a permanent armaments industry of vast proportions.

Added to this, three and one half million men and women are directly engaged in the defense establishment. We annually spend on military security more than the net income of all U.S. corporations.

This conjunction of an immense military establishment and a large arms industry is new in the American experience. The total influence—economic, political, even spiritual—is felt in every city, every statehouse, every office of the Federal Government.

We recognize the imperative need for this development. Yet we must not fail to comprehend its grave implications. Our toil, resources, and livelihood are all involved; so is the very structure of our society.

In the councils of government, we must guard against the acquisition of unwarranted influence, whether sought or unsought, by the military-industrial complex. The potential for the disastrous rise of misplaced power exists and will persist. We must never let the weight of this combination endanger our liberties or democratic processes. We should take nothing for granted. Only an alert and knowledgeable citizenry can compel the proper meshing of the huge industrial and military machinery of defense without peaceful methods and goals, so that security and liberty may prosper together.

Akin to, and largely responsible for the sweeping changes in our industrial-military posture, has been the technological revolution during recent decades. In this revolution, research has become central; it also becomes more formalized, complex, and costly. A steadily increasing share is conducted for, by, or at the direction of, the Federal Government.

Today, the solitary inventor, tinkering in his shop, has been overshadowed by task forces of scientists in laboratories and testing fields. In the same fashion, the free university, historically the fountainhead of free ideas and scientific discovery, has experienced a revolution in the conduct of research.

Partly because of the huge costs involved, a Government contract becomes virtually a substitute for intellectual curiosity. For every old blackboard there are now hundreds of new electronic computers.

The prospect of domination of the Nation's scholars by Federal employment, project allocations, and the power of money is ever present—and is gravely to be regarded.

Yet, in holding scientific research and discovery in respect, as we should, we must also be alert to the equal and opposite danger that public policy could itself become the captive of a scientific-technological elite.

It is the task of statesmanship to mold, to balance, and to integrate these and other forces, new, and old, within the principles of our democratic system —ever aiming toward the supreme goals of our free society.

Another factor in maintaining balance involves the element of time. As we peer into society's future, we—you and I, and our Government—must avoid the impulse to live only for today, plundering, for our own ease and convenience, the precious resources of tomorrow.

We cannot mortgage the material assets of our grandchildren without risking the loss also of their political and spiritual heritage. We want democracy to survive for all generations to come, not to become the insolvent phantom of tomorrow. . . .

Disarmament with mutual honor and confidence is a continuing imperative. Together we must learn how to compose differences, not with arms, but with intellect and decent purpose. Because this need is so sharp and apparent I confess that I lay down my official responsibilities in this field with a definite sense of disappointment. As one who has witnessed the horror and lingering sadness of war—as one who knows that another war could utterly destroy this civilization which has been so slowly and painfully built over thousands of years—I wish I could say tonight that a lasting peace is in sight.

Happily, I can say that war has been avoided. Steady progress toward our ultimate goal has been made. But so much remains to be done. As a private citizen, I shall never cease to do what little I can to help the world advance along that road.

BIOGRAPHICAL SKETCH
John Foster Dulles

It was a common refrain that John Foster Dulles had spent his entire life preparing to be secretary of state. He was the nephew of Woodrow Wilson's secretary of state during World War I, Robert Lansing; and the grandson of Benjamin Harrison's secretary of state, John Foster. As a partner of the prestigious New York law firm of Sullivan and Cromwell, he was a well-known Wall Street powerbroker, and from that position he had kept his hand in U.S. foreign policy. In 1907 he was part of the American delegation to the Hague Peace Conference, and in 1919 he was at Versailles. At the same time, he had always been a Republican Party operative, serving as an unofficial foreign policy advisor to several Republican presidential candidates. When Eisenhower chose Dulles as his secretary of state in 1953, it was hardly a surprise.

Dulles was an internationalist whose foreign policy views fell in well with those of Thomas Dewey, Arthur Vandenberg, Eisenhower, and even Truman. During the war he had worked hard to promote the proposed United Nations; and after the war he and Vandenberg were the chief architects of the postwar bipartisan foreign policy. In the late 1940s, Dulles was a Republican advisor to the Truman administration and in that capacity negotiated the Japanese peace treaty in 1951.

By 1952, however, Dulles had split with the Truman administration, especially on the administration's Asia policy, and had become the chief critic of Truman and his secretary of state, Dean Acheson. In an article in *Life* magazine, he was sharply critical of the administration's containment policy. He called for a new policy that would restore the initiative to the United States and free those being held under the oppression of world communism. As the 1952 presidential campaign got underway, Dulles began calling for "rollback" as an alternative to containment. He also argued for the "unleashing" of Chiang Kai-shek's Nationalist Chinese troops against Communist China.

Eisenhower's choice of Dulles satisfied those in the Republican Party— mostly from the party's right wing—who believed in the liberation of Eastern Europe ("rollback"), and (with General Douglas MacArthur) that the United States should in some way confront the power of Communist China. Eisenhower himself, however, seems never to have seriously contemplated any form of rollback—clearly, to have done so would have entailed a military invasion. He also had no interest in a wider war in Asia in support of the Nationalist Chinese—forces that had already been soundly defeated by Chinese Communist armies just four years earlier.

Dulles's harsh rhetoric intensified the hostility between East and West, even as it brought satisfaction to domestic hardliners. Historians have portrayed Dulles as the consummate cold warrior, someone who saw no room for neutrality in a black-and-white world of communists and anti-communists, a Presbyterian moralist who delivered long-winded speeches condemning atheistic communism and threatened the Soviets with massive retaliation. As part of this analysis, Ike was perceived as a chief executive who reigned but did not govern, placing Dulles in the role of the administration's chief foreign policy architect.

More recent research and analysis has shown that Eisenhower was, in fact, an activist president, and that his administration's foreign policy was a joint creation of the secretary and the president. At the same time, Dulles has emerged as a more complex figure. He had, in fact, considered genuine negotiations with the Soviets, did not always regard neutrality as immoral, and was cautious in dealing with atomic issues. Above all, Dulles accepted the basics of containment, and during his tenure as secretary of state he mostly preserved the foreign policy of the Truman-Acheson era. Throughout the crises in Hungary, the Suez, Lebanon, and at Dienbienphu, Dulles presided over a six-year period of peace in the Eisenhower administration.

Dulles died of cancer in 1959.

STUDY QUESTIONS

1. It was determined in the Kennedy administration that the Eisenhower-Dulles strategy of massive retaliation as a deterrent against Soviet aggression was inherently flawed. Why?
2. What is the reasoning behind the strategy of massive retaliation? How did economic forces push Eisenhower and Dulles in this direction?
3. What did Eisenhower fear from the military-industrial complex? How did he perceive the role of computers in the future? Were his fears in any way warranted?
4. Historians at one time saw Eisenhower as a hands-off president who left the day-to-day responsibilities and the decisions of the presidency to others. That perception has changed drastically in the last two decades. Discuss this change in perception.

FURTHER READINGS

Stephen Ambrose, *Eisenhower: The President* (1984).
Robert A. Divine, *Eisenhower and the Cold War* (1981).
Robert A. Divine, *The Sputnik Challenge* (1993).
Fred I. Greenstein, *The Hidden-Hand Presidency: Eisenhower as Leader* (1982).
Ronald Pruessen, *John Foster Dulles: The Road to Power* (1982).

5. The Fifties Lifestyle

The decade of the fifties was a time of optimism and prosperity, as the majority of Americans participated in a rapid economic expansion and a new culture of abundance. Fear that the nation would be plunged into postwar economic depression was completely forgotten; the world's largest economy produced a wealth of goods, available at department stores and on grocers' shelves throughout the country. Americans became conspicuous consumers. At the same time, the country was generally at peace. Communism, although still a cause of anxiety, had turned out not to be much of a domestic threat. The cold war itself was devolving into a contest for the hearts and minds of the third world nations that were gaining their independence from the disintegrating colonial empires. Of course, the decade had its problems and anxieties. There were harbingers of social conflict over racism and sexism; the country still had "pockets of poverty" (as economically stricken regions were called); and there was always the fear that a third world war might erupt. But generally, in the 1950s Americans had reason to believe that the future held promise and hope for a better life.

Of enormous importance for the decade was the baby boom. Between 1950 and 1960 the national population grew from about 150 million to 180 million; in 1957 alone there were 2.3 million births, more than in any other year in American history. The number of school-age children increased during the decade from 28 million to 42 million. But no one needed to see the census data to know that a baby boom was in progress. Babies were everywhere. The boom spiked demand for everything from housing to diapers, and as it did, the economy met the demand and continued growing.

Despite two serious recessions, the average annual family income rose from about $3,000 to $5,700 during the decade, and unemployment mostly held at about 4 percent (although it ran to over 6 percent during the 1957–58 recession). Through the decade, the United States, with only about 5 percent of the world's population, consumed over one-third of its goods and services.

The construction, electrical, and chemical industries flourished while traditional industries, such as railroads, coal mining, and textiles, began a slow decline. Car and truck sales averaged nearly 7 million per year. By 1960 there were 70 million cars on America's roads as families shifted from public transportation to the single "family car" to two cars and more. Even teenagers found both the need and the means to own their own "wheels." Every year it seemed that the cars produced by General Motors, Ford, and Chrysler got bigger, faster, wider. The population shift to newly built suburbs, facilitated by a rapidly expanding federally funded highway system, turned America into a car culture. A new car became the national status symbol, and advertisers linked automobile ownership with American values.

This economic growth fueled a culture that fed off the affluence. Leisure time, along with money to spend, led to cultural shifts and new interests and activities. American attitudes began to change toward everything from music to sex, from race to gender roles, from religion to entertainment. Many of these changes would cause huge cultural conflicts in the decades to come, but it all began here in the affluent fifties.

DOCUMENT 5.1
Jack Gould of the *New York Times* Pans Elvis
(September 1956)

Elvis Presley was the icon of the fifties. It might be argued that Marilyn Monroe or a baseball player or two might have a claim to that status, but somewhere above them stood Elvis. He excited the nation's youth with something new and different at a time when the adult world was fairly conformist. That made him and his followers seem like rebels.

Not surprisingly, much of adult America (particularly white middle-class America) feared Elvis, and in particular feared his music and its invitation to sex—as they saw it. Below is the reaction of New York Times *reporter Jack Gould. Elvis had made several TV appearances, one on the* Milton Berle Show, *in which his "gyrations" were recorded. Then he appeared on the* Steve Allen Show, *where he turned his rock 'n' roll style into slower ballads. On the* Ed Sullivan Show *the plan was to focus the cameras on Elvis above the waist. But that only drew attention to his sensuous facial expressions and "movements of the tongue," as Gould described it. Read more about Jack Gould in chapter 8.*

Looking back, it all seems silly. But, it can be argued, America's youth in the fifties needed Elvis.

SOURCE: Jack Gould, "Lack of Responsibility Is Shown by TV in Exploiting Teenagers," *New York Times* (September 16, 1956). Copyright © 1956 by the New York Times Agency. Reprinted by permission.

Television broadcasters cannot be asked to solve life's problems. But they can be expected to display adult leadership and responsibility in areas where they do have some significant influence. This they have hardly done in the case of Elvis Presley, entertainer and phenomenon.

Last Sunday on the Ed Sullivan show, Mr. Presley made another of his appearances and attracted a record audience. In some ways it was perhaps the most unpleasant of his recent three performances.

Mr. Presley initially disturbed adult viewers—and instantly became a martyr in the eyes of his teen-age following—for his striptease behavior on last spring's Milton Berle program. Then with Steve Allen he was much more sedate. On the Sullivan program he injected movements of the tongue and indulged in wordless singing that were singularly distasteful.

At least some parents are puzzled or confused by Presley's almost hypnotic power; others are concerned; perhaps most are a shade disgusted and content to permit the Presley fad to play itself out.

Neither criticism of Presley nor of the teen-agers who admire him is particularly to the point. Presley has fallen into a fortune with a routine that in one form or another has always existed on the fringe of show business; in his gyrating figure and suggestive gestures the teen-agers have found something that for the moment seems exciting or important.

Quite possibly Presley just happened to move in where society has failed the teen-ager. Certainly, modern youngsters have been subjected to a great deal of censure and perhaps too little understanding. Greater in their numbers than ever before, they may have found in Presley a rallying point, a nationally prominent figure who seems to be on their side. And, just as surely, there are limitless teenagers who cannot put up with the boy, either vocally or calisthenically.

Family counselors have wisely noted that ours is still a culture in a stage of frantic and tense transition. With even 16-year-olds capable of commanding $20 or $30 a week in their spare time, with access to automobiles at an early age, with communications media of all kinds exposing them to new thoughts very early in life, theirs indeed is a high degree of independence. Inevitably it has been accompanied by a lessening of parental control.

Small wonder, therefore, that the teen-ager is susceptible to overstimulation from the outside. He is at the age when an awareness of sex is both thoroughly natural and normal, when latent rebellion is to be expected. But what is new and a little discouraging is the willingness and indeed eagerness of reputable business men to exploit those critical factors beyond all reasonable grounds.

Television surely is not the only culprit. Exposé magazines, which once were more or less bootleg items, are now carried openly on the best newsstands.

The music-publishing business—as *Variety* most courageously has pointed out—has all but disgraced itself with some of the "rock 'n' roll" songs it has issued. Some of the finest recording companies have been willing to go right along with the trend, too.

Of all these businesses, however, television is in a unique position. First and foremost, it has access directly to the home and its wares are free. Second, the broadcasters are not only addressing themselves to the teen-agers but, much more importantly, also to the lower age groups. When Presley executes his bumps and grinds, it must be remembered by the Columbia Broadcasting System that even the 12-year-old's curiosity may be overstimulated. It is on this score that the adult viewer has every right to expect sympathetic understanding and cooperation from a broadcaster.

A perennial weakness in the executive echelons of the networks is their opportunistic rationalization of television's function. The industry lives fundamentally by the code of giving the public what it wants. This is not the place to argue the artistic foolishness of such a standard; in the case of situation comedies and other escapist diversions it is relatively unimportant.

But when this code is applied to teen-agers just becoming conscious of life's processes, not only is it manifestly without validity but it also is perilous. Catering to the interests of the younger generation is one of television's main jobs; because those interests do not always coincide with parental tastes should not deter the broadcasters. But selfish exploitation and commercialized overstimulation of youth's physical impulses is certainly a gross national disservice.

The issue is not one of censorship, which solves nothing; it is one of common sense. It is no impingement on the medium's artistic freedom to ask the broadcaster merely to exercise good sense and display responsibility. It is no blue-nosed suppression of the proper way of depicting life in the theater to expect stage manners somewhat above the level of the carnival sideshow.

In the long run, perhaps Presley will do everyone a favor by pointing up the need for earlier sex education so that neither his successors nor TV can capitalize on the idea that his type of routine is somehow highly tempting yet forbidden fruit. But that takes time, and meanwhile the broadcasters at least can employ a measure of mature and helpful thoughtfulness in not contributing further to the exploitation of the teenager.

With congested schools, early dating, the appeals of the car, military service, acceptance by the right crowd, sex and the normal parental pressures, the teen-ager has all the problems he needs.

To resort to the world's oldest theatrical come-on just to make a fast buck from such a sensitive individual is cheap and tawdry stuff. At least Presley is honest in what he is doing. That the teen-ager sometimes finds it difficult to feel respect for the moralizing older generation may of itself be an encouraging sign of his intelligence. If the profiteering hypocrite is above reproach and Presley isn't, today's youngsters might well ask what God do adults worship.

DOCUMENT 5.2
Game Show Scandals (1959)

The game show scandals of the mid-1950s might seem to be little more than a distasteful episode among the many broad cultural events of the immediate postwar years. But in fact the scandals changed the very nature of American television. Considering the importance of the medium, the scandals take on a greater significance.

The events were not complicated—or even surprising. Contestants on a television game show called Twenty-one *were prepped and given the answers to questions in an effort to make the show more dramatic, and thus increase ratings. Once the scandal was exposed, the two contestants, Herbert Stempel and Mark Van Doren, were subpoenaed to appear before a congressional committee to explain how the deception had been worked.*

The scandals revealed that these contestants, admired by millions, were in fact cheats, liars, and phonies. It also showed that the medium of television could not be trusted. By implication, then, might the networks' news broadcasts be fabricated or inaccurate? Was there any difference between the network news, Twenty-one, *and Saturday night wrestling? The scandal forced an abrupt change in the networks' policies. They shored up their credibility in all areas, but particularly in news coverage. News began to be emphasized, and network news became a staple—accurately covered and disseminated to the public with on-camera evidence that the story being reported was, in fact, the truth. Also as a result of the quiz show scandals the Federal Communications Commission ordered the three networks each to produce at least one public affairs program each week and to put an end to advertisers' manipulation of shows' contents. Consequently, as the many crises of the next decade unfolded, TV cameras were there to show the truth—and so was America.*

SOURCE: House Committee on Interstate and Foreign Commerce, *Investigation of Television Quiz Shows*, 86th Cong. 1st Sess. (October 6–10, 12, 1959), 1960.

Testimony of Herbert Stempel to the House Investigation of Television Quiz Shows

Chairman [Oren Harris (D-Ark), of the House Committee on Legislative Oversight]: Were you one of the contestants in the program referred to as *Twenty-one?*

Mr. [Herbert] **Stempel:**. I was, sir.

Chairman: At what time?

Mr. Stempel: I participated from October 17, 1956, to December 5, 1956. . . .

[Robert] **Lishman** [Chief Council for the committee]: The program, *Twenty-one*, was on the air for a period of about two years, from the fall of 1956 to the fall of 1958. We are about to watch a kinescopic recording of one of these quiz programs, *Twenty-one.*

The game is operated on very simple principles, similar to the card game *Twenty-one.* The two contestants are each placed in a soundproof isolation booth where they cannot hear what the other contestant is saying or what is being said to him. One of the contestants in the case of this show, Mr. Stempel, is the champion. This simply means he is the last winner in the show and has yet to be defeated.

The other contestant, in this case Mr. Van Doren, is the challenger and is trying to defeat the champion and become the new champion himself.

The challenger is told in what category questions will be asked. This category can be any subject from the entire range of human knowledge. After being told the category, he is then asked how many points he desires to play for. He may play for anywhere from one to eleven points. The higher the number of points he selects to play for, the more difficult will be the question in the announced category.

If he answers the question correctly, he gets the number of points for which he was playing. If not, he remains at zero.

The identical procedure, using the same category, is used for the champion. . . .

Mr. Lishman: Mr. Stempel, does the kinescopic showing of the television quiz show, *Twenty-one*, on November 28, 1956, which you have just seen, accurately reproduce the questions and the answers that were given to and by you at that time?

Mr. Stempel: It does, Mr. Lishman.

Mr. Lishman: Does the showing also accurately reproduce the mannerisms and the acting gestures which were used by you?

Mr. Stempel: Yes, sir.

Mr. Lishman: Does it reproduce the perspiration coming off your brow when you were attempting to answer what were theoretically the most extremely difficult questions?

Mr. Stempel: It does, sir.

Chairman: Mr. Stempel, did that reflect the condition within the booth that made you apparently so warm?

Mr. Stempel: Yes, sir. They have an air conditioning system in there and when I asked them to turn it on they gave some sort of excuse that it would make too much noise and refused to turn it on, thereby causing me to perspire profusely. . . .

Chairman: Being in such a closed place without any air at all, you would naturally perspire quite extensively?

Mr. Stempel: Yes, sir. Considering that they have very, very hot lights . . . which are used and the television cameras and so forth which have to use very strong lights. One would perspire.

Mr. Lishman: Now, Mr. Stempel, prior to your appearance on the show you have just seen, were you given by the producers of that show all the questions and all the answers to those questions which you were about to be asked on the show itself?

Mr. Stempel: I was, sir.

Mr. Lishman: Were you told which questions to answer correctly and which questions you should miss?

Mr. Stempel: I was, sir.

Mr. Lishman: Were you told how many points you should try for in every category?

Mr. Stempel: Yes, sir.

Mr. Lishman: In the first two games that you played with Mr. Van Doren on this show, were you told in advance that you would tie with Mr. Van Doren and precisely what the score would be?

Mr. Stempel: Yes, sir. In the first game I was told I would tie seventeen-to-seventeen, and in the second game there would be a twenty-one–twenty-one tie.

Mr. Lishman: Mr. Stempel, did you rehearse the questions and answers, the length of time you should take to answer, the types of gesture you should employ while answering the question with Mr. Daniel Enright, producer of this show, prior to your appearance on the show?

Mr. Stempel: I did, sir. . . . I received a call from a gentleman who identified himself as Mr. Daniel Enright and said that he had to see me in his office upon a very urgent matter. I thereupon told him that my wife had gone to the theater and I was babysitting that evening. He said he had to see me desperately and he would come out. He asked me for directions how to get to my home. I instructed him as to how he would get to my home. He came out about a half hour later. I recognized him from having met him before. At that time when he entered my house he was carrying an attaché case. He walked into my home. I offered him a seat, asked him if he wanted a drink and he refused it. Without further ado, he opened up the attaché case while sitting on my couch, pulled out a bunch of square cards, such as were eventually used as category cards on "Twenty-one," and proceeded to say the category is blank-blank, whatever it happened to be, and then would ask me questions sequentially from one to eleven.

Mr. Lishman: In other words, he was giving you a rehearsal or a dry run of the format of the *Twenty-one* program?

Mr. Stempel: Yes, sir; he was. I managed to answer the bulk of the questions and those which I did not know, he helped me on, and supplied the answers. After having done this, he very, very bluntly sat back and said with a smile, "How would you like to win $25,000?" I said to him, I was sort of taken aback, and I said, "Who wouldn't? . . ." He said something to the equivalent, "Play ball with me, kid, and you will do it," or words to that effect. Then he explained to me that I had been selected to go on the air as a contestant that very next evening. He was rehearsing me. . . . I would end up at eighteen points. Whereupon I would stop the game. Then we talked for a while about things I don't remember. Then he asked me, incidentally, where my wardrobe was, and I told him. He went and checked all my suits and selected a blue double breasted ill-fitting suit which had belonged to my deceased father-in-law, which I was intending to give to charity. Then he asked to look at my shirts. I went to the chest which I have and showed him my shirts. He said essentially that a blue shirt would be worn for television, whereupon he picked out a frayed collar blue shirt. He also instructed me to wear a wristwatch which ticked away like an alarm clock. It was a very cheap six dollar wristwatch. He also instructed me that I had to get what is known, as I understand it, a marine type white-wall haircut. This was the way I had to dress up. . . .

Mr. Lishman: Mr. Stempel, may I interrupt? While all this procedure was going on with Mr. Enright advising you as to your wardrobe, haircut, wristwatch and so on, what were you doing? What were your emotions as this was going on?

Mr. Stempel: I had been a poor boy all my life, and I was sort of overjoyed, and I took it for granted this was the way things were run on these programs. At first I had not realized when I first applied but then I was sort of taken aback. I was stunned. I didn't know what to say, Mr. Lishman.

Mr. Lishman: Did you tell Mr. Enright you would not do it?

Mr. Stempel: No, sir. I told him I would do it. . . .

Mr. Lishman: You told him you would?

Mr. Stempel: Yes, sir. . . .

Mr. Lishman: Now, Mr. Stempel, at this meeting with Mr. Enright prior to the showing on the seventeenth, did Mr. Enright again give you the categories and answers to questions which would be asked you in the evening? . . .

Mr. Stempel: Yes. He also told me at this time exactly how the questions were to be answered. In other words, I was to write down something like, "Take five seconds pause, stutter, say nine points." In other words, everything was explicit. He showed me how to bite my lip to show extreme tension. How to mop my brow. He told me specifically not to smear my brow, but rather to pat for optimum effect, as that created a more tense atmosphere. He told me how to breathe heavily into the microphone and sigh, such as this [witness sighs]. He taught me how to stutter and say in a very plaintive voice, "I will take nine, nine points." He also told me never to call Mr. Barry, Jack, but be very diffident, and call him Mr. Barry. That is the only way I was ever supposed to address him on television, whereas all the other contestants addressed him as Jack. As a matter of fact, I might say, apropos of this whole thing, that this was the hardest part of the show. Remembering the questions was quite easy, but the actual stage directions were the most difficult thing because everything had to be done exactly. . . .

Mr. Lishman: Mr. Stempel, in the instructions you were receiving from Mr. Enright, were you told that ties in the game were important in order to build up, let us say, tension and more attentive public interest in the program?

Mr. Stempel: Yes, sir. Also that Mr. Enright explained to me that he received approximately $10,000 a week . . . from Pharmaceuticals, Inc., as prize money, and that he had to arrange the games in such a way as to not go over the budget, because any moneys which were expended over $10,000 weekly came out of his pocket, and if he could keep the budget down, he made a little gravy, to use the phrase. . . .

Mr. Lishman: Let us fix the date when you were told you would lose.

Mr. Stempel: This would be on the 4th of December 1956. This was the day before the usual Tuesday meeting. I arrived at Mr. Enright's office, and suddenly on the couch in his office found an enormous pile of records which he very, very bluntly told me were mementos from the program of all the programs I had been on. In other words, all recordings of all the programs. After his assistants had left, I was told very bluntly, as he walked over to the blackboard, that I had done very well for the show, reached a certain plateau, and he drew a chalk mark, sort of going up the blackboard and then leveled it off, but said, "Now we find we are sort of at a plateau. We have to find a new champion. That is why you are going to have to go." Then he outlined the program for the evening, telling me I would miss on a question pertaining to what picture won the Academy Award in 1955, and the answer was "Marty," a picture I had seen three times, and I was also in the last question told to miss the last part of a three-part question dealing with the topic I had discussed in an American history course two days before.

Mr. Lishman: Was there a reason advanced to you as to why you should miss these apparently simple and easy questions?

Mr. Stempel: This was supposed to be the twist of the *Twenty-one* program. In other words, the omniscient genius was supposed to know all the hard answers, but miss on the easy ones, because the public would figure one of two things. Either in his very, very erudite studies he had either glossed over this and missed it, or it was intended as a sop to the public at large to make them say, "See, I knew the answer to this and the great genius, so and so, didn't." That is about the effect of it.

Mr. Lishman: Were you told to whom to lose?

Mr. Stempel: Yes, sir.

Mr. Lishman: Who.

Mr. Stempel: Charles Van Doren, sir.

Mr. Lishman: Did you lose as you were scheduled to lose? . . .

Mr. Stempel: Yes, sir.

Mr. Lishman: How much did you receive in total as your winnings?

Mr. Stempel: $49,500, sir. . . .

Mr. [Walter] Rogers (D-Tex): Both of you were dancing to the tune of the greenback, were you not?

Mr. Stempel: Yes. This again, of course, will bring up one final question. If I felt so badly about this, why did I not give the money back? I could not see returning it to Daniel Enright. . . .

Mr. Rogers: You mean you felt you had earned it by doing all this work?

Mr. Stempel: Yes. Actually, may I say I was not a quiz contestant in this program, in my opinion. I was an actor. . . .

DOCUMENT 5.3
Betty Friedan, *The Feminine Mystique* (1963)

Betty Friedan's book The Feminine Mystique *is usually identified as the opening salvo of the modern women's rights movement. Friedan uncovered the deep concerns of so many women in the late 1950s that society puts enormous pressures on women to become housewives—in fact ideal housewives—and douses any ambitions for careers outside the home and the family. This social pressure, Friedan continues, is, at best, often frustrating; and, at worst, debilitating. The result, she adds, is an empty, depressing existence for women as little more than extensions of their husbands.*

Friedan's themes seemed to awaken women to demand a more fulfilling life. That, it might be argued, was the foundation of a movement that led to demands for equality at all levels.

SOURCE: From *The Feminine Mystique* by Betty Friedan. Copyright © 1983, 1974, 1973, 1963 by Betty Friedan. Excerpt. Used by permission of W.W. Norton & Company, Inc.

The Problem That Has No Name

In the early 1960's *McCall's* has been the fastest growing of the women's magazines. Its contents are a fairly accurate representation of the image of the American woman presented, and in part created, by the large-circulation magazines. . . .

The image of women that emerges from this big, pretty magazine is young and frivolous, almost childlike; fluffy and feminine; passive; gaily content in a world of bedroom and kitchen, sex, babies, and home. The magazine surely does not leave out sex; the only passion, the only pursuit, the only goal a woman is permitted is the pursuit of a man. It is crammed full of food, clothing, cosmetics, furniture, and the physical bodies of young women, but where is the world of thought and ideas, the life of the mind and spirit? In the magazine women do no work except housework and work to keep their bodies beautiful and to get and keep a man. . . .

I sat one night at a meeting of magazine writers, mostly men, who work for all kinds of magazines, including women's magazines. The main speaker was a leader of the desegregation battle. Before he spoke, another man outlined the needs of the large women's magazine he edited:

"Our readers are housewives, full time. They're not interested in the broad public issues of the day. They are not interested in national or international affairs. They are only interested in the family and the home. They aren't interested in politics, unless it's related to an immediate need in the home, like the price of coffee. Humor? Has to be gentle, they don't get satire. Travel? We have almost completely dropped it. Education? That's a problem. Their own education level is going up. They've generally all had a high school education and many, college. They're tremendously interested in education for their children—fourth-grade arithmetic. You just can't write about ideas or broad issues of the day for women. That's why we're publishing 90 per cent service right now and 10 per cent general interest. . . ."

In 1939, the heroines of women's magazine stories were not always young, but in a certain sense they were younger than their fictional counterparts today. They were young in the same way that the American hero has always been young: they were New Women, creating with a gay determined spirit a new identity for women—a life of their own. There was an aura about them of becoming, of moving into a future that was going to be different from the past. The majority of heroines in the four major women's magazines (then *Ladies' Home Journal, McCall's, Good Housekeeping, Woman's Home Companion*) were career women—happily, proudly, adventurously, attractively career women—who loved and were loved by men. And the spirit, courage, independence, determination—the strength of character they showed in their work as nurses, teachers, artists, actresses, copywriters, saleswomen—were part of their charm. There was a definite aura that their individuality was something to be admired, not unattractive to men, that men were drawn to them as much for their spirit and character as for their looks. . . .

It is like remembering a long-forgotten dream, to recapture the memory of what a career meant to women before "career woman" became a dirty word in America. Jobs meant money, of course, at the end of the depression. But the readers of these magazines were not the women who got the jobs; career meant more than job. It seemed to mean doing something, being somebody yourself, not just existing in and through others. . . .

In 1949, the *Ladies' Home Journal* also ran Margaret Mead's *Male and Female.* All the magazines were echoing Farnham and Lundberg's *Modern Woman: The Lost Sex,* which came out in 1942, with its warning that careers and higher education were leading to the "masculinization of women with enormously dangerous consequences to the home, the children dependent on it and to the ability of the woman, as well as her husband, to obtain sexual gratification."

And so the feminine mystique began to spread through the land, grafted onto old prejudices and comfortable conventions which so easily give the past a stranglehold on the future. Behind the new mystique were concepts and theories deceptive in their sophistication and their assumption of accepted truth. These theories were supposedly so complex that they were inaccessible to all but a few initiates, and therefore irrefutable. It will be necessary to break through this wall of mystery and look more closely at these complex concepts, these accepted truths, to understand fully what has happened to American women.

The feminine mystique says that the highest value and the only commitment for women is the fulfillment of their own femininity. It says that the great mistake of Western culture, through most of its history, has been the undervaluation of this femininity. It says this femininity is so mysterious and intuitive and close to the creation and origin of life that man-made science may never be able to understand it. But however special and different, it is in no way inferior to the nature of man; it may even in certain respects be superior. The mistake, says the mystique, the root of women's troubles in the past is that women envied men, women tried to be like men, instead of accepting their own nature, which can find fulfillment only in sexual passivity, male domination, and nurturing maternal love.

But the new image this mystique gives to American women is the old image: "Occupation: housewife." The new mystique makes the housewife-mothers, who never had a chance to be anything else, the model for all women; it presupposes that history has reached a final and glorious end in the here and now, as far as women are concerned. Beneath the sophisticated trappings, it simply makes certain concrete, finite, domestic aspects of feminine existence—as it was lived by women whose lives were confined, by necessity, to cooking, cleaning, washing, bearing children—into a religion, a pattern by which all women must now live or deny their femininity.

Fulfillment as a woman had only one definition for American women after 1949—the housewife-mother. As swiftly as in a dream, the image of the American woman as a changing, growing individual in a changing world was shattered. Her solo flight to find her own identity was forgotten in the rush for the security of togetherness. Her limitless world shrunk to the cozy walls of home.

The transformation, reflected in the pages of the women's magazines, was sharply visible in 1949 and progressive through the fifties. "Femininity Begins at Home," "It's a Man's World Maybe," "Have Babies While You're Young," "How to Snare a Male," "Should I Stop Work When We Marry?" "Are You Training Your Daughter to be a Wife?" "Careers at Home," "Do Women Have to Talk So Much?" "Why GI's Prefer Those German Girls," "What Women Can Learn from Mother Eve," "Really a Man's World, Politics," "How to Hold On to a Happy Marriage," "Don't Be Afraid to Marry Young," "The Doctor Talks about Breast-Feeding," "Our Baby Was Born at Home," "Cooking to Me is Poetry," "The Business of Running a Home."

By the end of 1949, only one out of three heroines in the women's magazines was a career woman—and she was shown in the act of renouncing her career and discovering that what she really wanted to be was a housewife. In 1958, and again in 1959, I went through issue after issue of the three major women's magazines (the fourth, *Woman's Home Companion,* had died) without finding a single heroine who had a career, a commitment to any work, art, profession, or mission in the world, other than "Occupation: housewife." Only one in a hundred heroines had a job; even the young unmarried heroines no longer worked except at snaring a husband.

These new happy housewife heroines seem strangely younger than the spirited career girls of the thirties and forties. They seem to get younger all the time—in looks, and a childlike kind of dependence. They have no vision of the future, except to have a baby. The only active growing figure in their world is the child. The housewife heroines are forever young, because their own image *ends* in childbirth. Like Peter Pan, they must remain young, while their children grow up with the world. They must keep on having babies, because the feminine mystique says there is no other way for a woman to be a heroine. . . .

By the time I started writing for women's magazines, in the fifties, it was simply taken for granted by editors, and accepted as an immutable fact of life by writers, that women were not interested in politics, life outside the United States, national issues, art, science, ideas, adventure, education, or even their own communities, except where they could be sold through their emotions as wives and mothers. . . .

In 1960, a perceptive social psychologist showed me some sad statistics which seemed to prove unmistakably that American women under thirty-five are not interested in politics. "They may have the vote, but they don't dream about running for office," he told me. "If you write a political piece, they won't read it. You have to translate it into issues they can understand—romance, pregnancy, nursing, home furnishings, clothes. Run an article on the economy, or the race question, civil rights, and you'd think that women had never heard of them." Maybe they hadn't heard of them. Ideas are not like instincts of the blood that spring into the mind intact. They are communicated by education, by the printed word. The new young housewives, who leave high school or college to marry, do not read books, the psychological surveys say. They only read magazines. . . .

This is the real mystery: why did so many American women, with the ability and education to discover and create, go back home again, to look for "something more" in housework and rearing children? For paradoxically, in the same fifteen years in which the spirited New Woman was replaced by the Happy Housewife, the boundaries of the human world have widened, the pace of the world has quickened, and the very nature of human reality has become increasingly free from biological and material necessity. Does the mystique keep American woman from growing with the world? Does it force her to deny reality, as a woman in a mental hospital must deny reality to believe she is a queen? Does it doom women to be displaced persons, if not virtual schizophrenics, in our complex, changing world?

It is more than a strange paradox that as all professions are finally open to women in America, "career woman" has become a dirty word; that as higher education becomes available to any woman with the capacity for it, education for women has become so suspect that more and more drop out of high school and college to marry and have babies; that as so many roles in modern society become theirs for the taking, women so insistently confine themselves to one role. Why, with the removal of all the legal, political, economic, and educational barriers that once kept woman from being man's equal, a person in her own right, an individual free to develop her own potential, should she accept this new image which insists she is not a person but a "woman," by definition barred from the freedom of human existence and a voice in human destiny?

The feminine mystique is so powerful that women grow up no longer knowing that they have the desires and capacities the mystique forbids. But such a mystique does not fasten itself on a whole nation in a few short years, reversing the trends of a century, without cause. What gives the mystique its power? Why did women go home again?

DOCUMENT 5.4
Female Sexuality in the 1950s: "Myths That Imperil Married Love" (1958)

It seemed that in the fifties everyone had an opinion on sex and sexuality. Much of that conversation was stimulated by the publication of Kinsey's reports on sexuality, Sexual Behavior in the Human Male *(1948) and* Sexual Behavior in the Human Female *(1953). Kinsey, who died in 1956, purported to document how Americans worked their will in their bedrooms. His reports were flawed for several reasons, but his research seemed to open up a Pandora's box of questions and assumptions about sexuality.*

If there is anything humorous about all this questioning of "who's doing what to whom in whose bed," it was that men of authority tried to answer the questions about *women for* women. *In the article below (published in* Coronet *magazine in 1958) a prominent male marriage counselor gives advice to women that today might evoke a strong retort: "Speak for yourself."*

SOURCE: Hugo Bourdeau, "Myths That Imperil Married Love," *Coronet*, December 1958.

All across America, there is a widespread belief that sex—the need for it, the preparation for it, the presentation of it, the consummation of it—dominates a woman's life.

This is a delusion, a dangerous one.

That is my firm conviction after many years as a marriage counselor—a person whose business is understanding life. After interviewing thousands of married women and talking with leading authorities on family relations all over the country, I am convinced that the American woman is being vastly oversold on the importance of the physical act of love.

Biologically, sex is a hunger which needs to be appeased. Emotionally, it is an important adjunct to the love relationship. . . . Although the place of sex in marriage must not be minimized, it is not the critical factor that women are being led to believe. . . .

Unfortunately, however, the American woman today is told so many things that she often doesn't know what to believe. Sexual advice, detailed to the smallest, painfully clinical item, is hurled at her from every side. She is warned constantly that her marital happiness hinges upon "proper sexual adjustment." She is scolded about the response she ought to have, and how she should have it. She is made acutely aware that a "vigorous and harmonious sex relationship" with her husband is vital to a successful union. . . .

This unremitting propaganda has been only too successful. The American wife is beginning to feel that she must aggressively seek sexual satisfaction or her life will become hollow. She tortures herself by trying to live up to what she is told is normal feminine behavior. Finally, she comes to look upon sex, not as a natural and beautiful human relationship, but as a game to be played at, shrewdly and wisely.

From here, it is only one short step to the point where a woman begins to feel that she must even take responsibility for *initiating sex.* Not overtly, of course. But she is covertly urged and encouraged to create, in every possible way and by every possible allurement and guile, situations which will result in a sex experience.

Worse yet, the woman is made to feel not only that she must actively search for more sexual experience, but also seek the experience—the big big experience, the Experience that will make all other experiences seem pallid. . . .

What *should* a wife expect?

Should she expect complete transport, utter ecstatic gratification, failing which she must count that episode a failure? Of course not. She can experience ardor on numerous levels and in varying degrees, ranging from a sensation of pressure to convulsive explosion. Her desire as well as her enjoyment fluctuate markedly. There may be keenness or there may be a diffused glow of much lesser intensity.

A wife must not expect to attain orgasm at each experience and certainly ought not to feel cheated if she does not. Studies by the Margaret Sanger Research Bureau reveal that fully 66 percent of 8,500 women never, rarely or only occasionally achieve physical climax. Nevertheless, many report considerable and even profound satisfaction merely from contact with the male.

After marriage most women quickly become aware that sex actually does not color and control their lives, that most of the time sex is *not* uppermost in their minds. In fact, there are many hours of the day when it does not intrude at all! And there are many nights when they are not eager for love-making.

But the propaganda passions have been so insistent that they wonder if something is lacking in themselves. Some, fearing a loss of their husband's affection, feign passionate interest they do not really feel. Others run to doctors, wondering if they are losing vitality, and are often taken in by charlatans who prescribe quack pills and "shots" designed to restore their sex drives.

One thirty-two-year-old wife, fearful that her sex interest was not up to par, came to our agency for guidance. In the course of our discussion, she said timidly: "When my husband reaches for me in the dark, about half the time I am willing to be reached, but the other half I feel like begging him not to touch me. What's wrong with me?"

"Nothing!" I told her bluntly. I am explaining that millions of other wives, exhausted by children and housework at the end of the day[,] want nothing more than to sleep, that this was not only normal but a well-earned wifely prerogative. A woman does not need to be possessed by sex in the same way and to the same degree as a man.

As any woman can tell you—if you can get her to put down her marriage handbook long enough—a woman's natural sexual role is essentially passive. She wants to be overcome. She resents taking the initiative, even covertly.

Extremely few women have a built-in sexual aggressiveness; rarely indeed does a woman look at a man and automatically desire him. The late Dr. Alfred Kinsey proved this conclusively in his report on the human female. His statistics showed that male nudity seldom stimulates a woman, nor do pornographic movies, photographs and books.

This does not mean, of course, that a woman should be uncooperative or unimaginative in her relationships with her husband. When I say a woman's natural sexual role is essentially passive, I do not wish to imply that she may not derive equal enjoyment. In the intimacy of married love, she may take an active—even an eager—part. But there is no reason for her to push her instincts unnaturally or feel disappointed when she fails to reach a stirring physical climax.

Overemphasis on the importance of sexual climax for a woman is causing almost insurmountable problems for the male. Often a husband may become too determined to "satisfy" his wife's exaggerated idea of sexual climax. In his mechanical attempts to do so, naturalness in love is lost. Marriage relations become a contest, lacking spiritual depth and frequently wearisome for one or both partners. Or, failing to prove an impossible "maleness," the husband may often try to compensate by seeking the company of another woman, sometimes a prostitute whom he feels he can "dominate" more easily and completely.

On the other side of the coin, we find that if a wife has not obtained the gratification she thinks she should, she may decide to seek it outside the home. The current propaganda has convinced her she has an enormous experience coming to her, and she might as well make up her mind to go and claim it in the arms of another man. . . .

Depth of love is totally unrelated to sexual performance. Love-making may be as often or as infrequent as the temperaments of the individuals demand. There are no competitive standards to which one must conform, no "averages" of any sort which must be followed. That which makes a woman and her husband happy and contented is the only possible standard.

Forcing oneself out of this pattern of personal needs can only lead to un-happiness, even marital disaster

BIOGRAPHICAL SKETCH
James Dean

The fifties literally oozed pop culture icons. In music there were Elvis and Little Richard. In sports there were DiMaggio and Williams. And in the movies an entirely new group of actors hit the screens, ready to replace the receding hairlines of Bogart and Widmark. And they changed the nature of what it was to be cool. Leading the pack were Marlon Brando and James Dean, actors who reeked anger, sexuality, and (of course) contempt for their elders. Brando produced a number of strong characters throughout his early career in the fifties, but it was Dean, in a flash of just three movies, who created for posterity the movie character of the sullen, rebellious, sexy teenage punk. It can hardly be said that he invented cool, but if a character exists that can be called "modern cool," Dean invented it—or at least he was there for the creation.

James Dean was more than a flash-in-the-pan. True, from the time he hit the screen with *East of Eden* until he died, he had been a Hollywood movie star for less than two years and made only three movies—of which only *East of Eden* had been released. But his impact was enormous in that short time—certainly because his amazing talent was cut short so suddenly, but also because he developed a theatrical character that has hung on in films since then.

Dean was born in 1931 in rural northern Indiana. His family moved to California when he was five, but Dean was sent back to Indiana to live with relatives when his mother died. After graduating from high school, he returned to California and studied drama at UCLA for two years. In 1951, he took advantage of the new medium and appeared in an occasional television commercial, and he took a few small roles in films and on the stage.

At the suggestion of James Whitmore, who ran a successful acting workshop in Hollywood, Dean went to New York to work on the stage. There he appeared in an occasional television program before winning a small part in a Broadway play called *See the Jaguar.*

In 1954 Dean landed a Warner Brothers screen test and then the part of Cal Trask in John Steinbeck's *East of Eden.* In March 1955 he began shooting *Rebel Without a Cause*, the movie that would establish him as the brooding, troubled youth in a red jacket, a kid whose troubled turns had forced his family to move from place to place to avoid public embarrassment. His nature, however—no matter how innocent at times—seemed to draw him toward trouble.

In April, *East of Eden* opened in theaters across the country. The next month Dean wrapped up shooting Rebel and then joined the cast and crew of *Giant* in Marfa, Texas. His character, R.J., rose from slow-witted ranch hand to ruthless oil baron in just under four hours. With Rock Hudson, Elizabeth Taylor, and friend Dennis Hopper, the film had a wonderful cast and a strong epical story about the first half of the twentieth century on the Texas frontier, but its length was box office poison. It would be Dean's last movie.

One of Dean's passions was sports car racing. In 1955, with his *East of Eden* royalties, he bought a Porsche Spyder 550 to race in local California road rallies. On September 30, 1955, en route to a race near Salinas, a car pulled into the highway. Dean, age twenty-four, was killed instantly.

STUDY QUESTIONS

1. Have adult attitudes toward youth entertainment (specifically music) changed over time? Is there any relationship between the antics of Elvis Presley and the antics of Janet Jackson? Or Elvis Presley and Marilyn Manson?
2. What is the "feminine mystique"? How does Friedan define it? How does the conformity of women fit into the nature of the fifties? How does the *Coronet* article assume the manner in which women of the fifties were expected to act and react?
3. Historians of the twentieth century tend to see the century divided into decades. Can the fifties stand alone as an historical period? Why or why not?
4. If is true that the sixties was an explosion of cultural change, why might the fifties be seen as the origin of that change? Give examples.

FURTHER READINGS

Betty Friedan, *The Feminine Mystique* (1963).
David Halberstam, *The Fifties* (1993).
Joe Hyams, *James Dean: Little Boy Lost* (1993).
William O'Neill, *American High: The Years of Confidence, 1945–1960* (1986).

6 • The Cold War Heats Up During the Kennedy Administration

INTRODUCTION

It was during the administration of John F. Kennedy that the cold war reached its most dangerous phase. Within a three-year period, Kennedy and Soviet leader Nikita Khrushchev squared off over issues and incidents that threatened to push the world into a cataclysmic nuclear war. Both men needed strategic victories over the other to maintain their positions as national leaders just at the moment when nuclear power and the capability of new delivery systems had reached a new phase. As the arms race intensified, so did the rhetoric from both sides. The early sixties was a dangerous time.

When Kennedy came to office in January 1961, he established a foreign policy that deviated drastically from Eisenhower's New Look. Ike's foreign policy had relied heavily on the inexpensive strategies of nuclear threat and covert actions, mostly as a response to demands for a balanced budget from the Republican Right. Kennedy, however, believed that the communist threat was broad and varied, and he wanted more military options. He initiated a policy that would allow the United States to fight several types of wars (even several wars at once). This strategy became known as "flexible response," and it was devised to allow the U.S. military to respond to communist aggressions in several different ways. In his first message to Congress on defense, Kennedy described flexible response as a strategy that would "deter all wars, general or limited, nuclear or conventional, large or small—to convince all potential aggressors that any attack would be futile."

As part of flexible response, Kennedy wanted to deal with what he called "brushfires," small wars (usually perceived as communist-inspired insurgencies) that threatened U.S. interests abroad. Such brushfires were burning in Vietnam and Laos when Kennedy came to office; and later in his administration brushfires threatened to break out in parts of Africa and South Asia where several newly independent nations erupted into civil war.

But it was the situation in Cuba that challenged the Kennedy administration the most. There, the irascible Fidel Castro had joined the Soviet sphere of influence and established a communist regime just ninety miles off the Florida coast. A Soviet-dominated Cuba threatened the U.S. mainland directly; it also threatened U.S. interests in Latin America. When Kennedy came to office a plan was already in the works for an American-sponsored invasion of Cuba by a force of some 1,400 Cuban exiles. With some reluctance, Kennedy ordered the operation to go forward. The incident, which occurred at the Bay of Pigs in southern Cuba, was a disaster.

Cuba continued to be Kennedy's primary concern. On October 14, 1962, a U-2 reconnaissance plane photographed several missile sites under construction in Cuba. For the next thirteen days the United States and the Soviet Union faced each other in a showdown that brought the world to the brink of war. The two nations remained close to war until October 28, when Kennedy and Khrushchev reached a compromise. The Soviets agreed to remove the missiles from Cuba; Kennedy agreed not to invade Cuba and to remove U.S. long-range missiles from Turkey.

By the time Kennedy died in November 1963, the situation in Cuba had moderated, at least as a military danger; and U.S.-Soviet relations had become less strident. Both nations, it seemed, had been to the brink and had not liked what they saw. The situation in Vietnam, however, had heated up considerably, and was beginning to show the signs of the quagmire it would become under Lyndon Johnson's administration—and after. When Kennedy came to office he inherited a situation in which Eisenhower had committed about 800 U.S. advisors to the war in Vietnam. A thousand days later, there were nearly 17,000 U.S. advisors backed up by helicopter support units. U.S. pilots were flying sorties out of Bienhoa Air Base, providing transport and cover for the South Vietnamese army.

DOCUMENT 6.1
President John F. Kennedy's Inaugural Address (January 1961)

John F. Kennedy was the youngest man ever elected to the presidency. His youthful image alone gave many Americans hope that his administration would mark the beginning of a new era in the nation's history, a time of new ideas, a move away from what many saw as the Eisenhower doldrums. Whether or not the Kennedy administration lived up to that image of hope and change is another issue, but on a bitterly cold day in January 1961, many Americans saw a new beginning in their new president as he spoke to the nation of such things as hope, public service, and a new generation of leaders. The catchword of the day was vigor; *a popular Broadway play was* Camelot—*about a young and vigorous king and his dashing roundtable of advisors. For his admirers, Kennedy seemed to personify many of the challenges of the sixties that lay ahead.*

Kennedy and his advisors saw the victory over Richard Nixon in the 1960 campaign as a mandate for change and a call to an activist presidency. Kennedy's personal vigor (real or imagined) would be transformed into a vigorous administration. His inaugural speech was intended to convey this new beginning.

SOURCE: *Public Papers of the Presidents: John F. Kennedy, 1961,* 1–3.

We observe today not a victory of party but a celebration of freedom—symbolizing an end as well as a beginning—signifying renewal as well as change. For I have sworn before you and Almighty God the same solemn oath our forebears prescribed nearly a century and three-quarters ago.

The world is very different now. For man holds in his mortal hands the power to abolish all forms of human poverty and all forms of human life. And yet the same revolutionary beliefs for which our forebears fought are still at issue around the globe—the belief that the rights of man come not from the generosity of the state but from the hand of God.

We dare not forget today that we are the heirs of the first revolution. Let the word go forth from this time and place, to friend and foe alike, that the torch has been passed to a new generation of Americans—born in this century, tempered by war, disciplined by a hard and bitter peace, proud of our ancient heritage—and unwilling to witness or permit the slow undoing of those human rights to which this nation has always been committed, and to which we are committed today at home and around the world.

Let every nation know, whether it wishes us well or ill, that we shall pay any price, bear any burden, meet any hardship, support any friend, oppose any foe to assure the survival and the success of liberty.

This much we pledge—and more.

To those old allies whose culture and spiritual origins we share, we pledge the loyalty of faithful friends. United, there is little we cannot do in a host of cooperative ventures. Divided, there is little we can do—for we dare not meet a powerful challenge at odds and split asunder.

To those new states whom we welcome to the ranks of the free, we pledge our word that one form of colonial control shall not have passed away merely to be replaced by a more iron tyranny. We shall not always expect to find them supporting our view. But we shall always hope to find them strongly supporting their own freedom—and to remember that, in the past, those who foolishly sought power by riding the back of the tiger ended up inside.

To those people in the huts and villages of half the globe struggling to break the bonds of mass misery, we pledge our best efforts to help them help themselves, for whatever period is required—not because the Communists may be doing it, not because we seek their votes, but because it is right. If a free society cannot help the many who are poor, it cannot save the few who are rich. . . .

Finally, to those nations who would make themselves our adversary, we offer not a pledge but a request: that both sides begin anew the quest for peace, before the dark powers of destruction unleashed by science engulf all humanity in planned or accidental self-destruction.

We dare not tempt them with weakness. For only when our arms are sufficient beyond doubt can we be certain beyond doubt that they will never be employed.

But neither can two great and powerful groups of nations take comfort from our present course—both sides overburdened by the cost of modern weapons, both rightly alarmed by the steady spread of the deadly atom, yet both racing to alter the uncertain balance of terror that stays the hand of mankind's final war.

So let us begin anew—remembering on both sides that civility is not a sign of weakness, and sincerity is always subject to proof. Let us never negotiate out of fear. But let us never fear to negotiate.

Let both sides explore what problems unite us instead of belaboring those problems which divide us.

Let both sides, for the first time, formulate serious and precise proposals for the inspection and control of arms—and bring the absolute power to destroy other nations under the absolute control of all nations. . . .

And if a beach-head of cooperation may push back the jungle of suspicion, let both sides join in creating a new endeavor, not a new balance of power, but a new world of law, where the strong are just and the weak secure and the peace preserved.

All this will not be finished in the first one hundred days. Nor will it be finished in the first one hundred days of this Administration, nor perhaps even in our lifetime on this planet. But let us begin.

In your hands, my fellow citizens, more than mine, will rest the final success or failure of our course. Since this country was founded, each generation of Americans has been summoned to give testimony to its national loyalty. The graves of young Americans who answered the call to service surround the globe.

Now the trumpet summons us again—not as a call to bear arms, though arms we need—not as a call to battle, though embattled we are—but a call to bear the burden of a long twilight struggle, year in and year out, "rejoicing in hope, patient in tribulation," a struggle against the common enemies of man: tyranny, poverty, disease, and war itself.

Can we forge against these enemies a grand and global alliance, North and South, East and West, that can assure a more fruitful life for all mankind? Will you join that historic effort?

In the long history of the world, only a few generations have been granted the role of defending freedom in its hour of maximum danger. I do not shrink from this responsibility—I welcome it. I do not believe that any of us would exchange places with any other people or any other generation. The energy, the faith, the devotion which we bring to this endeavor will light our country and all who serve it—and the glow from that fire can truly light the world.

And so, my fellow Americans: ask not what your country can do for you—ask what you can do for your country.

My fellow citizens of the world: ask not what America will do for you, but what together we can do for the freedom of man.

Finally, whether you are citizens of America or citizens of the world, ask us here the same high standards of strength and sacrifice which we ask of you. With a good conscience our only sure reward, with history the final judge of our deeds, let us go forth to lead the land we love, asking His blessing and His help, but knowing that here on earth God's work must truly be our own.

DOCUMENT 6.2
Dean Rusk Recalls the Bay of Pigs Incident (April 1961)

The following document is Secretary of State Dean Rusk's recollection of the Bay of Pigs invasion of April 1961. Rusk was a career diplomat who worked his way to the top of the State Department in the postwar years. He is often described as a "hawk," a believer in the use of military action to work the nation's will against communist aggression.

When Rusk left office he vowed never to write a memoir. The following recollection comes from a series of interviews compiled by Rusk's son Richard and published in a volume titled As I Saw It.

It offers an excellent example of how presidents obtain information (and misinformation) in times of crises.

SOURCE: Dean Rusk (as told to Richard Rusk), *As I Saw It* (New York, 1990).

On April 17, 1961, a brigade of some fourteen hundred anti-Castro Cuban exiles organized, trained, armed, transported, and directed by the Central

Intelligence Agency, landed at the Bay of Pigs to overthrow Fidel Castro. CIA advisers assured the brigade that Castro's own men would defect, that the landings would inspire a popular uprising against Castro's regime, and that the American forces would back them up in case of trouble.

The exile force made it to the beaches, but the landing was opposed. The men fought bravely while their ammunition lasted, but they were quickly surrounded by tanks and twenty thousand Cuban soldiers. Two of their freighters containing ammunition, food, and medical supplies were sunk by Castro's planes, and President Kennedy forbade U.S. forces to go to the brigade's assistance. Castro's troops crushed the brigade in less than three days. The general uprising never took place, and Castro arrested two hundred thousand Cubans in Havana alone. Throughout the island he rounded up anyone suspected of underground connections.

The circumstances leading to this fiasco are well known. When Castro first seized power in 1959, he was supported by most Americans, relieved that former Cuban dictator Fulgencio Batista's repressive rule had finally ended. Soon afterward Castro even visited Washington and talked about replacing the Batista regime with a constitutional democracy, based upon free elections. Americans at first wanted to work with Castro. In fact, there is some classic television footage of Castro walking out of then Vice President Nixon's office and Nixon putting his arm around Castro and saying, "We're going to work with this man."

However, the relationship soured, and Castro angered Eisenhower . . . [and] Eisenhower broke off relations on January 3 [1961] seventeen days before the Kennedy inauguration. . . .

In subsequent briefings I discovered that the CIA had begun to train the Cuban exiles in Guatemala in 1960. They planned to launch a conventional assault and establish a foothold close to main population centers. . . . If the brigade did not succeed in the invasion, it would fall back into the hills and conduct guerrilla operations.

CIA planners may have remembered that Castro's own movement started small but eventually overthrew Batista. We had heard of widespread disillusionment in Cuba and had seen a steady stream of refugees fleeing the island. This gave us the impression that many Cubans did not like Castro and would do something about him if the opportunity arose. . . .

President Kennedy . . . decided to proceed, primarily on the advice of Allen Dulles and Richard Bissell at the CIA. The Joint Chiefs of Staff also supported the operation, but I am convinced they never looked at the plan as professional soldiers. They figured that since the whole show was a CIA operation, they would just approve it and wash their hands of it. Had the Joint Chiefs been responsible for the operation, my guess is they would have expressed serious reservations; for example, they would have spotted the great gap between the brigade's small size and its large operation.

I myself did not serve President Kennedy very well. Personally I was skeptical about the Bay of Pigs plan from the beginning. Most simply, the operation violated international law. There was no way to make a good legal case for an American-supported landing in Cuba. Also, I felt that an operation of this scale could not be conducted covertly. The landing and our involvement would become publicly known the moment the brigade started for the beach. We didn't grapple with that reality at all. Finally, having never seen actual evidence that Cuba was ripe for another revolution, I doubted that an uprising would spring up in support of this operation. . . . I should have pressed Kennedy to ask the Joint Chiefs a question that was never asked. Kennedy should have told the chiefs, "I may want to invade with American forces. How many men would we need to conduct the operation ourselves?" I am sure that the chiefs would have insisted upon sustained preliminary bombing and at least two divisions going ashore in initial landings, with full back up by the Army, Navy, Marines, and Air Force. In looking at the chief's total bill, Kennedy also would have noted the extraordinary contrast between what our professional military thought was needed and the puny resources of the Cuban brigade. . . . I knew that this thin brigade of Cuban exiles did not stand a snowball's chance in hell of success. I didn't relay this military judgment to President Kennedy because I was no longer in the military. . . .

I am not sure which specific argument convinced Kennedy finally to authorize the invasion. An overriding concern for him might have been the chance to overthrow Castro's regime. Cuba's move toward communism had been a deep shock to the American people, posing a real threat to the stability of other Latin American countries. Thus, Kennedy may have felt the operation worth the risk, if success meant a non-Communist Cuba and a loyal member of the Organization of American States (OAS). Cuba's focus on Marxist revolution was unsettling the hemisphere. . . .

And so the invasion went on as planned, and it ran into trouble from the beginning. Early Saturday morning, April 15, Cuban exile pilots flying prop-driven B-26s took off from an airfield in Nicaragua and attacked Castro's air force on the ground in Cuba. The raid damaged only a few planes. Equally ominous, the CIA cover story that the raid was the work of defectors from Castro's own air force fell to pieces when one B-26 made an emergency landing in Key West, alerting the American press. Not only did the raid fail to knock out Castro's air force, but it warned him that further action was imminent.

Early Monday morning, April 17, the exile force of fourteen hundred men reached the beaches at the Bay of Pigs after a difficult landing. The brigade met stiff resistance on the ground, and there was no popular uprising. Castro's few T-35s [Soviet tanks] raised havoc during the first two days, strafing the brigade on the beaches and sinking two supply ships. Sometime during this period, with the invasion suffering from inadequate air support, Richard Bissell and Charles Cabell of the CIA came to my office and asked my permission to launch a second B-26 strike against Cuban airfields. They claimed the second strike had already been authorized. My impression was that this had not been part of the plan, although I wasn't sure because I never had a written copy of the plan. I told them I couldn't authorize that strike. They persisted, and I invited them to call President Kennedy and ask him personally. They elected not to do so but later claimed that had that strike gone ahead, Castro's planes would not have hit the landing ships.

That was nonsense. A handful of obsolete B-26s could not have provided air cover for the landing or destroyed Castro's entire air force, as small as it was. Even if American planes had flown the mission, as some were advocating, a sustained and systematic operation would have been required; we didn't even know where Castro had hidden all his planes.

The Bay of Pigs invasion was an obvious blunder. The news of this disaster and the subsequent loss of life hit Kennedy hard. It also shook his confidence in people for whom he had great regard. It increased his tendency to be skeptical of everything he was told, a healthy attitude for any American president. I was especially concerned over what damage it would do to the administration and Kennedy's relations with Congress and our NATO allies.

Kennedy himself refused to deny his responsibility, as some White House aides suggested he do; some even hinted to the press that Kennedy was only carrying out an operation planned and organized by President Eisenhower. This infuriated Kennedy. We had had full chance to review the operation and make our own judgment, and he wasn't going to dump the failure on Eisenhower. He immediately held a press conference and took full responsibility. . . . He deeply resented any lack of solidarity in his own administration over this debacle. He remarked that "success has many fathers, but failure is an orphan," and he did not like it when some of his own people abandoned ship.

DOCUMENT 6.3
President John F. Kennedy Addresses the Nation on the Cuban Missile Crisis (October 22, 1962)

The most dangerous U.S.-Soviet confrontation of the entire cold war occurred in October 1962 when the Soviets placed short-range and medium-range missiles, armed with nuclear warheads, in Cuba. The Soviet premier, Nikita Khrushchev, was looking for a victory over the United States following the

Berlin crisis of late 1961, an incident that culminated in the Berlin Wall and appeared to be a defeat for the Eastern bloc. In Cuba, Khrushchev hoped to undermine U.S. prestige abroad (particularly in Latin America) while compensating for the growing American advantage in long-range ICBMs by placing Soviet weapons closer to U.S. borders. Once activated, the Soviet missiles, only ninety miles from U.S. soil, could hit every major American city except Seattle. They could also be used by the Soviets as a bargaining chip in future crises.

U-2 spy planes detected the missile sites on October 14. Kennedy immediately created Ex-Com (Executive Committee of the National Security Council) to deal with the crisis. Members of Ex-Com included Secretary of State Dean Rusk, Secretary of Defense Robert McNamara, National Security Advisor McGeorge Bundy, General Maxwell Taylor, former Secretary of State Dean Acheson, and the president's brother, Attorney General Robert Kennedy. Others who were present at various Ex-Com meetings included Vice President Lyndon Johnson and Adlai Stevenson.

As the Soviets rushed to complete their launch pads in Cuba, Ex-Com weighed its options. Eight days later, when Kennedy spoke to the nation, the members of Ex-Com had moderated their plans considerably. The crisis was resolved when Kennedy agreed to accept a Soviet offer to remove the missiles from Cuba in exchange for the removal of U.S. missiles from Turkey.

The Soviet Army Chief of Operations later recalled: "Nuclear catastrophe was hanging by a thread . . . and we weren't counting days or hours, but minutes." In the documentary Fog of War, *Robert McNamara, recalling these events, placed his thumb and forefinger as close together as he could for the camera, and said "We came this close to war."*

SOURCE: *Public Papers of the Presidents: John F. Kennedy, 1962, 806–9.*

Good evening my fellow citizens:

This government, as promised, has maintained the closest surveillance of the Soviet military buildup on the island of Cuba. Within the past week, unmistakable evidence has established the fact that a series of offensive missile sites is now in preparation on that imprisoned island. The purpose of these bases can be none other than to provide a nuclear strike capability against the Western Hemisphere. . . .

The characteristics of these new missile sites indicate two distinct types of installations. Several of them include medium range ballistic missiles, capable of carrying a nuclear warhead for a distance of more than one thousand nautical miles. Each of these missiles, in short, is capable of striking Washington, D.C., the Panama Canal, Cape Canaveral, Mexico City, or any other city in the southeastern part of the United States, in Central America, or in the Caribbean area.

Additional sites not yet completed appear to be designed for intermediate range ballistic missiles—capable of traveling more than twice as far—and thus capable of striking most of the major cities in the Western Hemisphere, ranging as far north as Hudson Bay, Canada, and as far south as Lima, Peru. In addition, jet bombers, capable of carrying nuclear weapons, are now being uncrated and assembled in Cuba, while the necessary air bases are being prepared. . . .

This action . . . contradicts the repeated assurances of Soviet spokesmen, both publicly and privately delivered, that the arms buildup in Cuba would retain its original defensive character, and that the Soviet Union had no need or desire to station strategic missiles on the territory of any other nation. . . .

For many years, both the Soviet Union and the United States . . . have deployed strategic nuclear weapons with great care, never upsetting the precarious *status quo* which insured that these weapons would not be used in the absence of some vital challenge. Our own strategic missiles have never been transferred to the territory of any other nation under a cloak of secrecy and deception; and our history—unlike that of the Soviets since the end of World War II—demonstrates that we have no desire to dominate or conquer any other nation or impose our system upon its people. Nevertheless, American citizens have become adjusted to living daily on the bull's-eye of Soviet missiles located inside the U.S.S.R. or in submarines.

In that sense, missiles in Cuba add to an already clear and present danger— although it should be noted the nations of Latin America have never previously been subjected to a potential nuclear threat.

But this secret, swift, and extraordinary buildup of Communist missiles—in an area well known to have a special and historical relationship to the United States and the nations of the Western Hemisphere, in violation of Soviet assurances, and in defiance of American and hemispheric policy—this sudden, clandestine decision to station strategic weapons for the first time outside of Soviet soil—is a deliberately provocative and unjustified change in the *status quo* which cannot be accepted by this country, if our courage and our commitments are ever to be trusted again by either friend or foe.

The 1930's taught us a clear lesson: aggressive conduct, if allowed to go unchecked, ultimately leads to war. This nation is opposed to war. We are also true to our word. Our unswerving objective, therefore, must be to prevent the use of these missiles against this or any other country, and to secure their withdrawal or elimination from the Western Hemisphere. . . .

Acting, therefore, in the defense of our own security and of the entire Western Hemisphere, and under the authority entrusted to me by the Constitution as endorsed by the resolution of the Congress, I have directed that the following initial steps be taken immediately:

First: To halt this offensive buildup, a strict quarantine on all offensive military equipment under shipment to Cuba is being initiated. All ships of any kind bound for Cuba from whatever nation or port will, if found to contain cargoes of offensive weapons, be turned back. . . .

Second: I have directed the continued and increased close surveillance of Cuba and its military buildup. . . . Should these offensive military preparations continue, thus increasing the threat to the hemisphere, further action will be justified. I have directed the armed forces to prepare for any eventualities; and I trust that in the interest of both the Cuban people and the Soviet technicians at the sites, the hazards to all concerned of continuing this threat will be recognized.

Third: It shall be the policy of this nation to regard any nuclear missile launched from Cuba against any nation in the Western Hemisphere as an attack by the Soviet Union on the United States, requiring a full retaliatory response upon the Soviet Union.

Fourth: As a necessary military precaution, I have reinforced our base at Guantanamo, evacuated today the dependents of our personnel there, and ordered additional military units to be on a standby alert basis.

Fifth: We are calling tonight for an immediate meeting of the Organ of Consultation under the Organization of American States, to consider this threat to hemispheric security and to invoke articles 6 and 8 of the Rio Treaty in support of all necessary action. . . .

Sixth: Under the Charter of the United Nations, we are asking tonight that an emergency meeting of the Security Council be convoked without delay to take action against this latest Soviet threat to world peace. Our resolution will call for the prompt dismantling and withdrawal of all offensive weapons in Cuba, under the supervision of U.N. observers, before the quarantine can be lifted.

Seventh and finally: I call upon Chairman Khrushchev to halt and eliminate this clandestine, reckless, and provocative threat to world peace and to stable relations between our two nations. I call upon him further to abandon this course of world domination, and to join in an historic effort to end the perilous arms race and to transform the history of man. He has an opportunity now to move the world back from the abyss of destruction—by returning to his government's own words that it had no need to station missiles outside its own territory, and withdrawing these weapons from Cuba—by refraining from any action which will widen or deepen the present crisis—and then by participating in a search for peaceful and permanent solutions. . . .

But it is difficult to settle or even discuss these problems in an atmosphere of intimidation. That is why this latest Soviet threat—or any other threat which is made either independently or in response to our actions this week—must and will be met with determination. Any hostile move anywhere in the world against the safety and freedom of peoples to whom we are committed—including in particular the brave people of West Berlin—will be met by whatever action is needed. . . .

My fellow citizens. Let no one doubt that this is a difficult and dangerous effort on which we have set out. No one can foresee precisely what course it will take or what costs or casualties will be incurred. Many months of sacrifice and self-discipline lie ahead—months in which both our patience and our will will be tested—months in which many threats and denunciations will keep us aware of our dangers. But the greatest danger of all would be to do nothing. . . .

Our goal is not the victory of might, but the vindication of right—not peace at the expense of freedom, but both peace and freedom, here in this hemisphere, and, we hope, around the world. God willing, that goal will be achieved.

Thank you and good night.

DOCUMENT 6.4
Kennedy and Vietnam. Two Interviews

In the annals of "what-if" history, one of the most analyzed questions has been: Would Kennedy have pulled out of Vietnam had he lived to serve a second term? Robert Dallek, in An Unfinished Life, John F. Kennedy, 1917–1963, *takes time with this question and concludes that Kennedy probably would have withdrawn U.S. troops after the 1964 election. Much of Dallek's evidence is drawn from a conversation that JFK had with Senator Mike Mansfield in the summer of 1963 in which Kennedy apparently said that he would withdraw from Vietnam, "But I can't do it until 1965—after I'm reelected. If I tried to pull out completely now . . . we would have another Joe McCarthy scare on our hands, but I can do it after I'm reelected."*

However, as late as September 1963, Kennedy, in a series of television interviews, was making statements that seemed to imply that he would stay the course in Vietnam—and he gave the reasons why he believed that a continued presence in Vietnam was necessary. Those reasons were many of the same ones that Lyndon Johnson cited in his continued escalation of the war in Vietnam. Kennedy may have wanted to leave Vietnam in 1965, but more likely he would have faced the same problems and the same foreign policy considerations that plagued Johnson through the remainder of the decade—and would very likely have reacted much the same way.

Below are two television interviews, just two months before Kennedy's assassination in Dallas, in which the president discusses a whole range of problems facing him in Vietnam, including his difficulties with the administration of President Ngo Dinh Diem, which had just begun a systematic repression of Buddhists who opposed the war. Diem would be overthrown and murdered on November 1 in a coup encouraged by Washington. Kennedy died in Dallas three weeks later.

SOURCE: Interview transcripts, Box 14, David Powers Paper, John F. Kennedy Library, Boston.

CBS interview, Walter Cronkite (September 2, 1963)

Cronkite: Mr. President, the only hot war we've got running at the moment is of course the one in Vietnam, and we have our difficulties there, quite obviously.

JFK: I don't think that unless a greater effort is made by the government to win popular support that the war can be won out there. In the final analysis, it is their war. They are the ones who have to win it or lose it. We can help them, we can give them equipment, we can send our men out there as advisers, but they have to win it—the people of Vietnam—against the communists. We are prepared to continue to assist them, but I don't think that the war can be won unless the people support the effort, and, in my opinion, in the last two months the government has gotten out of touch with the people. . . .

Cronkite: Do you think this government has time to regain the support of the people?

JFK: I do. With changes in policy and perhaps with personnel, I think it can. If it doesn't make those changes, I would think that the chances of winning it would not be very good.

Cronkite: Hasn't every indication from Saigon been that President Diem has no intention of changing his pattern?

JFK: If he does not change it, of course, that is his decision. He has been there ten years, and, as I say, he has carried this burden when he has been counted out on a number of occasions.

Our best judgment is that he can't be successful on this basis. We hope that he comes to see that; but in the final analysis it is the people and the government itself who have to win or lose this struggle. All we can do is help, and we are making it very clear. But I don't agree with those who say we should withdraw. That would be a great mistake. I know people don't like America to be engaged in this kind of an effort. Forty-seven

Americans have been killed in combat with the enemy, but this is a very important struggle even though it is far away.

We took all this—made this effort to defend Europe. Now Europe is quite secure. We also have to participate—we may not like it—in the defense of Asia.

NBC Interview, Chet Huntley and David Brinkley (September 9, 1963)

Huntley: Mr. President, in respect to our difficulties in South Vietnam, could it be that our government tends occasionally to get locked into a policy or an attitude and then finds it difficult to alter or shift that policy?

JFK: Yes, that is true. I think in the case of South Vietnam we have been dealing with a government which is in control, has been in control for ten years. In addition, we have felt for the last two years that the struggle against the communists was going better. Since June, however . . . we have been concerned about a deterioration, particularly in the Saigon area, which hasn't been felt greatly in the outlying areas but may spread. So we are faced with the problem of wanting to protect the area against the communists. On the other hand, we have to deal with the government there. That produces a kind of ambivalence in our efforts which exposes us to some criticism. We are using our influence to persuade the government there to take those steps which will win back support. That takes some time, and we must be patient. We must persist.

Huntley: Are we likely to reduce our aid to South Vietnam now?

JFK: I don't think . . . that would be helpful at this time. If you reduce your aid, it is possible you could have some effect upon the government structure there. On the other hand, you might have a situation which could bring about a collapse. Strongly in our mind is what happened in the case of China at the end of World War II, where China was lost—a weak government became increasingly unable to control events. We don't want that.

Brinkley: Mr. President have you had any reason to doubt this so-called "domino theory," that if South Vietnam falls, the rest of Southeast Asia will go behind it?

JFK: No, I believe it. I believe it. I think that the struggle is close enough. China is so large, looms so high just beyond the frontiers, that if South Vietnam went, it would not only give them an improved geographic position for a guerrilla assault on Malaya but would also give the impression that the wave of the future in Southeast Asia was China and the communists. So I believe it. . . .

Brinkley: With so much of our prestige, money, so on, committed in South Vietnam, why can't we exercise a little more influence there, Mr. President?

JFK: We have some influence. We have some influence and we are attempting to carry it out. I think we don't—we can't expect these countries to do everything the way we want to do them. They have their own interest, their own personalities, their own traditions. We can't make everyone in our image, and there are a good many people who don't want to go in our image. . . . We would like to have Cambodia, Thailand, and South Vietnam all in harmony, but there are ancient differences there. We can't make the world over, but we can influence the world. The fact of the matter is that with the assistance of the United States and SEATO [Southeast Asia Treaty Organization], Southeast Asia and indeed all of Asia has been maintained independent against a powerful force, the Chinese communists. What I am concerned about is that Americans will get impatient and say, because they don't like events in Southeast Asia or they don't like the government in Saigon, that we should withdraw. That only makes it easy for the communists. I think we should stay. We should use our influence in as effective a way as we can, but we should not withdraw.

BIOGRAPHICAL SKETCH
Robert McNamara

When John Kennedy came to the White House in January 1961, he lacked the foreign policy experience of his predecessor. Defense issues had played a prominent role in the presidential campaign, and it was expected that defense issues would probably occupy the new administration. Kennedy needed a strong secretary of defense. He first offered the position to the former secretary, Robert Lovett, but Lovett declined. Lovett did, however, recommend Robert S. McNamara.

McNamara was born in San Francisco in 1916. He graduated from the University of California in 1937 with a degree in economics and philosophy. He went on to receive a master's degree in business from Harvard, and in 1940 he returned to Harvard to teach in the business school. In 1943 he joined the Army Air Corps and served under General Curtis LeMay. McNamara was a part of the command structure that ordered the firebombing of Japanese cities in 1945.

After the war, in 1946, McNamara joined Ford Motor Company as manager of planning and financial analysis. He rose rapidly inside the corporate structure, and on November 9, 1960 (the day after Kennedy was elected president), McNamara was named president of Ford Motor Company—the first person outside the Ford family to hold that position. Five weeks later, McNamara joined Kennedy's cabinet.

The Kennedy-McNamara redesign of U.S. foreign policy was significantly different from the Eisenhower-Dulles New Look strategy. It was McNamara who rejected the Eisenhower-Dulles threat of massive retaliation as a deterrent for war, and replaced it with what he called "flexible response."

One aspect of flexible response was to increase the nation's conventional strength, designed to counter conventional military thrusts by the Soviets (or their proxies) just about anywhere on earth. Another was called "counterinsurgency," a plan for training American guerrillas (or their proxies) to fight communist guerrillas. The U.S. counterinsurgency force was the celebrated Green Berets. The Green Berets were trained to take the guerrilla war to the guerrillas, particularly in Vietnam.

Although McNamara rejected the old massive retaliation strategy, his own strategy of "assured destruction" was similar—although it was still within the context of flexible response. He characterized assured destruction as the capability "to deter deliberate nuclear attack upon the United States and its allies by maintaining a highly reliable ability to inflict an unacceptable degree of damage upon any single aggressor, or combination of aggressors, even after absorbing a surprise first strike." Thus in a retaliatory strike, the United States would still be able to destroy as much of 25 percent of the Soviet Union's population and 50 percent of its industrial capacity. That, then, would stand as a deterrent to a Soviet first strike. This strategy called for a significant increase in U.S. nuclear capability, and McNamara pushed for the modernization and expansion of weapons and delivery systems, culminating in an accelerated production and deployment of the Minuteman ICBM and Polaris missiles. By the time McNamara left office in 1968, the United States had deployed 54 Titan II and 1,000 Minuteman missiles on land, and 656 Polaris missiles on 41 nuclear submarines.

The Kennedy administration's first international crisis came in April 1961 when the Bay Pigs invasion turned into a military disaster in the swamps of southern Cuba. The dramatic failure of that mission was a great embarrassment to the administration, and McNamara later said that his principal regret was his recommendation to Kennedy to proceed with the operation. More successful from McNamara's point of view was the advice he gave Kennedy during the Cuban missile crisis in October 1962. As that crisis unfolded, McNamara ultimately supported the president's decision to quarantine Cuba to prevent Soviet ships from transporting more weapons to the island.

It was, however, the war in Vietnam that truly came to define McNamara. During the one thousand days of the Kennedy administration, U.S. military advisors to the Saigon government steadily increased—with

McNamara's concurrence—from just a few hundred under Eisenhower to about 17,000.

Following Kennedy's death, McNamara continued on at Defense in the Johnson administration. As the war escalated, McNamara became the focus of the tragedy as it unfolded—and the war became increasingly identified as "McNamara's war." The United States began sustained bombing in 1965, and a larger military force was sent to defend South Vietnam. That force grew to almost 535,000 by the summer of 1968; and the casualty lists mounted as the nation became more deeply involved.

Other than the presidents themselves, no one was more responsible for the escalation of America's involvement in Vietnam than McNamara. But through 1967 he gradually became skeptical about whether the war could be won by deploying more troops to South Vietnam and intensifying the bombing of the North. He traveled to Vietnam several times to study the situation, but he became more and more reluctant to approve the increases in troop levels requested by the military commanders. In November 1967, when McNamara failed to convince Johnson that the war could not be won, he resigned. He was named by Johnson to head the World Bank.

McNamara's memoir, *In Retrospect*, published in 1995, presented an account and analysis of the Vietnam War that dwelt heavily on his mistakes, his strong sense of guilt and regret. He wrote: "We of the Kennedy and Johnson administrations who participated in the decisions on Vietnam acted according to what we thought were the principles and traditions of this nation. We made our decisions in light of those values. Yet we were wrong, terribly wrong. We owe it to future generations to explain why."

STUDY QUESTIONS

1. Kennedy's inaugural speech is most often remembered for its call to service. But it is more than anything else a foreign policy speech. It is often argued, in fact, that it is an extremely threatening speech. Who is Kennedy threatening? How did Kennedy's statements here translate into actions later in his administration?
2. In the sixties it was often said that liberals believed in what was called "the perfectibility of mankind." What do you think this means, and do you see any aspects of this idea in Kennedy's inaugural speech?
3. There was plenty of blame to go around for the failure of the Bay of Pigs invasion. Who was to blame, and why?
4. What were Kennedy's reasons for staying the course in Vietnam?

FURTHER READINGS

Michael Beschloss, *The Crisis Years: Kennedy and Khrushchev, 1960–1963* (1991).

Ernest R. May and Philip D. Zelikow, eds., *The Kennedy Tapes: Inside the White House During the Cuban Missile Crisis* (2002).

Robert McNamara, *In Retrospect: The Tragedy and Lessons of Vietnam* (1995).

Mark J. White, ed., *The Kennedys and Cuba: The Declassified Documentary History* (2001).

Peter Wyden, *Bay of Pigs: The Untold Story* (1979).

7 • Lyndon Johnson's War

INTRODUCTION

The United States entered the war in Vietnam for much the same reason it entered the war in Korea—to stop what was perceived as the advancing forces of communism. The message to the world was clear: the United States would come to the aid of an aggrieved nation in the face of communist aggression.

But in the final analysis, the war in Vietnam proved the opposite. The American people showed that they would not endure the many hardships of that kind of war indefinitely. It also became clear in Vietnam that America's mechanized might—the force designed specifically to fight the Soviets on the broad plains of western Russia—was not terribly effective against an unmechanized land force that moved more men and materiel by bicycle than by truck. When General Curtis LeMay suggested to Lyndon Johnson that he bomb the North Vietnamese back to the Stone Age, some suggested that that might not be very far. Many Americans simply refused to believe that the U.S. military could not defeat what Johnson called a "fourth-rate raggedy-assed country," and so they began looking for answers to America's frustrations elsewhere, among the Washington politicians, the anti-war protesters, and the press.

America's involvement in Vietnam was couched in cold war rhetoric and the tenets and assumptions of the time: containment (communism must not be allowed to expand on any front), the domino theory (if one country falls to communism so will its neighbors), and the first lesson of World War II—that appeasement of an aggressor only brings on a wider war. But as it became clear, in the late 1960s, that a conventional military victory would not be possible in Vietnam, America's leaders began wrapping themselves in a sort of perverse Wilsonian rhetoric, suggesting that the United States sought a "peace with honor" and would be satisfied by a peace without victory.

In August 1964 North Vietnamese torpedo boats attacked the U.S. destroyer *Maddox* in the Tonkin Gulf. On August 5, the Senate voted 98 to 2 to give Johnson the power to "take all necessary measures to repel any armed attacks against the forces of the United States." Later the same day, the House vote on the Tonkin

Gulf Resolution was unanimous. In early February, an attack on U.S. forces at Pleiku pushed Johnson to begin bombing the North. Within three weeks, Johnson approved Operation Rolling Thunder, a massive sustained bombing operation against the North. In 1965 the United States flew 25,000 sorties against North Vietnam. By the end of 1966 the United States was sending in 12,000 sorties a month. In early March, Johnson sent the first U.S. combat troops to Vietnam: two Marine landing teams to protect the U.S. airbase at Danang. Lyndon Johnson was at war in Vietnam. America's nightmare had begun.

DOCUMENT 7.1
President Lyndon Johnson, "Why We Are in Vietnam" (April 1965)

One month after sending the first U.S. combat troops into Vietnam, President Johnson, in a landmark speech at Johns Hopkins University, explained to the nation his reasons for going to war. "Why," he asked, "must we take this painful road?" His explanation evoked the main tenets of America's cold war foreign policy, from the consequences of appeasement to falling dominoes.

Johnson's speech is, unfortunately, remembered only for the president's reasons for escalation and not for his vision of a peaceful world order, or even his simple concept that weapons are a manifestation of man's failures.

SOURCE: *Public Papers of the Presidents: Lyndon B. Johnson, 1963,* 394–99.

Tonight Americans and Asians are dying for a world where each people may choose its own path to change.

This is the principle for which our ancestors fought in the valleys of Pennsylvania. It is the principle for which our sons fight tonight in the jungles of Vietnam.

Vietnam is far away from this quiet campus. We have no territory there. Nor do we seek any. The war is dirty and brutal and difficult. And some too-young men, born into an America that is bursting with opportunity and promise, have ended their lives on Vietnam's steaming soil.

Why must we take this painful road?

Why must this nation hazard its ease, its interests, and its power for the sake of a people so far away? We fight because we must fight if we are to live in the world where every country can shape its own destiny, and only in such a world will our own freedom be finally secure.

This kind of world will never be built by bombs or bullets. Yet the infirmities of man are such that force must often precede reason, and the waste of the war [must often precede] the works of peace.

We wish that this were not so. But we must deal with the world as it is, if it is ever to be as we wish.

The world as it is in Asia is not a serene or peaceful place.

The first reality is that North Vietnam has attacked the independent nation of South Vietnam. Its object is total conquest.

Of course, some of the people of South Vietnam are participating in attacks on their own government. But trained men and supplies, orders and arms, flow in a constant stream from North to South.

This support is the heartbeat of the war. . . .

The confused nature of this conflict cannot mask the fact that it is the new face of an old enemy.

Over this war—and all Asia—is another reality: the deepening shadow of Communist China. The rulers in Hanoi are urged on by Peking. This is a regime which has destroyed freedom in Tibet, which has attacked India and has been condemned by the United Nations for aggression in Korea. It is a nation which is helping the forces of violence in almost every continent. The contest in Vietnam is part of a wider pattern of aggressive purpose.

Why are these realities our concern? Why are we in South Vietnam?

We are there because we have a promise to keep. Since 1954 every American President has offered support to the people of Vietnam. We have helped to build, and we have helped to defend. Thus, over many years, we have made a national pledge to help South Vietnam defend its independence.

And I intend to keep that promise.

To dishonor that pledge, to abandon this small and brave nation to its enemies, and to the terror that must follow, would be an unforgivable wrong.

We are also there to strengthen world order. Around the globe from Berlin to Thailand are people whose well-being rests in part on the belief that they can count on us if they are attacked. To leave Vietnam to its fate would shake the confidence of all these people in the value of an American commitment and in the value of America's word. The result would be increased unrest and instability, and even wider war.

We are also there because there are great stakes in the balance. Let no one think for a moment that retreat from Vietnam would bring an end to conflict. The battle would be renewed in one country and then another. The central lesson of our time is that the appetite of aggression is never satisfied. To withdraw from one battlefield means only to prepare for the next. We must say in Southeast Asia—as we did in Europe—in the words of the Bible: "Hitherto shalt thou come, but no farther."

There are those who say that all our effort there will be futile—that China's power is such that it is bound to dominate all Southeast Asia. But there is no end to that argument until all of the nations of Asia are swallowed up. . . .

Our objective is the independence of South Vietnam and its freedom from attack. We want nothing for ourselves—only that the people of South Vietnam be allowed to guide their own country in their own way.

We will do everything necessary to reach that objective and we will do only what is absolutely necessary.

In recent months attacks on South Vietnam were stepped up. Thus, it became necessary for us to increase our response and to make attacks by air. This is not a change of purpose. It is a change in what we believe that purpose requires.

We do this in order to slow down the aggression.

We do this to increase the confidence of the brave people of South Vietnam who have bravely borne this brutal battle for so many years with so many casualties.

And we do this to convince the leaders of North Vietnam—and all who seek to share their conquest—of a simple fact:

We will not be defeated.

We will not grow tired.

We will not withdraw, either openly or under the cloak of a meaningless agreement. . . .

We hope that peace will come swiftly. But that is in the hands of others besides ourselves. And we must be prepared for a long continued conflict. It will require patience as well as bravery—the will to endure as well as the will to resist. . . .

Such peace demands an independent South Vietnam securely guaranteed and able to shape its own relationships to all others, free from outside interference, tied to no alliance, a military base for no other country.

These are the essentials of any final settlement.

We will never be second in the search for such a peaceful settlement in Vietnam. . . .

The United Nations is already actively engaged in development in this area. As far back as 1961 I conferred with our authorities in Vietnam in connection with their work here. And I hope tonight that the Secretary General of the United Nations could use the prestige of his great office, and his deep knowledge of Asia, to initiate, as soon as possible, with the countries of that area, a plan for cooperation in increased development.

For our part, I will ask the Congress to join in a billion dollar American investment in this effort as soon as it is underway. And I hope that all other industrialized countries, including the Soviet Union, will join in this effort to replace despair with hope, and terror with progress.

The task is nothing less than to enrich the hopes and the existence of more than a hundred million people. And there is much to be done.

The vast Mekong River can provide food and water and power on a scale to dwarf even our own TVA. The wonders of modern medicine can be spread through villages where thousands die every year from lack of care. Schools can be established to train people in the skills that are needed to manage the process of development.

And these objectives, and more, are within the reach of a cooperative and determined effort. . . .

Well, this can be their world yet. Man now has the knowledge—always before denied—to make this planet serve the real needs of the people who live on it.

I know this will not be easy. I know how difficult it is for reason to guide passion, and love to master hate. The complexities of this world do not bow easily to pure and consistent answers. But the simple truths are there just the same. We must try.

This generation of the world must choose: destroy or build, kill or aid, hate or understand. We can do all these things on a scale never dreamed of before.

Well, we will choose life. In doing so we will prevail over the enemies within man, and over the natural enemies of all mankind.

DOCUMENT 7.2
Senator J. William Fulbright, "A Voodoo Foreign Policy" (May 1966)

Just a year after President Johnson's Johns Hopkins speech, Arkansas Senator J. William Fulbright spoke at the same university. Fulbright's speech was part of the Christian Herter Lecture Series at the Johns Hopkins School of Advanced International Studies in Washington, and was not intended as a response to Johnson's speech. But in many ways it was.

Fulbright was a good personal friend of President Johnson, and as chairman of the Senate Foreign Relations Committee had pushed through the president's Tonkin Gulf Resolution in August 1964. But Fulbright soon came to oppose the president's Vietnam policy, and, as he explained in his speech, became a supporter of (and even a spokesman for) anti-war activism as an expression of national pride and patriotism.

Anti-war dissent from a Senate heavyweight like Fulbright seemed to clear the way for a growing opposition to the war in both houses of Congress as the war escalated.

Document 7.2 is an excerpt of Fulbright's speech at Johns Hopkins—parts of which were later published in the New York Times Magazine *under the title "The Fatal Arrogance of Power." In 1967, Fulbright published a book with the title* The Arrogance of Power.

SOURCE: J. William Fulbright, *The Arrogance of Power* (1967).

To criticize one's country is to do it a service and to pay it a compliment. It is a service because it may spur the country to do better than it is doing; it is a compliment because it evidences a belief that the country can do better than it is doing.

Criticism may embarrass the country's leaders in the short run but strengthen their hands in the long run; it may destroy a consensus on policy while expressing a consensus on values. Woodrow Wilson once said that there was "such a thing as being too proud to fight." There is, or ought to be, such a thing as being too confident to conform, too strong to be silent in the face of apparent error. Criticism, in short, is more than a right: it is an act of patriotism—a higher form of patriotism, I believe, than the familiar rituals of national adulation.

This it is not pejorative but a tribute to say that America is worthy of criticism. If nonetheless one is charged with a lack of patriotism, I would reply with Albert Camus: "No, I didn't love my country, if pointing out what is unjust in what we love amounts to not loving. If insisting that what we love should measure up to the finest image we have to her amounts to not loving."

What is the finest image of America? To me it is the image of the composite—or, better still, a synthesis—of diverse peoples and cultures, come together in harmony, but not identity, in an open, receptive, generous and creative society.

We are an extraordinary nation, endowed with rich and productive land and a talented and energetic population. Surely a nation so favored is capable of extraordinary achievement, not only in the area of producing and enjoying great wealth—where our achievements have indeed been extraordinary—but also in the area of human and international relations—in which area, it seems to me, our achievements have fallen short of our capacity and promise. The question that I find intriguing is whether a nation so extraordinarily endowed as the United States can overcome that arrogance of power which has afflicted, weakened and, in some cases, destroyed great nations in the past.

The causes of the malady are a mystery but its recurrence is one of the uniformities of history: Power tends to confuse itself with virtue and a great nation is particularly susceptible to the idea that its power is a sign of God's favor, conferring upon it a special responsibility for other nations—to make them richer and happier and wiser, to remake them, that is, in its own shining image.

Power also tends to take itself for omnipotence. Once imbued with the idea of a mission a great nation easily assumes that it has the means as well as the duty to do God's work. The Lord, after all, surely would not choose you as His agent and then deny you the sword with which to work His will. . . .

There is a kind of voodoo about American foreign policy. Certain drums have to be beaten regularly to ward off evil spirits—for example, the male-dictions which are regularly uttered against North Vietnamese aggression, the "wild men" in Peking. . . . Certain pledges must be repeated every day lest the whole free world go to rack and ruin—for example, we will never go back on a commitment no matter how unwise; we regard this alliance or that as absolutely "vital" to the free world; and, of course, we will stand stalwart in Berlin from now until Judgment Day. Certain words must never be uttered except in derision—the word "appeasement," for example, comes as near as any word can to summarizing anything that is regarded by American policy makers as stupid, wicked and disastrous.

I do not suggest that we should heap praise on the Chinese Communists, dismantle NATO, abandon Berlin and seize every opportunity that comes along to appease our enemies. I do suggest the desirability of an atmosphere in which unorthodox ideas would arouse interest rather than horror, reflection rather than emotion. As likely as not, new proposals, carefully examined, would be found wanting and old policies judged sound; what is wanted is not change itself but the capacity for change.

Consider the idea of "appeasement." In a free and healthy political atmosphere it would elicit neither horror nor enthusiasm but only interest in what precisely its proponent had in mind. As Winston Churchill once said: "Appeasement in itself may be good or bad according to circumstances. . . . Appeasement from strength is magnanimous and noble and might be the surest and perhaps the only path to peace."

In addition to its usefulness for redeeming error and introducing new ideas, free and open criticism has a third, more abstract but no less important function in a democracy. It is therapy and catharsis for those who are troubled or dismayed by something their country is doing; it helps to reassert traditional values, to clear the air when it is full of tension and mistrust.

There are times in public life as in private life when one must protest, not solely or even primarily because one's protest will be politic or materially productive, but because one's sense of decency is offended, because one is fed up with political craft and public image, or simply because something goes against the grain. The catharsis thus provided may indeed be the most valuable of freedom's uses.

While not unprecedented, protests against a war in the middle of the war are a rare experience for Americans. I see it as a mark of strength and maturity that an articulate minority have raised their voices against the Vietnamese war and that the majority of Americans are enduring this dissent—not without anxiety, to be sure, but with better grace and understanding than would have been the case in any other war of the 20th century. . . .

Some of our superpatriots assume that any war the United States fights is a just war, if not indeed a holy crusade, but history does not sustain their view. No reputable historian would deny that the United States has fought some wars which were unjust, unnecessary or both—I would suggest the War of 1812, the Civil War and the Spanish-American War as examples. In a historical frame of reference it seems to me logical and proper to question the wisdom of our present military involvement in Asia.

Protesters against the Vietnamese war have been held up to scorn on the ground that they wish to "select their wars," by which it is apparently meant that it is hypocritical to object to this particular war while not objecting to war in general. I fail to understand what is reprehensible about trying to make moral distinctions between one war and another—between, for example, resistance to Hitler and intervention in Vietnam. From the time of Grotius to the drafting of the United Nations Charter, international lawyers have tried to distinguish between "just wars" and "unjust wars." It is a difficult problem of law and an even more difficult problem of morality, but it is certainly a valid problem.

Under the American Constitution the Congress—especially the Senate —has a particular responsibility in coping with such problems, yet in recent years the Congress has not fully discharged its obligations in the field of foreign relations. The reduced role of the Congress and the enhanced role of the President in the making of foreign policy are not the result merely of President Johnson's ideas of consensus; they are the culmination of a trend in the constitutional relationship between President and Congress that began in 1940—that is to say, at the beginning of this age of crisis.

The cause of the change is crisis itself. The President has the authority and resources to make decisions and take actions in an emergency; the Congress does not. Nor, in my opinion, should it; the proper responsibilities of the Congress are to reflect and review, to advise and criticize, to consent and to withhold consent.

In the past twenty-five years, American foreign policy has encountered a shattering series of crises and inevitably—or almost inevitably—the effort to cope with these has been an executive effort, while the Congress, inspired by patriotism, importuned by Presidents and deterred by lack of information, has tended to fall in line. The result has been an unhinging of traditional constitutional relationships; the Senate's constitutional powers of advice and consent have atrophied into what is widely regarded—though never asserted—to be a duty to give prompt consent with a minimum of advice. . . .

[O]n August 5, 1964, the Congress received an urgent request from President Johnson for the immediate adoption of a joint resolution regarding Southeast Asia. On August 7, after perfunctory committee hearings and a brief debate, the Congress, with only two Senators dissenting, adopted the resolution, authorizing the President "to take all necessary steps, including the use of armed force," against aggression in Southeast Asia.

The joint [Tonkin Gulf] resolution was a blank check signed by the Congress in an atmosphere of urgency that seemed at the time to preclude debate. Since its adoption, the Administration has converted the Vietnamese conflict from a civil war in which some American advisers were involved to a major international war in which the principal fighting unit is an American army of 250,000 men. Each time that Senators have raised questions about successive escalations of the war, we have had the blank check of August 7, 1964, waved in our faces as supposed evidence of the overwhelming support of the Congress for a policy in Southeast Asia which, in fact, has been radically changed since the summer of 1964.

All this is very frustrating to some of us in the Senate, but we have only ourselves to blame. Had we met our responsibility of careful examination of a Presidential request, had the Senate Foreign Relations Committee held hearings on the resolution before recommending its adoption, had the Senate debated the resolution and considered its implications before giving its overwhelming approval, we might have put limits and qualifications on our endorsement of future uses of force in Southeast Asia. . . .

I myself as chairman of the Foreign Relations Committee, served as floor manager of the Southeast Asia resolution and did all I could to bring about its prompt and overwhelming adoption. I did so because I was confident that President Johnson would use our endorsement with wisdom and restraint. I was also influenced by partisanship: an election campaign was in progress and I had no wish to make any difficulties for the President in his race against a Republican candidate* whose election I thought would be a disaster for the country. My role in the adoption of the resolution of August 7, 1964, is a source of neither pleasure nor pride to me today—although I do not regret the outcome of the election. . . .

DOCUMENT 7.3
Coming Home from Vietnam

Lynda Van Devanter served as an army nurse in Vietnam from June 1969 until June 1970. She was stationed with the 71st Evacuation Hospital in Pleiku, and later with the 67th Evacuation Hospital in Qui Nhon. In 1983 she wrote the best seller Home Before Morning, *describing her Vietnam*

---

*Arizona senator Barry Goldwater.

experience. The document below describes Van Devanter's return home to "the World," in 1970.

Lynda Van Devanter is discussed in more detail in the biographical sketch at the end of this chapter.

SOURCE: Lynda Van Devanter, *Home Before Morning: The Story of an Army Nurse in Vietnam.* University of Massachusetts Press; Reprint edition (April 1, 2001). Reprinted by permission.

When the soldiers of World War II came home, they were met by brass bands, ticker-tape parades, and people so thankful for their service that even those who had never heard a shot fired in anger were treated with respect. It was a time when words like honor, glory, and duty held some value, a time when a returning GI was viewed with esteem so high it bordered on awe. To be a veteran was to be seen as a person of courage, a champion of democracy, an ideal against which all citizens could measure themselves. If you had answered your country's call, you were a hero. And in those days, heroes were plentiful.

But somewhere between 1945 and 1970, words like bravery, sacrifice, and valor had gone out of vogue. . . . When I returned to my country in June of 1970, I began to learn a very bitter lesson. The values with which I had been raised had changed; in the eyes of most Americans, the military services had no more heroes, merely babykillers, misfits, and fools. I was certain that I was neither a babykiller nor a misfit. Maybe I was a fool. . . .

Be we didn't ask for a brass band. We didn't ask for a parade. We didn't even ask for much of a thank you. All we wanted was some transportation to San Francisco International Airport so we could hop connecting flights to get home to our families. We gave the Army a year of our lives, a year with more difficulties than most Americans face in fifty years. The least the Army could have done was give us a ride.

At Travis [Air Force Base] we were herded onto buses and driven to the Oakland Army Terminal where they dumped us around 5 A.M. with a "so long suckers" from the driver and a feeling that we were not more than warm bodies who had outlived their usefulness. Unfortunately, San Francisco International was at least twenty miles away. Since most of us had to get flights from there, wouldn't it have been logical to drop us at the airport? Or was I expecting too much out of the Army when I asked it to be logical?

I checked into commercial busses and taxis, but none were running. There was a transit strike on, and it was nearly impossible to get public transportation of any kind. So I hung one of my suitcases from my left shoulder, hefted my duffel bag onto my right shoulder, grabbed my overnight case with my left hand and my purse with my right, and struggling under the weight, walked out to the highway, where I stuck out my thumb and waited. I was no stranger to hitchhiking. It was the only way to get around in Vietnam. Back in 'Nam, I would usually stand on the flight line in my fatigues, combat boots, jungle hat, pigtails, and a smile. Getting a ride there was a cinch. In fact, planes would sometimes reach the end of the runway, then return to offer me a lift.

But hitchhiking in the real world, I was quickly finding out, was nowhere near as easy—especially if you were wearing a uniform. The cars whizzed past me during rush hour, while I patiently waited for a good Samaritan to stop. A few drivers gave me the finger. I tried to ignore them. Some slowed long enough to yell obscenities. One threw a carton of trash and another nearly hit me with a half-empty can of soda. Finally, two guys stopped in a red and yellow Volkswagen bus. The one on the passenger side opened his door. I ran to the car, dragging the duffel bag and other luggage behind me. I was hot, tired, and dirty.

"Going anywhere near the airport?" I asked.

"Sure am," the guy said. He had long brown hair, blue eyes framed by wire-rimmed glasses, and a full curly beard. There were patches on his jeans and a peace sign on his T-shirt. His relaxed, easy smile was deceptive.

I smiled back and lifted my duffel bag to put it inside the van. But the guy slammed the door shut. "We're going past the airport, sucker, but we don't take Army pigs." He spit on me. I was stunned. . . .

[He] floored the accelerator and [the two men in the car] both laughed uncontrollably as the VW spun its wheels for a few seconds, throwing dirt and stones back at me before it roared away. The drivers of other passing cars also laughed.

I looked down at my chest. On top of my nametag sat a big glob of brownish-colored saliva. I couldn't touch it. I didn't have the energy to wipe it away. Instead, I watched as it ran down my name tag and over a button before it was absorbed into the green material of my uniform.

I wasn't angry, just confused. I wanted to know why. Why would he spit on me? What had I done to him? To either of them? It might have been simple to say I had gone to war and they blamed me for killing innocent people, but didn't they understand that I didn't want this war any more than the most vocal of peace marchers? Didn't they realize that those of us who had seen the war firsthand were probably more antiwar than they were? That we had seen friends suffer and die? That we had seen children destroyed? That we had seen futures crushed?

Were they that naïve?

Or were they merely insensitive creeps who used the excuse of my uniform to vent their hostility toward all people?

I waited a few more hours, holding my thumb out until I thought my arm would fall off. After awhile, I stopped watching people as they hurled their insults. I had begun noticing the people who didn't scream as they drove by. I soon realized they all had something in common. It was what I eventually came to refer to as "the look." It was a combination of surprise at seeing a woman in uniform, and hatred for what they assumed I represented. Most of them never bothered to try to conceal it. "The look" would start around the eyes, as if they were peering right through me. Their faces would harden into stone. I was a pariah, a non-person so low that they believed they could squash me underfoot. . . .

Around 10:30 A.M., when I had given up and was sitting on my duffel bag . . . an old black man in a beat up '58 Chevy stopped and got out of his car. He walked with a limp and leaned forward as if he couldn't stand straight. His clothes were frayed and his face deeply lined. He ran his bony fingers through his gray-black hair, then shook his head and smiled. "I don't know where you're going, little girl," he said. "But I been by here four times since early morning and you ain't got a ride yet. I can't let you spend your whole life on the road." He was only headed for the other side of Oakland, but he said he'd rather go out of his way than see me stranded. He even carried my duffel bag to the trunk. As we drove south on 101, I didn't say much other than thank you, but my disillusionment was obvious.

"People ain't all bad, little girl," he said. "It's just some folks are crazy mixed up these days. You keep in mind that it's gotta get better, cause it can't get any worse."

BIOGRAPHICAL SKETCH
Lynda Van Devanter

Possibly the most unreported heroes of the Vietnam War were the military nurses, particularly those who served in active combat regions at evacuation hospitals. Every day they had to witness the horrors and the tragedies of the war. At the same time, they were often close to the fighting, even threatened by it.

Lynda Van Devanter served as an army nurse in Vietnam from June 1969 until June 1970. In 1979 she founded the Vietnam Veterans of America Women's Project. She served as the organization's executive director until 1984, and continued to be a national spokesperson for the contributions that nurses made to the war. She testified several times before Congress and other government agencies on behalf of the 7,465 women Vietnam veterans. In her later life she focused on those female veterans who continued to struggle with the effects of post-traumatic stress disorder and physical damage from the chemicals (herbicides and pesticides) used in Vietnam, including Agent Orange.

Van Devanter went to Vietnam full of patriotic pride and idealism. "If our boys were being blown apart, then somebody better be over there putting them back together again," she wrote before she left. But the idealism evaporated quickly as she experienced the gore, the noise, the fear, and the fatigue of war. She returned home to recurring nightmares and flashbacks—primary symptoms of post-traumatic stress disorder. She spiraled into uncontrolled drinking and crying, and finally ended up on welfare. Only under intensive therapy was she even able to discuss her Vietnam experiences.

In 1983 Van Devanter wrote the highly acclaimed *Home Before Morning*, a gritty account of her experiences as a nurse at Pleiku. She describes doctors and nurses in Vietnam indulging in drugs, sex, and alcohol to ease the pain of what they saw on the operating tables. It did a great deal to change American attitudes toward the women who served in the war. It was also the inspiration for the television series *China Beach*.

In November 2002, Van Devanter died of diseases associated with wartime exposure to chemical agents and pesticides.

STUDY QUESTIONS

1. Why, according to Johnson, was the U.S. involved in Vietnam? How did that reasoning relate to Truman's reasons for entering the war in Korea fifteen years earlier?
2. What are Fulbright's reasons for opposing the war? How does he justify those reasons?
3. How did Lynda Van Devanter describe her attitude toward the war? How did that differ from those who confronted her when she returned home? How did her view of the war mirror the nation's attitudes?

FURTHER READINGS

Larry Berman, *Lyndon Johnson's War: The Road to Stalemate in Vietnam* (1989).

J. William Fulbright, *The Arrogance of Power* (1967).

H.R. McMaster, *Dereliction of Duty: Lyndon Johnson, Robert McNamara, the Joint Chiefs of Staff, and the Lies That Led to Vietnam* (1997).

Robert McNamara, *In Retrospect: The Tragedy and Lessons of Vietnam* (1995).

James Olson and Randy Roberts, *Where the Domino Fell: America and Vietnam, 1945–1990* (1991).

Lynda Van Devanter, *Home Before Morning: The Story of an Army Nurse in Vietnam* (1983).

8 • Sixties Society and Culture

INTRODUCTION

The decade of the sixties, and the various cultural phenomena that emerged from it, has become nearly mythical in the collective mind of the postwar baby boom generation. It was a new style, new music, new freedoms, changing cultural mores and attitudes. In some analyses it was a reaction to what was perceived as the stifling and conformist fifties—a sort of anti-Eisenhower era.

Whatever it was that was different about the sixties, it was definitely youth generated. The result was, for the first time in American history, a youth culture that evolved into a distinct force in society with unique values, tastes, and aspirations. This helped produce what became popularly known as "the generation gap," an ideological struggle between this new youth and their elders, a sort of social conflict between the past and the present. Certainly, rebellious youth was not new, but in the sixties it was a cultural and social phenomenon, rather than simply one of life's many stages of development.

The generation gap was widened significantly by drug use. It is impossible to determine just how widely drugs were used by the nation's youth in the sixties. It is significant, however, that drug use was such a drastic departure from the nation's cultural norm—or at least the middle-class cultural norm—that it totally confounded the adult generation and opened a gulf between the generations that was difficult to bridge. For most of those who used drugs (or simply experimented with drugs) the drug of choice was usually marijuana. And its use was commonplace. At most universities, for instance, marijuana replaced social drinking. For other participants, the primary drug was LSD, a chemical hallucinogen that for some defined the entire era. LSD and its use is usually traced back to a drug cult founded in the Northeast by Timothy Leary, a one-time Harvard researcher-turned-cult-leader. Leary not only used and distributed the drug, he founded a sort of LSD philosophy of use that involved aspects of mind expansion and the revelation of personal truth through "dropping acid." "Remember man," Leary wrote, "a natural state is ecstatic wonder, ecstatic intuition, ecstatic accurate movement. Don't settle for less." It was nearly the decade's mantra that drug use somehow promoted peace, wisdom, and unity with the universe. For some reason adults did not understand.

Much of the fuel for this fire that was the sixties came from the media. Everything about the decade was different—just by definition—and that made for good press. Every innovation, every new clothing style, every new song release, every new art design, everything "sixties" was covered by the press until it was dragged through a well-worn process from innovation, to fancy, to fashion, to fad. What had begun as "youth culture" rapidly broadened into a style that truly meant all things to all Americans and embraced everything from clothing to politics. Quickly, the term "youth culture" no longer fit, and was replaced with the broader "counterculture."

The breadth of the counterculture is generally a result of how the movement is defined. Narrowly, it might be seen as a few hundred hippies on each coast. Broadly, it encompassed nearly every aspect of American society and culture. For some, it was little more than a physical presence—a hairstyle, a clothing style, a "look." For others it was a new way of seeing the world, a new philosophy, a new freedom.

It is still argued that the counterculture movement never ended, that it folded into the mainstream of the nation's culture. But certainly, by the early years of the 1970s, the uniqueness of the counterculture had worn off and—in some corners of society—a conservative reaction to the excesses of the decade had begun to set in. Possibly the youth of the sixties had become the adults of the seventies and now found little redemption in "sex, drugs, and rock 'n' roll." Or perhaps the end of the Vietnam War removed the primary reason for rebellion in the first place. For whatever reason, the marrow of the sixties became the stuff of nostalgia and myth, a past time of innocence and freedom.

DOCUMENT 8.1
Vaughn Meader, *The First Family* (1962)

Presidents, their families, and all other political and public figures are, today, fair game for parodists, comedians, and impressionists. But it was not always so. Presidents, in particular, were usually considered beyond the target range of humorists and impressionists. But in the 1950s the comedy album became a standard in middle-class households. And in 1962 a parody of the Kennedy family, The First Family, *was released. The star impressionist was Vaughn Meader, an otherwise little-known comedian who had John Kennedy's voice and inflections down so well that he was able to make a short career out of "doing" the president as a stand-up routine. Within four weeks of the album's release in late 1962, it had sold an amazing four million copies, outselling the sound track to* My Fair Lady.

*The following is a track from the album, titled "Economy Lunch." Besides
Meader, other characters are played by Chuck McCann, Earle Doud, Jim
Lehner, Bob McFadden, and others. The characters they play include French
president Charles de Gaulle, Cuban president Fidel Castro, German chancel-
lor Konrad Adenauer, Soviet premier Nikita Khrushchev, Egyptian president
Abdul Nasser, Israeli prime minister David Ben-Gurion, Ghanaian president
Kwame Nkrumah, and the president of Nationalist China, Chiang Kai-shek.*

*It is never good to explain humor, but it will help to know the following:
While on a trip to the United States in 1959, Castro and his entourage were
accused of cleaning chickens in their Manhattan hotel room; mayo (as in
mayonnaise) and Mao (as in Mao Zedong) have a similar sound; Khrushchev,
in an attempt to get attention at a UN conference, had taken his shoe off and
banged it on his desk; the Kennedy administration had been heavily criticized
in the press for throwing extravagant parties; and Lyndon Johnson was given
very little to do as vice president.*

SOURCE: Vaughn Meader, *The First Family*, Cadence Records, New York, 1962.

Press Secretary Pierre Salinger: Do you really think you can get away
  with this?
Kennedy: I've been criticized in the newspapers for the big parties and the
  state dinners. We've got to cut down—and economy starts at home.
Salinger: Alright, if you say so.
Kennedy: Alright gentlemen, let us be seated. Mr. Adenauer, if you'll sit next
  to your friend, Mr. de Gaulle. And Mr. Castro, if you'll sit here next to your
  friend, Mr. Khrushchev. And Mr. Nasser, if you'll sit here next to your friend,
  Mr. Ben-Gurion, oh, I'm sorry. *(Laughter.)* Mr. Nkrumah, if you will sit in
  between Mr. Ben-Gurion and Mr. Nasser. Then you can turn either way.
  (Laughter.) Now, ah, Mr. Chiang Kai-shek, would you please sit there next
  to Mr. Khrushchev? Now, before we get down to the business at hand, I
  thought a brief lunch would be in order. Now, instead of the usual food that
  we usually serve here, I thought we'd have a normal businessman's lunch,
  so I'm going to send down to the delicatessen store for some sandwiches.
  (Grumbling.) How does that strike you gentlemen? *(Noise of pounding.)*

  Mr. Khrushchev? Mr. Khrushchev? I appreciate your enthusiasm. Would
  you mind just taking your shoe off the table. *(Laughter.)*

  I think I'll have a peanut butter and jelly on whole wheat, with a side
  order of coleslaw and a hot fudge sundae. Mr. de Gaulle?
de Gaulle: Uch! *(Laughter.)* I would like to have dove under glass.
Kennedy: Ah, I'm sorry general, but we're only having sandwiches today.
de Gaulle: Then could I have a dove-under-glass sandwich? *(Laughter.)*

Kennedy: Alright, Pierre, a chicken salad on white for the general. Mr. Chiang Kai-shek?

Chiang: A club sandwich would be fine. Thank you so much.

Kennedy: Would you like a little mayo?

Chiang: Please, not to mention that name. *(Laughter.)*

Kennedy: I'm sorry. Mr. Nasser?

Nasser: I'll have a hot pastrami sandwich. I can never get it at home. *(Laughter.)*

Kennedy: What kind of bread?

Nasser: White toast, with lettuce and mayonnaise.

Ben-Gurion: Mr. Nasser.

Nasser: What do you want, Ben-Gurion?

Ben-Gurion: I know we don't get along. You never listen to me. Now you're fooling around with rockets. But this time please listen. Pastrami don't go with white bread and mayonnaise. *(Laughter.)* Have it on rye bread with mustard and a glass of tea and you'll enjoy. *(Laughter.)*

Kennedy: I think Mr. Ben-Gurion has a point there.

Nasser: Alright, I'll take a chance.

Ben-Gurion: Good boy. And if you like pastrami, next time you're in the neighborhood, drop by the house. My wife makes a gefilte fish—it melts in your mouth.

Nasser: We're going to have to get together, Mr. Ben-Gurion.

Ben-Gurion: My name is Ben-Gurion. You can call me Ben.

Nasser: My name is Abdul Nasser. You can call me Abe. *(Laughter.)*

Kennedy: Good. Now, fine. Mr. Khrushchev?

Khrushchev: You don't have to order special for me. I'll have a bit of everybody elses. *(Laughter.)*

Kennedy: Alright. Mr. Adenauer?

Adenauer: There's one sandwich here in America I love. I'll have a western sandwich.

Khrushchev: If Adenauer has a western sandwich, then I'll have an eastern sandwich.

Kennedy: There is no eastern sandwich.

Khrushchev: Then I want the eastern portion of his western sandwich. *(Laughter.)*

Kennedy: I'm sure we can negotiate on that subject. Mr. Castro?

Castro: I'll have a chicken sandwich with a live chicken. *(Laughter.)*

Kennedy: That leaves Mr. Nkrumah. What will you have sir?

Nkrumah: I'll have some watermelon.

Kennedy: Don't put me on, Mr. Nkrumah. *(Laughter.)*

Nkrumah: Alright. A ham and egg sandwich and a coke. *(Noise of pounding.)*

And I guess a bowl of borscht.

Kennedy: Okay, Pierre, put a rush on it.

   Later.

Kennedy: Gentlemen. Now that was a pleasant lunch. Now, under discussion today will be nuclear disarmament, followed by the U.N. bond issue, and a matter of the trade agreement. But first, there is a most important matter to settle. Mr. de Gaulle, yours was the chicken salad and coffee. That's a dollar forty. . . . *(Laughter.)*

End of sketch.

SCENE II, ACT IV
"White House Visitor"

Noise of steps in the snow.

Guard: Halt! Who goes there? Oh, go right ahead.

(Noise of steps in the snow.)

Guard: Where do you think you're going? Oh, I'm sorry. I didn't recognize you sir.

(Steps, now inside.)

Guard: Hey! No one is admitted beyond. . . . Oh! I'm sorry, sir. I didn't know it was you.

(Steps. Doorbell ringing. Door opens.)

Kennedy: Yes? Oh, it's you. What is it?

Child's voice: Can Caroline come out and play?

Kennedy: I'm sorry, young man, but she can't. She's in Italy with her mother.

Child's voice: Oh. Well, then, what's Lyndon doing?

(Laughter. End of sketch.)

DOCUMENT 8.2
Bob Dylan, "The Times They Are A-Changin'" (1963)

Bob Dylan sought to carry the torch of past folksingers who believed that music could be at the forefront of social change in America. His 1963 song, "The Times They Are A-Changin'," forecast a new day for the nation and for the nation's youth. For some, it set the stage for the age. For others, it was an anthem for the generation. It may have been the first cultural expression of what later became known as the generation gap.

With great songs like "The Times They Are A-Changin'" and "Blowin' in the Wind," Dylan became a folk icon, in the mold of Woody Guthrie from the past, and Peter, Paul, and Mary and Joan Baez from the fifties and sixties. But in 1965, at the Newport Folk Festival, Dylan bridged the gap between folk and rock. In a much celebrated (or maligned) event, he appeared before the assembled music lovers wearing black leather and playing an electric guitar. He was booed, and finally ostracized by the folkies, but he introduced a new type of music that would impact the culture: folk-rock.

In 2004, Dylan published a memoir, Chronicles: Volume 1, *in which he describes his revulsion at the iconic status that was ascribed to him by the sixties generation.*

Come gather 'round people
Wherever you roam
And admit that the waters
Around you have grown
And accept it that soon
You'll be drenched to the bone.
If your time to you
Is worth savin'
Then you better start swimmin'
Or you'll sink like a stone
For the times they are a-changin'.

Come writers and critics
Who prophesize with your pen
And keep you eyes wide
The chance won't come again
And don't speak too soon
For the wheel's still in spin
And there's no tellin' who
That it's namin'.
For the loser now
Will be later to win
For the times they are a-changin'.

Come senators, congressmen
Please heed the call
Don't stand in the doorway

Don't block up the hall
For he that gets hurt
Will be he who has stalled
There's a battle outside
And it's ragin'.
It'll soon shake your windows
And rattle your walls
For the times they are a-changin'.

Come mothers and fathers
Throughout the land
And don't criticize
What you can't understand
Your sons and your daughters
Are beyond your command
Your old road is
Rapidly agin.'
Please get out of the new one
If you can't lend a hand
For the times they are a-changin'.

The line it is drawn
The curse it is cast
The slow one now
Will later be fast
As the present now
Will later be past
The order is
Rapidly fadin.'
And the first one now
Will later be last
For the times they are a-changin'.

DOCUMENT 8.3
Jack Gould of the *New York Times* Pans the Beatles
(February 10, 1964)

*Unless you were a teenager in 1964, the arrival of the Beatles at Kennedy
Airport (recently renamed for the assassinated president) in New York may
not have seemed an important event—just another rock'n'roll band, this time*

from Liverpool instead of Lubbock. But the Beatles changed American music and American pop culture. The "Fab Four," as the press insisted on calling John, Paul, George, and Ringo, brought to America a new sound and a new style, both of which were immensely popular and worth imitating. The style was immediately copied by other rock bands (at first in England and then in the United States), and the Beatles' style became the style of American youth from coast to coast. It all seemed to evolve and change throughout the next decade, but much of what was identifiable as the 1960s and well into the next decade (at least in music, style, and pop culture) could be traced to that winter day in early February when the lads from Liverpool invaded America.

Jack Gould of the New York Times *never seemed to get it, at least when it came to rock'n'roll. As television critic for the* Times, *Gould covered America's growing love affair with TV from the late 1940s until the mid-1970s. Often called the "conscience of the industry," Gould led the national press in analyzing and criticizing the quality of programming. His taste was hardly high brow, but he saw television as an outlet for cultural programming—and he disliked the "low culture" that emerged with the new music of the 1950s and 1960s. In September 1956 (Document 5.1), Gould wrote that Elvis Presley, in his appearance on the* Ed Sullivan Show, *had "no discernable singing ability." Eight years later (Document 8.3), Gould reviewed the Beatles' performance on the same Sunday night variety show and found them little more than "the world's highest paid recreational directors."*

SOURCE: *New York Times,* February 10, 1964. © 1964, by the New York Times Agency. Printed with permission.

The cynical turnover in teen-age trauma received recognition last night in the businesslike appearance of the Beatles on the "Ed Sullivan Show" over the Columbia Broadcasting System. The boys hardly did for daughter what Elvis Presley did for her older sister or Frank Sinatra did for mother.

The Liverpool quartet, borrowing the square hairdo used every morning on television by Captain Kangaroo, was composed of conservative conformists. In furthering Britain's comeback as an international influence, they followed established procedure for encouraging self-determination in underdeveloped areas.

The pretext of a connection with the world of music, a matter left to separate consideration below, was perfunctorily sustained by the Beatles. But in the quick intelligence beneath their bangs, there appeared to be a bemused awareness that they might qualify as the world's highest-paid recreation directors.

In their sophisticated understanding that the life of a fad depends on the

performance of the audience and not on the stage, the Beatles were decidedly effective. In their two sets of numbers, they allowed the healing effect
of group therapy to run its course under the discipline of Mr. Sullivan, the
chaperon of the year.

Televised Beatlemania appeared to be a fine mass placebo, and thanks undoubtedly are due Britain for a recess in winter's routine. Last night's sedate
anticlimax speaks well for continuing British-American understanding. The
British always were much more strict with children.

DOCUMENT 8.4
What They Watched: Top Ten TV Shows, 1960–1969

*In 1950, television was little more than a novelty, accessible only to a little
over 10 percent of households—mostly on the East Coast—who had to squint
at their tiny, flickering black and white screens. By mid-decade, however,
the primary TV genres were firmly in place. The sitcom, the Western, the TV
drama, and the variety show were all well established. The TV game show
and sports broadcasts (mostly boxing and wrestling) rounded out evening
entertainment, and soap operas and down-sized game shows kept mostly
housewives entertained during the day.*

*But by 1960 television had become the nation's primary entertainment
staple. By then, 88 percent—or some 40 million—of American households
owned televisions. At times, some 10,000 sets were being hooked up each
day. As journalist Theodore White wrote, "Within a single decade the medium
has exploded to a dimension in shaping the American mind that rivals that of
America's schools and churches."*

*During the sixties, the various genres mostly matured. The TV West-
ern reached its high point with* Bonanza *and* Gunsmoke *before it finally
waned and died out. The variety show that originated in the fifties with the
great* Milton Berle Show *(a.k.a.* Texaco Star Theater*) and the* Sid Caesar
Show*, was little more than filmed vaudeville. But in the 1960s, that form
reached its zenith with programs such as the* Red Skelton Hour, *which
hit the top ten in 1961, and the* Dean Martin Show *later in the decade. It
was, however, the sitcom that became the most enduring of the TV genres.
The decade of the fifties saw some of the best (and worst) sitcoms ever
produced.* I Love Lucy *and* The Honeymooners *have stood the tests of
time with perpetual reruns. Not far behind were the* Donna Reed Show,
Father Knows Best, Leave It to Beaver, Ozzie and Harriet, *and countless
others that varied widely in quality and humor. By the late sixties, the
sitcom came to dominate the evening's entertainment, pushing out most*

other types of entertainment as both the Western and the variety show lost their footing in the ratings.

In ratings of the 1960s below, it is interesting to note that only one game show rose to the top ten through the entire decade (the Price Is Right *in 1960–61). Following the game show scandals of the year before (see Document 5.2) the big money shows like* Twenty-one *were banished from evening programming, although shows of lesser production continued on daytime television. In the 1968–69 programming year, among the top ten was* Julia, *starring Diahann Carroll, the first African American to star in a successful television series. She paved the way for* The Bill Cosby Show, *which reached the number eleven spot a year later.*

Among the TV listings below, several shows defy classification, particularly Candid Camera, Batman, *and* Rowan and Martin's Laugh-In.

SOURCE: Fiftiesweb.com/TV-ratings-60s.

1960–1961
1. Gunsmoke (Western)
2. Wagon Train (Western)
3. Have Gun Will Travel (Western)
4. The Andy Griffith Show (Sitcom)
5. The Real McCoys (Sitcom)
6. Rawhide (Western)
7. Candid Camera
8. Untouchables (Drama)
9. The Price is Right (Game show)
10. The Jack Benny Show (Variety)

1961–1962
1. Wagon Train (Western)
2. Bonanza (Western)
3. Gunsmoke (Western)
4. Hazel (Sitcom)
5. Perry Mason (Drama)
6. The Red Skelton Hour (Variety)
7. The Andy Griffith Show (Sitcom)
8. The Danny Thomas Show (Sitcom)
9. Dr. Kildare (Drama)
10. Candid Camera

1962–1963
1. The Beverly Hillbillies (Sitcom)
2. Candid Camera
3. The Red Skelton Hour (Variety)
4. Bonanza (Western)
5. The Lucy Show (Sitcom)
6. The Andy Griffith Show (Sitcom)
7. Ben Casey (Drama)
8. The Danny Thomas Show (Sitcom)
9. The Dick Van Dyke Show (Sitcom)
10. Gunsmoke (Western)

1963–1964
1. The Beverly Hillbillies (Sitcom)
2. Bonanza (Western)
3. The Dick Van Dyke Show (Sitcom)
4. Petticoat Junction (Sitcom)
5. The Andy Griffith Show (Sitcom)
6. The Lucy Show (Sitcom)
7. Candid Camera
8. The Ed Sullivan Show (Variety)
9. The Danny Thomas Show (Sitcom)
10. My Favorite Martian (Sitcom)

1964–1965

1. Bonanza (Western)
2. Bewitched (Sitcom)
3. Gomer Pyle, USMC (Sitcom)
4. The Andy Griffith Show (Sitcom)
5. The Fugitive (Drama)
6. The Red Skelton Hour (Variety)
7. The Dick Van Dyke Show (Sitcom)
8. The Lucy Show (Sitcom)
9. Peyton Place (Drama)
10. Combat (Drama)

1965–1966

1. Bonanza (Western)
2. Gomer Pyle, USMC (Sitcom)
3. The Lucy Show (Sitcom)
4. The Red Skelton Hour (Variety)
5. Batman
6. The Andy Griffith Show (Sitcom)
7. Bewitched (Sitcom)
8. The Beverly Hillbillies (Sitcom)
9. Hogan's Heroes (Sitcom)
10. Batman

1966–1967

1. Bonanza (Western)
2. The Red Skelton Hour (Variety)
3. The Andy Griffith Show (Sitcom)
4. The Lucy Show (Sitcom)
5. The Jackie Gleason Show (Variety)
6. Green Acres (Sitcom)
7. Daktari (Drama)
8. Bewitched (Sitcom)
9. The Beverly Hillbillies (Sitcom)
10. Gomer Pyle, USMC (Sitcom)

1967–1968

1. The Andy Griffith Show (Sitcom)
2. The Lucy Show (Sitcom)
3. Gomer Pyle, USMC (Sitcom)
4. Gunsmoke (Western)
5. Family Affair (Sitcom)
6. Bonanza (Western)
7. The Red Skelton Hour (Variety)
8. The Dean Martin Show (Variety)
9. The Jackie Gleason Show (Variety)
10. Saturday Night at the Movies

1968–1969

1. Rowan and Martin's Laugh-in
2. Gomer Pyle, USMC (Sitcom)
3. Bonanza (Western)
4. Mayberry RFD (Sitcom)
5. Family Affair (Sitcom)
6. Gunsmoke (Western)
7. Julia (Sitcom)
8. The Dean Martin Show (Variety)
9. Here's Lucy (Sitcom)
10. The Beverly Hillbillies (Sitcom)

1969–1970

1. Rowan and Martin's Laugh-In
2. Gunsmoke (Western)
3. Bonanza (Western)
4. Mayberry RFD (Sitcom)
5. Family Affair (Sitcom)
6. Here's Lucy (Sitcom)
7. The Red Skelton Hour (Variety)
8. Marcus Welby, MD (Drama)
9. Walt Disney's Wonderful World of Color
10. The Doris Day Show (Variety)

BIOGRAPHICAL SKETCH
Janis Joplin

The rock era of the sixties produced some meteoric talent. Unfortunately, a few of those who produced that music were unable to handle the fame—and often the money that went along with it. By the end of the sixties some of the greatest figures in rock were dead, most often of excessive substance abuse. One of those tragic figures was Janis Joplin, a young woman from east Texas with an amazing ability to belt out blues rock. At age twenty-seven, at just the moment she became a rock legend, she died of a drug overdose.

It is no secret that drugs were a part of the sixties youth culture, but in the world of rock superstardom, drug use often progressed to drug abuse. Much of this had to do with youthful exuberance, excessive disposable income, and occasionally, substances supplied by record producers and promoters intent on keeping their artists in a state of blissful peonage.

When Janis Joplin began her career, in the mid- to late sixties, there were very few female rock singers—either as individuals or as lead singers in rock groups. Grace Slick had broken through as the lead singer of Jefferson Airplane, but she was considered an aberration in the all-male world of rock. Not only did Janis Joplin begin her career as a lead singer, she quickly split from her group and headed out on her own as a solo act. And that was a first in rock music history.

Janis Joplin was born in 1943 into a working-class family in the oil refinery town of Port Arthur, Texas. From her earliest days, she was classified as both musically talented and socially eccentric. As early as fourteen she had already come into contact with the music of blues legends like Huddie "Leadbelly" Ledbetter and Bessie Smith. By the time she was eighteen, she was singing in clubs in Austin and Houston.

In 1963, after two years in college, Janis hitchhiked to California, where she quickly fell in with the hippie movement and began singing in clubs and coffeehouses near Los Angeles. The lifestyle, however, seemed to absorb her and she began abusing alcohol and amphetamines. By the mid-1960s, being drunk on stage had, in fact, become a popular part of her act.

Her answer to her growing substance abuse problem was to return to Port Arthur, to her family, and to get away from the lifestyle that seemed to be destroying her. She returned to college, and tried to fit back into small-town life. Within a year, however, she had returned to California.

In 1967 she joined Big Brother and the Holding Company, a little-known West Coast band, and almost immediately she took the group to the top of the rock charts. Their album *Cheap Thrills*, with live versions of "Piece of My Heart" and "Ball and Chain," stayed at the number one spot on the *Billboard* charts for eight weeks and made Joplin and Big Brother one of the great rock bands of the late 1960s. But within a year, "creative differences," exacerbated by excessive substance abuse, caused the band to break up. With plenty of corporate support, Janis made the obvious jump to a solo career.

In 1970, she began production of a new album, *Pearl*. In October, just as the album was completed, Janis Joplin was found dead in a Los Angeles hotel. She died of a heroin overdose; those close to her described her death as accidental. *Pearl* was released posthumously and includes the two songs that have made Janis Joplin a music legend: "Me and Bobby McGee" and "(Oh, Lord Won't You Buy Me a) Mercedes Benz." She was inducted into the Rock 'n' Roll Hall of Fame in 1995.

STUDY QUESTIONS

1. Dylan's "The Times They Are A-Changin'" is usually described as a warning. What is the warning? Who is Dylan warning? What might be the consequences if the warning is not heeded?
2. What made the Beatles so different and exciting in 1964? Was the idolization of the Beatles really so different from the reaction of American youth to other music performers in the past or future?
3. How did the press impact sixties culture? Was the press used to *sell* the outrageous as much as it reported the outrageous? If so, how did that impact the era?

FURTHER READINGS

David Burner, *Making Peace with the Sixties* (1996).

Lewis L. Gould, ed., *Watching Television Coming of Age:* The New York Times *Reviews of Jack Gould* (2002).

Allen J. Matusow, *The Unraveling of America: A History of Liberalism in the 1960s* (1984).

William O'Neill, *Coming Apart: An Informal History of America in the 1960s* (1971).

Theodore Roszak, *The Making of a Counterculture* (1995).

9 • Political Trends on the Left and the Right

INTRODUCTION

The fifteen years following the election of John Kennedy were marked by significant challenges to a tradition of consensus in America. That was particularly true in society and popular culture, where it was perhaps the most visible, but it was also true in national politics.

The challenge to the political consensus manifested itself in the formation of two significant movements, both often described as radical; both, however, remained well within the mainstream of American politics. These two movements, the "New Left" and the "New Right," were mostly youth-driven, at least in their infancies; and both movements grew to influence the two main political parties.

The New Left was driven more by the call for social, economic, and political justice based on the equality of race, gender, and class than by the old leftist-Marxist dogma that socialism would replace the decadence of capitalism. The New Left was also spurred on by the successes of the civil rights movement, fear of nuclear holocaust, and revulsion for government irresponsibility and corporate greed. It was the nation's youth, the New Left often argued, that should be the avant-garde of this movement.

The New Right was a conscious step away from what conservatives called the Republican Party's me-too-ism, or the view that the Republican Party leadership had, at least since 1940, tried to match the liberalism of the Democrats. Conservatives in the sixties called for a new conservatism that focused on downsizing the federal government, supporting states' rights, resisting communism, reducing government regulation of industry, and reaffirming the market economy. Again, the vigor of the New Right was found in the youth of the Republican Party—people like William F. Buckley, Jr., William Rusher, and M. Stanton Evans, and organizations like the Young Americans for Freedom. Within their own party, they rejected the "middle roadism" of

Eisenhower and the social liberalism of Nelson Rockefeller in favor of the principled bluntness of Barry Goldwater. Goldwater's nomination in 1964 was a triumph for the New Right and the beginning of the conservative domination of the Republican Party that would reach fruition with Ronald Reagan's presidency.

The sixties also produced a new political realignment. Through the forties and fifties, the Democrats had slowly embraced the civil rights movement. That stance alienated white southerners, many of whom gradually made their way into the Republican Party. By the mid-sixties, the Republicans had built an effective geographic coalition that included the South, the Midwest, and the Southwest, and took the GOP from a minority party (as it had been since 1936) to a contender in the national political arena. By the mid-seventies, the two parties were beginning to show signs of parity. As the population of the Sunbelt (the South and Southwest) began to increase through the sixties and seventies, that region emerged as a bastion of conservatism—and GOP power increased dramatically into the next decades.

DOCUMENT 9.1
The "Sharon Statement" (October 1960) and the "Port Huron Statement" (June 1962)

Just a few weeks before the 1960 presidential contest between John Kennedy and Richard Nixon a group of young conservatives met at the home of William F. Buckley, Jr., in Sharon, Connecticut, to draft a statement of principles for a new, youth-generated, conservative movement. Their impulse had come, at least in part, from Senator Barry Goldwater's book, Conscience of a Conservative, *published a few months earlier. The group had determined that Nixon's candidacy (as an extension of Eisenhower's middle-of-the-road presidency) supported a series of policies much too liberal for their tastes. The "Sharon Statement" is touted often by conservatives today as the first statement of principles of the modern conservative movement.*

About a year after the "Sharon Statement," some sixty members of a student organization known as Students for a Democratic Society (SDS) met at a United Auto Workers conference center in Port Huron, Michigan, to draft a statement of principles for their organization. Their leader was Tom Hayden, a University of Michigan graduate student and editor of the student newspaper. The SDS aimed to speak for the youth of the early sixties. However, the organization made an attempt to lead the anti-war movement as the decade progressed, and was, in some ways, swallowed up by it.

SOURCE: *National Review* (September 1960).

The Sharon Statement

In this time of moral and political crises, it is the responsibility of the youth of America to affirm certain eternal truths.

We, as young conservatives, believe:

That foremost among the transcendent values is the individual's use of his God-given free will, whence derives his right to be free from the restrictions of arbitrary force;

That liberty is indivisible, and that political freedom cannot long exist without economic freedom;

That the purpose of government is to protect those freedoms through the preservation of internal order, the provision of national defense, and the administration of justice;

That when government ventures beyond these rightful functions, it accumulates power, which tends to diminish order and liberty;

That the *Constitution of the United States* is the best arrangement yet devised for empowering government to fulfill its proper role, while restraining it from the concentration and abuse of power;

That the genius of the *Constitution*—the division of powers—is summed up in the clause that reserves primacy to the several states, or to the people, in those spheres not specifically delegated to the Federal government;

That the market economy, allocating resources by the free play of supply and demand, is the single economic system compatible with the requirements of personal freedom and constitutional government, and that it is at the same time the most productive supplier of human needs;

That when government interferes with the work of the market economy, it tends to reduce the moral and physical strength of the nation; that when it takes from one man to bestow on another, it diminishes the incentive of the first, the integrity of the second, and the moral autonomy of both;

That we will be free only so long as the national sovereignty of the United States is secure; that history shows periods of freedom are rare, and can exist only when free citizens concertedly defend their rights against all enemies;

That the forces of international Communism are, at present, the greatest single threat to these liberties;

That the United States should stress victory over, rather than coexistence with, this menace; and

That American foreign policy must be judged by this criterion: does it serve the just interests of the United States?

SOURCE: Tom Hayden, et al. (Students for a Democratic Society), *The Port Huron Statement* (June 1962). This text, made available by the Sixties Project, is copyright © 1993 by the author or by Vietnam Generation, Inc., all rights reserved. Reprinted by permission.

The Port Huron Statement

We are people of this generation, bred in at least modest comfort, housed now in universities, looking uncomfortably to the world we inherit.

When we were kids the United States was the wealthiest and strongest country in the world; the only one with the atom bomb, the least scarred by modern war, an initiator of the United Nations that we thought would distribute Western influence throughout the world. Freedom and equality for each individual, government of, by, and for the people—these American values we found good, principles by which we could live as men. Many of us began maturing in complacency.

As we grew, however, our comfort was penetrated by events too troubling to dismiss. First, the permeating and victimizing fact of human degradation, symbolized by the Southern struggle against racial bigotry, compelled most of us from silence to activism. Second, the enclosing fact of the Cold War, symbolized by the presence of the Bomb, brought awareness that we ourselves, and our friends, and millions of abstract "others" we knew more directly because of our common peril, might die at any time. We might deliberately ignore, or avoid, or fail to feel all other human problems, but not these two, for these were too immediate and crushing in their impact, too challenging in the demand that we as individuals take the responsibility for encounter and resolution.

While these and other problems either directly oppressed us or rankled our consciences and became our own subjective concerns, we began to see complicated and disturbing paradoxes in our surrounding America. The declaration "all men are created equal . . ." rang hollow before the facts of Negro life in the South and the big cities of the North. The proclaimed peaceful intentions of the United States contradicted its economic and military investments in the Cold War *status quo.* . . .

Not only did tarnish appear on our image of American virtue, not only did disillusion occur when the hypocrisy of American ideals was discovered, but we began to sense that what we had originally seen as the American Golden Age was actually the decline of an era. The worldwide outbreak of revolution against colonialism and imperialism, the entrenchment of totalitarian states, the menace of war, overpopulation, international disorder, supertechnology—these trends were testing the tenacity of our own commitment to democracy and freedom and our abilities to visualize their application to a world in upheaval. . . .

Some would have us believe that Americans feel contentment amidst prosperity—but might it not better be called a glaze above deeply-felt anxieties about their role in the new world? And if these anxieties produce a developed indifference to human affairs, do they not as well produce a yearning to believe there *is* an alternative to the present, that something *can* be done to change circumstances in the school, the workplace, the bureaucracies, the government? It is to this latter yearning, at once the spark and engine of change, that we direct our present appeal. The search for truly democratic alternatives to the present, and a commitment to social experimentation with them, is a worthy and fulfilling human enterprise, one which moves us and, we hope, others today. On such a basis do we offer this document of our convictions and analysis: as an effort in understanding and changing and conditions of humanity in the late twentieth century, an effort rooted in the ancient, still unfulfilled conception of man attaining determining influence over his circumstances of life. . . .

If student movements for change are still rarities on the campus scene, what is commonplace there? The real campus, the familiar campus, is a place of private people, engaged in their notorious "inner emigration." It is a place of commitment to business-as-usual, getting ahead, playing it cool. It is a place of mass affirmation of the Twist,* but mass reluctance toward the controversial public stance.

Rules are accepted as "inevitable," bureaucracy as "just circumstances," irrelevance as "scholarship," selflessness as "martyrdom," politics as "just another way to make people, and an unprofitable one, too." . . .

Tragically, the university could serve as a significant source of social criticism and an initiator of new modes and molders of attitudes. But the actual intellectual effect of the college experience is hardly distinguishable from that of any other communications channel—say, a television set—passing on the stock truths of the day. Students leave college somewhat more "tolerant" than when they arrived, but basically unchallenged in their values and political orientations. With administrators ordering the institution, and faculty [ordering] the curriculum, the student learns by his isolation to accept elite rule within the university, which prepares him to accept later forms of minority control. The real function of the educational system—as opposed to its more rhetorical function of "searching for the truth"—is to impart the key information and styles that will help the student get by, modestly but comfortably, in the big society beyond.

Look beyond the campus, to America itself. That student life is more intellectual, and perhaps more comfortable, does not obscure the fact that the fundamental qualities of life on the campus reflect the habits of society at large. The fraternity president is seen at the junior manager levels; the sorority

---

*A popular dance in the sixties.

queen has gone to Grosse Pointe; the serious poet burns for a place, any place, to work; the once-serious and never-serious poets work at the advertising agencies. The desperation of people threatened by forces about which they know little and of which they can say less; the cheerful emptiness of people "giving up" all hope of changing things; the faceless ones polled by Gallup who listed "international affairs" fourteenth on their list of "problems" but who also expected thermonuclear war in the next few years; in these and other forms, Americans are in withdrawal from public life, from any collective effort in directing their own affairs. . . .

We live amidst a national celebration of economic prosperity while poverty and deprivation remain an unbreakable way of life for millions in the "affluent society," including many of our own generation. We hear glib references to the "welfare state," "free enterprise," and "shareholder's democracy" while military defense is the main item of "public" spending and obvious oligopoly and other forms of minority rule defy real individual initiative or popular control. Work, too, is often unfulfilling and victimizing, accepted as a channel to status or plenty, if not a way to pay the bills, rarely as a means of understanding and controlling self and events. In work and leisure the individual is regulated as part of the system, a consuming unit, bombarded by hard-sell, soft-sell, lies and semi-true appeals to his basest drives. He is always told that he is a "free" man because of "free enterprise." . . .

The most spectacular and important creation of the authoritarian and oligopolistic structure of economic decision-making in America is the institution called "the military-industrial complex" by former President Eisenhower—the powerful congruence of interest and structure among military and business elites which affects so much of our development and destiny. Not only is ours the first generation to live with the possibility of world-wide cataclysm—it is the first to experience the actual social preparation for cataclysm, the general militarization of American society. . . .

Since our childhood these two trends—the rise of the military and the installation of a defense-based economy—have grown fantastically. The Department of Defense, ironically the world's largest single organization, is worth $160 billion, owns 32 million acres of America and employs half the 7.5 million persons directly dependent on the military for subsistence, has an $11 billion payroll which is larger than the net annual income of all American corporations. Defense spending in the Eisenhower era totaled $350 billions and President Kennedy entered office pledged to go even beyond the present defense allocation of 60 cents from every public dollar spent. Except for a war-induced boom immediately after "our side" bombed Hiroshima, American economic prosperity has coincided with a growing dependence on military outlay—from 1911 to 1959 America's Gross National Product of $5.25 trillion included $700 billion in goods and services purchased for the defense effort, about one-seventh of the accumulated GNP. This pattern has included the steady concentration of military spending among a few corporations. In 1961, 86 percent of Defense Department contracts were awarded without competition. The ordnance industry of 100,000 people is completely engaged in military work; in the aircraft industry, 94 percent of 750,000 workers are linked to the war economy; shipbuilding, radio and communications equipment industries commit forty percent of their work to defense; iron and steel, petroleum, metal-stamping and machine shop products, motors and generators, tools and hardware, copper, aluminum and machine tools industries all devote at least 10 percent of their work to the same cause. . . .

Every effort to end the Cold War and expand the process of world industrialization is an effort hostile to people and institutions whose interests lie in perpetuation of the East-West military threat and the postponement of change in the "have not" nations of the world. Every such effort, too, is bound to establish greater democracy in America.

DOCUMENT 9.2
President Lyndon B. Johnson Describes the "Great Society" (May 22, 1964)

Historians sometimes like to judge presidents by their vision for the nation. Here, President Lyndon Johnson presents his vision, the Great Society. This ambitious social program (which is not specifically spelled out in this speech) was the stepchild of the liberal Democratic programs that began in earnest with Franklin Roosevelt's New Deal, followed by Harry Truman's Fair Deal and John Kennedy's New Frontier. Following the New Deal, however, such liberal programs had limited success. Very little of Truman's Fair Deal was passed by Congress, stymied mostly by a conservative coalition of southerners and Republicans; and Kennedy's New Frontier programs were kept locked up by a similar coalition when the president was assassinated in November 1963.

Six months after Kennedy's death, Lyndon Johnson picked up the gauntlet of postwar liberalism. In the following speech, delivered at the University of Michigan, Johnson promises to realize the potential of a Great Society. And quickly, in one brief burst of reform, he moved from promises to action. Before Congress adjourned in the fall of 1965 it had passed an amazing eighty-nine bills, enacting the entire Democratic reform agenda in just nine months. Great Society hallmarks included federal aid to education, Medicare, Medicaid, and the Civil Rights acts of 1964 and 1965.

In the final analysis, however, much of the Great Society failed, either because of underfunding in the face of wartime expenses and a weakening economy, or because the reform mood gave way to ideological and political polarization. The Vietnam War ended and the Great Society atrophied at about the same time, giving many Americans the impression that the four-decade-long era of liberal reform at home and U.S. dominance abroad was over.

SOURCE: *Public Papers of the Presidents: Lyndon B. Johnson, 1963–1965* (Washington, DC: USGPO, 1965).

I have come here today from the turmoil of your Capital to the tranquility of your campus to speak about the future of your country.

The purpose of protecting the life of our Nation and preserving the liberty of our citizens is to pursue the happiness of our people. Our success in that pursuit is the test of our success as a Nation.

For a century we labored to settle and to subdue a continent. For half a century we called upon unbounded invention and untiring industry to create an order of plenty for all of our people.

The challenge of the next half century is whether we have the wisdom to use that wealth to enrich and elevate our national life, and to advance the quality of our American civilization.

Your imagination, your initiative, and your indignation will determine whether we build a society where progress is the servant of our needs, or a society where old values and new visions are buried under unbridled growth. For in your time we have the opportunity to move not only toward the rich society and the powerful society, but upward to the Great Society.

The Great Society rests on abundance and liberty for all. It demands an end to poverty and racial injustice, to which we are totally committed in our time. But that is just the beginning.

The Great Society is a place where every child can find knowledge to enrich his mind and to enlarge his talents. It is a place where leisure is a welcome chance to build and reflect, not a feared cause of boredom and restlessness. It is a place where the city of man serves not only the needs of the body and the demands of commerce but the desire for beauty and the hunger for community.

It is a place where man can renew contact with nature. It is a place which honors creation for its own sake and for what it adds to the understanding of the race. It is a place where men are more concerned with the quality of their goals than the quality of their goods.

But most of all, the Great Society is not a safe harbor, a resting place, a final objective, a finished work. It is a challenge constantly renewed, beckoning us toward a destiny where the meaning of our lives matches the marvelous products of our labor.

So I want to talk to you today about three places where we begin to build the Great Society—in our cities, in our countryside, and in our classrooms.

Many of you will live to see the day, perhaps fifty years from now, when there will be 400 million Americans—four-fifths of them in urban areas. In the remainder of this century urban population will double, city land will double, and we will have to build homes, highways, and facilities equal to all those built since this country was first settled. So in the next forty years we must rebuild the entire urban United States.

Aristotle said: "Men come together in cities in order to live, but they remain together in order to live the good life." It is harder and harder to live the good life in American cities today.

The catalog of ills is long: There is the decay of the centers and the despoiling of the suburbs. There is not enough housing for our people or transportation for our traffic. Open land is vanishing and the old landmarks are violated. . . .

Our society will never be great until our cities are great. Today the frontier of imagination and innovation is inside those cities and not beyond their borders. New experiments are already going on. It will be the task of your generation to make the American city a place where future generations will come, not only to live but to live the good life. . . .

A second place where we begin to build the great Society is in our countryside. We have always prided ourselves on being not only America the strong and America the free, but America the beautiful. Today that beauty is in danger. The water we drink, the food we eat, the very air we breathe, are threatened with pollution. Our parks are overcrowded, our seashores overburdened. Green fields and dense forests are disappearing. . . .

For once the battle is lost, once our natural splendor is destroyed, it can never be recaptured. And once man can no longer walk with beauty or wonder at nature his spirit will wither and his sustenance be wasted.

A third place to build the Great Society is in the classrooms of America. There your children's lives will be shaped. Our society will not be great until every young mind is set free to scan the farthest reaches of thought and imagination. We are still far from that goal.

Today eight million adult Americans, more than the entire population of Michigan, have not finished five years of school. Nearly twenty million have not finished eight years of school. Nearly fifty-four million—more than one-quarter of all America—have not even finished high school. Each year more than 100,000 high school graduates, with proven ability, do not enter college because they cannot afford it. . . .

In many places classrooms are overcrowded and curricula are outdated. Most of our qualified teachers are underpaid, and many of our paid teachers are unqualified. So we must give every child a place to sit and a teacher to learn from. Poverty must not be a bar to learning, and learning must offer an escape from poverty.

But more classrooms and more teachers are not enough. We must seek an education system which grows in excellence as it grows in size. This means better training for our teachers. It means preparing youth to enjoy their hours of leisure as well as their hours of labor. It means exploring new techniques of teaching, to find new ways to stimulate the love of learning and the capacity for creation.

These are three of the central issues of the Great Society. While our government has many programs directed at those issues, I do not pretend that we have the full answer to those problems.

But I do promise this: We are going to assemble the best thought and the broadest knowledge from all over the world to find those answers for America. I intend to establish working groups to prepare a series of White House conferences and meetings—on the cities, on natural beauty, on the quality of education, and on other emerging challenges. And from these meetings and from this inspiration and from these studies we will begin to set our course toward the Great Society.

The solution to these problems does not rest on a massive program in Washington, nor can it rely solely on the strained resources of local authority. They require us to create new concepts of cooperation, a creative federalism, between the National Capital and the leaders of the local community. . . .

For better or worse, your generation has been appointed by history to deal with those problems and to lead America toward a new age. You have the chance never before afforded to any people in any age. You can help build a society where the demands of morality, and the needs of the spirit, can be realized in the life of the Nation.

So, will you join in this battle to give every citizen the full equality which God enjoins and the law requires, whatever his belief, or race, or the color of his skin?

Will you join in the battle to give every citizen an escape from the crushing weight of poverty?

Will you join in the battle to make it possible for all nations to have an enduring peace—as neighbors and not as mortal enemies?

Will you join in the battle to build the Great Society, to prove that our material progress is only the foundation on which we will build a richer life of mind and spirit?

There are those timid souls who say this battle cannot be won; that we are condemned to a soulless wealth. I do not agree. We have the power to shape the civilization that we want. But we need your will, your labor, your hearts, if we are to build that kind of society.

Those who came to this land sought to build more than just a new country. They sought a new world. So I have come here today to your campus to say that you can make their vision our reality. So let us from this moment begin our work so that in the future men will look back and say: It was then, after a long and weary way, that man turned the exploits of his genius to the full enrichment of life.

DOCUMENT 9.3
Barry Goldwater, "Extremism Is No Vice" (June 1964)

Barry Goldwater's acceptance speech at the 1964 Republican National Convention in San Francisco was one of the most dynamic—and controversial—of the era. Delivered at possibly the most raucous Republican convention since Teddy Roosevelt tried to unseat incumbent president William Howard Taft in 1912, it was a call to arms for conservatives and the new conservatism.

    Goldwater's speech was exciting and dramatic, but when he let loose with "extremism in the defense of liberty is no vice, . . . [and] moderation in the pursuit of justice is no virtue," he lit up the hall. It was certainly a rallying point for the faithful on that summer evening in San Francisco, but the statement hung over Goldwater like a dark cloud for the remainder of the campaign—and some would say for the rest of his life. No matter how he tried to explain what he meant, it was always understood that he was willing to accept right-wing extremists into his campaign at the expense of Nelson Rockefeller and the Republican moderates. The Saturday Evening Post *commented: "That statement deserves to be the 'Rum, Romanism and Rebellion' of this election, and Barry Goldwater deserves to be defeated for it alone, no matter how much he tries to clown it away. He knows what he meant by it."*

SOURCE: *Official Report of the Proceedings of the Twenty-eighth Republican National Convention*, 413–19.

My fellow Republicans, our cause is too great for any man to feel worthy of it. Our task would be too great for any man, did he not have with him the heart and the hands of this great Republican Party. And I promise you tonight that every fiber of my being is consecrated to our cause, that nothing shall be lacking from the struggle that can be brought to it by enthusiasm, by devotion, and plain hard work.

    In this world, no person—no party—can guarantee anything, but what we can do and what we shall do is to deserve victory, and victory will be ours.

    The good Lord raised this mighty Republic to be a home for the brave and to flourish as the land of the free—not to stagnate in the swampland of collectivism, not to cringe before the bully of communism.

Now, my fellow Americans, the tide has been running against freedom. Our people have followed false prophets. We must, and we shall, return to proven ways—not because they are old, but because they are true. We must, and we shall, set the tide running again in the cause of freedom.

And this party, with its every action, every word, every breath, and every heartbeat, has but a single resolve, and that is freedom. . . .

During four futile years, the administration which we shall replace has distorted and lost its vision. It has talked and talked and talked and talked the words of freedom, but it has failed and failed and failed in the works of freedom.

Now, failure cements the wall of shame in Berlin. Failures blot the sands of shame at the Bay of Pigs. Failures mark the slow death of freedom in Laos. Failures infest the jungles of Vietnam. And failures haunt the houses of our once great alliances, and undermine the greatest bulwark ever erected by free nations—the NATO community.

Failures proclaim lost leadership, obscure purpose, weakening will, and the risk of inciting our sworn enemies to new aggressions and to new excesses.

And because of this administration, we are tonight a world divided—we are a nation becalmed. We have lost the brisk pace of diversity and the genius of individual creativity. We are plodding at a pace set by centralized planning, red tape, rules without responsibility, and regimentation without recourse. Rather than useful jobs in our country, people have been offered bureaucratic make-work. Rather than moral leadership, they have been given bread and circuses, spectacle, and, yes, they've even been given scandals.

Tonight there is violence in our streets, corruption in our highest offices, aimlessness among our youth, anxiety among our elderly. And there is a virtual despair among the many who look beyond material success toward the inner meaning of their lives.

And where examples of morality should be set, the opposite is seen. Small men, seeking great wealth or power, have too often and too long turned even the highest levels of public service into mere personal opportunity.

Now, certainly, simple honesty is not too much to demand of men in government. We find it in most. Republicans demand it from everyone—no matter how exalted or protected his position might be.

The growing menace to personal safety, to life, to limb and property, in homes, in churches, on the playgrounds, and places of business, particularly in our great cities, is the mounting concern of every thoughtful citizen in the United States. Security from domestic violence, no less than from foreign aggression, is the most elementary and fundamental purpose of any government.

A government that cannot fulfill this purpose is one that cannot long command the loyalty of its citizens. History demonstrates that nothing prepares the way for tyranny more than the failure of public officials to keep the streets from bullies and marauders.

We Republicans see all this as more, much more than the result of mere political differences, or of mere political mistakes. We see this as the result of a fundamentally and absolutely wrong view of man, his nature, and his destiny. . . .

Those who seek absolute power, even though they seek it to do what they regard as good, are simply demanding the right to enforce their own version of heaven on earth, and let me remind you they are the very ones who always create the most hellish tyrannies.

Absolute power does corrupt, and those who seek it must be suspect and must be opposed. Their mistaken course stems from false notions of equality. Equality, rightly understood as our founding fathers understood it, leads to liberty and to the emancipation of creative differences; wrongly understood, as it has been so tragically in our time, it leads first to conformity and then to despotism. . . .

Now, I needn't remind you, or my fellow Americans regardless of party, that Republicans have shouldered this hard responsibility and marched in this cause before. It was Republican leadership under Dwight Eisenhower that kept the peace, and passed along to this administration the mightiest arsenal for defense the world has ever known.

And I needn't remind you that it was the strength and the unbelievable will of the Eisenhower years that kept the peace by using our strength—by using it in the Formosa Strait and in Lebanon, and by showing it courageously at all times.

It was during those Republican years that the thrust of Communist imperialism was blunted. It was during those years of Republican leadership that this world moved closer not to war but closer to peace than at any other time in the last three decades.

And I needn't remind you that it's been during Democratic years that our strength to deter war has stood still and even gone into a planned decline. It has been during Democratic years that we have weakly stumbled into conflicts—timidly refusing to draw our own lines against aggression—deceitfully refusing to tell even our people of our full participation—and tragically letting our finest men die on battlefields unmarked by purpose, unmarked by pride, or the prospect of victory.

Yesterday it was Korea. Tonight it is Vietnam. Make no bones of this. Don't try to sweep this under the rug. We are at war in Vietnam. And yet the president, who is the commander-in-chief of our forces, refuses to say whether or not the objective over there is victory, and his Secretary of Defense continues to mislead and misinform the American people. . . .

And I needn't remind you—but I will—that it has been during Democratic years that a billion persons were cast into Communist captivity and their fate cynically sealed.

Today, in our beloved country, we have an administration which seems eager to deal with communism in every coin known—from gold to wheat, from consulates to confidence, and even human freedom itself.

The Republican cause demands that we brand communism as the principal disturber of peace in the world today. Indeed, we should brand it as the only significant disturber of the peace. And we must make clear that until its goals of conquest are absolutely renounced, and its relations with all nations tempered, communism and the governments it now controls are enemies of every man on earth who is or wants to be free. . . .

And beyond all that, we see and cherish diversity of ways, diversity of thoughts, of motives and accomplishments. We don't seek to live anyone's life for him—we seek only to secure his rights, guarantee him opportunity to strive, with government performing only those needed and constitutionally sanctioned tasks which cannot otherwise be performed.

We Republicans seek a government that attends to its inherent responsibilities of maintaining a stable monetary and fiscal climate—encouraging a free and a competitive economy, and enforcing law and order.

Thus do we seek inventiveness, diversity, and creative difference within a stable order. For we Republicans define government's role, where needed, at many, many levels—preferably the one closest to the people involved: our towns and our cities, then our counties, then our states, then our regional contacts, and only then the national government. That, let me remind you, is the ladder of liberty built by decentralized power. On it, also, we must have balance between the branches of government at every level.

Balance, diversity, creative difference—these are the elements of Republican equation. Republicans agree on these elements, and they heartily agree to disagree on many, many of their applications. But we have never disagreed on the basic fundamental issues of why you and I are Republicans.

This is a party for free men, not for blind followers and not for conformists. . . .

Anyone who joins us in all sincerity, we welcome. Those who do not care for our cause, we don't expect to enter our ranks in any case. And let our Republicanism, so focused and so dedicated, not be made fuzzy and futile by unthinking and stupid labels.

I would remind you that extremism in the defense of liberty is no vice. And let me remind you also that moderation in the pursuit of justice is no virtue.

The beauty of the very system we Republicans are pledged to restore and revitalize, the beauty of this federal system of ours, is in its reconciliation of diversity with unity. We must not see malice in honest differences of opinion, and no matter how great, so long as they are not inconsistent with the pledges we have given to each other in and through our Constitution.

Our Republican cause is not to level out the world or make its people conform in computer-regimented sameness. Our Republican cause is to free our people and light the way for liberty throughout the world. Ours is a very human cause for very humane goals. This party, its good people, and its unquestionable devotion to freedom will not fulfill the purposes of this campaign which we launch here now until our cause has won the day, inspired the world, and shown the way to a tomorrow worthy of all our yesteryears.

I repeat, I accept your nomination with humbleness, with pride, and you and I are going to fight for the goodness of our land. Thank you.

DOCUMENT 9.4
Time Attempts to Define the "Silent Majority" (January 1970)

In November 1969 President Richard Nixon spoke to the nation on Vietnam. It was a frank speech, an attempt to tell the nation why the United States had gotten involved in the war and what the various options were for withdrawal. Near the end of the speech he said: "And so tonight—to you, the great silent majority of my fellow Americans—I ask for your support." The press immediately grasped the phrase "silent majority" and began trying to define it. Two months after Nixon's speech, Time *magazine passed over the Apollo 11 and Apollo 12 astronauts and chose for its "man of the year" edition "The Middle American," a possibly broader definition of Nixon's "silent majority." As the document below makes apparent, defining Middle America was not a simple task.*

SOURCE: "The Middle Americans," *Time,* January 5, 1970. © 1970 TIME Inc., reprinted by permission.

The Supreme Court had forbidden it, but they prayed defiantly in a school in Netcong, N.J., reading the morning invocation from the *Congressional Record.* In the state legislatures, they introduced more than 100 Draconian bills to put down campus dissent. In West Virginia, they passed a law absolving police in advance of guilt in any riot deaths. In Minneapolis they elected a police detective to be mayor.

Everywhere, they flew the colors of assertive patriots. Their car windows were plastered with American-flag decals, their ideological totems. In the bumper-sticker dialogue of the freeways, they answered "Make Love Not War" with "Honor America" or "Spiro is My Hero." They sent Richard Nixon to the White House and two teams of astronauts to the moon. They were both exalted and afraid. The mysteries of space were nothing, after all, compared with the menacing confusions of their own society.

The American dream that they were living was no longer the dream as advertised. They feared that they were beginning to lose their grip on the country. Others seemed to be taking over—the liberals, the radicals, the defiant young, a communications industry that they often believed was lying to them. The *Saturday Evening Post* folded, but the older world of Norman Rockwell icons was long gone anyway. No one celebrated them: intellectuals dismissed their lore as banality. Pornography, dissent and drugs seemed to wash over them in waves, bearing some of their children away.

But in 1969 they began to assert themselves. They were "discovered" first by politicians and the press, and then they started to discover themselves. In the Administration's voices—especially in the Vice President's and the Attorney General's—in the achievements and the character of the astronauts, in a murmurous and pervasive discontent, they sought to reclaim their culture. It was their interpretation of patriotism that brought Richard Nixon the time to pursue a gradual withdrawal from the war. By their silent but newly felt presence, they influenced the mood of government and the course of legislation, and this began to shape the course of the nation and the nation's course in the world. The Men and Women of the Year were the Middle Americans. . . .

Middle Americans both physically and ideologically inhabit the battleground of change, and they feel themselves are most threatened by it. Taxes hit them the hardest, and yet they feel that they have less and less voice in where and how their money is spent. The Woman of the Year, perhaps even more than her husband, senses the chaos. Often enough, inflation determines the diet she feeds her family. She is anxious about safety in the streets. She worries about her children being bussed, about the sex education to which they are subjected, the drugs they might pick up at school, the smut for sale on the drugstore newsstand and the neighborhood movie screen. For too long no one has seemed to care about the Middle Americans' concerns. They have felt ignored while angry minorities dominated the headlines and the Government's domestic action. If not ignored, they have been treated with condescension. . . .

The culture no longer seems to supply many heroes, but Middle Americans admire men like Neil Armstrong and to some extent, Spiro Agnew. California Governor Ronald Reagan and San Francisco State College President S.I. Hayakawa have won approval for their hard line on dissent. Before his death last year, Dwight Eisenhower was listed as the most admired man in the nation—and Middle America cast much of the vote. In death, John Kennedy is also a hero. Ironically, Robert Kennedy had the allegiance of much of Middle America along with his constituency of blacks and the young. Whatever their politics, both Kennedys had an idealism about America, a pride about it to which Middle Americans responded because they shared it.

Middle America's villains are less easily singled out. Yippie Abbie Hoffman or [Students for a Democratic Society] leaders like Mark Rudd are hardly important enough by themselves to constitute major devils. With such faceless groups as the Weathermen, they merely serve as symbols of all the radicals who pronounce the country evil and ripe for destruction. Disliked, too, are the vaguely identified "liberals" and "intellectuals" who are seen as sympathizing with the radicals. Perhaps the most authentic individual villains to Middle America are the Black Panther leaders, Eldridge Cleaver and Bobby Seale. . . .

Who precisely are the Middle Americans? Columnist Joseph Kraft gave the term currency in late 1967. They make up the core of the group that Richard Nixon now invokes as the "forgotten Americans" or "the Great Silent Majority," though Middle Americans themselves may not be a majority of the U.S. All Americans doubtless share some Middle American beliefs, and many Middle Americans would disagree among themselves on some issues. The lower middle class, including blue-collar workers, service employees and farm workers, numbers some 40 million. Many of the nation's 20 million elderly citizens, frequently living on fixed incomes, are Middle American. So is a substantial portion of the 36 million white-collar workers. Although a hard figure is not possible, the total of Middle Americans possibly approaches 100 million, or half the U.S. population.

The Middle Americans tend to be grouped in the nation's heartland more than on its coasts. But they live in Queens, New York, and Van Nuys, California, as well as in Skokie and Chillicothe. They tend toward the middle-aged and the middlebrow. They are defined as much by what they are not as what they are. As a rule, they are not the poor or the rich. Still, many wealthy business executives are Middle Americans. H. Ross Perot, the Texas millionaire who organized a group called "United We Stand, Inc." to support the President on the war, is an example. Few blacks march in the ranks of Middle America. Nor do the nation's intellectuals, its liberals, its professors, its surgeons. Many general practitioners, though are Middle Americans. Needless to say, Middle America offers no haven to the New Left, although Middle Americans might count a number of old leftists—unionists, for example—in their numbers. They are not extremists of the right despite the fact that some of them voted for George Wallace in 1968. They are both Republicans and Democrats: many cast their ballots for Richard Nixon, but it may be that nearly as many voted for Hubert Humphrey.

Above all Middle America is a state of mind, a morality, a construct of values and prejudices and a complex of fears. The Man and Woman of the Year represent a vast, unorganized fraternity bound together by a roughly similar way of seeing things.

The American mood during the past year has been unquestionably calmer than it was in 1968, which seemed to be the violent crescendo for the '60s. A new Administration given to understatement—on the part of the President if not the Vice President—soothed the national psyche. When Spiro Agnew erupted against television and newspaper commentators and against dissent's "effete corps of impudent snobs," Middle America was further comforted—and also aroused to an intimation of its own potential strength. The flights of Apollo 11 and 12 were a quintessential adventure of American technology and daring. . . . The astronauts themselves were paragons of Middle American aspiration. Redolent of charcoal cookouts, their vocabularies an engaging mix of space jargon and "gee whiz," the space explorer gave back to Middle America where such things still matter; that among Neil Armstrong's extraterrestrial bag-gage was a special badge of his college fraternity, Phi Delta Theta. He used it symbolically to establish Moon Alpha Chapter. . . . Americans, particularly Middle Americans, reveled in the lunar landings precisely because they were victories purely accomplished: in Viet Nam, in the various slums, in the pol-luted environment, no clear victories seemed possible any longer. . . .

Nixon himself is the embodiment of Middle America. There is opportunity for everyone, his mother taught him back in Whittier, California—work hard, love your country, never give up. . . .

The rising level of crime frightens the Middle American, and when he speaks of crime, though he does not like to admit it, he means blacks. On the one hand, Middle America largely agrees with the advances toward equality made by blacks in the past ten years.

Middle Americans express respect for moderate black leaders like Roy Wilkins and Whitney Young—which is easy enough. Middle Americans would generally like to see the quality of black education improve. But the idea of sacrificing their own children's education to a long-range improvement for blacks appalls them. . . .

Open admissions programs at universities strike Middle Americans an un-fair and illogical violations of the merit system. Beyond that, they see a bias toward blacks in conventional admissions policies. "If anything," says Futurist Herman Kahn, "they believe that a black face helps. A Middle American can't send his kid to Harvard, but he knows the black man down the street can, if the boy is bright enough." Middle American workers frequently feel that blacks are given preferential treatment in job hiring. Says Harvard Psychiatrist Robert Coles, who has made a study of the grievances of Middle America: "They say that the Negro should be given jobs, but only so long as he does not go faster than they had to go." . . .

No one expresses the ideology of the Nixonian nation on dissent better than historian Daniel Boorstin, whose book, *The Decline of Radicalism*, Nixon sometimes studies in a secluded den in the Executive Office Building. For an academic, Boorstin is almost ferocious about dissent: "Disagreement is the lifeblood of democracy, dissention is its cancer. Disagreers seek solutions to common problems, dissenters seek power for themselves." In a section on the "Rise of Minority Veto," which must be Agnew's text, he writes: "Small groups have more power than ever before. . . . We are witnessing the explosive rebellion of small groups, who reject the American past, deny their relation to the community. This activism, this new barbarism, cannot last if the nation is to survive." To that, Middle America offers a resounding amen. Middle Americans believe that the radical young are operating in a vast misunderstanding of their nation. Brandeis political scientist John Roche tells an anecdote about the Chicago convention trouble. As he was being collared by a cop, a dissident shouted: "Long live the dictatorship of the proletariat!" Raising his nightstick, the cop retorted "I am the proletariat." Bash, bash.

Viet Nam, the war, which has claimed so many of its sons, leaves Middle America in a moral perplexity. Most probably agree that the U.S. commitment was a mistake in the first place. Yet they want "an honorable withdrawal." The idea of a U.S. defeat troubles them. . . .

The My Lai massacre has only deepened the confusion. Many Middle Americans stoutly refuse to believe that it even occurred. This was true of 49% of those polled by the *Minneapolis Tribune* last month. When they do believe that the massacre happened, they attribute it to battlefield error and not to the malignancy of American soldiers. Middle America teeters on the edge of a different fear: What if all that death and maiming were to amount to little or nothing, if so much sacrifice made no real difference to Southeast Asia, to the containment of Communism? American sons keep coming homeward in zippered plastic body bags, and a sizable percentage of Americans tell the pollsters that they believe Viet Nam will eventually turn Communist in any case. . . .

Treadmill inflation has betrayed Middle America's faith in the work ethic; American affluence seems indefinitely expandable, all right, but prices expand just as rapidly, or more so. Last year, despite his wage increases, the average American worker barely broke even in actual buying power. . . .

The present shift to the right is in one perspective illusory. Since the start of the New Deal, the tide of the nation has flowed to the left. Middle America is now swimming against the tide in some issues, but the current is likely to continue, carrying it ever more leftward. The mass of Americans have grown steadily more tolerant over the last few generations. One can glimpse the changes in small incidents of the popular culture. When Ingrid Bergman became adulterously pregnant by Roberto Rossellini in 1949, she was all but stoned out of the country. Mia Farrow and André Previn, anticipating the joys of unwed motherhood and fatherhood, have aroused only minor indignation. Middle Americans accept Bayard Rustin as an eminently sensible black moderate now, but only a few years ago they thought him a firebrand. The idea of socialized medicine gives apoplexy to the patients. Middle Americans have more or less accepted the principles of guaranteed annual income, of coexistence with Communism. . . .

If the U.S. is to go forward as Nixon has promised, Middle America must be led to assist change rather than resent and resist it, to help shape the future rather than try to preserve an already vanished America. In that task, a presidential prophet might find himself surprisingly honored in Middle American country. The Man and Woman of the Year still want to believe in America and the American dream. It has dimmed for too many, sometimes because of their failed expectations, sometimes because of the assaults on their complacency. Yet if the dream were to be redefined properly for them, Middle Americans could again provide abundantly that felicitous mixture of idealism and sound common sense on which the U.S. was founded.

BIOGRAPHICAL SKETCH
Barry Goldwater

Since at least the 1930s, the Republican Party had been in a very bad way. The Roosevelt-Truman juggernaut had dominated American politics from 1933 to 1953. The New Deal coalition, pulled together by FDR in 1936, had generally held together at least through 1948 and had proven to be unbeatable in national elections. Consequently, the Republicans were forced to the sidelines as a sort of loyal opposition. Their only real influence, it seemed, was to affect Democratic Party legislation as much as possible.

At the same time, the party was terribly divided. The moderate Republicans had taken a general stance of carrying on the Democratic Party's programs and policies—but with less spending and more efficiency. This wing of the party was led, from the late 1940s on through the mid-1960s, by Thomas Dewey, the party's losing candidate in 1944 and again in the 1948 debacle. He was succeeded by Nelson Rockefeller through the 1970s. It is significant that both men had served as governors of New York and, apparently, saw the need for social programs in states with large urban areas.

The more conservative wing of the Republican Party, often called the Old Guard, never seemed to gain control again after Roosevelt's emergence as leader of the Democrats in the early 1930s. It was they who had controlled the Republican Party through the 1920s and early 1930s, until Roosevelt's election, and they still, in the 1950s, carried the stigma of being the group most responsible for the Great Depression. Their leader in the 1940s and into the early1950s was Robert Taft, a brilliant, but dour, politician who wanted to be president, but did not have the personality or the temperament for that role. When Taft died in 1953, the Republican Party began to change—if for no other reason than that the Old Guard began looking for new leadership.

The 1950s were a frustrating time for the Republican Right. Eisenhower continually talked of moving down the middle of the road, and for Republican conservatives that meant he was much too liberal for their tastes. His vice president, Richard Nixon, had come up through the party ranks as a conservative, but as the 1960 campaign approached, Nixon saw the advantages of running down the middle of Ike's road, and he abandoned the right. When Nixon lost the 1960 election to John Kennedy, the Old Guard argued with some effect that (with the exception of Eisenhower) the moderates had lost every election since 1936. It was time for the party's right wing to step out of the shadows and into the sunlight.

Of course, they needed a candidate, and that would be Barry Goldwater. Goldwater was just what the conservatives needed. He was from Arizona, and he carried a sort of a Western cowboy persona. He was good looking, fairly young, and active. He even flew jets for the Arizona National Guard. Goldwater had taken his place as the savior of the party's right wing by openly breaking with Eisenhower. In a rousing speech on the Senate floor in 1956, Goldwater charged the president with being influenced by socialists and "aping the New Deal." Then in 1958, Goldwater published *Conscience of a Conservative*, which quickly became the bible of the new conservative movement.

Republican conservatives hoped that in the 1964 campaign they could offer the nation an alternative to the liberalism of John Kennedy and the Democrats. They expected that a campaign between Goldwater and Kennedy would offer a choice to the American people—a choice they had not had since the 1930s. The 1964 campaign, they said, would be a "choice, not an echo." And Goldwater was ready.

But everything changed in November 1963 when Kennedy was assassinated and Lyndon Johnson moved into the White House. Johnson was considered a conservative, from the conservative wing of the Democratic Party. From Texas, Johnson had a foothold in both the South and the West, regions where Goldwater hoped to take his message and win votes. There was, it seemed, no longer such a stark choice. Goldwater considered not running, but his friends and advisors prevailed and he entered the race against Johnson.

The campaign was of little consequence. The broad public was not prepared for Goldwater's right-wing politics, and the Johnson campaign succeeded in portraying Goldwater as an itchy trigger finger that should not be near the nuclear button. Johnson won a spectacular landslide.

Political pundits wrote the obituary for the Republican Right: they would never recover from such a trouncing. But near the end of the campaign, Ronald Reagan (then in the process of making the transition from film star to politician) came on board the Goldwater campaign. Reagan made a mesmerizing speech on Goldwater's behalf over national television. It did little to boost Goldwater's campaign in its last dying days, but leaders of the Republican Right—now again looking for a new leader—saw Reagan's future. Goldwater and Reagan were only casual acquaintances, but Reagan had come to see Goldwater as his John the Baptist, his teacher and mentor. Although the Right was pounded in 1964, it was truly the beginning of its resurgence. In January 1981, under Reagan's leadership, it would take control of the government.

Barry Goldwater was born in Phoenix in 1909. In 1929, after a year at college, he began his business career at the family department store in Phoenix. He served as a pilot in the Asian theater in World War II. After the war he organized the Arizona Air National Guard and became a brigadier general in 1959. After serving three years on the Phoenix city council, he was elected to the U.S. Senate in 1952, and was reelected in 1958. Following his failed bid for the presidency in 1964, he won back his Senate seat in 1968 and was reelected in 1974, and again in 1980. He retired from the Senate in 1986. A maverick to the end, he often parted ways with the Republican Party leadership even after the conservatives took the helm. He died in 1998.

STUDY QUESTIONS

1. The Sharon Statement is more ideological than specific. How does that compare to the Port Huron Statement?
2. What might be the reasons for the emergence of these two, almost simultaneous, political statements from the nation's youth, each one from the opposite end of the national political spectrum?
3. "FDR's New Deal was an exercise in pragmatism. His liberal followers in office, however, have turned Franklin's pragmatism into pie-in-the-sky idealism." Discuss this statement as it might relate to Lyndon Johnson and his Great Society.
4. Many "mainstream" Republicans thought Goldwater had made it impossible for their party to win in 1964—and they were right.

Why do you think Goldwater's speech was so disturbing to these Republicans?

5. *Time* does not seem quite sure whether Middle Americans in 1970 were liberal or conservative. It fact, the article appears very contradictory. Or not. Discuss.

FURTHER READINGS

Terry Anderson, *The Movement and the Sixties: Protest in America from Greensboro to Wounded Knee* (1995).

John A. Andrew III, *Lyndon Johnson and the Great Society* (1998).

Robert Alan Goldberg, *Barry Goldwater* (1995).

Lisa McGirr, *Suburban Warriors: The Origins of the New American Right* (2001).

William L. O'Neill, *Coming Apart: An Informal History of the 1960s* (1971).

10 • Civil Rights Victories and Divisions

INTRODUCTION

The civil rights movement reached its crescendo in the 1960s. Martin Luther King, Jr., took the battle against racial segregation to Birmingham, Alabama, in the spring of 1963 and showed the nation that racism and violence went hand in hand in the South. In August, a March on Washington was planned to push Congress into passing the bill that would become the Civil Rights Act of 1964, but the event became the crowning glory of the entire movement—topped off by King's unforgettable "I Have a Dream" speech. The next year, the Student Nonviolent Coordinating Committee (SNCC) organized a voting rights drive in Mississippi that became known as the Freedom Summer, and again Americans were shown (usually over television) that southern whites would use violence to maintain their whites-only system. Then in 1965, events in two cities in Alabama—Selma and Montgomery—made it clear to the nation that blacks in the South were being denied the vote. That revelation, at least in part, led to the Voting Rights Act of 1965. This success, along with the Civil Rights Act, put an end to legal segregation and illegal voting practices in the South. For some, this was the culmination of the movement, an end to a legal system that kept African Americans as second-class citizens. For others, however, the legislation that passed Congress was a long way from establishing equality—and there was much more to do.

It quickly became apparent that two problems made further steps toward equality more difficult. One was a growing white backlash, a general resistance from some corners of white society where racial equality was perceived as encroachment. A second problem was a debilitating moderate-radical split in the movement itself.

The most visible personification of the white backlash was George Wallace, the governor of Alabama. Wallace first gained notoriety when, in his inaugural address in 1963, he brought the crowd to its feet with his words "segregation now; segregation tomorrow; segregation forever." Just five months later he promised he would not allow the desegregation of the University of Alabama. "I will stand in the schoolhouse door," he declared. The confrontation in Tuscaloosa that followed was only of symbolic significance, but Wallace was catapulted to a national figure, the champion of the resistance. Almost immediately he began a run for the presidency.

Wallace's 1964 presidential campaign would have been barely a blip on the political screen except for his own discovery that there were voters in the North with Southern convictions—voters in the North who believed what George Wallace believed and would vote for him. Wallace entered primaries in Wisconsin, Indiana, and Maryland and did surprisingly well, particularly in industrial areas where workers apparently feared for their jobs under the system of racial equality being proposed in the civil rights legislation before Congress. Wallace never left the Democratic Party, but he unleashed a backlash that would bolster the Republican Party for decades to come—at least into the late 1980s.

The split in the civil rights movement emerged as King's southern, church-based, nonviolent movement came to seem too moderate and too compromising for some impatient, and often young, northern, urban African Americans. It might be argued that a strain of radicalism had always been a part of African American politics, a radicalism that manifested itself in "back-to-Africa" movements, separatism, and black nationalism. The radicalism in the early sixties was given voice most prominently by Malcolm X, the chief spokesman for the Nation of Islam, and its founder, Elijah Mohammed. In 1965 Malcolm was murdered. But the black nationalist message was quickly picked up by several young black leaders who took organizations such as SNCC and CORE (Congress of Racial Equality) in the radical direction, away from King's nonviolent protests.

DOCUMENT 10.1
Fannie Lou Hamer Recalls Her Attempts to Register and Vote (1962)

Fannie Lou Hamer was a leader of the civil rights movement, and known to many Americans as a primary figure in the Mississippi Freedom Democratic Party (MFDP) at the 1964 Democratic National Convention in Atlantic City, New Jersey.

Hamer's early life, as she moved from a barely educated sharecropper to active civil rights worker, was an amazing journey from ignorance to political awareness and activism. In 1962 she came into contact with grassroots civil rights leader Robert Parish Moses, who convinced her to register and vote.

*Her attempts to register are recounted below in a 1972 interview conducted
as part of the Mississippi Oral History Program at the University of Southern Mississippi in Hattiesburg. Hamer's life is recounted in the biographical
sketch at the end of this chapter.*

SOURCE: Fannie Lou Hamer Interview, Mississippi Oral History Program, University
of Southern Mississippi, Hattiesburg, Mississippi.

McMillan: Tell us about your efforts to vote.

Hamer: Well, I didn't know anything about voting; I didn't know anything
about registering to vote. One night I went to church. They had a mass meeting. And I went to church, and they talked about how it was our right, that
we could register and vote. They were talking about [how] we could vote
out people that we didn't want in office, [people] we thought that wasn't
right, that we could vote them out. That sounded interesting enough to
me that I wanted to try it. I had never heard, until 1962, that black people
could register and vote.

McMillan: Never heard that in your life?

Hamer: I'd never heard that; we hadn't heard anything about registering to vote
because when you see this flat land in here, when the people would get out of
the fields if they had a radio, they'd be too tired to play it. So we didn't know
what was going on in the rest of the state, even much less in other places.

McMillan: When you were a child at school, did the books you had say
anything about voting or democracy?

Hamer: Never! I'd never even heard that that was in the Constitution. I never
heard anything about it. In fact, the first time I was aware that Mississippi
had a constitution was when I tried to register to vote, and they gave me a
section of the Constitution of Mississippi to write—to copy—and then to give
a reasonable interpretation of it. I didn't know that we had that right. . . .

McMillan: When you first tried to vote, where was that?

Hamer: Well, when I first tried to register it was in Indianola. I went to Indianola
on the thirty-first of August in 1962; that was to try to register. When we got
there—there was eighteen of us went that day—so when we got there, there
were people there with guns and just a lot of strange-looking people to us.

We went on in the circuit clerk's office, and he asked us what did we want;
and we told him what we wanted. We wanted to try to register. He told us
that all of us would have to get out of there except two. So I was one of
the two persons that remained inside. . . . We stayed in to take the literacy
test. So the registrar gave me the sixteenth section of the Constitution of
Mississippi. He pointed it out in the book and told me to look at it and then
copy it down just like I saw it in the book. Put a period where a period was

supposed to be, a comma and all of that. After I copied it down he told me that right below that to give a real reasonable interpretation, then interpret what I had read. That was impossible. I had tried to give it, but I didn't even know what it meant, much less to interpret it. . . .

McMillan: Did you think it was dangerous that first time you tried?

Hamer: I had a feeling that [it was]; I don't know why, but I just had a feeling. . . . I didn't know it was going to be as much involved as it finally was. But I had a feeling that we might be arrested.

McMillan: What happened when you got back? Did anything happen? Did you lose your home?

Hamer: Well, when we got back I went on out to where I had been staying for eighteen years, and the landowner had talked to my husband and told him I had to leave the place. My little girl, the child I raised, met me and told me that the landowner was mad and I might have to leave.

So during the time that my husband was talking about it, I was back in the house. The landowner drove up and asked him [if I had] made it back. [My husband] told him I had. I got up and walked out on the porch, and he [asked] me did [my husband] tell me what he said. I told him, "He did." He said, "Well, I mean that, you'll have to go down and withdraw your registration, or you'll have to leave the place." . . .

McMillan: So you had to leave right away?

Hamer: I had to leave that same night.

McMillan: Your husband stayed on to finish the crop?

Hamer: He stayed on because [the landowner] told him the next morning that if he left he wouldn't give us any of our belongings. But if [my husband would] help him harvest the crop, well, he'd give us the rest of our things. . . .

McMillan: Where did you go then, Mrs. Hamer, after you had to leave the house on the plantation? . . .

Hamer: I started staying with some people. . . . Then my husband got frightened and carried me to my niece's. And after he carried me there, then they shot in that house that I was staying with those people—they shot in that house. . . .

McMillan: So you were turned down then; your registration effort failed?

Hamer: It failed.

McMillan: When did you finally succeed?

Hamer: Well, after coming back to Ruleville, I went to Tallahatchie County and stayed awhile . . . and we went back . . . to take the literacy test again.

McMillan: 1962?

Hamer: The registrar gave me another section of the Constitution. [It] was the 49th section of the Constitution of Mississippi, dealing with the House of Representatives. He told me to copy that down and to give a reasonable interpretation. I copied that, but we had got hold of [a copy] of the Constitution of Mississippi and had been able to study it. Some of the people from the [SNCC] would help us to try to interpret it, so that time I gave a reasonable enough interpretation. When I went back to see about it . . . I had passed the literacy test. . . .

McMillan: I see. So then you voted. When did you first vote?

Hamer: Well, the first attempt that I tried to vote, I didn't really get to vote. I went up to vote—that was in a primary election. . . . We went up to vote that day, and I didn't have two poll tax receipts. I hadn't been paying poll tax, and I didn't have two prior years. They told me I couldn't vote because I didn't have two poll tax receipts.

McMillan: So you couldn't vote that time. When did you finally cast your vote?

Hamer: The first vote I cast, I cast my first vote for myself, because I was running for Congress. The first vote—I voted for myself.

DOCUMENT 10.2
George Wallace, "The Civil Rights Movement Is a Hoax" (July 1964)

Through the spring of 1964, George Wallace entered three presidential primaries (Wisconsin, Indiana, and Maryland) and did much better than anyone ever expected. As governor of Alabama, he was not considered much of a political draw in these states. But he had concluded that many northern whites opposed the Johnson administration's civil rights bill, then before Congress. It was no secret that Wallace's message was race, but he couched his arguments in the language of states' rights and he won followers throughout the country—particularly in industrial regions where the economies were not strong and jobs were uncertain.

On July 4, 1964, the day after Lyndon Johnson signed the Civil Rights Act into law, Wallace spoke to a wild crowd at an abandoned stock car track south of Atlanta. On the bill with Wallace were Mississippi governor Ross Barnett, Georgia Klan leader Calvin Craig, and Atlanta restaurant owner (and future Georgia governor) Lester Maddox. During Barnett's speech, several members from SNCC were nearly killed by the crowd when they began booing Barnett. By the time Wallace stepped to the podium the audience had turned into a mob.

Wallace withdrew from the race on July 19.

SOURCE: George C. Wallace Speech, Atlanta, Georgia (July 4, 1964), Speech Collection, Alabama Department of Archives and History, Montgomery, Alabama.

We come here today in deference to the memory of those stalwart patriots who on July 4, 1776, pledged their lives, their fortunes, and their sacred honor to establish and defend the proposition that governments are created by the people, empowered by the people, derive their just powers from the consent of the people, and must forever remain subservient to the will of the people.

Today, 188 years later, we celebrate that occasion and find inspiration, and determination, and courage to preserve and protect the great principles of freedom enunciated in the Declaration of Independence.

It is therefore a cruel irony that the President of the United States has only yesterday signed into law the most monstrous piece of legislation ever enacted by the United States Congress. It is a fraud, a sham, and a hoax. This bill will live in infamy. To sign it into law at any time is tragic. To do so upon the eve of the celebration of our independence insults the intelligence of the American people.

It dishonors the memory of countless thousands of our dead who offered up their very lives in defense of principles which this bill destroys. Never before in the history of this nation have so many human and property rights been destroyed by a single enactment of the Congress. It is an act of tyranny. It is the assassin's knife stuck in the back of liberty. . . .

Today, this tyranny is imposed by the central government which claims the right to rule over our lives under sanction of the omnipotent black-robed despots who sit on the bench of the United States Supreme Court.

This bill is fraudulent in intent, in design, and in execution. It is misnamed. Each and every provision is mistitled. It was rammed through the Congress on the wave of ballyhoo, promotions, and publicity stunts reminiscent of P.T. Barnum. It was enacted in an atmosphere of pressure, intimidation, and even cowardice, as demonstrated by the refusal of the United States Senate to adopt an amendment to submit the bill to a vote of the people.

To illustrate the fraud—it is not a Civil Rights Bill. It is a Federal Penal Code. It creates federal crimes which would take volumes to list and years to tabulate because it affects the lives of 192 million American citizens. Every person in every walk and station of life and every aspect of our daily lives becomes subject to the criminal provisions of this bill. It threatens our freedom of speech, of assembly, of association, and makes the exercise of these freedoms a federal crime under certain conditions.

It affects our political rights, our right to trial by jury, our right to the full use and enjoyment of our private property, the freedom from search and seizure of our private property and possessions, the freedom from harassment by federal police and, in short, all the rights of individuals inherent in a society of free men. . . .

[A] federal judge may still try one without a jury under the provisions of this bill. . . . [A] federal judge may still order busing from one neighborhood school to another. They have done it; they will continue to do it. As a matter of fact, it is but another evidence of the deceitful intent of the sponsors of this bill for them to claim that it accomplished any such thing.

It was left-wing radicals who led the fight in the Senate for the so-called Civil Rights Bill now about to enslave our nation. We find Senator Hubert Humphrey telling the people of the United States that "nonviolent" demonstrations would continue to serve a good purpose through a "long, busy and constructive summer." Yet this same Senator told the people of this country that passage of this monstrous bill would ease tensions and stop demonstrations. This is the same Senator who has suggested, now that the Civil Rights Bill is passed, that the President call the fifty state Governors together to work out ways and means to enforce this rotten measure.

There is no need for him to call on me. I am not about to be a party to anything having to do with the law that is going to destroy individual freedom and liberty in this country. . . .

I am having nothing to do with this so-called civil rights bill. The liberal left-wingers have passed it. Now let them employ some pinknik social engineers in Washington, D.C. to figure out what to do with it. . . .

However, we will not be intimidated by the vultures of the liberal left-wing press. We will not be deceived by their lies and distortions of truth. We will not be swayed by their brutal attacks upon the character and reputation of any honest citizen who dares stand up and fight for liberty. . . . These editors, like many other left-wingers in the liberal press, are not influenced by tradition. Theirs is a tradition of the scalawags. Their mealy-mouthed platitudes disgrace the honored memory of their predecessors. . . .

The only reason [the Civil Rights Act] is the Supreme Law of the Land today is because we have a President who cares so little for freedom that he would send the armed forces into the states to enforce the dictatorial decree. . . . Today . . . we have actually witnessed the invasion of the states of Arkansas, Mississippi, and Alabama by the armed forces of the United States, and maintained in the state against the will of the people and without consent of state legislatures. It is a form of tyranny worse than that of King George III, who had sent mercenaries against the colonies. Because today the federal judicial tyrants have sanctioned the use of brother against brother and father against son by federalizing the National Guard. . . .

Let us look at the record further with respect to the court's contribution to the destruction of the concept of God and the abolition of religion. The federal court rules that your children shall not be permitted to read the Bible in our public school systems.

Let me tell you this, though. We still read the Bible in Alabama schools and as long as I am Governor we will continue to read the Bible no matter what the Supreme Court says.

Federal courts will not convict a "demonstrator" invading and destroying private property. But the federal courts rule you cannot say a simple "God is great, God is good, we thank Thee for our food," in kindergartens supported by public funds. . . .

But yet there is hope. There is yet a spirit of resistance in this country which will not be oppressed. And it is awakening. And I am sure there is an abundance of good sense in this country which cannot be deceived. I have personal knowledge of this. Thirty-four percent of the Wisconsin Democrats supported the beliefs you and I uphold and expound. Thirty percent of the Democrats in Indiana joined us in fighting this grab for executive power by those now in control in Washington. And, listen to this, forty-three percent of the Democrats in Maryland, practically in view of the nation's Capital, believe as you and I believe.

So, let me say to you today, take heart, millions of Americans believe just as we in this great region of the United States believe. I shall never forget last spring as I stood in the midst of a great throng of South Milwaukee supporters at one of the greatest political rallies I have ever witnessed. A fine-looking man grabbed my hand and said: "Governor, I've never been south of South Milwaukee, but I am a Southerner!" Of course, he was saying he believed in the principles and philosophy of the southern people. . . . Being a southerner is no longer geographic. It's a philosophy and an attitude—one destined to be a national philosophy, embraced by millions of Americans, which shall assume the mantle of leadership and steady a governmental structure in these days of crises.

Certainly I am a candidate for President of the United States. If the left-wingers do not think I am serious, let them consider this. I am going to take our fight to the people—the court of public opinion—where truth and common sense will eventually prevail. . . .

A left-wing monster has risen up in this nation. It has invaded the government. It has invaded the news media. It has invaded the leadership of many of our churches. It has invaded every phase and aspect of the life of freedom-loving people. It consists of many and various and powerful interests, but it has combined into one massive drive and is held together by the cohesive power of the emotion, setting forth civil rights as supreme to all. But, in reality, it is a drive to destroy the rights of private property, to destroy the freedom and liberty of you and me.

And, my friends, where there are no property rights, there are no human rights. Red China and Soviet Russia are prime examples. Politically evil men have combined and arranged themselves against us. The good people of this nation must now associate themselves together, else we will fall one by one, an unpitied sacrifice in a struggle which threatens to engulf the entire nation. . . .

I ask that you join with me and that together, we give an active and courageous leadership to the millions of people throughout this nation who look with hope and faith to our fight to preserve our constitutional system of government with its guarantees of liberty and justice for all within the framework of our priceless freedoms.

DOCUMENT 10.3
Charles Hamilton Defines Black Power (April 1968)

If the Black Power movement in the 1960s had a theoretician it was Charles Hamilton. He, along with Stokley Carmichael, tried several times to define Black Power, a phrase that was becoming more and more abstract as the decade of the sixties drew to a close. The essay below is another attempt by Hamilton to define the movement. He begins by explaining the difficulty of his endeavor.

SOURCE: *New York Times Magazine* (April 14, 1968). Reprinted by permission.

Black Power has many definitions and connotations in the rhetoric of race relations today. To some people, it is synonymous with premeditated acts of violence to destroy the political and economic institutions of this country. Others equate Black Power with plans to rid the civil rights movement of whites who have been in it for years. The concept is understood by many to mean hatred of and separation from whites; it is associated with calling whites "honkies" and with shouts of "Burn, baby, burn!" Some understand it to be the use of pressure-group tactics in the accepted tradition of the American political process. And still others say that Black Power must be seen first of all as an attempt to instill a sense of identity and pride in black people.

Ultimately, I suspect, we have to accept the fact that, in this highly charged atmosphere, it is virtually impossible to come up with a single definition satisfactory to all.

Even as some of us try to articulate our idea of Black Power and the way we relate to it and advocate it, we are categorized as "moderate" or "militant" or "reasonable" or "extremist." "I can accept your definition of Black Power," a listener will say to me. "But how does your position compare with what Stokely Carmichael said in Cuba or with what H. Rap Brown said in Cambridge, [Maryland]?" Or, just as frequently, some young white New Left advocate will come up to me and proudly announce: "You're not radical enough. Watts, Newark, Detroit—that's what's happening, man! You're nothing but a reformist. We've got to blow up this society. Read Che or Debray or Mao." All I can do is shrug and conclude that some people believe that making a revolution in this country involves rhetoric, Molotov cocktails and being under 30.

To have Black Power equated with calculated acts of violence would be very unfortunate. First, if black people have learned anything over the years, it is that he who shouts revolution the loudest is one of the first to run when the action starts. Second, open calls to violence are a sure way to have one's ranks immediately infiltrated. Third—and this is as important as any reason—violent revolution in this country would fail; it would be met with the kind of repression used in Sharpeville, South Africa, in 1960, when 67 Africans were killed and 186 wounded during a demonstration against apartheid. It is clear that America is not above this. There are many white bigots who would like nothing better than to embark on a program of black genocide, even though the imposition of such repressive measures would destroy civil liberties for whites as well as blacks. Some whites are so panicky, irrational and filled with racial hatred that they would welcome the opportunity to annihilate the black community. This was clearly shown in the senseless murder of Dr. Martin Luther King Jr., which understandably—but none the less irrationally—prompted some black militants to advocate violent retaliation. Such cries for revenge intensify racial fear and animosity when the need—now more than ever—is to establish solid, stable organizations and action programs. . . .

Black Power rejects the lessons of slavery and segregation that caused black people to look upon themselves with hatred and disdain. To be "integrated" it was necessary to deny one's heritage, one's culture, to be ashamed of one's black skin, thick lips and kinky hair. . . . The black man must change his demeaning conception of himself; he must develop a sense of pride and self-respect. Then, if integration comes, it will deal with people who are psychologically and mentally healthy, with people who have a sense of their history and of themselves as whole human beings. . . .

This brings us to a consideration of the external problems of the black community. It is clear that black people will need the help of whites at many places along the line. There simply are not sufficient economic resources—actual or potential—in the black community for a total, unilateral, boot-strap operation. Why should there be? Black people have been the target of deliberate denial for centuries, and racist America has done its job well. This is a serious problem that must be faced by Black Power advocates. On the one hand, they recognize the need to be independent of "the white power structure." And on the other, they must frequently turn to that structure for help—technical and financial. Thus, the rhetoric and the reality often clash.

Resolution probably lies in the realization by white America that it is in her interest not to have a weak, dependent, alienated black community inhabiting the inner cities and blowing them up periodically. Society needs stability, and as long as there is a sizable powerless, restless group within it which considers the society illegitimate, stability is not possible. However it is calculated, that situation calls for black-white rapprochement, which may well come only through additional confrontations and crises. More frequently than not, the self-interest of the dominate society is not clearly perceived until the brink is reached.

DOCUMENT 10.4
President Lyndon Johnson, Special Message to Congress on Civil Rights (March 1965)

The summer of 1964 saw the passage of the Civil Rights Act, but it also saw unparalleled violence. In the fall, President Johnson ordered work to begin on a tough voting rights bill, and he asked Congress for the measure in his State of the Union speech in January 1965. The bill stalled in Congress, and in March, Martin Luther King led a march on Selma, Alabama, to dramatize the need for a voting rights bill—and to show the nation, again, that the South would use extreme and open violence to maintain its racist system. Alabama officials accommodated King by brutally attacking the marchers in the presence of national television.

In the midst of the crisis, the president delivered the following message to Congress. It may have been Johnson's greatest speech, even his finest hour. It is an excellent example of a president of the United States evoking the moral authority of his office to lead the nation in time of crisis. On August 5, 1965, the Voting Rights Act passed Congress on a rising tide that was a combination of public revulsion over white violence in the South and Lyndon Johnson's own political and legislative skills.

SOURCE: *Public Papers of the Presidents: Lyndon B. Johnson, 1965,* 281–87.

I speak tonight for the dignity of man and the destiny of Democracy. I urge every member of both parties, Americans of all religions and of all colors, from every section of this country, to join me in that cause.

At times, history and fate meet at a single time in a single place to shape a turning point in man's unending search for freedom. So it was at Lexington and Concord. So it was a century ago at Appomattox. So it was last week in Selma, Alabama. There, long suffering men and women peacefully protested the denial of their rights as Americans. Many of them were brutally assaulted. One good man—a man of God—was killed. . . .

Rarely in any time does an issue lay bare the secret heart of America itself. Rarely are we met with a challenge, not to our growth or abundance, or our welfare or our security, but rather to the values and the purposes and the meaning of our beloved nation. The issue of equal rights for American Negroes is such an issue. And should we defeat every enemy, and should we double our wealth and conquer the stars, and still be unequal to this issue, then we will have failed as a people and as a nation. For, with a country as with a person, "what is a man profited if he shall gain the whole world, and lose his own soul?"

There is no Negro problem. There is no Southern problem. There is no Northern problem. There is only an American problem.

And we are met here tonight as Americans—not as Democrats or Republicans; we're met here as Americans to solve that problem.

This was the first nation in the history of the world to be founded with a purpose.

The great phrases of that purpose still sound in every American heart, North and South: "All men are created equal." "Government by consent of the governed." "Give me liberty or give me death." And those are not just clever words, and those are not just empty theories. In their name Americans have fought and died for two centuries and tonight around the world they stand there as guardians of our liberty risking their lives. Those words are promised to every citizen that he shall share in the dignity of man. This dignity cannot be found in a man's possessions. It cannot be found in his power or in his position. It really rests on his right to be treated as a man, equal in opportunity to all others. It says that he shall share in freedom. He shall choose his leaders, educate his children, provide for his family according to his ability and his merits as a human being. . . .

Many of the issues of civil rights are very complex and most difficult. But about this there can and should be no argument: every American citizen must have an equal right to vote. There is no reason which can excuse the denial of that right. There is no duty which weighs more heavily on us than the duty we have to insure that right. Yet the harsh fact is that in many places in this country, men and women are kept from voting simply because they are Negroes.

Every device of which human ingenuity is capable has been used to deny this right. The Negro citizen may go to register only to be told that the day is wrong, or the hour is late, or the official in charge is absent. And if he persists and, if he manages to present himself to the registrar, he may be disqualified because he did not spell out his middle name, or because he abbreviated a word on the application. And if he manages to fill out an application, he is given a test. The registrar is the sole judge of whether he passes this test. He may be asked to recite the entire *Constitution,* or explain the most complex provisions of state law.

And even a college degree cannot be used to prove that he can read and write. For the fact is that the only way to pass these barriers is to show a white skin. Experience has clearly shown that the existing process of law cannot overcome systematic and ingenious discrimination. No law that we now have on the books, and I have helped to put three of them there, can insure the right to vote when local officials are determined to deny it. In such a case, our duty must be clear to all of us. The Constitution says that no person shall be kept from voting because of his race or his color.

We have all sworn an oath before God to support and to defend that Constitution. We must now act in obedience to that oath. Wednesday, I will send to Congress a law designed to eliminate illegal barriers to the right to vote. The broad principles of that bill will be in the hands of the Democratic and Republican leaders tomorrow. After they have reviewed it, it will come here formally as a bill. I am grateful for this opportunity to come here tonight at the invitation of the leadership to reason with my friends, to give them my views and to visit with my former colleagues. . . .

There is no issue of state's rights or national rights. There is only the struggle for human rights. I have not the slightest doubt what will be your answer. But the last time a President sent a civil rights bill to the Congress it contained a provision to protect voting rights in Federal elections. That civil rights bill was passed after eight long months of debate. And when that bill came to my desk from the Congress for signature, the heart of the voting provision had been eliminated.

This time, on this issue, there must be no delay, or no hesitation, or no compromise with our purpose. We cannot, we must not, refuse to protect the right of every American to vote in every election that he may desire to participate in.

And we ought not, and we cannot, and we must not wait another eight months before we get a bill. We have already waited one hundred years and more and the time for waiting is gone. So I ask you to join me in working long hours and nights and weekends, if necessary, to pass this bill. And I don't make that request lightly, for, from the window where I sit, with the problems of our country, I recognize that from outside this chamber is the outraged conscience of a nation, the grave concern of many nations and the harsh judgment of history on our acts.

But even if we pass this bill the battle will not be over. What happened in Selma is part of a far larger movement which reaches into every section and state of America. It is the effort of American Negroes to secure for themselves the full blessings of American life. Their cause must be our cause too. Because it's not just Negroes, but really it's all of us, who must overcome the crippling legacy of bigotry and injustice.

And we shall overcome.

As a man whose roots go deeply into Southern soil, I know how agonizing racial feelings are. I know how difficult it is to reshape the attitudes and the structure of our society. But a century has passed—more than one hundred years—since the Negro was freed. And he is not fully free tonight. It was more than one hundred years ago that Abraham Lincoln—a great President of another party—signed the Emancipation Proclamation. But emancipation is a proclamation and not a fact.

A century has passed—more than one hundred years—since equality was promised, and yet the Negro is not equal. A century has passed since the day of promise, and the promise is un-kept. The time of justice has now come, and I tell you that I believe sincerely that no force can hold it back. It is right in the eyes of man and God that it should come, and when it does, I think that day will brighten the lives of every American. For Negroes are not the only victims. How many white children have gone uneducated? How many white families have lived in stark poverty? How many white lives have been scarred by fear, because we wasted energy and our substance to maintain the barriers of hatred and terror?

And so I say to all of you here and to all in the nation tonight that those who appeal to you to hold on to the past do so at the cost of denying you your future. This great, rich, restless country can offer opportunity and education and hope to all—all, black and white, North and South, sharecropper and city dweller. These are the enemies: poverty, ignorance, disease. They are our enemies, not our fellow man, not our neighbor.

And these enemies too—poverty, disease and ignorance—we shall overcome. . . .

The bill I am presenting to you will be known as a civil rights bill. But in a larger sense, most of the program I am recommending is a civil rights program. Its object is to open the city of hope to all people of all races, because all Americans must have the right to vote, and we are going to give them that right.

All Americans must have the privileges of citizenship, regardless of race, and they are going to have those privileges of citizenship regardless of race.

But I would like to caution you and remind you that to exercise these privileges takes much more than just legal rights. It requires a trained mind and a healthy body. It requires a decent home and the chance to find a job and the opportunity to escape from the clutches of poverty.

Of course people cannot contribute to the nation if they are never taught to read or write; if their bodies are stunted from hunger; if their sickness goes untended; if their life is spent in hopeless poverty, just drawing a welfare check. . . .

This is the richest, most powerful country which ever occupied this globe. The might of past empires is little compared to ours. But I do not want to be the president who built empires, or sought grandeur, or extended dominion.

I want to be the president who educated young children to the wonders of their world. I want to be the president who helped to feed the hungry and to prepare them to be taxpayers instead of tax eaters. I want to be the president who helped the poor to find their own way and who protected the right of every citizen to vote in every election. I want to be the president who helped to end hatred among his fellow men and who promoted love among the people of all races, all regions and all parties. I want to be the president who helped to end war among the brothers of this earth.

And so . . . I came down here to ask you to share this task with me. And to share it with the people that we both work for. . . .

Above the pyramid on the Great Seal of the United States it says in Latin, "God has favored our undertaking." God will not favor everything that we do. It is rather our duty to divine His will. But I cannot help but believe that He truly understands and that He really favors the undertaking that we begin here tonight.

BIOGRAPHICAL SKETCH
Fannie Lou Hamer

It is easy to find the voices of the elite in the civil rights movement, those African American leaders with advanced degrees, who parlayed with presidents and world leaders, and whose faces appeared often on television and in the newspapers. It is harder to find the voices of the movement's grassroots leadership, the men and women who knocked on the doors, organized the drives, took the force of the truncheons in Mississippi and Alabama, and who risked their lives for the movement. Fannie Lou Hamer was one of those grassroots leaders.

Hamer was born in Montgomery County, Mississippi, in October 1917. The granddaughter of slaves, and the last of twenty children to a family of sharecroppers, she left school before her twelfth birthday for what was to be a life in the cotton fields in the upper Mississippi delta. She married in 1944 and moved, with her husband, Pap, to a plantation near Ruleville where they became sharecroppers.

In the early sixties, as the civil rights movement was just gaining its strength, Hamer became intrigued by a Mississippi voting rights drive led by the Student Nonviolent Coordinating Committee (SNCC), and began attending meetings in Ruleville.

In late August 1962, Hamer and a group from Ruleville traveled by bus to nearby Indianola, Mississippi, to register to vote. They were turned away. When she returned to her home she was told by the landowner to leave the property. A year later, after several additional attempts, she was allowed to register.

Her success drove her to help other African Americans in Mississippi to register, and eventually she became a field secretary for SNCC.

The Mississippi Democratic Party was an all-white organization that every four years sent an all-white delegation to the Democratic Party's national convention. In 1964 Hamer and other members of SNCC decided to challenge that exclusionary practice by forming an alternative, integrated, party, the Mississippi Freedom Democratic Party (MFDP), and sending a delegation to the Democratic National Convention in Atlantic City.

In an impassioned speech before the credentials committee of the Democratic Party (which happened to be televised), Hamer told of her attempts to register to vote and her experiences in helping others to register. She included in her story the following series of events that took place near Winona, Mississippi, after she was arrested when some of the workers she was traveling with used a "whites only" waiting room:

> Three white men came into my room. One was a state highway policeman. They said they were going to make me wish I was dead. They made me lay down on my face and they ordered two Negro prisoners to beat me with a blackjack. That was unbearable. The first prisoner beat me until he was exhausted. Then the second Negro began to beat me. They beat me until I was hard, 'til I couldn't bend my fingers or get up when they told me to. That's how I got this blood clot in my eye—the sight's nearly gone now. My kidney was injured from the blows they gave me on my back.

Her testimony was so poignant and moving that it threatened to disrupt the entire convention if the credentials committee chose to seat the MFDP delegates instead of the Mississippi "Regulars," as the all-white delegation was called. President Johnson, fearing that a seating of the MFDP might divide the party and push the South into revolt, orchestrated a news conference that preempted Hamer's testimony. In the end, the Regulars were seated and the MFDP was given two "at large" seats. Hamer, now leading the MFDP along with Robert Moses, refused to accept the compromise.

Hamer continued to work in Mississippi by organizing grassroots anti-poverty projects, including several farm cooperatives, throughout the state.

She also worked most of the remainder of her life to unite the black and white factions of the Mississippi Democratic Party.

At her funeral in March 1977, Andrew Young, then mayor of Atlanta and former ambassador to the United Nations, said: "Women were the spine of our movement. It was women, going door-to-door, speaking with their neighbors, meeting in voter-registration classes together, organizing through their churches that gave the vital momentum and energy to the movement. Mrs. Hamer . . . shook the foundations of this nation."

STUDY QUESTIONS

1. What impact might someone like Fannie Lou Hamer have had on the civil rights movement compared to, say, Martin Luther King, Jr., or Malcolm X? How did the message, goals, and tactics of these three civil rights leaders differ?
2. How did George Wallace's stand on race change the political nature of the South in the 1960s? Why were southerners Democrats? Although Wallace never became a Republican, many southerners in this period did. Why?
3. What impact did U.S. foreign policy in the 1960s have on the civil rights movement? Why did many Americans believe it was important to solve the nation's race problems in the face of the Soviet challenge?

FURTHER READINGS

Dan T. Carter, *The Politics of Rage: George Wallace and the Origins of the New Conservatism, and the Transformation of American Politics* (1995).
David Garrow, *Protest at Selma* (1978).
Stephan Lesher, *George Wallace, American Populist* (1994).
Chana Kai Lee, *For Freedom's Sake: The Life of Fannie Lou Hamer* (1999).
Doug McAdam, *Freedom Summer* (1988).
Kay Mills, *This Little Light of Mine: The Life of Fannie Lou Hamer* (1993).

11 • Polarization and Protest

INTRODUCTION

The sixties were a time of protest—even radicalism. The cameras may have focused on a few high-profile areas (New York, Washington, Berkeley), but protest and radicalism in the sixties were truly a national phenomenon.

Recent scholarship has tended to see the civil rights movement as the source for all the other movements that emerged during the decade. Perhaps because the civil rights movement was so righteous and moral in its objectives, the violent resistance to it radicalized large numbers of young people. From that point on, one movement seems to have built upon another until the decade exploded into a cascade of social and political movements. The Vietnam War added fuel to the fire. There were civil rights movements for African Americans, Native Americans, Mexican Americans, women, gays and lesbians, and just about any other group that felt oppressed by America's white, male-dominated society. Radical political movements emerged on both the left and the right. There was radicalism in music, the visual arts, and religion.

The question that is always begged about the sixties is, did it promote positive social change, or was it, as historian Richard Hofstadter called it, "The Age of Rubbish"? Did the movements of the decade succeed in changing the nation for the better? Since most of the era's movements tended to spring from the left, many liberal "baby boomers" today remember those years nostalgically, as a time of hope. Many conservatives, in contrast, condemn the sixties as having opened the floodgates to a degeneration of social values, racial conflicts, and the attempted curtailment of economic freedoms. The arguments will undoubtedly continue.

If there was any one quality that characterized the sixties radical movements it was impatience. Young people wanted social change, and they wanted it now. Gradualism, as the saying went at the time, was forever. Much of sixties animosity from the left was directed at liberalism—or more specifically liberal politicians and leaders who had promised much but delivered little. It was the liberal politicians who implored the radicals to avoid confrontation, to slow down, and embrace gradual progress. Lyndon Johnson and Martin Luther King were often targets of radical protest.

DOCUMENT 11.1
The "Weatherman Manifesto" (1969)

In much the same way as the civil rights movement developed a moderate-radical split, the New Left (the radical youth movement that had its origins in the Port Huron Statement and the formation of the Students for a Democratic Society, SDS) experienced a split as the decade of the sixties came to a close. A group within the SDS concluded that the organization was not radical enough, and they split off to form the Weather Underground, named after a line in a Bob Dylan song.

The Weathermen dabbled in domestic terrorism, flirted with the Black Panthers, and, for the most part, lived outside the law. They were often idealized by young radicals (and would-be radicals) as revolutionary heroes. In fact, they accomplished little other than focusing enmity on the left; and life on the run—underground—was difficult, unrewarding, and dangerous. Several served jail time, and three Weathermen managed to blow themselves up while making bombs in a Greenwich Village apartment.

In many ways, the Weather Underground reflects how the idealism of the early 1960s had drastically deteriorated.

Lin Piao (Lin Biao), quoted below, was to have been Mao Zedong's successor. During the Cultural Revolution, there were rumors that Lin was conspiring to overthrow Mao in a coup. In 1971, as Lin tried to escape China, his airplane disappeared over Mongolia.

SOURCE: "You Don't Need a Weatherman to Know Which Way the Wind Blows" (June 1969). Students for a Democratic Society Papers. State Historical Society of Wisconsin, Madison, Wisconsin.

> The contradiction between the revolutionary peoples of Asia, Africa, and Latin America, and the imperialists headed by the United States is the principal contradiction in the contemporary world. The development of this contradiction is promoting the struggle of the people of the whole world against U.S. imperialism and its lackeys.
>
> Lin Piao, *Long Live the Victory of the People's War!*

People ask, what is the nature of the revolution that we talk about? Who will it be made by, and for, and what are its goals and strategy?

The overriding consideration in answering these questions is that the main struggle going on in the world today is between U.S. imperialism and the national liberation struggles against it. . . .

So the very first question people in this country must ask in considering the question of revolution is where they stand in relation to the United States as an oppressor nation, and where they stand in relation to the masses of people throughout the world whom U.S. imperialism is oppressing. . . .

It is in this context that we must examine the revolutionary struggles in the United States. We are within the heartland of a world-wide monster, a country so rich from its world-wide plunder that even the crumbs doled out to the enslaved masses within its borders provide for material existence very much above the conditions of the masses of people of the world.

The U.S. empire, as a world-wide system, channels wealth, based upon the labor and resources of the rest of the world, into the United States. The relative affluence existing in the United States is directly dependent upon the labor and natural resources of the Vietnamese, the Angolans, the Bolivians and the rest of the peoples of the Third World. All of the United Airlines Astrojets, all of the Holiday Inns, all of Hertz's automobiles, your television set, car and wardrobe already belong, to a large degree, to the people of the rest of the world. . . .

The goal is the destruction of U.S. imperialism and the achievement of a classless world: world communism. Winning state power in the U.S. will occur as a result of the military forces of the U.S. overextending themselves around the world and being defeated piecemeal; struggle within the U.S. will be a vital part of this process, but when the revolution triumphs in the U.S. it will have been made by the people of the whole world. For socialism to be defined in national terms within so extreme and historical an oppressor nation as this is only imperialist national chauvinism on the part of the movement. . . .

The crisis in imperialism has brought about a breakdown in bourgeois social forms, culture and ideology. The family falls apart, kids leave home, women begin to break out of traditional "female" and "mother" roles. There develops a "generation gap" and a "youth problem." Our heroes are no longer struggling businessmen, and we also begin to reject the ideal career of the professional and look to Mao, Che, the Panthers, the Third World, for our models, for motion. We reject the elitist, technocratic bullshit that tells us only experts can rule, and look instead to leadership from the people's war of the Vietnamese.

Chuck Berry, Elvis, the Temptations brought us closer to the "people's culture" of Black America. The racist response to the civil rights movement revealed the depth of racism in America, as well as the impossibility of real change through American institutions. And the war against Vietnam is not "the heroic war against the Nazis"; it's the big lie, with napalm, burning through everything we had heard this country stood for. Kids begin to ask questions: Where is the Free World? And who do the pigs protect at home?

A major focus in our neighborhood and citywide work is the pigs, because they tie together the various struggles around the state as the enemy, and thus point to the need for a movement oriented toward power to defeat it.

The pigs are the capitalist state, and as such define the limits of all political struggles; to the extent that a revolutionary struggle shows signs of success, they come in and mark the point it can't go beyond. . . . Our job is not to avoid the issue of the pigs as "diverting" from anti-imperialist struggle, but to emphasize that they are our real enemy if we fight that struggle to win. . . .

Long Live the Victory of the People's War!

DOCUMENT 11.2
Ronald Reagan Recalls the 1969 Berkeley Riots

Ronald Reagan was governor of California from 1967 to 1975—at the height of the Vietnam War and the height of the student protest movement. He won the election in November 1966 by appealing to a growing white middle-class backlash against the counterculture movement, the anti-war movement, and the civil rights movement. America's youth first learned of Reagan-the-politician by his statement that a hippie was someone who "dresses like Tarzan, has hair like Jane, and smells like Cheetah."

The excerpt below is from Reagan's post-presidential memoir, An American Life, *and refers to incidents surrounding a confrontation near the University of California campus at Berkeley in the spring of 1969 when a large number of students "confiscated" a section of land that had been left abandoned by the university. They called it People's Park. The university responded by bull- dozing the land and erecting a fence to keep out the students. That sparked a riot along Telegraph Avenue in which shotgun-wielding policemen shot and injured between fifty and one hundred rioters. One died. Reagan restored order by sending in 3,000 National Guardsmen.*

All ellipses below are in the original.

SOURCE: Ronald Reagan, *An American Life* (New York, 1990). Reprinted with permission of Simon and Schuster Adult Publishing Group from *An American Life* by Ronald Reagan. Copyright © 1990 by Ronald W. Reagan.

During the peak of unrest on our college campuses, student leaders from the nine campuses of the University of California asked to see me in Sacramento. I was delighted to see them. During those days, if I'd visited one of their campuses, I'd have started a riot. When I'd been campaigning, I was cheered by students because I was running against an incumbent who was part of the establishment. Now *I* was the establishment.

When the delegation arrived in the capitol, some were barefoot and several were wearing torn T-shirts; when I entered the room, they sat silently where they were, some sprawled out on the floor. No one stood up. Then their spokesman began:

"Governor, we want to talk to you, but I think you should realize that it's impossible for you to understand us. . . . It's sad, but it's impossible for the members of your generation to understand your own children. . . .

"You weren't raised in a time of instant communications or satellites and computers solving problems in seconds that previously took hours or days or even weeks to solve. You didn't live in an age of space travel and journeys to the moon, of jet travel or high speed electronics. . . ."

While he paused to take a breath, I said: "You're absolutely right. We didn't have those things when we were your age. We invented them." . . .

When it began, perhaps students at the University of California had grounds for grievances against the institution they had entered: Full of dreams and full of ambition, they had been herded into gigantic classes and handed over to a faculty they seldom saw, one that spent most of its time on "research," and turned over its responsibility to teach to inexperienced teaching assistants not much older than the students themselves. The students were given little attention as individuals.

I understood their sense of alienation, but whatever the source of this alienation, it was expropriated by the articulate agitators—many of whom had never been inside a college classroom—who then turned it into an ugly force that could not be tolerated.

A great educational institution became paralyzed. In later years, some participants in those revolutionary days have tried to look back on them as heroic and noble.

Whatever it might have been at the beginning, the upheaval that shook so many of our campuses when I was governor wasn't a gallant or idealistic rebellion to right some wrongs: It was violent anarchy; the campuses were literally set afire by rioting mobs in the name of "free speech."

During one eleven-month period, there were eight bombings and attempted bombings at the Berkeley campus of the university alone; during those eleven months, the police confiscated more than two hundred rifles, pistols, and shotguns and nearly a thousand sticks of dynamite and dozens of Molotov cocktails. . . .

These were stormy times, but I'll never forget one very quiet moment during that period. One day, I arrived at the University of California campus in San

Diego for a meeting of the Board of Regents and there was a huge crowd of demonstrators waiting outside.

The security people told me to remain in the car so that they could drive around to the rear entrance of the building away from the demonstrators. Well, I didn't want to do that. I told them I'd walk through the front door of the university administration building as I was supposed to.

It was a long walk, about 150 yards, to the building. On one side was a knoll and on the other side a smaller rise; both areas were packed with demonstrators all the way from the street to the front door of the building, and I had to take that long walk between them by myself.

The protesters had decided to hold a silent demonstration, with not a sound, and everyone just standing and glaring at me as I made the walk; the silence had an effect and pretty soon it began to seem like a very long walk and I was feeling a little uncomfortable. I had almost reached the building when one girl left the crowd and started descending from the knoll, headed right for me, and I thought, Lord, what have they got planned now? As I approached her, she was waiting for me and she held out her hand and I took it. Then her voice broke the stark silence and said: "I just want to tell you, I like everything you're doing as governor."

I'll never forget the sound of her voice rising out of the silent crowd. I was going on into the building, she was going to be left outside with her peers in a crowd with whom she had had the courage to disagree.

In subsequent years, sometimes when I had a decision to make and the easy way out was to go along with the crowd, I have thought about this young woman's demonstration of courage. And I have always felt terrible that afterward I didn't try to learn her name so that I could tell her how much it had meant to me that day.

Once the National Guardsmen restored order on the campuses, no more policemen or other people were attacked by rioters and peace began to be restored to our universities.

DOCUMENT 11.3
The "Redstockings Manifesto" and the Rise of Radical Feminism (1969)

Radical feminism was born out of many of the same pressures that spurred other radical movements in the sixties and seventies. Moderate reform groups did not go far enough to solve the needs of a more radical minority. In this case, NOW (the National Organization for Women) was not radical enough for a group that split away and formed the more radical Redstockings.

The Redstockings Manifesto (July 7, 1969)

After centuries of individual and preliminary political struggle, women are uniting to achieve their final liberation from male supremacy. Redstockings is dedicated to building this unity and winning our freedom.

Women are an oppressed class. Our oppression is total, affecting every facet of our lives. We are exploited as sex objects, breeders, domestic servants, and cheap labor. We are considered inferior beings, whose only purpose is to enhance men's lives. Our humanity is denied. Our prescribed behavior is enforced by the threat of physical violence. . . .

We identify the agents of our oppression as men. Male supremacy is the oldest, most basic form of domination. All other forms of exploitation and oppression (racism, capitalism, imperialism, etc.) are extensions of male supremacy: men dominate women, a few men dominate the rest. All power structures throughout history have been male-dominated and male oriented. Men have controlled all political, economic and cultural institutions and backed up this control with physical force. They have used their power to keep women in an inferior position. *All men* receive economic, sexual, and psychological benefits from male supremacy. *All men* have oppressed women.

Attempts have been made to shift the burden of responsibility from men to institutions or to women themselves. We condemn these arguments as evasions. Institutions alone do not oppress; they are merely tools of the oppressor. To blame institutions implies that men and women are equally victimized, obscures the fact that men benefit from the subordination of women, and gives men the excuse that they are forced to be oppressors. On the contrary, any man is free to renounce his superior position provided that he is willing to be treated like a woman by other men.

We also reject the idea that women consent to or are to blame for their own oppression. Women's submission is not the result of brainwashing, stupidity, or mental illness but of continual, daily pressure from men. We do not need to change ourselves, but to change men.

The most slanderous evasion of all is that women can oppress men. The basis for this illusion is the isolation of individual relationships from their political context and the tendency of men to see any legitimate challenge to their privileges as persecution. . . .

Our chief task at present is to develop female class consciousness through sharing experience and publicly exposing the sexist foundation of all our institutions. Consciousness-raising is not "therapy," which implies the existence of individual solutions and falsely assumes that the male-female relationship is purely personal, but the only method by which we can ensure that our program for liberation is based on the concrete realities of our lives.

The first requirement for raising class consciousness is honesty, in private and in public, with ourselves and other women.

We identify with all women. We define our best interest as that of the poorest, most brutally exploited woman.

We repudiate all economic, racial, educational or status privileges that divide us from other women. We are determined to recognize and eliminate any prejudices we may hold against other women.

We are committed to achieving internal democracy. We will do whatever is necessary to ensure that every woman in our movement has an equal chance to participate, assume responsibility, and develop her political potential.

We call on all our sisters to unite with us in struggle.

We call on all men to give up their male privileges and support women's liberation in the interest of our humanity and their own.

In fighting for our liberation we will always take the side of women against their oppressors. We will not ask what is "revolutionary" or "reformist," only what is good for women.

The time for individual skirmishes has passed. This time we are going all the way.

DOCUMENT 11.4
The Legend of Stonewall and Gay Activism (July 1969)

In the late 1960s gay Americans considered themselves to be oppressed in much the same way as did black Americans and Hispanics. Many homosexuals hid their way of life; others congregated in gay communities and frequented all-gay establishments. The largest gay bar in New York was the Stonewall Inn, located in the West Village in lower Manhattan. In July 1969 New York City police raided the bar and arrested the patrons—presumably on charges of "indecency." As writer and participant Robert Amsel recalled years later in an article in The Advocate, *the situation escalated from light protest to violence. Outrage over the event was a catalyst for the growth of a nationwide gay-rights/gay-pride movement. For gay Americans, Stonewall became their Selma.*

SOURCE: Robert Amsel, "A Walk on the Wild Side of Stonewall," *The Advocate* (September 15, 1987).

The legend of Stonewall was born as another legend died. On Sunday, June 22, 1969, Judy Garland was found dead from a pill overdose in her London home. An older generation of homosexuals had idolized Judy, as much for her suffering as her talent. Her unsuccessful marriages, her dependence on pills and liquor, and her resilience—the ability to rise when she was down—gave them hope that whatever their oppression, they too could find the strength to carry on.

But now Judy was down and would stay down, and the old gay way of endurance seemed to pass with her.

But while the flags hung at half mast on Fire Island, new flags were about to be raised on the streets of Greenwich Village. Friday afternoon, June 27, Judy was buried. Saturday morning, June 28, the raid on the Stonewall Inn began. "We will endure" became "We shall overcome."

The Stonewall Inn was located at 53 Christopher Street, off Sheridan Square. It was an after-hours "private club" for members only. Anyone who could scrounge up three bucks could become a member for the evening. . . . The former owners had been burned out and the bar had remained vacant for a year. Its new owners slapped black paint on the already smoke-blackened walls, and with minimum overhauling were ready for business. It was still a fire trap. It was also a dope drop and the suspected source of a minor hepatitis epidemic six months prior to the raid. Its two large rooms—one a dance area, the other a bar—were generally sardine-packed with young men, including drag queens, hippies, street people, and uptown boys slumming. Many customers were under 18, the legal drinking age. Some were runaways. Some had nowhere to go.

For whatever strange reason, the police that summer decided to launch an all-out attack on illegal clubs throughout the city. . . . Prior to Stonewall, there had been raids on other gay after-hours clubs, the Sewer and the Snake Pit, both aptly named. The Tele-Star and the Checkerboard had closed down not long before. By the time the cops hit the Stonewall, the customers were angry, frustrated, and, more important, running out of places to go.

Deputy Inspector Seymour Pine led eight plainclothes officers (including two women) into the Stonewall at 3 a.m. It was a hot night and a full moon was shining over Sheridan Square. The employees were arrested for selling liquor without a license. The customers were allowed to leave, one at a time. They waited outside for their friends. Many had been in such raids before, some in the past few weeks.

One straight observer referred to the gathering as "festive" with those exiting the club striking poses, swishing and camping. Then [there was] a sudden mood change when the paddy wagon arrived and the bartender, doorman, three drag queens and a struggling lesbian were shoved inside. There were catcalls and cries to topple the paddy wagon. . . . The crowd threw coins at the police and shouted "Pigs!" Coins progressed to bottles. The crowd was closing in. Pine and his detectives moved quickly back into the Stonewall and locked themselves in. . . .

Police reinforcements arrived en masse. . . . [*Village Voice* reporter] Howard Smith went outside [of the bar] and took . . . notes. He returned inside to discover that the police had vented their anger by smashing all the mirrors, juke boxes, phones, toilets, and cigarette machines. No one but the police had been inside, but the courts would later find them innocent of vandalism.

[Saturday night riot]

Stonewall management found it difficult to keep their customers inside Saturday night, since all the action was outside. Shouts of "Gay Power!" and "Liberate Christopher Street!" echoed along Sixth and Seventh avenues, and Greenwich Avenue. . . . The battle cry raged the length of Christopher Street.

There was a strong feeling of gay community and a strong fighting spirit, an intoxicating sense of release. It was "us against them, and by God, we're winning." Crowds were growing, as if from the pavement. . . . [The] owner of a gay bookstore in the Village reported that some gay men were barricading the streets and not allowing heterosexual drivers to pass. A car of newlyweds was half lifted before the openmouthed bride and groom were allowed to drive on.

New York's Tactical Police Force (TPF) arrived on the scene. They were helmeted and carried clubs. They had rescued Pine and his men the morning before, but were unprepared for the guerrilla warfare that awaited them.

These streets were gay territory. Gay people knew every doorway, alley and side street and where they would lead. They knew how to split up the TPF and run them in circles. Men on roofs or in rooms overlooking Christopher Street hurled bottles at the cops. When the cops looked up, no one could be seen.

Two TPF men chased a gay guy down a side street. Gay bystanders started running with their brother. Before long, a large group was running. A man at the head of the group suddenly held out his arms and yelled, "Stop!" The group stopped. "There are two pigs and how many of us?" A moment of meaningful silence. The two cops had also stopped, were looking at one another and then at the crowd. The group leader grinned. "Get the bastards!" About face. The cops were now running at full gallop, a lynch mob on their heels. "Catch'em! Fuck'em!"

The crowd dispersed by 3 a.m.

Sunday night was quiet. Monday and Tuesday nights' crowds started to gather again, but outbreaks were few. . . . The next night, Wednesday, July 2, events took a brutal turn. The TPF men used their nightsticks indiscriminately. "At one point," [Dick] Leitsch [of the *Mattachine Newsletter*—a gay-oriented publication] wrote, "7th Avenue from Christopher to West 10th looked like a battlefield in Vietnam. Young people, many of them queens, were lying on the sidewalk, bleeding from the head, face, mouth, and even the eyes. Others were nursing bruised and often bleeding arms, legs, backs, and necks." . . .

After Wednesday the riots petered out and the politicizing began. [The] Gay Liberation Front (GLF) was a new group of young male and female homosexuals, which formed in late July. . . . [The] GLF had a leftist ideology and an anarchic structure. They were sort of a gay SDS [Students for a Democratic Society], and opted for revolution and whatever means were necessary to achieve it. They aligned themselves with and supported all other radical groups of the period. . . . Many smaller groups sprang up as well. All the groups suffered from infighting, out-fighting and egos in conflict. But age-old barriers were breaking down. Gay people in other parts of the country were starting to emerge from their closets. California's heavily gay cities of San Francisco and Los Angeles had their own gay renaissance. New organizations spread throughout the land. A year later, diverse gay groups and independent gays marched in brotherhood and sisterhood. Annual gay pride days would follow. . . .

A decade after Stonewall, in this carefree, extra-fertile soil, a deadly virus was imported. It quietly, swiftly spread before anyone was the wiser. AIDS [has produced] a backlash stronger and more lethal than anything we knew in our cozy closets. Homophobes always feared that gayness might rub off. Now they fear that death might rub off along with it. . . .

And that is why Stonewall should be remembered today. It doesn't matter that it was a firetrap, that the police may have been doing us a favor. It doesn't matter that the gutsier fighters were drags and street kids. . . . What matters is the communal gay spirit. . . . Unless we recapture that spirit and do battle, we'll be ripe for . . . a time when "camp" is something that follows "concentration."

BIOGRAPHICAL SKETCH
Cesar Chavez

The success of the African American civil rights movement in the postwar years had an impact on other groups—particularly the nation's other large minority group, the Mexican Americans. Much of this awakening can be credited directly to Cesar Chavez, an aggressive farm labor leader who took on what seemed the almost impossible task of organizing the nation's five million Mexican American migrant workers.

This group was left out of the advancements in labor organization that took place during the New Deal era. With no leadership and no real voting power, Mexican American migrants were not able to organize, and never fell under the protection of the minimum wage or Social Security laws, which almost always excluded farm workers. The result was that a majority of these people lived in the worst kind of poverty. Most lived in barrios in large cities or in primitive shelters provided (with no regulation or minimum standards) by growers. And a-dollar-a-day wages were still common in Southern California and south Texas in the immediate postwar years.

The cycle was all too familiar. Mexican Americans received the least education of all the minority groups, were paid the least, lived in the worst conditions, and consequently, had fewer opportunities. They had little hope of escaping poverty. This, of course, made them second-class citizens. Schools were often segregated, and in Texas and California it was illegal to teach classes in any language but English—which kept most Mexican American kids out of school and in the fields. In 1968, the Johnson administration passed the Bilingual Education Act, but even that did not end the practice in much of the Southwest.

It was Cesar Chavez who gave Mexican Americans leadership; he also gave identity and hope to the millions of the nation's migrant farm workers.

Chavez was born in southern Arizona to a fairly prosperous family, considering the general condition of the Mexican American community at the time. They owned their own ranch—some one hundred acres in the Gila Valley—and a local store. But all that was lost in Anglo land swindles during the Great Depression. The Chavez family was forced to join the thousands of Mexican American migrants who worked the fields of California. Cesar received only an eighth-grade education, about average for a Mexican American child at the time. African Americans received an average of ten years of education; whites, twelve.

In 1948, at age twenty-one, Chavez took part in his first strike to protest low wages and poor working conditions for California's migrant farm workers. The strike was a failure, and the owners forced the workers back to the fields. Following the strike, Chavez joined the Community Service Organization, and in 1958 he became general director. He realized that the organization needed a strategy of direct action—a strategy that would bring attention to the plight of migrant workers, organize them, and ultimately better their conditions. The strategy that had the greatest appeal—the strategy that had the most possibility for success—was the strategy of non-violence, as it was espoused by Gandhi and Martin Luther King, Jr. And, like King and Gandhi, Chavez used it to great success.

In 1962 Chavez formed his own organization, first called the National Farm Workers Association (NFWA), and in 1965 he led a strike of California's grape-pickers. In a campaign that caught the imagination of the nation, the NFWA encouraged all Americans to boycott table grapes as a show of support for the workers. Possibly the most important result of the strike was the extensive national press coverage that often revealed, on television, the poor living conditions of the migrant workers. That, in turn, put pressure on growers and politicians to deal with the problems and poverty that migrant workers faced.

In 1968 Chavez began fasting—intent on drawing additional public attention to the plight of the farm workers. Through the 1970s the United Farm Workers (changed from the NFWA) organized strikes and boycotts, particularly against the California grape and lettuce growers. In the 1980s, Chavez fasted and led a series of boycotts to protest the use of pesticides on grapes.

He died on April 23, 1993.

Cesar Chavez's greatest contribution to civil rights for Mexican Americans was that he became the leader of a movement that had no leaders and no spokesmen. He organized the nation's farm workers, and he brought to the nation's attention the plight of a minority group that was badly exploited and almost invisible inside the nation's social and economic system.

STUDY QUESTIONS

1. Why do you think Reagan used the parable of the girl supporter?
2. Cesar Chavez actually lost most strikes he led. How, then, did his work do so much to help Mexican American farm workers?
3. The sixties seemed littered with manifestos; it seemed every organization felt a need to write down its objectives. Do you see any relationship between any of these writings? How about the Redstockings and the Weathermen? Whom were they rebelling against?

FURTHER READINGS

Terry Anderson, *The Movement and the Sixties: Protest in America from Greensboro to Wounded Knee* (1995).

David Burner, *Making Peace with the Sixties* (1996).

Todd Gitlin, *The Sixties: Years of Hope, Days of Rage* (1987).

Allen J. Matusow, *The Unraveling of America: A History of Liberalism in the 1960s* (1984).

Milton Viorst, *Fire in the Streets: America in the 1960s* (1979).

12 • Nixon and the End of U.S. Involvement in Indochina

INTRODUCTION

The two foreign policy events that marked Richard Nixon's administration were the prosecution of the war in Vietnam and the president's historic trip to China in 1972. One closed a door on the past; the other opened a window to the future.

During the 1968 presidential campaign, candidate Nixon told the nation that he had a plan to end the war in Vietnam—and that he would spell out that plan when he took office. Nixon clearly wanted to end the war quickly. He saw what it had done to Johnson and the Democrats at a time when their domestic policies were generally popular. In January 1969, just after he took the oath of office, Nixon told an aide: "I'm not going to end up like LBJ. . . . I'm going to stop that war. Fast."

Nixon's campaign pledge, revealed after he took office, was what he called "peace with honor." It revolved mostly around his policy of "Vietnamization," a plan to turn the war over to the army of South Vietnam as U.S. troops were gradually withdrawn. The South Vietnamese would then continue the fight against the communist forces with U.S. money and materiel. For cynics, Nixon's policy was much less than peace with honor; it was essentially an exit strategy preceded by a declaration of victory.

Nixon also hoped to stifle the anti-war movement at home by ending the then-current draft system and replacing it with a lottery—a system that would send to war only those with low lottery numbers, determined by individuals' birthdays, in a national drawing. The plan was intended to make the draft more equitable.

Much of this worked—or at least it was popular at the time. Vietnamization was embraced by moderates, who hoped the plan would avoid a humiliating military defeat. The lottery seemed to quiet the protesters—at least those who drew high numbers.

Another aspect of Nixon's strategy was to begin a secret bombing of Cambodia and Laos. For fourteen months after his inauguration, Nixon authorized some 3,600 B-52 sorties that dropped over 110,000 tons of bombs on eastern Cambodia—a nation that had declared neutrality in the war but could not keep the Viet Cong from establishing base camps on its eastern and southern border. Only after those fourteen months, in 1970, did Nixon acknowledge this expansion of the war.

The United States withdrew from Vietnam in early 1973. The war had cost the country somewhere between $112 billion and $155 billion, along with a great deal of credibility. On the battlefield, 45,943 U.S. soldiers were killed in action. Another 10,298 were killed in non-combat incidents, and an additional 2,477 were designated as missing in action and presumed dead. Of the total number, 20,553 were killed in the last four years of the war. In early 1975 the army of North Vietnam overran the South and the war ended.

If Nixon's prosecution of the Vietnam War was not successful, his visit to China in 1972 changed the general dynamic of world foreign policy. It was truly a foreign policy victory for Nixon, just as the war in Indochina was coming to a difficult end.

By 1970 China and the United States had come to need each other—or at least they thought they did. By that date, the Chinese–Soviet ideological divorce had become so hostile that the two communist powers were fighting a border war along the Ussuri River in eastern Siberia. Mao Zedong, the Chinese "supreme leader," hoped that a closer association with Washington might help Beijing stave off any further Soviet aggressions. Mao also hoped to convince the United States to end its long-time recognition of Taiwan as the sole government representing the Chinese people—and recognize Beijing. Nixon's trip to China began that process.

In turn, Nixon hoped that by moving closer to Beijing he could "play the China card," that is, gain concessions from Moscow by threatening to assist China against Soviet aggressions. At the same time, Nixon thought that he might convince China to pressure Hanoi to come to terms at the peace table and end that agony. In fact, neither of those hopes came to fruition.

DOCUMENT 12.1
President Richard Nixon on the Vietnamization of the War
(November 1969)

During the 1968 campaign, Nixon said several times that he had a plan to end the war in Vietnam, but he refused to reveal any specifics of his plan until after the election. The cornerstone of that plan was the Vietnamization of the war, a plan to replace American soldiers with Vietnamese soldiers.

A cynic said that the plan would do little more than change the skin color of the bodies.

After one year in office, Nixon went to the American people to explain his plan of Vietnamization. In the speech, Nixon refers to the "silent majority." He had used the phrase in his campaign to describe those Americans who quietly supported the U.S. role in Vietnam and opposed the boisterous excesses of the era. Nixon had, in fact, discovered a significant voting bloc that the Republicans would finally mobilize. There were large numbers of conservative Americans who believed strongly in fighting communism in Vietnam, and who were just as passionately repelled by all that encompassed the sixties "revolution," in everything from sex to race.

SOURCE: *Public Papers of the Presidents: Richard M. Nixon, 1969,* 901–9.

Good evening, my fellow Americans.

Tonight I want to talk to you on a subject of deep concern to all Americans and to many people in all parts of the world: the war in Vietnam. I believe that one of the reasons for the deep division about Vietnam is that many Americans have lost confidence in what their government has told them about our policy. The American people cannot and should not be asked to support a policy which involves the overriding issues of war and peace unless they know the truth about that policy.

Tonight, therefore, I would like to answer some of the questions that I know are on the minds of many of you listening to me. . . .

Now, let me begin by describing the situation I found when I was inaugurated on January 20.

The war had been going on for four years. 31,000 American had been killed in action.

The training program for the South Vietnamese was behind schedule. 540,000 Americans were in Vietnam with no plans to reduce the number. No progress had been made at the negotiations in Paris and the United States had not put forth a comprehensive peace proposal. The war was causing deep division at home and criticism from many of our friends as well as our enemies abroad.

In view of these circumstances there were some who urged that I end the war at once by ordering the immediate withdrawal of all American forces. From a political standpoint this would have been a popular and easy course to follow. After all, we became involved in the war while my predecessor was in office. I could blame the defeat, which would be the result of my action, on him and come out as the peacemaker. Some put it to me quite bluntly. This was the only way to avoid allowing Johnson's war to become Nixon's war.

But I had a greater obligation than to think only of the years of my administration and of the next election. I had to think of the effect of my decision on the next generation and on the future of peace and freedom in America and in the world.

Let us all understand that the question before us is not whether some Americans are for peace and some Americans are against peace. The question at issue is not whether Johnson's war becomes Nixon's war. The great question is: How can we win America's peace?

Well, let us turn now to the fundamental issue. Why, and how, did the United States become involved in Vietnam in the first place? Fifteen years ago North Vietnam, with the logistical support of Communist China and the Soviet Union, launched a campaign to impose a communist government on South Vietnam by instigating and supporting a revolution. In response to the request of the government of South Vietnam, President Eisenhower sent economic aid and military equipment to assist the people of South Vietnam in their efforts to prevent a communist takeover. Seven years ago, President Kennedy sent 16,000 military personnel to Vietnam as combat advisers. Four years ago, President Johnson sent American combat forces to South Vietnam.

Now, many believe that President Johnson's decision to send American combat forces to South Vietnam was wrong. And many others—I among them—have been strongly critical of the way the war has been conducted. But the question facing us today is: Now that we are in the war, what is the best way to end it?

In January, I could only conclude that the precipitate withdrawal of American forces from Vietnam would be a disaster, not only for South Vietnam, but for the United States and for the cause of peace. . . .

For the United States, this first defeat in our nation's history would result in a collapse of confidence in American leadership—not only in Asia but throughout the world. Three American Presidents have recognized the great stakes involved in Vietnam and understood what had to be done. In 1963, President Kennedy, with his characteristic eloquence and clarity, said: "We want to see a stable government there, carrying on a struggle to maintain its national independence. We believe strongly in that. We are not going to withdraw from that effort. In my opinion, for us to withdraw from that effort would mean a collapse not only of South Vietnam, but Southeast Asia. So we are going to stay there."

President Eisenhower and President Johnson expressed the same conclusion during their terms of office. For the future of peace, precipitate withdrawal would thus be a disaster of immense magnitude. A nation cannot remain great if it betrays its allies and lets down its friends. Our defeat and humiliation in South Vietnam without question would promote recklessness in the councils of those great powers who have not yet abandoned their goals of world conquest. This would spark violence wherever our commitments help maintain the peace—in the Middle East, in Berlin, eventually even in the Western Hemisphere. Ultimately, this would cost more lives. It would not bring peace; it would bring more war. For these reasons, I rejected the recommendation that I should end the war by immediately withdrawing all of our forces. I chose instead to change American policy on both the negotiating front and battlefront. . . .

Before any American troops were committed to Vietnam, a leader of another Asian country expressed this opinion to me when I was traveling in Asia as a private citizen. He said: "When you are trying to assist another nation defend its freedom, U.S. policy should be to help them fight the war, but not to fight the war for them." Well, in accordance with this wise counsel, I have laid down . . . three principles as guidelines for future American policy toward Asia:

First, the United States will keep all of its treaty commitments.

Second, we shall provide a shield if a nuclear power threatens the freedom of a nation allied with us or of a nation whose survival we consider vital to our security.

Third, in cases involving other types of aggression, we shall furnish military and economic assistance when requested in accordance with our treaty commitments. But we shall look to the nation directly threatened to assume the primary responsibility of providing the manpower for its defense.

After I announced this policy, I found that the leaders of the Philippines, Thailand, Vietnam, South Korea, and other nations which might be threatened by Communist aggression, welcomed this new direction in American foreign policy. The defense of freedom is everybody's business, not just America's business. And it is particularly the responsibility of the people whose freedom is threatened.

In the previous administration, we Americanized the war in Vietnam. In this administration, we are Vietnamizing the search for peace. The policy of the previous administration not only resulted in our assuming the primary responsibility for fighting the war, but even more significantly we did not adequately stress the goal of strengthening the South Vietnamese so that they could defend themselves when we left. . . .

After five years of Americans going into Vietnam, we are finally bringing men home. By December 15, over 60,000 men will have been withdrawn from South Vietnam, including 20 percent of all of our combat forces.

The South Vietnamese have continued to gain in strength. As a result they have been able to take over combat responsibilities from our American troops. . . .

My fellow Americans, I am sure you can recognize from what I have said that we really only have two choices open to us if we want to end this war. I can order an immediate, precipitate, withdrawal of all Americans from Vietnam without regard to the effects of that action. Or we can persist in our search for a just peace through a negotiated settlement if possible, or through continued implementation of our plan for Vietnamization . . . in which we will withdraw all our forces from Vietnam on a schedule in accordance with our program, as the South Vietnamese become strong enough to defend their own freedom.

I have chosen this second course. It is not the easy way. It is the right way. It is a plan which will end the war and serve the cause of peace, not just in Vietnam, but in the Pacific and in the world. . . .

Let historians not record that when America was the most powerful nation in the world we passed on the other side of the road and allowed the last hopes for peace and freedom of millions of people to be suffocated by the forces of totalitarianism.

And so tonight to you, the great silent majority of my fellow Americans, I ask for your support. I pledged in my campaign for the presidency to end the war in a way that we could win the peace. I have initiated a plan of action which will enable me to keep that pledge.

The more support I can have from the American people, the sooner that pledge can be redeemed—for the more divided we are at home, the less likely the enemy is to negotiate at Paris.

Let us be united for peace. Let us also be united against defeat. Because let us understand, North Vietnam cannot defeat or humiliate the United States. Only Americans can do that. . . .

Thank you and goodnight.

DOCUMENT 12.2
John Kerry, Testimony Before the House Foreign Relations Committee (April 22, 1971)

In 1971 John Kerry held a great deal of credibility. He was a highly decorated Vietnam veteran who, like many other veterans, had come home disenchanted with the war effort and then finally became actively opposed to the war. Moreover, he was intelligent, articulate, and well educated. As the spokesman for Vietnam Veterans Against the War, Kerry was asked to testify before the House Foreign Relations Committee. His prepared speech is excerpted below.

Kerry's testimony was covered on national news, and Kerry quickly became a hero to the nation's youth who opposed the war. Following the war, Kerry was able to turn his anti-war activism into a political career. In 1982 he became Massachusetts' lieutenant governor. Two years later he was elected to the Senate and then reelected three times. He served nineteen years on the Senate Foreign Relations Committee.

In 2004 Kerry won the Democratic Party's presidential nomination and lost to President George Bush in the November election. His well-publicized opposition to the war was used by the Republican Party against him in that campaign.

SOURCE: Congressional Record—Senate, April 23, 1971.

I would like to talk, representing all those veterans, and say that several months ago, in Detroit, we had an investigation at which over 150 honorably discharged, and many very highly decorated, veterans testified to war crimes committed in Southeast Asia. These were not isolated incidents, but crimes committed on a day-to-day basis, with the full awareness of officers at all levels of command. It is impossible to describe to you exactly what did happen in Detroit—the emotions in the room, and the feelings of the men who were reliving their experiences in Vietnam. They relived the absolute horror of what this country, in a sense, made them do.

They told stories that, at times, they had personally raped, cut off ears, cut off heads, taped wires from portable telephones to human genitals and turned up the power, cut off limbs, blown up bodies, randomly shot at civilians, razed villages in fashion reminiscent of Genghis Khan, shot cattle and dogs for fun, poisoned food stocks, and generally ravaged the countryside of South Vietnam, in addition to the normal ravage of war and the normal and very particular ravaging which is done by the applied bombing power of this country. . . .

I would like to talk to you a little bit about what the result is of the feelings these men carry with them after coming back from Vietnam. The country doesn't know it yet, but it has created a monster, a monster in the form of millions of men who have been taught to deal, and to trade, in violence, and who are given the chance to die for the biggest nothing in history; men who have returned with a sense of anger and a sense of betrayal which no one has yet grasped.

As a veteran and one who felt this anger, I would like to talk about it. We are angry because we feel we have been used in the worst fashion by the administration of this country.

In 1970, at West Point, Vice President Agnew said, "some glamorize the criminal misfits of society while our best men die in Asian rice paddies to preserve the freedom which most of those misfits abuse," and this was used as a rallying point for our effort in Vietnam. But for us, as boys in Asia whom the country was supposed to support, his statement is a terrible distortion from which we can only draw a very deep sense of revulsion. Hence the anger of some of the men who are here in Washington today. It is a distortion because we in no way consider ourselves the best men of this country, because those he calls misfits were standing up for us in a way that nobody else in this country dared to, because so many who have died would have returned to this country to join the misfits in their efforts to ask for an immediate withdrawal from South Vietnam, because so many of those best men have returned as quadriplegics and amputees, and they lie forgotten in Veterans' Administration hospitals in this country which fly the flag which so many have chosen as their own personal symbol. And we cannot consider ourselves America's best men when we are ashamed of and hated for what we were called on to do in Southeast Asia.

In our opinion, and from our experience, there is nothing in South Vietnam which could happen that realistically threatens the United States of America. And to attempt to justify the loss of one American life in Vietnam, Cambodia, or Laos by linking such loss to the preservation of freedom, which those misfits supposedly abuse, is to us the height of criminal hypocrisy, and it is that kind of hypocrisy which we feel has torn this country apart.

We found that not only was it a civil war, an effort by a people who had for years been seeking their liberation from any colonial influence whatsoever, but, also, we found that the Vietnamese, whom we had enthusiastically molded after our own image, were hard-put to take up the fight against the threat we were supposedly saving them from.

We found most people didn't even know the difference between communism and democracy. They only wanted to work in rice paddies without helicopters strafing them and bombs with napalm burning their villages and tearing their country apart. They wanted everything to do with the war, particularly with this foreign presence of the United States of America, to leave them alone in peace, and they practiced the art of survival by siding with whichever military force was present at a particular time, be it Viet Cong, North Vietnamese or American.

We found also that, all too often, American men were dying in those rice paddies for want of support from their allies. We saw first hand how monies from American taxes were used for a corrupt dictatorial regime. We saw that many people in this country had a one-sided idea of who was kept free by the flag, and blacks provided the highest percentage of casualties. We saw Vietnam ravaged equally by American bombs and search-and-destroy missions as well as by Viet Cong terrorism—and yet we listened while this country tried to blame all of the havoc on the Viet Cong.

We rationalized destroying villages in order to save them. We saw America lose her sense of morality as she accepted very coolly a Mi Lai, and refused to give up the image of American soldiers who hand out chocolate bars and chewing gum.

We learned the meaning of free-fire zones—shooting anything that moves—and we watched while America placed a cheapness on the lives of Orientals.

We watched the United States' falsification of body counts, in fact the glorification of body counts. We listened while, month after month, we were told the back of the enemy was about to break. We fought using weapons against "Oriental human beings" with quotation marks around that. . . .

Now we are told that the men who fought there . . . can exercise the incredible arrogance of "Vietnamizing" the Vietnamese.

Each day, to facilitate the process by which the United States washes her hands of Vietnam, someone has to give up his life so that the United States doesn't have to admit something that the entire world already knows, so that we can't say that we have made a mistake. Someone has to die so that President Nixon won't be, and these are his words, "the first President to lose a war. . . ."

We wish that a merciful God could wipe away our own memories of that service as easily as this administration has wiped away their memories of us. But all that they have done, and all that they can do by this denial, is to make more clear than ever our own determination to undertake one last mission: To search out and destroy the last vestige of this barbaric war, to pacify our own hearts, to conquer the hate and fear that have driven this country these last ten years and more. And more. And so, when thirty years from now our brothers go down the street without a leg, without an arm, or a face, and small boys ask why, we will be able to say "Vietnam" and not mean a desert, not a filthy obscene memory, but mean instead where America finally turned, and where soldiers like us helped it in the turning.

DOCUMENT 12.3
Shanghai Communiqué (February 1972)

The United States and the People's Republic of China (PRC) had treated each other as enemies since the communist takeover in China in 1949. They had fought a war in Korea. They had accused each other of acts of open aggression, and both had supported the other's enemies in military conflicts. As late as 1970, Washington had continued to maintain its position that the Nationalist Chinese on Taiwan comprised the only legitimate government of the Chinese people. At the same time, Beijing continued its open support of the communist forces fighting the United States in Vietnam.

In 1970, however, things began to change. The ideological split between China and the Soviet Union erupted into border clashes in Siberia, leading China's supreme leader, Mao Zedong, to look to the United States as a possible ally against further Soviet aggressions. Mao also hoped that a warming of relations might reduce Washington's commitment to Taiwan. In January, Chinese officials asked for talks with the United States, and later that year the two began a simple dialogue facilitated through Pakistan, a nation friendly to both countries. In April 1971 the Chinese unexpectedly reached out by inviting an American table tennis team, then on tour in Japan, to China for a series of matches. The Americans were soundly trounced, but within three months Henry Kissinger was in Beijing making arrangements for President Nixon's visit. Nixon made the announcement that he would go to China in July 1971.

Nixon's trip to China seemed a bizarre turn of events for anyone who knew Nixon's history. An American president who had built his political career as an anti-communist hardliner was sitting down with Mao Zedong, the communist dictator and theoretician. After much bickering, U.S. and Chinese officials issued the Shanghai Communiqué, a general agreement to disagree on most issues of substance. Possibly the most important aspect of the communiqué was the U.S. agreement to recognize "one China," governed from Beijing—a China that included Taiwan.

SOURCE: *Public Papers of the Presidents: Richard M. Nixon, 1972, 376–79.*

The leaders of the People's Republic of China and the United States of America found it beneficial to have this opportunity, after so many years without contact, to present candidly to one another their views on a variety of issues. They reviewed the international situation in which important changes and great upheavals are taking place and expounded their respective positions and attitudes.

The Chinese side stated: Wherever there is oppression, there is resistance. Countries want independence, nations want liberation and the people want revolution—this has become the irresistible trend of history. All nations, big or small, should be equal. Big nations should not bully the small and strong nations should not bully the weak. China will never be a superpower and it opposes hegemony and power politics of any kind. The Chinese side stated that it firmly supports the struggles of all the oppressed people and nations for freedom and liberation and that the people of all countries have the right to choose their social systems according their own wishes and the right to safeguard the independence, sovereignty and territorial integrity of their own countries and oppose foreign aggression, interference, control and subversion. All foreign troops should be withdrawn to their own countries. The Chinese side expressed its firm support to the peoples of Vietnam, Laos and Cambodia in their efforts for the attainment of their goal and its firm support to the seven-point proposal of the Provisional Revolutionary Government of the Republic of South Viet Nam and the elaboration of February this year on the two key problems in the proposal, and to the Joint Declaration of the Summit Conference of the Indochinese Peoples. It firmly supports the eight-point program for the peaceful unification of Korea put forward by the government of the Democratic People's Republic of Korea on April 12, 1971, and the stand for the abolition of the "U.N. Commission for the Unification and Rehabilitation of Korea." It firmly opposes the revival and outward expansion of Japanese militarism and firmly supports the Japanese people's desire to build an independent, democratic, peaceful and neutral Japan. It firmly maintains that India and Pakistan should, in accordance with the United Nations resolutions on the Indo-Pakistan question, immediately withdraw all their forces to their respective territories and to their own sides of the ceasefire line in Jammu and Kashmir and firmly supports the Pakistan government and people in their struggle to preserve their independence and sovereignty and the people of Jammu and Kashmir in their struggle for the right of self-determination.

The U.S. side stated: Peace in Asia and peace in the world requires efforts both to reduce immediate tensions and to eliminate the basic causes of conflict. The United States will work for a just and secure peace. *Just,* because it fulfills the aspirations of peoples and nations for freedom and progress. *Secure,* because it removes the danger of foreign aggression. The United States supports individual freedom and social progress for all the peoples of the world, free of outside pressure or intervention. The United States believes that the effort to reduce tensions is served by improving communication between countries that have different ideologies so as to lessen the risks of confrontation through accident, miscalculation or misunderstanding. Countries should treat each other with mutual respect and be willing to compete peacefully, letting performance be the ultimate judge. No country should claim infallibility and each country should be prepared to reexamine its own attitudes for the common good. The United States stressed that the peoples of Indochina should be allowed to determine their destiny without outside intervention; its constant primary objective has been a negotiated solution; the eight-point proposal put forward by the Republic of Vietnam and the United States on January 27, 1972 represents a basis for the attainment of that objective; in the absence of a negotiated settlement the United States envisages the ultimate withdrawal of all U.S. forces from the region consistent with the aim of self-determination for each country of Indochina. The United States will maintain its close ties with and support for the Republic of Korea; the United States will support efforts of the Republic of Korea to seek a relaxation of tension and increased communication on the Korean peninsula. The United States places the highest value on its friendly relations with Japan; it will continue to develop the existing close bonds. Consistent with the United Nations Security Council Resolution of December 21, 1971, the United States favors the continuation of the ceasefire between India and Pakistan and the withdrawal of all military forces to within their own territories and to their own sides of the ceasefire line in Jammu and Kashmir; the United States supports the right of the peoples of South Asia to shape their own future in peace, free of military threat, and without having the area become the subject of great power rivalry.

There are essential differences between China and the United States in their social systems and foreign policies. However, the two sides agreed that countries, regardless of their social systems, should conduct their relations on the principles of respect for the sovereignty and territorial integrity of all states, non-aggression against other states, non-interference in the internal affairs of other states, equality and mutual benefit, and peaceful coexistence. International disputes should be settled on this basis, without resorting to the use or threat of force. The United States and the People's Republic of China are prepared to apply these principles to their mutual relations. . . .

Both sides are of the view that it would be against the interests of the peoples of the world for any major country to collude with another against other countries, or for major countries to divide up the world into spheres of interest.

The two sides reviewed the long-standing serious disputes between China and the United States. The Chinese side reaffirmed its position: the Taiwan question is the crucial question obstructing the normalization of relations between China and the United States; the government of the People's Republic of China is the sole legal government of China; Taiwan is a province of China which has long been returned to the motherland; the liberation of Taiwan is China's internal affair in which no other country has the right to interfere; and all U.S. forces and military installations must be withdrawn from Taiwan. The Chinese government firmly opposes any activities which aim at the creation of "one China, one Taiwan," "one China, two governments," "two Chinas," an "independent Taiwan" or advocate that "the status of Taiwan remains to be determined."

The U.S. side declared: The United States acknowledges that all Chinese on either side of the Taiwan Strait maintain there is but one China and that Taiwan is a part of China. The United States Government does not challenge that position. It reaffirms its interest in a peaceful settlement of the Taiwan question by the Chinese themselves. With this prospect in mind, it affirms the ultimate objective of the withdrawal of all U.S. forces and military installations from Taiwan. In the meantime, it will progressively reduce its forces and military installations on Taiwan as the tension in the area diminishes. . . .

Both sides view bilateral trade as another area from which mutual benefit can be derived, and agreed that economic relations based on equality and mutual benefit are in the interest of the peoples of the two countries. They agree to facilitate the progressive development of trade between their two countries. . . .

President Nixon, Mrs. Nixon and the American party expressed their appreciation for the gracious hospitality shown them by the government and people of the People's Republic of China.

BIOGRAPHICAL SKETCH
Henry Kissinger

Henry Kissinger is widely regarded as one of the greatest American statesmen of the twentieth century. He influenced American foreign policy as early as the Kennedy administration, and was the principal architect of foreign policy in the Nixon and Ford administrations between 1969 and 1977. There have been few other figures in the American twentieth century (except for the presidents themselves) who have had such impact on the nation's foreign policy.

Kissinger was born into a middle-class Jewish family in Furth, Germany, in 1923. In 1938 his family fled the Nazi anti-Semitism of the time, settling in New York. In 1943, Kissinger became a naturalized citizen and joined the U.S. Army, serving in Europe as an interpreter and intelligence officer. After the war, he pursued a brilliant academic career at Harvard, where he became a professor of international affairs in 1957.

At least in part because of his book *Nuclear Weapons and Foreign Policy* (1957), Kissinger's advice was sought after by national political leaders. He became a part-time foreign policy advisor to the Kennedy administration in the early sixties, and is usually credited with devising JFK's "flexible response" strategy, arguing the need for both conventional and nuclear forces in response to Soviet aggressions.

Through the sixties, Kissinger continued to advise the Johnson administration, but he also served as a behind-the-scenes advisor to several Republicans, particularly Nelson Rockefeller, who ran unsuccessfully for his party's nomination in 1964 and again in 1968. When Nixon was elected in 1968, he appointed Kissinger as his national security advisor. With Nixon's support, Kissinger immediately concentrated the foreign policy structure of the administration under the authority of the National Security Council, effectively circumventing and limiting the power of the State Department and the secretary of state.

Kissinger often expressed his lack of faith in the American moralistic approach to its cold war foreign policy: the assumption that the American system was morally superior to the Soviet system, and therefore it would ultimately win out. He argued for a more pragmatic approach that recognized the Soviet Union as a rival superpower in a balance of power and a threat of equal force. Once a perception of equality was accepted by both sides, areas of cooperation could be pursued. The policy became known as "détente."

In 1969 Kissinger began secret talks with North Vietnam in an attempt to bring a favorable end to the war. In 1973, he shared the Nobel Peace Prize with North Vietnamese negotiator Le Duc Tho for secretly negotiating conditions for an American withdrawal from Vietnam.

In 1971 Kissinger made contact with Chinese officials and formalized the arrangements for President Nixon to visit China in February of the next year. Nixon's China visit threatened to reorganize the world order by changing the international balance of power from a two-power cold war struggle to a triangle of three competing powers. The new order threatened the Soviet Union's equal place in the world with a possible U.S.-Chinese anti-Soviet alliance. That alliance was never realized, but the threat of it forced the Soviets to moderate their hard-line stance in many areas, and it brought China back into the world order. It was one of the most significant turning points in American foreign policy since the end of World War II.

Kissinger was also instrumental in brokering an end to the 1973 Yom Kippur War between Israel, Egypt, and Syria. He followed up with intensive "shuttle diplomacy" in an effort to arbitrate a permanent peace in the region.

Kissinger was named secretary of state in Nixon's second term, while he continued to hold the position of national security advisor. During the Watergate crisis, it is widely perceived that Nixon was so burdened by those events that he allowed Kissinger to operate the nation's foreign policy on his own accord, with no significant presidential input. When Nixon resigned in August 1974, Kissinger continued on in the Ford administration and retained his positions and his unprecedented influence in the nation's foreign affairs.

It was during the Ford years that Kissinger's policies came under fire, mostly from the members of Republican Right, who opposed détente. They considered the policy an appeasement of the communist aggressor, and a willingness to accept the status quo. They also argued that détente allowed the Soviet Union to build its military arsenal at America's expense.

Kissinger has his detractors. They have argued that many of his policies failed, and that they often came at the cost of human rights. Although détente eased tensions in the mid-1970s, the policy ultimately failed when U.S.-Soviet relations hardened in the late 1970s. In 1975 South Vietnam collapsed following what Kissinger had called a "decent interval" after the U.S. withdrawal. And he failed to win a lasting peace in the Middle East, one of his primary goals. In addition, Kissinger is often blamed for the massive bombings of Cambodia in the early Nixon administration, a policy that led to the rise of Pol Pot, the Khmer Rouge, and genocide. He is also credited with ordering the overthrow of the democratically elected government of Salvador Allende in Chile and supporting Allende's brutal successor, Augusto Pinochet.

Today, Kissinger is the chairman of an international consulting firm, Kissinger and Associates. He is a popular speaker, and appears often as a foreign policy analyst on news programs.

STUDY QUESTIONS

1. Who made up Nixon's silent majority? Had this group gone by any other names in the past? How did this group match up with Nixon's political support throughout the nation?
2. Why was John Kerry's anti-war activism so important at a time when anti-war activism was widespread in the nation?
3. How did the Shanghai Communiqué change the U.S.-Soviet-Chinese diplomatic equation? How did it change the U.S.-Taiwan-Chinese diplomatic equation?
4. How did Henry Kissinger's view of America's role in the world differ from the views of those who went before him?

FURTHER READINGS

Larry Berman, *No Peace, No Honor: Nixon, Kissinger, and Betrayal in Vietnam* (2002).
Douglas Brinkley, *Tour of Duty: John Kerry and the Vietnam War* (2004).
Henry Kissinger, *Years of Renewal* (2000).
Robert D. Schulzinger, *Henry Kissinger, Doctor of Diplomacy* (1989).

13 • The Environmental and Consumer Movements

INTRODUCTION

The modern American environmental movement had its birth in the postwar years with the realization that many achievements of modern science and industry were destructive of the natural environment. For some twenty years, environmentalists fought industry (with government joining in on one side or the other at different times) over the effects of industrial waste, chemicals, and pollution on the environment. In the 1970s, the environmental movement matured, going from a movement that fought industrial encroachment of the environment into one that began to see the long-term and profound relationship between the earth and its inhabitants.

World War II stimulated the development of "miracle products," new chemicals and synthetic materials that promised a more comfortable life, and agricultural abundance as a result of pesticides, herbicides, and new chemical fertilizers. But by the late 1950s and early 1960s it was apparent that pesticide and herbicide use, particularly, had exacted a huge price on the environment. Rachel Carson's book *Silent Spring* was an indictment of the damage done to the environment by the pesticide industry. She showed that between the end of the war and 1960, pesticide use had increased by 400 percent. Farmers in the United States were spraying some 650 million pounds of pesticides every year. That in itself was an amazing revelation, but Carson's main contribution was to show, in addition, that the chemicals remained in the environment indefinitely, filtering through the soil, contaminating the ground water, and eventually finding their way into the food chain. The warning was clear: pesticides were destroying the environment.

The success of Carson's book prodded the government to act further. In 1964 President Johnson established the Task Force on Environmental Pollution, which addressed not only the problem of pesticides, but also the emissions produced from coal-burning factories and power plants, and, for the first time, auto exhaust emissions. A year later, the Water Quality Act, pushed through Congress by Johnson, toughened an old Truman administration regulation. This new measure required all states to monitor water quality or face federal intervention. The Clean Water Restoration Act, passed in 1966, expanded the 1965 law; it also authorized $3.5 billion to clean up the nation's water and waterways.

Water cleanup generally went hand in hand with a similar movement for better air quality. Atmospheric pollution was a serious problem in many areas of the country by the early 1960s—particularly in the urban corridors of the Northeast and in Southern California. But most other large urban areas in the nation were also affected, along with parts of the country where coal was the primary fuel for household use, in industry, and in the production of electric power. In 1967 the Air Quality Act covered a variety of pollution sources, including auto emissions.

By the late 1960s it had become clear that major sectors of private industry would not voluntarily clean up the environment, and that the states did not have the resources (or in many cases, the will) to force industry to do so. Environmental protection was then perceived as a national problem requiring federal action. In 1969, Congress passed the National Environmental Policy Act, which required environmental impact statements for all major projects that could potentially affect the environment.

As the environmental movement progressed, a growing consumer movement sprang up alongside it. And what Rachel Carson was to environmentalism, Ralph Nader was to consumerism. In 1965 Nader published *Unsafe at Any Speed,* an attack on the American auto industry—particularly General Motors and its Chevrolet Corvair. The Corvair, according to Nader, had been cobbled together quickly to meet the growing demand for smaller cars in the face of competition from Japanese and German imports. The result, according to Nader, was a car that was unsafe—at any speed. He went on to argue that Detroit's interests were directed more toward flash than safety, with almost no concern for the welfare of the consumer following the sale of the automobile. Nader's book led to passage, in 1966, of the National Traffic and Motor Vehicle Safety Act. Through the next decade, advocacy groups, known universally as "Nader's Raiders," lobbied against all kinds of dangerous consumer products.

In 1970, the Environmental Protection Agency (EPA) was formed to enforce the growing body of federal environmental laws. That year, the EPA finally acted on the warnings from Rachel Carson and banned the use of DDT and other toxic pesticides, and began monitoring the use of all commercial pesticides.

DOCUMENT 13.1
Rachel Carson, *Silent Spring* (1962)

Rachel Carson was a marine biologist with the U.S. Fish and Wildlife Service when she published Silent Spring *in 1962. She had gained some fame in the early 1950s as the writer of a best-selling series of nature essays,* The Sea Around Us, *but her continued work drove her to become increasingly alarmed about the effects of pesticides and herbicides on the environment. She was particularly concerned about the impact of DDT, one of the many postwar wonder chemicals billed by the agriculture and food production industries as the key to a future of worldwide abundance. The result was* Silent Spring, *a carefully researched book on the dangers of pesticides in the environment. This excerpt is from a chapter called "Beyond the Dreams of the Borgias."*

Over increasingly large areas of the United States, spring now comes unheralded by the return of the birds, and the early mornings are strangely silent where once they were filled with the beauty of bird song. This sudden silencing of the song of birds, this obliteration of the color and beauty and interest they lend to our world have come about swiftly, insidiously, and unnoticed by those whose communities are as yet unaffected. . . .

To millions of Americans, the season's first robin means that the grip of winter is broken. Its coming is an event reported in newspapers and told eagerly at the breakfast table. And as the number of migrants grows and the first mists of green appear in the woodlands, thousands of people listen for the first dawn chorus of the robins throbbing in the early morning light. But now all is changed, and not even the return of the birds may be taken for granted.

The survival of the robin, and indeed of many other species as well, seems fatefully linked with the American elm, a tree that is part of the history of thousands of towns from the Atlantic to the Rockies, gracing their streets and their village squares and college campuses with majestic archways of green. Now the elms are stricken with a disease that afflicts them throughout their range, a disease so serious that many experts believe all efforts to save the elms will in the end be futile. It would be tragic to lose the elms, but it would be doubly tragic if, in vain efforts to save them, we plunge vast segments of our bird populations into the night of extinction. Yet this is precisely what is threatened.

The so-called Dutch elm disease entered the United States from Europe about 1930 in elm burl logs imported for the veneer industry. It is a fungus disease; the organism invades the water conducting vessels of the tree, spreads by spores carried in the flow of sap, and by its poisonous secretions as well as by mechanical clogging causes the branches to wilt and the tree to die. The disease is spread from diseased to healthy trees by elm bark beetles. The galleries which the insects have tunneled out under the bark of dead trees become contaminated with spores of the invading fungus, and the spores adhere to the insect body and are carried wherever the beetle flies. Efforts to control the fungus disease of the elms have been directed largely toward control of the carrier insect. In community after community, especially throughout the strongholds of the American elm, the Midwest and New England, intensive spraying has become a routine procedure.

What this spraying could mean to bird life, and especially to the robin, was first made clear by the work of two ornithologists at Michigan State University, Professor George Wallace and one of his graduate students, John Mehner. When Mr. Mehner began work for the doctorate in 1954, he chose a research project that had to do with robin populations. This was quite by chance, for at that time no one suspected that the robins were in danger. But even as he undertook the work, events occurred that were to change its character and indeed to deprive him of his material.

Spraying for Dutch elm disease began in a small way on the university campus in 1954. The following year the city of East Lansing (where the university is located) joined in, spraying on the campus was expanded, and, with local programs for gypsy moth and mosquito control also under way, the rain of chemicals increased to a downpour.

During 1954, the year of the first light spraying, all seemed well. The following spring the migrating robins began to return to the campus as usual. Like the bluebells in Tomlinson's haunting essay "The Lost Wood," they were "expecting no evil" as they reoccupied their familiar territories. But soon it became evident that something was wrong. Dead and dying robins began to appear on the campus. Few birds were seen in their normal foraging activities or assembling in their usual roosts. Few nests were built; few young appeared. The pattern was repeated with monotonous regularity in succeeding springs. The sprayed area had become a lethal trap in which each wave of migrating robins would be eliminated in about a week. Then new arrivals would come in, only to add to the numbers of doomed birds seen on the campus in the agonized tremors that precede death.

"The campus is serving as a graveyard for most of the robins that attempt to take up residence in the spring," said Dr. Wallace. But why? At first he suspected some disease of the nervous system, but soon it became evident that "in spite of the assurances of the insecticide people that their sprays were 'harmless to birds' the robins were really dying of insecticidal poisoning; they exhibited the well-known symptoms of loss of balance, followed by tremors, convulsions, and death."

Several facts suggested that the robins were being poisoned, not so much by direct contact with the insecticides as indirectly, by eating earthworms. Campus earthworms had been fed inadvertently to crayfish in a research project and all the crayfish had promptly died. A snake kept in a laboratory cage had gone into violent tremors after being fed such worms. And earthworms were the principal food of robins in the spring. . . . The trees are sprayed in the spring (usually at the rate of 2 to 5 pounds of DDT per 50-foot tree, which may be the equivalent of as much as *23 pounds per acre* where elms are numerous) and often again in July, at about half this concentration. Powerful sprayers direct a stream of poison to all parts of the tallest trees, killing directly not only the target organism, the bark beetle, but other insects, including pollinating species and predatory spiders and beetles. The poison forms a tenacious film over the leaves and bark. Rains do not wash it away. In the autumn the leaves fall to the ground, accumulate in sodden layers, and begin the slow process of becoming one with the soil. In this they are aided by the toil of the earthworms, who feed in the leaf litter, for elm leaves are among their favorite foods. In feeding on the leaves the worms also swallow the insecticide, accumulating and concentrating it in their bodies. . . . Undoubtedly some of the earthworms themselves succumb, but others survive to become "biological magnifiers" of the poison. In the spring the robins return to provide another link in the cycle. As few as 11 large earthworms can transfer a lethal dose of DDT to a robin. And 11 worms form a small part of a day's rations to a bird that eats 10 to 12 earthworms in as many minutes.

Not all robins receive a lethal dose, but another consequence may lead to the extinction of their kind as surely as fatal poisoning. The shadow of sterility lies over all the bird studies and indeed lengthens to include all living things within its potential range. There are now only two or three dozen robins to be found each spring on the entire 185-acre campus of Michigan State University, compared with a conservatively estimated 370 adults in this area before spraying. In 1954 every robin nest under observation by Mehner produced young. Toward the end of June, 1957, when at least 370 young birds (the normal replacement of the adult population) would have been foraging over the campus in the years before spraying began, Mehner could find *only one young robin.* A year later Dr. Wallace was to report: "At no time during the spring or summer [of 1958] did I see a fledgling robin anywhere on the main campus, and so far I have failed to find anyone else who has seen one there."

DOCUMENT 13.2
Ralph Nader, *Unsafe at Any Speed* (1965)

There has always been a strong relationship between environmentalism and consumerism—if for no other reason than both movements view corporate and industrial America as the primary offenders. An important connector is Ralph Nader, a strong consumer advocate who pushed hard for improvement in the nation's environmental quality.

Ralph Nader's Unsafe at Any Speed, *excerpted here, was published in 1965, just three years after Carson's* Silent Spring, *and it took the identical view of corporate and industrial America as greedy abusers of power. Nader argued that the giant auto makers had created a monopoly in the United States by engaging in superficial competition over model styles. He also asserted that the automobile manufacturers were building vehicles that could cause serious injury, even in low-speed crashes. In 1966, at least partially in response to Nader's writings, Congress passed the National Traffic and Motor Vehicle Safety Act.*

SOURCE: Ralph Nader, *Unsafe at Any Speed* (New York, 1965). Reprinted by permission.

For over a half century the automobile has brought death, injury, and the most inestimable sorrow and deprivation to millions of people. With Medea-like intensity, this mass trauma began rising sharply four years ago, reflecting new and unexpected ravages by the motor vehicle. A 1959 Department of Commerce report projected that 51,000 persons would be killed by automobiles in 1975. That figure will probably be reached in 1965, a decade ahead of schedule. . . .

Highway accidents were estimated to have cost this country in 1964, $8.4 billion in property damage, medical expenses, lost wages, and insurance overhead expenses. Add an equivalent sum to comprise roughly the indirect costs and the total amounts to over two percent of the gross national product. But these are not the kind of costs which fall on the builders of motor vehicles (excepting a few successful law suits for negligent construction of the vehicle) and thus do not pinch the proper foot. Instead, the costs fall to users of vehicles, who are in no position to dictate safer automobile designs.

In fact, the gigantic costs of the highway carnage in this country support a service industry. A vast array of services—medical, police, administrative, legal, insurance, automotive repair, and funeral—stand equipped to handle the direct and indirect consequences of accident injuries. Traffic accidents create economic demands for these services running into billions of dollars. It is in the post-accident response that lawyers and physicians and other specialists labor. This is where the remuneration lies and this is where the talent and energies go. Working in the area of prevention of these casualties earns few fees. Consequently our society has an intricate organization to handle direct and indirect aftermaths of collisions. But the true mark of a humane society must be what it does about *prevention* of accident injuries, not the cleaning up of them afterward.

Unfortunately, there is little in the dynamics of the automobile accident industry that works for its reduction. Doctors, lawyers, engineers and other specialists have failed in their primary professional ethic: to dedicate themselves to the prevention of accident injuries. The roots of the unsafe vehicle problem are so entrenched that the situation can be improved only by the forging of new instruments of citizen action. When thirty practicing physicians picketed for safe auto design at the New York International Automobile Show on April 7, 1965, their unprecedented action was the measure of their desperation over the inaction of the men and institutions in government and industry who have failed to provide the public with the vehicle safety to which it is entitled. The picketing surgeons, orthopedists, pediatricians and general practitioners marched in protest because the existing medical, legal and engineering organizations have defaulted.

A great problem of contemporary life is how to control the power of economic interests which ignore the harmful effects of their applied sciences and technology. The automobile tragedy is one of the most serious of these man-made assaults on the human body. The history of that tragedy reveals many obstacles which must be overcome in the taming of any mechanical or biological hazard which is a by-product of industry or commerce. Our society's obligation to protect the "body rights" of its citizens with vigorous resolve and ample resources requires the precise, authoritative articulation and front-rank support which is being devoted to civil rights.

This country has not been entirely laggard in defining values relevant to new contexts of a technology laden with risks. The postwar years have witnessed an historic broadening, at least in the courts, of the procedural and substantive rights of the injured and the duties of manufacturers to produce a safe product. Judicial decisions throughout the fifty states have given living meaning to Walt Whitman's dictum, "If anything is sacred, the human body is sacred." Mr. Justice Jackson in 1953 defined the duty of the manufacturers by saying, "Where experiment or research is necessary to determine the presence or the degree of danger, the product must not be tried out on the public, nor must the public be expected to possess the facilities or the technical knowledge to learn for itself of inherent but latent dangers. The claim that a hazard was not foreseen is not available to one who did not use foresight appropriate to his enterprise."

It is a lag of almost paralytic proportions that these values of safety concerning consumers and economic enterprises, reiterated many times by the judicial branch of government, have not found their way into legislative policy-making for safer automobiles. Decades ago legislation was passed changing the pattern of private business investments to accommodate more fully the safety value on railroads, in factories, and more recently on ships and aircraft. In transport, apart from the motor vehicle, considerable progress has been made in recognizing the physical integrity of the individual. There was the period when railroad workers were killed by the thousands and the editor of *Harper's* could say late in the last century: "So long as brakes cost more than trainmen, we may expect the present sacrificial method of car-coupling to be continued." But injured train-men did cause the railroads some operating dislocations; highway victims cost the automobile companies next to nothing and the companies are not obligated to make use of developments in science-technology that have demonstrably opened up opportunities for far greater safety than any existing safety features lying unused on the automobile companies' shelves.

A principal reason why the automobile has remained the only transportation vehicle to escape being called to meaningful public account is that the public has never been supplied the information nor offered the quality of competition to enable it to make effective demands through the marketplace and through government for a safe, nonpolluting and efficient automobile that can be produced economically. The consumer's expectations regarding automotive in-novations have been deliberately held low and mostly oriented to very gradual annual style changes. The specialists and researchers outside the industry who could have provided the leadership to stimulate this flow of information by and large chose to remain silent, as did government officials.

The persistence of the automobile's immunity over the years has nourished the continuance of that immunity, recalling Francis Bacon's insight. "He that will not apply new remedies must expect new evils, for time is the greatest innovator."

The accumulated power of decades of effort by the automobile industry to strengthen its control over car design is reflected today in the difficulty of even beginning to bring it to justice. The time has not come to discipline the automobile for safety; that time came over four decades ago. But that is not cause to delay any longer what should have been accomplished in the nineteen-twenties.

DOCUMENT 13.3
Love Canal. Testimony Before the Senate Subcommittee on Environmental Pollution and Hazardous Waste (March 1979)

Love Canal was one of several environmental wake-up calls in the last decades of the twentieth century. The situation there made it clear that the disposal of hazardous waste could ultimately destroy the environment.

Love Canal was a neighborhood of about thirty-five square blocks in southeastern Niagara Falls, New York. In 1947, before the area was developed for residential use, Hooker Chemical and Plastics Corporation (a subsidiary of Occidental Petroleum) began dumping toxic waste in the area. Over a five-year period, Hooker dumped some 20,000 cubic yards of waste at the site. In 1952 it was determined that the site was filled to capacity, and Hooker covered the waste. That same year, Hooker sold the site to the city of Niagara Falls. In the sales agreement, Hooker included a seventeen-line statement that explained the dangers of the site.

The city built a school, and then residences were constructed in the area. By 1976 it was apparent that something was wrong. The residents of Love Canal had high rates of cancer and birth defects. The children at the school were often sick. The Love Canal Homeowners' Association went on a three-year fight to convince the state of New York, and then the U.S. government, that the problems affecting the residents at Love Canal were being caused by the chemical dump. By 1978, Love Canal had become a media event, and in August of that year, President Jimmy Carter declared Love Canal a "federal emergency." In 1980, the Environmental Protection Agency announced that blood tests had shown that the residents of Love Canal had suffered chromosome damage. Eventually, the federal government relocated eight hundred families and reimbursed them for the loss of their homes.

Occidental Petroleum spent over $200 million to clean up the site, and Congress passed the Superfund law, holding polluters accountable for the environmental damage they create.

The document below is the testimony of a Love Canal resident. His frustration with the process is apparent. All italics are in the original document.

SOURCE: Testimony of James L. Clark before the Subcommittee on Environmental Pollution and Resource Protection of the Committee on the Environment and Public Works, U.S. Senate, 96th Cong. 1st sess. (March 28–29, 1979), 8–23.

Gentlemen:

My name is James L. Clark. I am a disabled American Veteran having served approximately fourteen years in various paratroop, Green Beret and guard units. I have lived over eight years in the Love Canal area. Since living there my family has suffered many serious health problems. The adverse health affects in that area are real. These people need to be immediately evacuated from that contaminated area. . . .

The New York State Health Department's attempt to disprove the illnesses seems to be working against the purpose of a health department.

With all the contaminants found, one can only assume that there is a definite risk to the population of the Love Canal area.

We had another suicide discovered this past Friday. A twenty-two year old male shot himself. No one knows why, nor will they know why the next one will do it. This is a fact of life we live with everyday.

New York State Health Commissioner, Dr. David Axelrod's statement before the Congressional Subcommittee that: "The cancer data could not be substantiated," is ludicrous. New York State law requires that all cancer and tumors be reported to the New York State Health Department. Besides our area has one of the finest cancer research institutes in the world—Roswell Park Memorial Institute in Buffalo—and New York City has Sloane Kettering Institute. Why can't cancer findings be substantiated?

The "Blue Ribbon Panel" that was secretly assembled to look into the health problems [with] no names revealed to the public—was an absolute insult to our intelligence. . . . When a panel rules on a matter affecting the health and lives of my family, I would like to know who they are, if they are qualified individuals who can tell what is wrong and what course of action is to be taken to alleviate any problems. I have *received no answer.* . . .

This document from the state tells of the fact that the ambient air in the Love Canal area is infested with chlorinated hydrocarbons eighty times greater than in downtown Niagara Falls, which isn't too sweet.

The New York State Health Commissioner at every meeting simply states there is a risk of flying in an airplane, that there is a risk in crossing a street. We want to know what the risk is of living in an environment with known human carcinogens where the quantities are eighty times greater than in the downtown air of an industrial city (Niagara Falls). . . .

Hooker's role in this entire affair has been to launch a massive advertising campaign—in essence claiming that the victims caused the problem by moving into the area and disturbing the clay cap. The Love Canal dump, according to Hooker, was done in the most scientific, expert manner of the times—"a secure landfill"—meeting all the requirements of a secure landfill: isolation, barrier, sealed vault, clay cap, etc. *All of this is readily disputed by this 1952 photo showing it leaching into the river.*

Why wasn't it corrected then? Why are we using approximately the same technique now? It did not work then, and it will not work now, nor ten years from now by the state's own admission.

The whole remedial plan—their six inch pipe—is only an engineering hypothesis that has yet to be proven. . . . This remedial plan was drawn up between [the] City, State, Hooker, and an engineering firm which happens to be a Hooker business associate. The construction work for this plan was awarded, *without bid,* to another Hooker business associate—The Newco Chemical Corporation. Our city manager, who awarded the contract for the construction work, resigned and moved to Florida to work for Newco.

If the construction work had been implemented all at once, instead of in three phases there might have been the possibility of containing some of the chemicals. Just the other day, north of the completed construction site, this fact was clearly shown by chemicals leaching from the ground, running into the storm sewers, and into the Niagara River for three days. After news coverage, the remedial construction crew instigated emergency procedures. . . . In the next three days, over 12,000 gallons of leachate were sucked up. I wonder how much they did not contain from going into the river.

With hundreds of chemicals, of dioxin, of radiation, how much longer will these people be forced to stay?

Niagara Falls itself is a scenic wonder. Why are they allowing [it] to be turned into a chemical dump? . . .

There is no such thing as a secure landfill. While being the greatest industrial nation in the world, we are using antiquated methods of waste disposal and of regulating it. *What we are actually doing is regulating the slow, systematic poisoning of our citizens.*

The people want this dumping to stop. We have letters from unions and religious leaders to this effect. The technology for a total, safe method of waste treatment exists. We must initiate a national program on the mandatory industrial high temperature incineration of these wastes.

But this solution cannot be left to private industry. It has been proven time and time again that industry will not police its own garbage even though laws and regulations exist. I know it is not by design or intention, but a situation could exist where a company that pollutes forms another company to clean up the pollution at the taxpayer's expense.

A national program would be expensive, but we cannot afford not to start it. What is one child's worth? What is the next Love Canal worth? We cannot victimize our nation's children through carelessness and greed.

The Niagara frontier will be a perfect place to initiate a pilot program with over fifty chemical dumps identified and more being built. . . .

Gentlemen, to show what the Love Canal really means, a little girl in the neighborhood asked me to show you this photo. Her condition came about when the "remedial" digging started and it has grown steadily worse. Several doctors have said it is definitely not teenage acne. Last Friday she was taken to Roswell Park Memorial Institute. They did not know what is causing the severe rash. That girl, Gentlemen, is my daughter.

DOCUMENT 13.4
"To Our Friends Beyond the Radius, Hi!" An Open Letter from the Vicinity of Three Mile Island (April 1979)

During the 1970s there was an active anti-nuclear campaign, particularly in New Hampshire, California, and Washington, where nuclear plant construction was proposed. The protests revolved around plant safety, and in 1979 the protesters' warnings—or at least their fears—were realized when an accident at Three Mile Island (TMI), near Harrisburg, Pennsylvania, threatened to spew radioactive material over the Northeast. The intensity of the event was heightened by the coincidental release of the movie China Syndrome, *a fictionalized version of what happened (or what might have happened) at TMI.*

In the document below, a newspaper reporter in Harrisburg is whistling through the graveyard as he takes a fairly lighthearted look at the obviously frightening situation in and around TMI following the accident. He refers to a Lina Wertmuller film. The title is The End of the World in Our Usual Bed in a Night Full of Rain. *The film was made in 1978 and stars Candice Bergen.*

Bill Blando, the writer of the story below, is a reporter for the Harrisburg Patriot.

SOURCE: Bill Blando, "An Open Letter from Harrisburg: To Our Friends Beyond the Radius, Hi!" The Harrisburg *Patriot* (April 5, 1979). Reprinted by permission.

Yes, we're still here. And, we glow only with pride, having survived (so far) the radiation scare and the media blitz.

Thanks for the calls. We know you were worried. So were we. Still are. But right now, we're OK, calm but cautious. To paraphrase the awful Lina Wertmuller film with the almost-accurate title, most of us remain in our usual beds, not yet experiencing the end of the world.

This has been some kind of week, as our favorite sportscasters say. The first couple of days, starting last Wednesday, served as an attention-getting device. The big day was Friday, to start a very long weekend for us and the technicians at Three Mile Island Nuclear Generating Station who bring power to a lot of people mostly outside of the Harrisburg area. In those three days, such terms as "evacuation," "rems and millirems," "meltdown," "hydrogen bubble," "nuclear explosion" and "to err on the side of caution" fell from the tips of many tongues. . . .

Not listening to the radio in the early bright, I missed the initial announcement, but Betty, my ever-alert wife, called from her job to tell me that something new and different was happening in the radiation story, adding that perhaps I'd better get cracking, if not packing.

I flipped on the radio switch, and there was the familiar rock sound—nothing unusual yet. But then it came, in familiar Wellesian tones, "We interrupt this program. . . ."

The phrase was to be echoed and re-echoed throughout the day and, like the old Mercury Theatre of the Air dramatization, in . . . shorter intervals.

At one point, the station I turned to—a CBS outlet, coincidentally the same network that was destroyed over the air by Mr. Welles—interrupted one of its Spectrum speakers, trying to evaluate the social significance of a movie called *Norma Rae,* three times.

First, it was to hear a civil defense official remind us to be ready to evacuate, "although there was no evacuation yet," and to plan to bring only basic necessities, such as glasses and prescription medicines.

The second cut-off came when an official from the federal Nuclear Regulatory Agency urged area residents to stay indoors.

Finally, after the third interruption, the Spectrum speaker was abandoned altogether, this time in favor of a telephone conversation with Gov. Dick Thornburgh, which was given the playback treatment.

One of the speakers, I forget which one, advised us that "there is no reason to panic at this time." The question which begged to be asked was, "at what time would there be reason?"

But there are important things to be done in an evacuation, obviously. First, it is necessary to re-establish communications with one's spouse, if only to say goodbye.

Unfortunately, the home phone was dead. That meant seeking a pay phone that might work, which meant going outdoors, thereby violating the advice to remain indoors. There were other chores, too—gassing up the car and tapping the reserves for a little traveling money.

I was not alone in my mission.

I lucked out at the gas station, pulling right into it and up to the pump.

The attendant, who doubles as a mechanic assured me that "this is the slowest it's been all day. You should have been here earlier," he added. "All I've been doing is pumping gas."

While talking, his pumps were attacked by cars from three sides.

"Aren't you afraid," he asked, "of being outside?" He took my payment and shrugged, and as I drove off, vehicles were backed up on both sides of the pumps with the last car in line straddling the incline between the station and the sidewalk, with its tail hanging out over the street.

At the bank, I wasn't so lucky, but the long lines moved quickly. Perhaps it was an act of subconscious faith that I didn't withdraw all of my meager funds.

I asked the girl if the bank people planned on locking themselves in the vault until the whole thing blew away.

"No," she said without a smile. "It might be safer, but I'm going home and hope it's all right."

Meanwhile over the radio, a spokesman for the Metropolitan Edison Co., which operates the stricken nuclear plant, was explaining that it was "not an uncontrolled emission" which touched off the dangers of the day. "It was planned," he said emphatically, proceeding to charge the governor and everyone else with "overreacting." There was "no danger," he said, adding that the evacuation alert was ill-advised. . . .

Later, I heard stories about overly protective and nervous parents storming schools to yank their kin out. I can only imagine how harrowing such displays might have been for the children left behind.

Chores completed, I reported to work. "You should have been here a little while ago," I was told upon entering *The Patriot* newsroom. "It's been a wild and crazy place. More phone calls than a telethon, and even a lunch hour siren in the Capitol area to trigger a bit of panic in the streets."

Reporters from all over the country streamed in and out, getting calls, making calls and typing reams of copy on portable machines of different sizes and colors.

A couple of radios were blaring incoherently in different corners of the newsroom along with the squawking of a couple of police radios. There was even a TV set playing, but for the most part ignored.

Despite all the activity, the air hung heavy with skepticism, "You just can't believe what anyone says," was a phrase repeated over and over. One of the younger reporters said he had just been "speaking with a nuclear expert for two hours and I couldn't understand anything he said."

Later, exchanging views with Barker Howland, the genial elder statesman of our newsroom who holds the title of religion writer, among others, he remarked that he'd bet "church attendance would be up this weekend. It goes back to the old adage about there being no atheists in a fox hole."

He should know that territory, being an ex-Navy chaplain. "There's only one thing I can compare this to," he said referring to the day's events. "I have the same feeling now that I had when a bunch of us were left at an airstrip in Korea and the [commanding officer] told us, 'Sorry boys, you're on your own. That was the last plane today.'

"Yes, it was that same feeling, knowing that that was the last plane, watching it fly off and not being on it."

That's probably as good a way as any to end this, because Howland, at least, had something to compare it to. And I, quite frankly, didn't.

But, how was your week?

BIOGRAPHICAL SKETCH
Ralph Nader

Ralph Nader is widely recognized as the founder of the consumer rights movement. He was instrumental in creating the Environmental Protection Agency, the Occupational Safety and Health Administration, and the Consumer Product Safety Commission. He has always worked for the rights of consumers and the general public, a role that has repeatedly brought him into conflict with both business and government.

Nader was born in Winsted, Connecticut, to Lebanese immigrants. The family took seriously their responsibilities as American citizens and their part in the national democracy, and they felt a strong duty to instill that responsibility in their only child. Another major influence on Ralph's life was the works of the early muckrakers, particularly Ida Tarbell, Lincoln Steffens, and Upton Sinclair, whose writings and investigations forced changes in America at the turn of the last century.

Nader attended Princeton, and then Harvard Law School, a place he described as a "high-priced tool factory, only instead of tools and dies, they were producing hired advocates for corporate law firms and corporations." While at Harvard, Nader began to take an interest in the engineering design of automobiles. In 1959 he published an article in the *Nation* magazine titled "The Safe Car You Can't Buy." He criticized Detroit auto manufacturers for focusing on style, price, and performance—all at the cost of safety.

In 1963, after several years of working as a lawyer in Hartford, Connecticut, Nader arrived in Washington to work for Assistant Secretary of Labor Daniel Patrick Moynihan. He also worked as an unpaid advisor to a Senate subcommittee, chaired by Connecticut senator Abraham Ribicoff, which was exploring the possibility of federal regulation of auto safety.

In 1964 he began expanding his *Nation* article into a book, and published *Unsafe at Any Speed: The Designed-in Dangers of the American Automobile* (1965). His primary target was the Corvair, General Motors' new "sporty" answer to the small European and Japanese cars just coming onto the American market. Nader determined that the Corvair had a faulty rear suspension that caused it to skid and then flip over. He also showed that GM knew of the problem and failed to address it, simply blaming "nuts behind the wheel" rather than design problems.

Although *Unsafe at Any Speed* would finally become one of the seminal writings on American consumerism, it did not, at first, sell well, despite friendly reviews. It did, however, stir the interest of General Motors. GM hired several private detectives and went to extraordinary lengths to harass and discredit Nader. *The New Republic* magazine broke the GM harassment story, and Ribicoff's subcommittee summoned GM executives to explain their actions, and then finally apologize—all on national television. Nader sued for invasion of privacy and won an out-of-court settlement of $425,000. The national exposure made his book a bestseller. He used the money to expand his advocacy efforts, which launched the modern consumer movement.

His lobbying efforts pushed Congress to pass the National Traffic and Motor Vehicle Safety Act in 1966; a year later, he lobbied for the passage of the Wholesome Meat Act, which regulated the inspection of beef and poultry and imposed federal standards on slaughterhouses. He was also instrumental in the passage of the Freedom of Information Act and the 1970 Clean Air Act.

In 1969, Nader founded the Center for the Study of Responsive Law, a nonprofit organization staffed mostly by young law students known universally as "Nader's Raiders." The organization studied and released reports on consumer issues. In 1971 he founded Public Citizen, which represents consumer interests in government.

In the early 1990s, Nader turned from activist to candidate. His primary platform has always been that the nature of the national two-party system makes both parties too dependent on big-money donors. In 1992 he ran for president as a write-in candidate. In 1996, he made almost no splash running on the Green Party ticket. In 2000, however, running again as the Green Party candidate, Nader pulled almost three million votes and earned the wrath of the Democrats as a spoiler. Nader polled nearly 100,000 votes in Florida, considerably more than the number the Democratic candidate, Al Gore, needed to carry the state and take the election.

Nader's 2004 candidacy was a lesson on why third parties have never succeeded in the United States. During the campaign, the Republicans worked hard to get Nader on as many state ballots as possible—under the assumption that he would draw votes from John Kerry, the Democratic candidate—while the Democrats tried to keep him off the ballot. Third parties tend to split one party and thus aid the other. In the final analysis, Nader had no impact on the 2004 election.

STUDY QUESTIONS

1. What (according to the testimony of the Love Canal resident) were the problems at Love Canal? What were his solutions?
2. What is Ralph Nader's primary argument against the auto industry? How has Ralph Nader's consumerism changed the nation?
3. What is the relationship between environmentalism and consumerism? How have these two movements matured in the last decade?

FURTHER READINGS

Peter Borrelli, ed., *Crossroads: Environmental Priorities for the Future* (1988).

Adeline Gordon, *Love Canal* (1982).

Ralph Nader, *Crashing the Party: Taking on Corporate Government in an Age of Surrender* (2002).

Kirkpatrick Sale, *The Green Revolution: The American Environmental Movement, 1963–1992* (1993).

J. Samuel Walker, *Three Mile Island: A Nuclear Crisis in Historical Perspective* (2004).

14 • The Tragedy of Watergate

INTRODUCTION

As the election of 1972 approached, several of President Richard Nixon's special assistants had come to the conclusion that the national interest required that just about any action should be taken to ensure Nixon's reelection in November. In June, several members of the Committee to Re-Elect the President organized a burglary of Democratic Party offices at the Watergate Building in Washington. The raids were led by G. Gordon Liddy, a White House official; James McCord, a member of the Committee to Re-Elect the President; E. Howard Hunt, an ex-CIA operative; and several anti-Castro Cubans recruited for the job. During a second break-in, the group was caught. Evidence at the scene connected the burglars to Liddy and to the Committee to Re-Elect.

The *Washington Post* broke the story, and continued to investigate the events. Liddy, Hunt, McCord, and their Cuban accomplices all pleaded guilty. The judge in the case, John Sirica, however, believed that the case went deeper than these few men. In March 1973, McCord, in a letter to Sirica, charged that the White House had approved of the burglaries and then pressured the burglars into silence with offers of hush money. Then, McCord continued, the White House conspired to cover up all administration involvement. McCord's letter prompted the Senate to set up a special Watergate committee to investigate further.

The case began to break open when John Dean, special counsel to the president, who feared that he was being marked as the fall guy for the administration, agreed to turn his version of the story over to federal prosecutors. At about the same time, Jeb Magruder, the deputy chairman at the Committee to Re-elect, told the Watergate committee that orders for the break-ins had come directly from Attorney General John Mitchell.

In April 1973 Nixon went before the nation and explained that in dealing with the nation's business he had failed to monitor properly his reelection campaign. He spoke of "overzealous subordinates," and announced the resignation of two of his closest advisors, H.R. Haldeman and John Erlichman.

He then announced the appointment of a special prosecutor, Harvard Law professor Archibald Cox, and promised him "complete independence" in investigating the incident.

The testimonies of Dean and Magruder before the Senate Watergate committee linked Nixon to the cover-up from the beginning, but Nixon continued to insist that there had been no cover-up. Then on July 16, 1973, ex-presidential aide Alexander Butterfield testified that recording equipment had been installed in the Oval Office. Special Prosecutor Cox requested segments of the tapes, but Nixon, citing separation of powers and the confidentiality of the presidency, refused to release the tapes. When Cox protested that Nixon was in violation of a court ruling to turn over the tapes, Nixon fired Cox. Two top officials in the Justice Department quit in protest. Finally, in April 1974 Nixon agreed to hand over transcripts of the tapes; and then under further pressure he released edited segments of the tapes. Those tapes released, however, contained sizable gaps, erasures, and obvious omissions. A new special prosecutor, Leon Jaworski, indicted forty-one people in the case, and named the president as an "unindicted co-conspirator."

In the House of Representatives, twenty-four Democrats and fourteen Republicans worked together on articles of impeachment. On July 24, the Supreme Court ordered the White House to turn over sixty-four tapes dealing with the events of the summer of 1972. On that same day, the House Judiciary Committee began a televised debate on impeachment. On August 5 Nixon released the tapes. The tape of a conversation on June 23, 1972 (Nixon's first day back in the White House after the Watergate break-ins), showed that Nixon had been involved in the cover-up from nearly the beginning.

Republicans on the House Judiciary Committee switched their votes in favor of impeachment. Several leading Republican senators, including Barry Goldwater, visited the White House and encouraged Nixon to resign, insisting that he would be removed from office if the impeachment proceedings were allowed to play out. On August 9, 1974, President Richard Nixon became the first president to resign from office. A month later, on September 8, President Gerald R. Ford decided it would be best to put the agony of Watergate behind the nation and issued a presidential pardon to Nixon.

Watergate was the most serious political scandal in American history. Government power had been used to subvert the political process, and then to initiate a cover-up at the highest levels of the administration. Many tied the Watergate scandal to the rise of the "imperial presidency," a trend toward presidential supremacy that had developed since the end of World War II. It was also rooted in a cold war mentality that justified any activity to overcome an enemy, especially one that had the strategic advantage of not having to answer to its people.

The long, drawn-out agony of Watergate (coming just as the United States pulled out of Vietnam) dragged the country into a sort of national depression, with its military might in question and its political leadership under suspicion.

DOCUMENT 14.1
The *Washington Post* Breaks the Story: "Five Held in Plot to Bug Democrats' Office" (June 18, 1972)

The Watergate story was broken in the Washington Post *by Bob Woodward and Carl Bernstein, two young reporters who were assigned to cover metropolitan news. In fact, the* Post's *prominent national affairs reporters had balked at covering the story because they had been intimidated by earlier administration campaigns against the press.*

Woodward and Bernstein continued to write about Watergate through the remainder of 1972, but initially their stories did not have wide impact, even though they continued to uncover information. Their work was significant because it kept the story alive through 1972 and continued to ask important questions. Without that, the scandal would certainly have disappeared. Below is the first Washington Post *story covering the Watergate break-ins.*

SOURCE: © 1972, *The Washington Post* (June 18, 1972). Reprinted with permission.

Five Held in Plot to Bug Democrats' Office

Five men, one of whom said he is a former employee of the Central Intelligence Agency, were arrested at 2:30 a.m. yesterday in what authorities described as an elaborate plot to bug the offices of the Democratic National Committee here.

Three of the men were native-born Cubans and another was said to have trained Cuban exiles for guerilla activity after the 1961 Bay of Pigs invasion. They were surprised at gun-point by three plainclothes officers of the metropolitan police department in a sixth floor office at the plush Watergate, 2600 Virginia Avenue, NW, where the Democratic National Committee occupies the entire floor.

There was no immediate explanation as to why the five suspects would want to bug the Democratic National Committee offices or whether or not they were working for any other individuals or organizations.

A spokesman for the Democratic National Committee said records kept in those offices "are not of a sensitive variety, although there are financial records and other such information."

Police said two ceiling panels in the office of Dorothy V. Bush, Secretary of the Democratic Party, had been removed. Her office is adjacent to the office of Democratic National Chairman Lawrence F. O'Brien. Presumably, it would have been possible to slide a bugging device through the panels in that office to a place above the ceiling panels in O'Brien's office. . . .

Police said the men had with them at least two sophisticated devices capable of picking up and transmitting all talk, including telephone conversations. In addition, police found lock-picks and door jimmies, almost $2,300 in cash, most of it in $100 bills with serial numbers in sequence. The men also had with them one walkie-talkie, a short wave receiver that could pick up police calls, 40 rolls of unexposed film, two 35 millimeter cameras and three pen-sized tear gas guns.

Near where they were captured were two open file drawers, and one national committee source conjectured that the men were preparing to photograph the contents.

In court yesterday, one suspect said the men were "anti-communists" and the others nodded agreement. The operation was described in court by prosecutor Earl J. Silbert as "professional" and "clandestine." One of the Cuban natives, *The Washington Post* learned, is now a Miami locksmith. . . .

All were charged with felonious burglary and with possession of implements of crime. All . . . were ordered held on $50,000 bail. . . .

The early morning arrests occurred about 40 minutes after a security guard at the Watergate noticed that a door connecting a stairwell with the hotel's basement garage had been taped so it would not lock.

The guard, 24-year-old Frank Wills, removed the tape but when he passed by about 10 minutes later a new piece had been put on. Wills then called police.

Three officers from the tactical squad responded and entered the stairwell. From the basement to the sixth floor they found every door leading from the stairwell to a hallway of the building had been taped to prevent them from locking. At the sixth floor, where the stairwell door leads directly into the Democratic National Committee offices, they found the door had been jimmied. . . .

When the officers entered an office occupied by a secretary to Stanley Grieg, deputy party chairman, one of the suspects jumped up from behind a desk, put his hands in the air and cried "Don't Shoot," police said. . . .

In [the] thirty-minute arraignment, Assistant U.S. Attorney Earl Silbert, the No. 2 man in the chief prosecutor's office, unsuccessfully urged the court to order the five men held without bond.

Silbert argued that the men had no community ties and would be likely to leave the country to avoid trial. He said they gave false names to the police after they were arrested and refused to cooperate. "They were caught red-handed," Silbert said. . . .

Contributing to this story were *Washington Post* staff writers Bob Woodward, Carl Bernstein, Bart Barnes, Kirk Scharfenberg, Martin Weil, Claudia Levy, Abbott Combes, and Tim O'Brien.

DOCUMENT 14.2
Goldwater Eases Nixon Out (August 1974)

Following the release of the Oval Office tapes in early August, it became apparent that the House Judiciary Committee would go through the impeachment process. Nixon vowed to fight, and Senate leaders met to begin arrangements for a trial. In an attempt to avoid a protracted trial that would certainly embroil the nation in further agonies, Nixon's new chief of staff, Alexander Haig, began to engineer an effort to ease Nixon toward his own decision to resign. He approached the Senate's most prominent Republicans, including Barry Goldwater, the party's 1964 candidate and elder statesman. With senators Hugh Scott and John Rhodes at his side, Goldwater visited Nixon in the Oval Office on August 7. Goldwater recounted that event in his memoir, Goldwater, *published in 1988.*

SOURCE: Barry Goldwater (with Jack Casserly), *Goldwater* (New York, 1988).

[Dean] Burch invited me to his home with [Nixon's chief of staff, General Alexander] Haig the following day, Wednesday, August 7. The meeting was the general's idea. He wanted to speak with me before I saw the President late that afternoon. Haig said that Nixon wanted [Hugh] Scott and [John] Rhodes there, too. The President wanted as broad a picture as possible on what the Republicans might do.

Haig described Nixon as a man dancing on the point of a pin. He was someone who could be set off at any one of several directions. It would be best not to demand or even suggest that he resign. Every time that had happened in the past, Nixon had reacted defiantly. The best thing to do would be to show him there was no way out except quit or lose a long, bitter battle that would be good for no one—the country, Nixon, his family, or the party. Haig summed everything up succinctly: The President needs to know that there are no more alternatives, no options. . . .

Later, Scott and I met Rhodes at the White House. We waited in a nearby office before seeing Nixon. None of us was in the mood to talk. We knew what we had to do. All of us were aware of Nixon's moodiness, his habit of trying to conceal his real thoughts, the unpredictability of his character. The minutes seemed like hours. Finally the phone rang, and we were invited to the Oval Office. The White House had just issued a statement. The President had no intention of resigning.

Nixon put his feet up on the desk, leaned back in his swivel chair, and began reminiscing about the past. It was as if we were a foursome of old golfing partners sitting on the shady lawn of some nineteenth hole, listening to stories about games gone by, and sipping tall, cool drinks.

I didn't buy it—not one bit. I was sitting directly in front of Nixon with Scott and Rhodes at my side. I was looking at the public man, waiting for the private person to emerge.

Slowly his voice began to harden. Some of the men who had campaigned with him—fought the wars over the years—had turned against him. Yes, he remembered them well. His voice was becoming remote now, and the sound of the words was lengthening, as though he were alone listening to his own voice.

Suddenly, sharply, Nixon ended his soliloquy. He snapped at Rhodes that the situation—meaning impeachment—in the House was not good. Before Rhodes could answer, Nixon abruptly clumped his feet on the floor, wheeled his chair around, and faced Scott. Scott turned to me, saying I would be the spokesman for the group. For a split second, Nixon stopped. He had not planned it this way. Goldwater face to face. He stared at me, then said, "Okay, Barry, go ahead."

This was no time to mince words, I said, "Things are bad."

Nixon: "Less than a half dozen votes [out of one hundred votes in the Senate] ?" His voice dripped with sarcasm. His jaw automatically jutted out as his eyes narrowed.

"Ten at most," I said. "Maybe less. Some aren't firm."

The President asked Scott if he agreed. He did.

I could see that Nixon's blood pressure was rising. Now was the time to warn him without causing him to make some reckless, suicidal move. I said, "I took a nose count in the Senate today. You have four firm votes. The others are really undecided. I'm one of them."

I hit him as directly and as hard as I could. It didn't seem to hurt him. Nixon turned to Rhodes, who said the situation was about the same in the House.

For the first time since I entered the room, the President paused. He looked at all three of us. I was on the verge of tears—of humiliation, not sorrow.

Nixon leaned over the desk toward Rhodes and asked, "Do I have any options?" . . .

Rhodes replied, "I want to tell the people outside that we didn't discuss any options."

Nixon snapped his agreement, stressing, "It's my decision."

There was no modulation in Nixon's voice now. He spoke in a monotone. He was not interested in a pardon or amnesty. He would make the decision in the best interests of the country. It was going to be all right. He would make it so.

The President stood and thanked us for coming. We shook hands. Haig was waiting for us. We told him there had been no demands and no deals, but Nixon now knew beyond any doubt that one way or another his presidency was finished. None of us doubted the outcome. He would resign. . . .

My office was bedlam when I returned. It overflowed with reporters, and the phones were ringing off their hooks. I quickly slipped into my office and phoned Mrs. Katharine Graham, owner of *The Washington Post*. My opinion of the *Post* hadn't changed. We opposed one another. But now the country came first.

I told Mrs. Graham what had happened in the Oval Office—that Nixon was wobbling and could go off in any direction, depending on how the media, particularly the *Post*, handled the story. Could they play it cool for just one day, refrain from saying Nixon was finally finished . . . there was no telling what he would do. As things stood, I believed he would resign.

The *Post* was as circumspect as it could be the following morning, Thursday, August 8. Since 1953, when I entered the Senate, I have taken second place to no one in my criticism of the *Post*. And I'm well aware that the newspaper led every news organization across the country in uncovering the ungodly mess we call Watergate. However, that morning stands out in my mind as the *Post*'s finest hour. It may have spared the nation the agony of impeachment and a long, wrenching aftermath.

Mrs. Graham never mentioned the subject to me. I understand why. Newspapers call their own shots. There are times in the history of the nation, however, when the media should put their country above themselves. That hasn't happened with some in the past generation, but the *Post* did it on August 8. I will never forget their recognition of responsibility as long as I live.

President Nixon resigned that evening, effective at noon on Friday, August 9. Vice President Ford was sworn in as President at that hour in the East Room of the White House.

I watched Nixon's address on television with tears in my eyes. Despite his long record of political treachery, my heart ached for him and his family. It was, in the end, ironic that he had betrayed himself and become his own executioner.

DOCUMENT 14.3
"I Have Never Been a Quitter." President Richard Nixon's Resignation Statement (August 8, 1974)

On August 8, 1974, the day after Goldwater, Scott, and Rhodes told Nixon that there really was no hope of staying in office, the president addressed the country. In a somber tone he announced that he would resign from office.

He seemed to understand that his resignation would go a long way toward ending the agony of Watergate and move the country toward a much-needed healing.

It is significant that Nixon remained defiant in his speech and made no attempt to apologize for what he had done. Years later he would be more repentant, but in 1974 he seemed to say to the American people that he did not believe he had done anything wrong.

SOURCE: *Public Papers of the Presidents: Richard M. Nixon, 1974,* 626–30.

In all the decisions I have made in my public life, I have always tried to do what was best for the nation. Throughout the long and difficult period of Watergate, I have felt it was my duty to persevere, to make every possible effort to complete the term of office to which you elected me.

In the past few days, however, it has become evident to me that I no longer have a strong enough political base in the Congress to justify continuing that effort. As long as there was such a base, I felt strongly that it was necessary to see the constitutional process through to its conclusion, that to do otherwise would be unfaithful to the spirit of that deliberately difficult process and a dangerously destabilizing precedent for the future.

But with the disappearance of that base, I now believe that the constitutional purpose has been served, and there is no longer a need for the process to be prolonged.

I would have preferred to carry through to the finish whatever the personal agony it would have involved, and my family unanimously urged me to do so. But the interest of the nation must always come before any personal considerations.

From the discussions I have had with congressional and other leaders, I have concluded that because of the Watergate matter I might not have the support of the Congress that I would consider necessary to back the very difficult decisions and carry out the duties of this office in the way the interests of the nation would require.

I have never been a quitter. To leave office before my term is completed is abhorrent to every instinct in my body. But as President, I must put the interest of America first. America needs a full-time President and a full-time Congress, particularly at this time with problems we face at home and abroad.

To continue to fight through the months ahead for my personal vindication would almost totally absorb the time and attention of both the President and the Congress in a period when our entire focus should be on the great issues of peace abroad and prosperity without inflation at home.

Therefore, I shall resign the presidency effective at noon tomorrow. Vice President Ford will be sworn in as President at that hour in this office.

As I recall the high hopes for America with which we began this second term, I feel a great sadness that I will not be here in this office working on your behalf to achieve those hopes in the next two-and-a-half years. But in turning over direction of the government to Vice President Ford, I know, as I told the nation when I nominated him for that office ten months ago, that the leadership of America will be in good hands.

In passing this office to the Vice President, I also do so with the profound sense of the weight of responsibility that will fall on his shoulders tomorrow and, therefore, of the understanding, the patience, the cooperation he will need from all Americans.

As he assumes that responsibility, he will deserve the help and the support of all of us. As we look to the future, the first essential is to begin healing the wounds of this nation, to put the bitterness and divisions of the recent past behind us, and to rediscover those shared ideals that lie at the heart of our strength and unity as a great and as a free people.

By taking this action, I hope that I will have hastened the start of that process of healing which is so desperately needed in America.

I regret deeply any injuries that may have been done in the course of the events that led to this decision. I would say only that if some of my judgments were wrong, and some were wrong, they were made in what I believed at the time to be the best interest of the nation.

To those who have stood with me during these past difficult months, to my family, my friends, to many others who joined in supporting my cause because they believed it was right, I will be eternally grateful for your support.

And to those who have not felt able to give me your support, let me say I leave with no bitterness toward those who have opposed me, because all of us, in the final analysis, have been concerned with the good of the country, however our judgments might differ.

So, let us all now join together in affirming that common commitment and in helping our new President succeed for the benefit of all Americans.

I shall leave this office with regret at not completing my term, but with gratitude for the privilege of serving as your President for the past five-and-a-half years. These years have been a momentous time in the history of our nation and the world. They have been a time of achievement in which we can all be proud, achievements that represent the shared efforts of the administration, the Congress, and the people. . . .

For more than a quarter of a century in public life I have shared in the turbulent history of this era. I have fought for what I believed in. I have tried to the best of my ability to discharge those duties and meet those responsibilities that were entrusted to me.

Sometimes I have succeeded and sometimes I have failed, but always I have taken heart from what Theodore Roosevelt once said about the man in the arena, "whose face is marred by dust and sweat and blood, who strives valiantly, who errs and comes short again and again because there is not effort without error and shortcoming, but who does actually strive to do the deed, who knows the great enthusiasms, the great devotions, who spends himself in a worthy cause, who at the best knows in the end the triumphs of high achievements and who at the worst, if he fails, at least fails while daring greatly."

I pledge to you tonight that as long as I have a breath of life in my body, I shall continue in that spirit. I shall continue to work for the great causes to which I have been dedicated throughout my years as a Congressman, a Senator, a Vice President, and President, the cause of peace not just for America but among all nations, prosperity, justice, and opportunity for all of our people.

There is one cause above all to which I have been devoted and to which I shall always be devoted for as long as I live.

When I first took the oath of office as President five-and-a-half years ago, I made this sacred commitment, to consecrate my office, my energies, and all the wisdom I can summon to the cause of peace among nations.

I have done my very best in all the days since to be true to that pledge. As a result of these efforts, I am confident that the world is a safer place today, not only for the people of America but for the people of all nations, and that all of our children have a better chance than before of living in peace rather than dying in war.

This, more than anything, is what I hoped to achieve when I sought the presidency. This, more than anything, is what I hope will be my legacy to you, to our country, as I leave the presidency.

To have served in this office is to have felt a very personal sense of kinship with each and every American. In leaving it, I do so with this prayer: May God's grace be with you in all the days ahead.

BIOGRAPHICAL SKETCH
Mark Felt/Deep Throat

In all of modern journalism there has been no greater mystery than the identity of Deep Throat, the anonymous informant who kept *Washington Post* journalists Bob Woodward and Carl Bernstein on the right path as they exposed the Watergate scandal. "Who was Deep Throat?" has been among the most compelling questions of modern American history, dissected in books, movies, thousands of articles, and hundreds of television programs. Nearly every figure in the Nixon administration, from Henry Kissinger to John Dean, from speechwriter Patrick Buchanan to television journalist Diane Sawyer, has been a suspect in the mystery. Woodward added to the drama by stating several times that he would not identify Deep Throat while the informant still lived.

In the early summer of 2005 the mystery came to an end. An article in *Vanity Fair* identified Mark Felt, the number two man at the FBI during the Watergate investigations, as Deep Throat. Felt immediately confirmed the story, and the next day, Woodward and the *Post* confirmed that Felt was, indeed, Deep Throat. Felt, 91 and feeble, appeared on television news programs from his daughter's home in California and waved to cameras—seemingly triumphant and proud.

Felt had always been considered a possible candidate for Deep Throat. A 1992 article in *Atlantic* argued that Felt was Deep Throat. But Felt had always vehemently denied the connection. In a 1979 memoir, *The FBI Pyramid*, Felt wrote: "I never leaked information to Woodward and Bernstein or anyone else!"

The name "Deep Throat" was a combination of a journalistic phrase "deep cover," or "deep background," meaning a highly confidential source, and the title of a notorious pornographic movie. It was the "dirty, porny nickname," the *Washington Post* asserted the day following the announcement, that gave Deep Throat part of his mystique.

According to the account in Woodward and Bernstein's *All the President's Men*, Woodward (and not Bernstein) met with Deep Throat seven times in parking garages and other out-of-the-way places. They sent signals to each other, such as a flag on Woodward's balcony or a note stuck inside his morning newspaper, as an indicator of a need to meet.

The clandestine meetings between Woodward and Felt supplied context and confirmation for some of the *Post's* most explosive Watergate stories. Perhaps most importantly, the *Post* articles kept the Watergate story alive in the press, which then fueled further investigations by Congress.

Felt told Woodward that there was a connection between the Watergate break-ins and the White House, that Nixon's campaign committee had orchestrated the break-ins, and that Attorney General John Mitchell and Nixon himself had been aware of all the events from the beginning.

Felt's motives for leaking information to Woodward were complex. J. Edgar Hoover, the founding director of the FBI, died in the spring of 1972. Felt, second in command at the FBI, expected to be named to head the agency, but Nixon passed over Felt and named L. Patrick Grey, an outsider. Felt was not only furious that he had been passed over for the top job, he believed that Nixon intended to use Grey to dominate the agency (stripping it of its historic independence) and steer it clear of all Watergate investigations. Felt, then, became something of a disgruntled employee, while at the same time intending to expose the corruption inside the Nixon administration.

Immediately following the 2005 announcement, Felt's daughter let it be known that she hoped that the revelation would generate income for the family. Clearly, she suspected that when her father died it would be Woodward who would reap all the rewards of those events; she believed her father deserved some of the credit. That, in turn, led to a great deal of criticism from those who saw Felt as a betrayer of his government who now wanted to cash in on the events. Felt immediately signed lucrative book and movie deals. Within two months of Felt's announcement, Woodward had a book on the shelves recounting his side of the story.

STUDY QUESTIONS

1. How might Nixon's actions (and the actions of those around him) have related to a national mentality that resulted from the cold war and Vietnam? How, possibly, were the actions of a few zealots in the White House justified (in their minds) by the lessons learned from the cold war and Vietnam?
2. Historians have pointed to a "post-Watergate backlash." How did that backlash manifest itself in foreign policy, politics, and finally in political reform?
3. "Speculative history" is occasionally useful. How could Nixon have better handled this incident? How might the nation have been changed as a result?
4. What were Mark Felt's motives? What did he have to gain by keeping Woodward informed of the White House cover-up? Do you think Felt acted for personal interest, or in the national interest?

FURTHER READINGS

Stephen E. Ambrose, *Nixon: Ruin and Recover, 1973–1990* (1991).
John Dean, *Blind Ambition* (1976).
Joan Hoff, *Nixon Reconsidered* (1994).
Stanley I. Kutler, *The Wars of Watergate* (1997).
Theodore H. White, *Breach of Faith: The Fall of Richard Nixon* (1975).
Bob Woodward and Carl Bernstein, *All the President's Men* (1974).

15 • Feminism and American Society

INTRODUCTION

In the late 1960s and early 1970s women began to change their perceptions of themselves and their role in society. The result was a strong women's movement that gained momentum through the 1970s. The movement's leadership came from several areas, but the National Organization for Women (NOW) was at the forefront. NOW focused its efforts in four primary areas: equality for women before the law, equal pay for equal work, government-supported child-care centers, and abortion rights.

This new attitude brought new opportunities for women—but not necessarily equality. Between 1970 and 1974 the number of women enrolled in medical schools, law schools, and graduate schools doubled. In 1972, President Nixon signed the Education Act, including Title IX, which mandated gender equality in college sports. Magazines for women had been published since the turn of the twentieth century, but in the early 1970s magazines appeared on the newsstands that focused on feminist issues rather than housekeeping. The most important of these was *Ms.* edited by Gloria Steinem. Women even found equality in *Playboy*-style soft pornography with *Playgirl*.

The two most contentious aspects of the women's movement were the fights over the Equal Rights Amendment and abortion rights.

A constitutional amendment giving American women equal rights under the Constitution (and thus equal rights under the law) was first proposed by Alice Paul's National Woman's Party in the 1920s. That proposed amendment stated simply: "Equality of rights under the law shall not be denied on account of sex." The Equal Rights Amendment (ERA) was introduced into every session of Congress (and either rejected or not taken up) between 1923 and 1970. Then in 1972, with the new feminism gaining strength, Congress finally passed the amendment. The ERA was then sent out to the states for ratification. Thirty-eight states needed to approve the ERA for it to become a constitutional amendment, and in just over a year thirty-two states ratified the amendment with little fanfare or controversy.

But in mid-1973 the forces of opposition begin to rally their troops. Led by Phyllis Schlafly, a St. Louis lawyer and mother of six, the Stop ERA campaign quickly gained momentum. Schlafly argued that the ERA would take from women rights they already enjoyed, such as the right to be supported by a husband, the right to be exempt from military service, and the right to special job protections. Schlafly and the opponents of the ERA even insisted that the amendment would bring an end to separate bathrooms for men and women.

By the mid-1970s it was clear that the ERA was suffering from a national backlash against all types of reform. Polls showed that women (more than men) had come to see feminism as a threat to the traditional family, and many Americans had begun to lump the ERA with radical feminism, abortion rights, and even gay rights. A 1975 Gallup Poll showed that 63 percent of men supported the ERA, while only 54 percent of women felt the same way.

The Stop ERA movement succeeded. By 1977 state ratifications ceased, and (following several battles in state legislatures) a few states rescinded their earlier decisions to ratify. The deadline for ratification was 1979. Congress voted to extend the deadline for another three and an half years, but in 1982, with no further movement, the ERA was declared a dead issue.

For many in the woman's movement the most important issue that remained was the right to abortion, the right to end an unwanted pregnancy. Several states had passed laws making abortion illegal, with the result that thousands of women each year risked their lives by turning to "back-alley" abortions. Because abortion was illegal, abortion providers were, of course, not regulated and answered to no one. By the mid-1970s, leaders in the women's movement began to see the right to abortion as part of a woman's right to control her own body. Without that control, they argued, women could never be equal.

In 1973, feminists and civil libertarians challenged a Texas law that made abortion a felony. The case involved a young woman who did not believe she could afford to raise a child. Justice Harry Blackmun, writing for the court majority, cited the absolute right of privacy as the constitutional basis for striking down the Texas law. The right of privacy, Blackmun wrote, "was broad enough to encompass a woman's decision whether or not to terminate her pregnancy." The Court decided further that a woman had an absolute right to an abortion within the first trimester, when the fetus was considered "not viable," or not able to live outside the mother's womb. In the second trimester, when a fetus might be viable, Blackmun wrote that states could regulate but not outlaw abortions. Only in the third trimester, the last thirteen weeks of pregnancy, could state laws prohibit abortions.

The decision put an end to back-alley abortions, but it produced tremendous public dissent. The Catholic Church had ruled as far back as 1869 that life begins at the moment of conception, so that abortion would be tantamount to murder. But the primary opposition to the ruling came from the Protestant religious Right, which saw abortion not only as murder, but as an affront to the traditions of the American family. By the late 1970s, abortion had become a political issue, even an acid test for some single-issue voters.

DOCUMENT 15.1
Gloria Steinem, Testimony Before the Senate Judiciary Committee on the Equal Rights Amendment (1970)

In 1970 Gloria Steinem testified before the Senate Judiciary Committee on the need to pass the Equal Rights Amendment. The amendment passed Congress but failed to gain ratification by the states.

Steinem's arguments below seem little more than the common wisdom today. But at that time she was definitely bucking an all-white male hierarchy in America, and her statements seemed radical. As an example, her statement here followed testimony before the same committee that tried to show that women were physically inferior to men, and thus should not be given equal rights.

SOURCE: Statement of Gloria Steinem. The Equal Rights Amendment: Hearings Before the Senate Subcommittee on Constitutional Amendments (of the Committee on the Judiciary), 91st Cong. 2d sess., 1970.

During twelve years of working for a living, I have experienced much of the legal and social discrimination reserved for women in this country. I have been refused service in public restaurants, ordered out of public gathering places, and turned away from apartment rentals; all for the clearly-stated, sole reason that I am a woman. And all without the legal remedies available to blacks and other minorities. I have been excluded from professional groups, writing assignments on so-called "unfeminine" subjects such as politics, full participation in the Democratic Party, jury duty, and even from such small male privileges as discounts on airline fares. Most important to me, I have been denied a society in which women are encouraged, or even allowed to think of themselves as first-class citizens and responsible human beings.

However, after two years of researching the status of American women, I have discovered that in reality, I am very, very lucky. Most women, both wage-earners and housewives, routinely suffer more humiliation and injustice than I do.

As a freelance writer, I don't work in the male-dominated hierarchy of an office. Women, like blacks and other visibly different minorities, do better in individual professions such as the arts, sports, or domestic work; anything in which they don't have authority over white males. I am not one of the millions of women who must support a family. Therefore, I haven't had to go on welfare because there are no day-care centers for my children while I work, and I haven't had to submit to the humiliating welfare inquiries about my private and sexual life, inquiries from which men are exempt. I haven't had to brave the sex bias of labor unions and employers, only to see my family subsist on a median salary 40 percent less than the male median salary. . . .

I hope this committee will hear the personal daily injustices suffered by many women—professionals and day laborers, women housebound by welfare as well as by suburbia. We have all been silent for too long. But we won't be silent anymore.

The truth is that all our problems stem from the same sex based myths. We may appear before you as white radicals or the middle-aged middle class or black soul sisters, but we are all sisters in fighting against these outdated myths. Like racial myths, they have been reflected in our laws. Let me list a few.

That women are biologically inferior to men. In fact, an equally good case can be made for the reverse. Women live longer than men, even when the men are not subject to business pressures. Women survived Nazi concentration camps better, keep cooler heads in emergencies currently studied by disaster-researchers, are protected against heart attacks by their female sex hormones, and are so much more durable at every stage of life that nature must conceive 20-to-50 percent more males in order to keep the balance going. . . .

Another myth [is] that women are already treated equally in this society. I am sure there has been ample testimony to prove that equal pay for equal work, equal chance for advancement, and equal training or encouragement is obscenely scarce in every field, even those—like food and fashion industries—that are supposedly "feminine."

A deeper result of social and legal injustice, however, is what sociologists refer to as "Internalized Aggression." Victims of aggression absorb the myth of their own inferiority, and come to believe that their group is in fact second class. Even when they themselves realize they are not second class, they may still think their group is, thus the tendency to be the only Jew in the club, the only black woman on the block, the only woman in the office.

Women suffer this second class treatment from the moment they are born. They are expected to be, rather than achieve, to function biologically rather than learn. A brother, whatever his intellect, is more likely to get the family's encouragement and education money, while girls are often pressured to conceal ambition and intelligence. . . .

Another myth [is] that American women hold great economic power. Fifty-one percent of all shareholders in this country are women. That is a favorite male-chauvinist statistic. However, the number of shares they hold is so small that the total is only 18 percent of all the shares. Even those holdings are often controlled by men.

Similarly, only 5 percent of all the people in the country who receive $10,000 a year or more, earned or otherwise, are women. And that includes the famous rich widows.

The constantly repeated myth of our economic power seems less testimony to our real power than to the resentment of what little power we do have.

Another myth [is] that children must have full-time mothers. . . . The truth is that most American children seem to be suffering from too much mother, and too little father. Part of the program of Women's Liberation is a return of fathers to their children. If laws permit women equal work and pay opportunities, men will then be relieved of their role as sole breadwinner. Fewer ulcers, fewer hours of meaningless work, equal responsibility for his own children: these are a few of the reasons that Women's Liberation is Men's Liberation too. . . .

Another myth [is] that the women's movement is not political, won't last, or is somehow not "serious." When black people leave their nineteenth century roles, they are feared. When women dare to leave theirs, they are ridiculed. We understand this; we accept the burden of ridicule. It won't keep us quiet anymore.

Similarly, it shouldn't deceive male observers into thinking that this is somehow a joke. We are 51 percent of the population; we are essentially united on these issues across boundaries of class or race or age; and we may well end by changing this society more than the civil rights movement. That is an apt parallel. We, too, have our right wing and left wing, our separatists, gradualists, and Uncle Toms. But we are changing our own consciousness, and that of the country. . . . Women's bodies will no longer be owned by the state for the production of workers and soldiers; birth control and abortion are facts of everyday life. The new family is an egalitarian family. . . .

Finally, I would like to say one thing about this time in which I am testifying.

I had deep misgivings about discussing this topic when National Guardsmen are occupying our campuses, the country is being turned against itself in a terrible polarization, and America is enlarging an already inhuman and unjustifiable war. But it seems to me that much of the trouble in this country has to do with the "masculine mystique"; with the myth that masculinity somehow depends on the subjugation of other people. It is a bipartisan problem; both our past and current presidents seem to be victims of this myth, and to behave accordingly.

Women are not more moral than men. We are only uncorrupted by power. But we do not want to imitate men, to join this country as it is, and I think our very participation will change it. Perhaps if women were elected leaders—and there will be many of them—they will not be so likely to dominate black people or yellow people or men; anybody who looks different from us.

After all, we won't have our masculinity to prove.

DOCUMENT 15.2
Phyllis Schlafly Recalls Her Victory over the ERA (June 1997)

The Stop ERA movement was much more powerful than the ERA advocates ever imagined. It was well organized and well led by Phyllis Schlafly, a St. Louis attorney and conservative political activist who had first gained prominence in the 1964 election campaign with her book A Choice Not an Echo. *The Stop ERA movement had behind it a strong backlash against the women's liberation movement. Schlafly and her supporters finally convinced state legislators (who would decide ratification in the states) that the ERA movement was really just the groundwork for a broader agenda that included abortion rights, same-sex marriages, and compulsory military service for women. Despite the fact that Gallup polls showed that a majority of Americans (both men and women) supported the amendment, it failed in 1982 when time ran out on ratification and fewer than three-fourths of the states had ratified it. Below is Schlafly's recollection of those events.*

SOURCE: Phyllis Schlafly, "Beating the Bra Burners," *George* (June 1997). Copyright © Phyllis Schlafly. Reprinted by permission.

A giant rainbow of balloons hovered high over the dais in the Omni Shoreham ballroom in Washington, D.C. Some 1,400 battle-weary but triumphant Stop ERA volunteers gathered to savor their victory when the proposed equal rights amendment died at midnight on June 30, 1982.

Amid the clamor, a hotel security guard rushed toward the emcee, Representative Bob Dornan of California, with urgent news: The hotel had received a phone call that a bomb had been planted in the ballroom. But the Stop ERA revelers just had to laugh. No need to evacuate. We anticipated that a bomb threat would be the radical feminists' final insult, and police dogs had already sniffed out the room.

It was the last day of a ten-year David-and-Goliath struggle waged across America. A little band of women, headquartered in the kitchen of my home on the bluffs of the Mississippi in Alton, Illinois, had defeated the big guns. The odds against us could not have been greater. The ERA drew the support of presidents (Richard Nixon, Gerald Ford, and Jimmy Carter), would-be presidents of all political stripes (from Ted Kennedy to George Wallace), all members of Congress except eight in the Senate and twenty-four in the House, all the pushy women's organizations, a consortium of thirty-five women's magazines, and 99 percent of the media.

In March 1972, Congress sent ERA to the states for their legislatures to approve, and its ratification by the necessary three-fourths of the fifty states seemed inevitable. But the unstoppable was stopped by our unflappable ladies in red. They descended on state capitols wearing their octagonal STOP ERA buttons. They treated legislators to home-baked bread. And they sweetly and persistently made their case that ERA was a fraud: It would actually take away legal rights that women possessed, such as the right of an eighteen-year-old girl to be exempt from the military draft and the right of a wife to be supported by her husband.

Pro-ERA advocates argued that women wanted absolute equality anyway. That line didn't sell in Middle America. A noisy tax-funded national women's confab in November 1977 had showcased ERA's hidden agenda: abortion funding and same-sex unions. The noose around ERA was tightening.

The war over these ideas included annual clashes in key states. But the decisive battle (i.e., what Midway was to World War II) took place in Springfield, Illinois, on June 18, 1980. If we could win in this northern industrial state, then we could triumph in pro-ERA territory, and other states might swing our way. President Carter rang up Democratic legislators, luring votes for ERA with talk of new federal housing projects for their districts. Back in 1978, Governor James Thompson phoned Republican legislators, reportedly promising "jobs, roads, and bridges" for a yes vote. . . .

After the votes were tallied, ABC's Nightline caught Eleanor Smeal, president of the National Organization for Women, in the Illinois House gallery. "There is something very powerful out against us," she said. "And certainly it isn't people." The Stop ERAers knew the source of their power: prayer and the truth.

ERA activists persisted in desperate tactics at that crucial statehouse. In May and June of 1982, an excommunicated Mormon, Sonia Johnson, led a hunger strike in the rotunda, while upstairs other pro-ERAers chained themselves to the door of the senate chamber. On June 25, ERA supporters went to a slaughterhouse, purchased plastic bags of pigs' blood, and used it to spell out the names of the legislators they hated most on the capitol's marble floor. The lawmakers found these tactics, well, unpersuasive. Victory was sealed on June 30, 1982, and many politicians paid tribute. But the day's heroes were the women who came from the 15 states that never ratified ERA and from the five states that bravely rescinded their previous ratifications.

DOCUMENT 15.3
The Boston Women's Health Book Collective, *Our Bodies,*
Ourselves **(1971)**

The short piece below is from Our Bodies, Ourselves, *a sort of bible for the*
feminist movement in the 1970s. The book included discussions of everything
from feminism to biological, reproductive, and sexual functions. Our Bodies,
Ourselves *was published as a fairly inexpensive paperback. It graced the*
shelves of nearly every feminist and would-be feminist in America. Below is
an analysis of a discussion between several of the founding members of the
Health Book Collective about the role of women in American society.

SOURCE: From "Our Changing Sense of Self." Abridged with permission of Simon
& Schuster Adult Publishing Group from *Our Bodies, Ourselves,* by Boston Women's
Health Book Collective. Copyright © 1971, 1973 Boston Women's Health Book
Collective.

Our Changing Sense of Self

Changing Our Internalized Sexist Values

When we started talking to each other we came to realize how deeply in-
grained was our sense of being less valuable than men. In my home I always
had a sense that my father and brother were more important than my mother
and myself. My mother and I shopped, talked to each other, and had friends
over—this was considered silly. My father was considered more important—he
did the real work of the world.

Rediscovering Activity

Talking to each other, we realized that many of us shared a common perception of men—that they all seemed to be able to turn themselves on and to do
things for themselves. We tended to feel passive and helpless and to expect
and need men to do things for us. We were trained to give our power over to
men. We had reduced ourselves to objects. We remained children, helpless
and giving other people power to define us and objectify us.

As we talked together we realized that one of our central fantasies was our
wish to find a man who could turn us on, to do for us what we could not do
for ourselves, to make us feel alive and affirm our existence. It was as if we
were made of clay and man would mold us, shape us, and bring us to life. This
was the material of our childhood dreams: "Someday my prince will come."

We were always disappointed when men did not accomplish this impossible task for us. And we began to see our passive helpless ways of handing power over to others as crippling to us. What became clear to us was that we had to change our expectations for ourselves. There was no factual reason why we could not assert and affirm our own existence and do and act for ourselves.

There were many factors that affected our capacity to act. For one, the ideal woman does less and less as her class status rises. Most of us, being middle class, were brought up not to do very much. Also, the kind of activity that is built into the traditional female role is different in quality from masculine activity. Masculine activity (repairing a window, building a house) tends to be sporadic, concrete, and have a finished product. Feminine activity (comforting a crying child, preparing a meal, washing laundry) tends to be repetitive, less tangible, and have no final durable product. Here again our sense of inferiority came into play. We had come to think of our activity as doing nothing—although essential for maintaining life—and of male activity as superior. We began to value our activity in a new way. We and what we did were as valuable as men and what they did.

On the other hand, we tried to incorporate within us the capacity to do more "male" product-oriented [activities]. . . .

We have also come to enjoy physical activity as well as mental and emotional activity. Again, the realm of physical strength is traditionally male. Once again we realized that we were active in our own ways, but we did not value them. As we looked at the details of our lives—the shopping and the cleaning—we realized that we used up a lot of physical energy every day but that we had taken it for granted and thought of it as nothing. We did avoid heavy, strenuous activity. . . .

We are learning to do new things—mountain climbing, canoeing, karate, auto mechanics.

Rediscovering Our Separateness

During this period of building up our own sense of ourselves we tried to find out what we were like on our own, what we could do on our own. We discovered resources we never thought we had. Either because we had been dependent on men to do certain things for us or because we had been so used to thinking of ourselves as helpless and dependent, we had never tried.

It is hard. We are forever fighting a constant, inner struggle to give up and become weak, dependent, and helpless again. . . .

As we have come to feel separate we try to change old relationships and/or try to enter new relationships in new ways. We now also feel positive about our needs to be dependent and connect with others. We have come to value long-term commitments, which we find increasingly rare in such a changing society, just as we value our new separateness.

DOCUMENT 15.4
Justice Harry Blackmun for the Court in
Roe v. Wade (1973)

Below is an excerpt from Justice Harry Blackmun's decision for the majority of the justices of the Supreme Court in the case of Roe v. Wade. In the portion of his decision included here, Blackmun surveys abortion practices, laws, and beliefs through history. The final decision of the majority of the court was based on a woman's constitutional right to absolute privacy.

SOURCE: *Roe v. Wade,* 410 U.S. 113 (1973).

Jane Roe, a single woman who was residing in Dallas County, Texas, instituted this federal action in March 1970 against the District Attorney of the county. She sought a declaratory judgment that the Texas criminal abortion statutes were unconstitutional on their face, and an injunction restraining the defendant from enforcing the statutes.

Roe alleged that she was unmarried and pregnant; that she wished to terminate her pregnancy by an abortion "performed by a competent, licensed physician, under safe, clinical conditions"; that she was unable to get a "legal" abortion in Texas because her life did not appear to be threatened by the continuation of her pregnancy; and that she could not afford to travel to another jurisdiction in order to secure a legal abortion under safe conditions. She claimed that the Texas statutes were unconstitutionally vague and that they abridged her right of personal privacy, protected by the First, Fourth, Fifth, Ninth, and Fourteenth Amendments. By an amendment to her complaint Roe purported to sue "on behalf of herself and all other women" similarly situated. . . .

Before addressing this claim, we feel it desirable briefly to survey, in several aspects, the history of abortion, for such insight as that history may afford us, and then to examine the stated purposes and interests behind the criminal abortion laws.

It perhaps is not generally appreciated that the restrictive criminal abortion laws in effect in a majority of States today are of relatively recent vintage. Those laws, generally proscribing abortion or its attempt at any time during pregnancy except when necessary to preserve the pregnant woman's life, are not of ancient or even of common-law origin. Instead, they derive from statutory changes effected, for the most part, in the latter half of the 19th century.

1. Ancient attitudes: These are not capable of precise determination. We are told that at the time of the Persian Empire abortifacients were known and that criminal abortions were severely punished. We are also told, however, that abortion was practiced in Greek times as well as in the Roman Era, and that "it was resorted to without scruple." The Ephesian, Soranos, often described as the greatest of the ancient gynecologists, appears to have been generally opposed to Rome's prevailing free-abortion practices. He found it necessary to think first of the life of the mother, and he resorted to abortion when, upon this standard, he felt the procedure advisable. Greek and Roman law afforded little protection to the unborn. If abortion was prosecuted in some places, it seems to have been based on a concept of a violation of the father's right to his offspring. Ancient religion did not bar abortion.

2. The Hippocratic Oath: What then of the famous Oath that has stood so long as the ethical guide of the medical profession and that bears the name of the great Greek [460(?)–377(?) BCE], who has been described as the Father of Medicine, the "wisest and the greatest practitioner of his art," and the "most important and most complete medical personality of antiquity," who dominated the medical schools of his time, and who typified the sum of the medical knowledge of the past? The Oath varies somewhat according to the particular translation, but in any translation the content is clear: "I will give no deadly medicine to anyone if asked, nor suggest any such counsel; and in like manner I will not give to a woman a pessary to produce abortion," or "I will neither give a deadly drug to anybody if asked for it, nor will I make a suggestion to this effect. Similarly, I will not give to a woman an abortive remedy."

Although the Oath is not mentioned in any of the principal briefs in this case . . . it represents the apex of the development of strict ethical concepts in medicine, and its influence endures to this day. . . .

3. The common law: It is undisputed that at common law, abortion performed before "quickening"—the first recognizable movement of the fetus in utero, appearing usually from the 16th to the 18th week of pregnancy—was not an indictable offense. The absence of a common-law crime for pre-quickening abortion appears to have developed from a confluence of earlier philosophical, theological, and civil and canon law concepts of when life begins. These disciplines variously approached the question in terms of the point at which the embryo or fetus became "formed" or recognizably human, or in terms of when a "person" came into being, that is, infused with a "soul" or "animated." A loose consensus evolved in early English law that these events occurred at some point between conception and live birth. This was "mediate animation." Although Christian theology and the canon law came to fix the point of animation at forty days for a male and eighty days for a female, a view that persisted until the 19th century, there was otherwise little agreement about the precise time of formation or animation. There was agreement, however, that prior to this point the fetus was to be regarded as part of the mother, and its destruction, therefore, was not homicide. . . .

4. English statutory law: England's first criminal abortion statute . . . came in 1803. It made abortion of a quick fetus a capital crime, but in it provided lesser penalties for the felony of abortion before quickening, and thus preserved the "quickening" distinction. This contrast was continued in the general revision of 1828. It disappeared, however, together with the death penalty, in 1837 and did not reappear in the Offenses Against the Person Act of 1861 that formed the core of English anti-abortion law until the liberalizing reforms of 1967. In 1929, the Infant Life (Preservation) Act came into being. Its emphasis was upon the destruction of "the life of a child capable of being born alive." It made a willful act performed with the necessary intent a felony. It contained a proviso that one was not to be found guilty of the offense "unless it is proved that the act which caused the death of the child was not done in good faith for the purpose only of preserving the life of the mother." . . .

5. The American law: In this country, the law in effect in all but a few States until mid-19th century was the pre-existing English common law. Connecticut, the first State to enact abortion legislation, adopted in 1821 [a law] that . . . related to a woman "quick with child." The death penalty was not imposed. Abortion before quickening was made a crime in that State only in 1860. In 1828, New York enacted legislation that, in two respects, was to serve as a model for early anti-abortion statutes. First, while barring destruction of an unquickened fetus as well as a quick fetus, it made the former only a misdemeanor, but the latter second-degree manslaughter. Second, it incorporated a concept of therapeutic abortion by providing that an abortion was excused if it "shall have been necessary to preserve the life of such mother, or shall have been advised by two physicians to be necessary for such purpose." By 1840, when Texas had received the common law, only eight American States had statutes dealing with abortion. It was not until after the War Between the States that legislation began generally to replace the common law. . . .

Gradually, in the middle and late 19th century the quickening distinction disappeared from the statutory law of most States and the degree of the offense and the penalties were increased. By the end of the 1950's, a large majority of the jurisdictions banned abortion, however and whenever performed, unless done to save or preserve the life of the mother. The exceptions, Alabama and the District of Columbia, permitted abortion to preserve the mother's health. Three States permitted abortions that were not "unlawfully" performed or that were not "without lawful justification," leaving interpretation of those standards to the courts. In the past several years, however, a trend toward liberalization of abortion statutes has resulted in adoption, by about one-third of the States, of less stringent laws. . . .

6. The position of the American Medical Association: An AMA Committee on Criminal Abortion was appointed in May 1857. It presented its report to the Twelfth Annual Meeting. That report observed that the Committee had been appointed to investigate criminal abortion "with a view to its general suppression." It deplored abortion and its frequency and it listed three causes of "this general demoralization:"

"The first of these causes is a wide-spread popular ignorance of the true character of the crime—a belief, even among mothers themselves, that the fetus is not alive till after the period of quickening.

"The second of the agents alluded to is the fact that the profession[als] themselves are frequently supposed careless of fetal life. . . ."

The Committee then offered, and the Association adopted, resolutions protesting "against such unwarrantable destruction of human life," calling upon state legislatures to revise their abortion laws, and requesting the cooperation of state medical societies "in pressing the subject." . . .

Except for periodic condemnation of the criminal abortionist, no further formal AMA action took place until 1967. In that year, the Committee on Human Reproduction urged the adoption of a stated policy of opposition to induced abortion, except when there is "documented medical evidence" of a threat to the health or life of the mother, or that the child "may be born with incapacitating physical deformity or mental deficiency," or that a pregnancy "resulting from legally established statutory or forcible rape or incest may constitute a threat to the mental or physical health of the patient," two other physicians "chosen because of their recognized professional competence have examined the patient and have concurred in writing," and the procedure "is performed in a hospital accredited by the Joint Commission on Accreditation of Hospitals." The providing of medical information by physicians to state legislatures in their consideration of legislation regarding therapeutic abortion was "to be considered consistent with the principles of ethics of the American Medical Association." This recommendation was adopted by the House of Delegates. . . .

7. The position of the American Public Health Association: In October 1970, the Executive Board of the APHA adopted Standards for Abortion Services. These were five in number:

> "a. Rapid and simple abortion referral must be readily available through state and local public health departments, medical societies, or other nonprofit organizations.
> b. An important function of counseling should be to simplify and expedite the provision of abortion services; it should not delay the obtaining of these services.

c. Psychiatric consultation should not be mandatory. . . .

d. A wide range of individuals from appropriately trained, sympathetic volunteers to highly skilled physicians may qualify as abortion counselors.

e. Contraception and/or sterilization should be discussed with each abortion patient." . . .

8. The position of the American Bar Association: At its meeting in February 1972 the ABA House of Delegates approved, with seventeen opposing votes, the Uniform Abortion Act that had been drafted and approved the preceding August by the Conference of Commissioners on Uniform State Laws. . . .

Some of the argument . . . rests on the theory that a new human life is present from the moment of conception. The state's interest and general obligation to protect life then extends, it is argued, to prenatal life. Only when the life of the pregnant mother herself is at stake, balanced against the life she carries within her, should the interest of the embryo or fetus not prevail. Logically, of course, a legitimate state interest in this area need not stand or fall on acceptance of the belief that life begins at conception or at some other point prior to live birth. In assessing the state's interest, recognition may be given to the less rigid claim that as long as at least potential life is involved, the state may assert interests beyond the protection of the pregnant woman alone. . . .

The Constitution does not explicitly mention any right of privacy. In a line of decisions, however . . . the [Supreme] Court has recognized that a right of personal privacy, or a guarantee of certain areas or zones of privacy, does exist under the Constitution. . . . This right of privacy . . . is broad enough to encompass a woman's decision whether or not to terminate her pregnancy. The detriment that the state would impose upon the pregnant woman by denying this choice altogether is apparent. Specific and direct harm medically diagnosable even in early pregnancy may be involved. Maternity, or additional offspring, may force upon the woman a distressful life and future. Psychological harm may be imminent. Mental and physical health may be taxed by child care. There is also the distress, for all concerned, associated with the unwanted child, and there is the problem of bringing a child into a family already unable, psychologically and otherwise, to care for it. In other cases, as in this one, the additional difficulties and continuing stigma of unwed motherhood may be involved. All these are factors the woman and her responsible physician necessarily will consider in consultation.

On the basis of elements such as these, appellant and some amici argue that the woman's right is absolute and that she is entitled to terminate her pregnancy at whatever time, in whatever way, and for whatever reason she alone chooses. With this we do not agree. Appellant's arguments that Texas either has no valid interest at all in regulating the abortion decision, or no interest strong enough to support any limitation upon the woman's sole determination, are unpersuasive. . . .

Although the results are divided, most of these courts have agreed that the right of privacy, however based, is broad enough to cover the abortion decision; that the right, nonetheless, is not absolute and is subject to some limitations; and that at some point the state interests as to protection of health, medical standards, and prenatal life, become dominant. We agree with this approach. . . .

A. The appellee and certain amici argue that the fetus is a "person" within the language and meaning of the Fourteenth Amendment. In support of this, they outline at length and in detail the well-known facts of fetal development. If this suggestion of personhood is established, the appellant's case, of course, collapses, for the fetus' right to life would then be guaranteed specifically by the Amendment. The appellant conceded as much on reargument. On the other hand, the appellee conceded on reargument that no case could be cited that holds that a fetus is a person within the meaning of the Fourteenth Amendment. . . .

All this, together with our observation, supra, that throughout the major portion of the 19th century prevailing legal abortion practices were far freer than they are today, persuades us that the word "person," as used in the Fourteenth Amendment, does not include the unborn. This is in accord with the results reached in those few cases where the issue has been squarely presented. . . .

B. The pregnant woman cannot be isolated in her privacy. She carries an embryo and, later, a fetus, if one accepts the medical definitions of the developing young in the human uterus. . . . As we have intimated above, it is reasonable and appropriate for a state to decide that at some point in time another interest, that of health of the mother or that of potential human life, becomes significantly involved. The woman's privacy is no longer sole and any right of privacy she possesses must be measured accordingly.

Texas urges that, apart from the Fourteenth Amendment, life begins at conception and is present throughout pregnancy, and that, therefore, the state has a compelling interest in protecting that life from and after conception. We need not resolve the difficult question of when life begins. When those trained in the respective disciplines of medicine, philosophy, and theology are unable to arrive at any consensus, the judiciary, at this point in the development of man's knowledge, is not in a position to speculate as to the answer.

It should be sufficient to note briefly the wide divergence of thinking on this most sensitive and difficult question. There has always been strong support for the view that life does not begin until live birth. This was the belief of the Stoics. It appears to be the predominant, though not the unanimous, attitude of the Jewish faith. It may be taken to represent also the position of a large segment of the Protestant community, insofar as that can be ascertained; organized groups that have taken a formal position on the abortion issue have generally regarded abortion as a matter for the conscience of the individual and her family. As we have noted, the common law found greater significance in quickening. Physicians and their scientific colleagues have regarded that event with less interest and have tended to focus either upon conception, upon live birth, or upon the interim point at which the fetus becomes "viable," that is, potentially able to live outside the mother's womb, albeit with artificial aid. Viability is usually placed at about seven months (28 weeks) but may occur earlier, even at 24 weeks.

In areas other than criminal abortion, the law has been reluctant to endorse any theory that life, as we recognize it, begins before live birth or to accord legal rights to the unborn except in narrowly defined situations and except when the rights are contingent upon live birth. . . . In short, the unborn have never been recognized in the law as persons in the whole sense. . . .

With respect to the state's important and legitimate interest in the health of the mother, the "compelling" point, in the light of present medical knowledge, is at approximately the end of the first trimester. This is so because of the now-established medical fact . . . that until the end of the first trimester mortality in abortion may be less than mortality in normal childbirth. It follows that, from and after this point, a state may regulate the abortion procedure to the extent that the regulation reasonably relates to the preservation and protection of maternal health. Examples of permissible state regulation in this area are requirements as to the qualifications of the person who is to perform the abortion; as to the licensure of that person; as to the facility in which the procedure is to be performed, that is, whether it must be a hospital or may be a clinic or some other place of less-than-hospital status; as to the licensing of the facility; and the like.

This means, on the other hand, that, for the period of pregnancy prior to this "compelling" point, the attending physician, in consultation with his patient, is free to determine, without regulation by the state, that, in his medical judgment, the patient's pregnancy should be terminated. If that decision is reached, the judgment may be effectuated by an abortion free of interference by the state. . . .

Measured against these standards . . . the Texas Penal Code, in restricting legal abortions to those "procured or attempted by medical advice for the purpose of saving the life of the mother," sweeps too broadly. The statute makes no distinction between abortions performed early in pregnancy and those performed later, and it limits to a single reason, "saving" the mother's life, the legal justification for the procedure. The statute, therefore, cannot survive the constitutional attack made upon it here.

This conclusion makes it unnecessary for us to consider the additional challenge to the Texas statute asserted on grounds of vagueness. . . .

This holding, we feel, is consistent with the relative weights of the respective interests involved, with the lessons and examples of medical and legal history, with the lenity of the common law, and with the demands of the profound problems of the present day. The decision leaves the State free to place increasing restrictions on abortion as the period of pregnancy lengthens, so long as those restrictions are tailored to the recognized state interests. The decision vindicates the right of the physician to administer medical treatment according to his professional judgment up to the points where important state interests provide compelling justifications for intervention. Up to those points, the abortion decision in all its aspects is inherently, and primarily, a medical decision, and basic responsibility for it must rest with the physician. If an individual practitioner abuses the privilege of exercising proper medical judgment, the usual remedies, judicial and intra-professional, are available.

Our conclusion . . . is . . . of course, that the Texas abortion statutes, as a unit, must fall. . . .

Concurring: Mr. Chief Justice Burger
Concurring: Mr. Justice Douglas
Dissenting: Mr. Justice White

BIOGRAPHICAL SKETCH
Gloria Steinem

Prior to the 1960s, the feminist movement in America had been dormant for several decades. In World War II, women took on the jobs and the responsibilities of the men who fought the war. But when the war ended, women were encouraged to return to their kitchens; in fact, it was considered patriotic to give up jobs to returning soldiers. What followed was a fairly strict division of labor, with men working outside the home and women staying at home.

The successes of the civil rights movement for African Americans, along with the growth of the movement against the Vietnam War, set the stage for the birth of several other activist movements, including a new women's liberation movement. That movement had many divisions and many leaders, but none was more visible than Gloria Steinem, an activist journalist who had pulled herself up from the poverty of her youth to become a primary figure in one of the most important movements of the age.

Gloria Steinem was born in Toledo, Ohio, in the midst of the Depression. Her mother was a teacher. Her father was an itinerant antique salesman who dragged his family from antique shop to antique shop between California and Florida. It is probably of some significance that he was the son of noted suffragette Pauline Steinem. He abandoned the family when Gloria was only eight, leaving his two daughters to take care of their mother, who suffered from an increasingly debilitating depression. Their situation, during the war, can only be described as bitter poverty.

From that bad situation, fifteen-year-old Gloria Steinem moved to Washington, D.C., to live with her older sister. Good grades got her into Smith College. She graduated in 1956. After a two-year fellowship to India, she moved to New York and began writing freelance articles for popular magazines. She drew the attention of the publishing world with a two-part series for *Show* magazine that took a behind-the-scenes look at the working life of a Playboy bunny. Perceived as glamorous girls in a glamorous job, the bunnies, Steinem wrote, were actually sexually exploited, underpaid, and overworked. The catch to the articles was that Steinem had worked undercover as a bunny to do the research, allowing her to speak firsthand.

In 1968, Steinem joined the founding staff of *New York* magazine. She also became politically active in this period, assisting in the campaigns of liberal candidates, particularly Eugene McCarthy, Robert Kennedy, and George McGovern. It was in 1968 that Steinem first came into direct contact with the women's liberation movement when she attended a meeting of the feminist group the Redstockings to cover the organization for a story. She found herself drawn to the issue of abortion, and the dangers of "back-alley" abortions in late-1960s America. Her commitment to liberal causes of the time provided a natural path toward a career as a leader in the feminist movement, which continued to grow and strengthen into the 1970s.

In 1971 she helped organize the National Women's Political Caucus to encourage women to vote in the 1972 election. At the Democratic Party convention that year, Steinem fought for a pro-choice plank in the party platform, and challenged the seating of several all-male state delegations to the convention. Her efforts helped place women's issues into the political arena.

In that same year, Steinem founded *Ms.* magazine, the first mass-circulation feminist publication. The magazine became the primary vehicle for women's rights issues, and as editor, Steinem became the nation's foremost spokesperson on feminist issues.

STUDY QUESTIONS

1. How does Justice Blackmun reach his decision based on the history of abortion?
2. Discuss Steinem's "myths" that stifled women's progress. How are similar myths explained by the women in the document *Our Bodies, Ourselves?*
3. Why did Phyllis Schlafly and (what became a majority of) American women come to oppose the Equal Rights Amendment? Is not constitutional equality basic to the American purpose?

FURTHER READINGS

Susan Faludi, *Backlash: The Undeclared War against American Women* (1992).
Christina Hoff-Sommers, *Who Stole Feminism? How Women Have Betrayed Women* (1995).
Mary Ann Mason, *The Equality Trap* (1988).
Miriam Schneir, *Feminism in Our Time: The Essential Writings, World War II to the Present* (1994).
Winifred D. Wandersee, *On the Move: American Women in the 1970s* (1988).

16 • The Emergence of Ronald Reagan and the New Right

INTRODUCTION

Ronald Reagan's election to the presidency in 1980 was a victory for a resurgent American conservatism, the first in some sixty years. The coalition that Reagan pulled together was not very cohesive. In fact, not unlike the Democrats, the members of the coalition seldom got along, but they found themselves united by a few basic convictions—and, of course, by Reagan himself.

What united Reagan conservatives was a disdain for what they perceived as the liberal mismanagement of government over the last fifty years, along with a general fear of social change that they believed was being pushed on the nation by a liberal minority. High taxes, conservatives often argued, supported welfare programs, so they pushed for drastic reductions to both. They attacked busing to integrate schools and affirmative action to achieve equal opportunity; and they attacked laws and rulings that supported equal rights for women or for gays and lesbians. They opposed gun control laws, favored capital punishment, and opposed abortion rights and the *Roe v. Wade* decision. They found abhorrent court rulings that outlawed prayer in public schools.

In the foreign policy arena, Reagan conservatives saw the evils of communism as a threat to capitalism and the freedoms it provided. They demanded a strong military with the force to contain, and, if necessary, destroy communism in order to rid the world of that evil. All foreign policy strategies seemed to find their way back to that one simple dictum.

Many of the Reagan Republicans called themselves new conservatives, or neoconservatives. Fundamentally, there was little to separate them from the Republican Old Guard of decades past. However, they believed that the nation should play a greater role in world events. They also embraced the religious Right and that group's ardent belief in "family values," a new calling for conservatives.

Reagan's personal appeal and his abilities to pull this conservative coalition together changed the nature of American politics in the 1980s. The Republicans had been, in the past, a loyal opposition that might have an impact on legislation, but little more. Occasionally, an Eisenhower-like figure who appealed to the political center could win the White House. Reagan, however, brought the Republicans political parity, an equal place in the nation's political arena for the immediate future.

DOCUMENT 16.1
"Government Is Not the Solution." President Ronald Reagan's Inaugural Address (January 1981)

Ronald Reagan's inaugural address presented a new vision for the nation. It was a vision that was markedly conservative, a point that is abundantly clear in his repeated calls for downsizing the national government. But it was also, nevertheless, a national vision, and that is what separates Reagan from presidents who have governed not as leaders, but as managers.

In this address, Reagan also shows his optimism, which for many Americans from across the political spectrum was a wonderfully refreshing attitude at a time when the nation seemed in decline both at home and abroad.

Even those who disagreed with Reagan's policies could admire an optimistic president with a national vision.

SOURCE: *Public Papers of the Presidents: Ronald Reagan, 1981* (Washington, D.C.: USGPO, 1982), 1–4.

My fellow Americans: . . .

The business of our nation goes forward. These United States are confronted with an economic affliction of great proportions. We suffer from the longest and one of the worst sustained inflations in our national history. It distorts our economic decisions, penalizes thrift, and crushes the struggling young and the fixed-income elderly alike. It threatens to shatter the lives of millions of our people.

Idle industries have cast workers into unemployment, causing human misery and personal indignity. Those who do work are denied a fair return for their labor by a tax system which penalizes successful achievement and keeps us from maintaining full productivity.

But great as our tax burden is, it has not kept pace with public spending.

For decades, we have piled deficit upon deficit, mortgaging our future and our children's future for the temporary convenience of the present. To continue this long trend is to guarantee tremendous social, cultural, political, and economic upheavals.

You and I, as individuals, can, by borrowing, live beyond our means, but for only a limited period of time. Why, then, should we think that collectively, as a nation, we are not bound by that limitation?

We must act today in order to preserve tomorrow. And let there be no misunderstanding—we are going to begin to act, beginning today.

The economic ills we suffer have come upon us over several decades. They will not go away in days, weeks, or months, but they will go away. They will go away because we, as Americans, have the capacity now, as we have had in the past, to do whatever needs to be done to preserve this last and greatest bastion of freedom.

In the present crisis, government is not the solution to our problem. . . .

We hear much of special interest groups. Our concern must be for a special interest group that has been too long neglected. It knows no sectional boundaries or ethnic and racial divisions, and it crosses political party lines. It is made up of men and women who raise our food, patrol our streets, man our mines and our factories, teach our children, keep our homes, and heal us when we are sick—professionals, industrialists, shopkeepers, clerks, cabbies, and truck-drivers. They are, in short, "We the people," this breed called Americans.

Well, this administration's objective will be a healthy, vigorous, growing economy that provides equal opportunity for all Americans, with no barriers born of bigotry or discrimination. Putting America back to work means putting all Americans back to work. Ending inflation means freeing all Americans from the terror of runaway living costs. All must share in the productive work of this "new beginning" and all must share in the bounty of a revived economy. With the idealism and fair play which are the core of our system, we can have a strong and prosperous America at peace with itself and the world.

So, as we begin, let us take inventory. We are a nation that has a government—not the other way around. And this makes us special among the nations of the earth. Our government has no power except that granted it by the people. It is time to check and reverse the growth of government which shows signs of having grown beyond the consent of the governed.

It is my intention to curb the size and influence of the federal establishment and to demand recognition of the distinction between the powers granted to the federal government and those reserved to the states or to the people. All of us need to be reminded that the federal government did not create the states; the states created the federal government.

Now, so there will be no misunderstanding, it is not my intention to do away with government. It is, rather, to make it work—work with us, not over us; to stand by our side, not ride on our back. Government can and must provide opportunity, not smother it; foster productivity, not stifle it.

If we look to the answer as to why, for so many years, we achieved so much, prospered as no other people on earth, it was because here, in this land, we unleashed the energy and individual genius of man to greater extent than has ever been done before. Freedom and the dignity of the individual have been more available and assured here than in any other place on earth. The price for this freedom at times has been high, but we have never been unwilling to pay that price.

It is no coincidence that our present troubles parallel and are proportionate to the intervention and intrusion in our lives that result from unnecessary and excessive growth of government.

It is time for us to realize that we are too great a nation to limit ourselves to small dreams. We are not, as some would have us believe, doomed to an inevitable decline. I do not believe in a fate that will fall on us no matter what we do. I do believe in a fate that will fall on us if we do nothing. So, with all the creative energy at our command, let us begin an era of national renewal. Let us renew our determination, our courage, and our strength. And let us renew our faith and our hope.

We have every right to dream heroic dreams. Those who say that we are in a time when there are no heroes just don't know where to look. You can see heroes every day going in and out of factory gates. Others, a handful in number, produce enough food to feed all of us and then the world beyond. You meet heroes across a counter—and they are on both sides of that counter. There are entrepreneurs with faith in themselves and faith in an idea to create new jobs, new wealth and opportunity. They are individuals and families whose taxes support the government and whose voluntary gifts support church, charity, culture, arts, and education. Their patriotism is quiet but deep. Their values sustain our national life. . . .

Can we solve the problems confronting us? Well, the answer is an unequivocal and emphatic "yes." To paraphrase Winston Churchill, I did not take the oath I have just taken with the intention of presiding over the dissolution of the world's strongest economy.

In the days ahead I will propose removing the roadblocks that have slowed our economy and reduced productivity. Steps will be taken aimed at restoring the balance between the various levels of government. Progress may be slow—measured in inches and feet, not miles—but we will progress. It is time to reawaken this industrial giant, to get government back within its means, and to lighten our punitive tax burden. And these will be our first priorities, and on these principles, there will be no compromise. . . .

To those neighbors and allies who share our freedom, we will strengthen our historic ties and assure them of our support and firm commitment. We will match loyalty with loyalty. We will strive for mutually beneficial relations. We will not use our friendship to impose on their sovereignty, for our own sovereignty is not for sale.

As for the enemies of freedom, those who are potential adversaries, they will be reminded that peace is the highest aspiration of the American people. We will negotiate for it, sacrifice for it; we will not surrender for it—now or ever.

Our forbearance should never be misunderstood. Our reluctance for conflict should not be misjudged as a failure of will. When action is required to preserve our national security, we will act. We will maintain sufficient strength to prevail if need be, knowing that if we do so we have the best chance of never having to use that strength.

Above all, we must realize that no arsenal, or no weapon in the arsenal of the world, is so formidable as the will and moral courage of free men and women. It is a weapon our adversaries in today's world do not have. It is a weapon that we as Americans do have. Let that be understood by those who practice terrorism and prey upon their neighbors.

I am told that tens of thousands of prayer meetings are being held on this day, and for that I am deeply grateful. We are a nation under God, and I believe God intended for us to be free. It would be fitting and good, I think, if on each inauguration day in future years it should be declared a day of prayer. . . .

We are Americans. God bless you, and thank you.

DOCUMENT 16.2
T. Boone Pickens, "My Case for Reagan" (1984)

T. Boone Pickens personified the American self-made man. In 1958, at age twenty-eight, he started Mesa Petroleum Company with only $2,500. By the mid-1980s Mesa had become the largest independent oil company in the nation. In the process, Pickens perfected the business strategy of buying companies, breaking them up, and selling off the individual parts. To his detractors, he was a corporate raider. Fortune *magazine called him the "most hated man in America" because his hostile takeovers and corporate restructurings put people out of work. But he was a hero to shareholders who saw their stock values increase as he streamlined the companies he acquired and pushed out CEOs who were more concerned with their own salaries and perquisites than with shareholders' dividends.*

Pickens was a winner in the game of free enterprise. Ronald Reagan was his political champion.

In the 1984 presidential campaign, the Democrats chose Jimmy Carter's vice president, Walter Mondale, to run against Reagan.

SOURCE: Published in *Fortune* and reprinted by arrangement with the author.

When businessmen consider why they should support President Reagan's reelection, their analysis should come down to two important questions: What has allowed their companies to grow and prosper? What makes business opportunities in America different from those in any other country?

The answer is free enterprise. Our economic system is what keeps Americans employed, clothed, housed, and nourished. That system makes it possible for every American to attain his or her dream of material or spiritual wealth. It truly makes ours the land of opportunity. This year voters will have a clear choice between a President who believes in retaining the maximum amount possible of the nation's wealth in the private sector and a challenger who supports a greater role for government.

More than any other president in the last thirty years, Ronald Reagan understands the importance of free enterprise. He knows that this country's markets should be allowed to operate freely and competitively. That's the philosophy he brought to the White House in 1981, and we've seen how beneficial the results are. Since President Reagan took office, inflation has dropped from nearly 14 percent to approximately 4 percent, and the prime rate has fallen from 20 percent to 13 percent.

By reducing government intervention, Reagan has injected a new competitive spirit into the marketplace. There is now an atmosphere that encourages business efficiency. For example, merger and acquisition activity, properly undertaken within the constraints of antitrust laws, has allowed companies and even entire industries to restructure and become more efficient and financially sound. Shareholders have reaped the rewards of their investments, and the government has received additional revenues as taxes are paid on those gains.

In contrast, [Democratic presidential candidate in 1984] Walter Mondale does not appear to understand what makes America work. His proposals would more heavily tax individuals and corporations, inhibit capital formation, and use government as the primary means to stimulate employment.

The cheapest, most effective way to create jobs is to encourage business growth, not to devise complicated and costly federal programs. Ronald Reagan has proved that. His policies have invigorated the market and put more Americans to work. Economic recovery is the best jobs programs this country has had. A record 107 million people are currently employed, five million more than when the Carter-Mondale Administration left office.

But Reagan has done even more for the average worker than stimulate employment. Through his tax policies, Americans are now taking home more pay. They have more money for their children's education, a new home, retirement, and investments. Some forty-two million Americans have invested in shares of publicly owned companies, either directly or through mutual funds, compared with thirty million in 1980. We've seen tangible evidence that Ronald Reagan's policies are working for America. That's important for everyone in this country. The health of U.S. business is critical to our nation's survival. We do, indeed, have a responsibility to support candidates who understand that principle—a responsibility not just to ourselves but to all citizens.

I am frequently asked by high school and college students how they can attain success from modest beginnings. My answer is simple. Like many business executives, I owe my success to the free enterprise system. I started with a good education, $2,500 in capital, and an opportunity to do something—the sky was the limit, and fortunately the same opportunity still exists.

The American free enterprise spirit is something we will be able to maintain only under a Reagan Administration. While Walter Mondale tells us that his plan for this country is better, we've seen what better means: Mondale's recent speeches have promised increased government intervention in the market and our lives and disincentives in the form of higher taxes.

The ill effects of the Carter-Mondale Administration were far-reaching: double-digit inflation—the worst since 1946—unemployment, skyrocketing interest rates, and a crumbling economy. There is no reason to believe that a Mondale-Ferraro Administration would be any different in philosophy or outcome.

All of us realize the importance of strong leadership. It is the greatest attribute any President can have and should be a prime asset of the nation. Lack of leadership ability is one of my greatest concerns about a Mondale-Ferraro Administration. Mondale has given no indication of having such ability either as Carter's Vice President or on his own. How could a nation possibly trust the affairs of state to a person who could not make a decision as to whether Bert Lance or Charles Manatt would chair his party?

America need not take that chance when it is blessed with an incumbent President who has proven leadership qualities. Ronald Reagan has been able to instill a new sense of pride and confidence in our nation. Gone are the days of Carter-Mondale defeatism and national malaise.

In 1980 the American people realized the disastrous economic brink on which this country teetered. They wanted a change for the better, and they chose a president who accomplished that goal. On November 6, Americans will once again ask themselves if a change is in order. I think the resounding answer will be that they wish to stay the course Reagan has charted. We're no longer on the brink of disaster; both feet are planted firmly on solid ground, and the future looks bright.

I'm supporting President Reagan and Vice President Bush for those reasons, and I unabashedly ask others to support them as well. I make no apology for political participation. At stake in this election is the future of the free enterprise system. A commitment from the business community, not just a check, is required to prevent another give-away-now, pay-later disaster. And that commitment will mean for future Americans a vigorous free market, the opportunity to succeed, and an attainable American Dream.

DOCUMENT 16.3
"The New American Revolution." President Ronald Reagan's State of the Union Address (January 1985)

In the 1984 campaign, President Reagan annihilated his Democratic opponent, Walter F. Mondale. With a landslide mandate in his hands, Reagan went before the American people in January 1985 and recounted the economic successes of his first term. He seemed to be saying to his critics that his plan worked—despite liberal cynicism, economists' skepticism, and criticism from the press and various pundits. He called his economic successes a New American Revolution because, he argued, his administration had changed the way Washington did business.

Reagan also mentions his Strategic Defense Initiative (SDI). Its detractors called the program "Star Wars," claiming that it was mostly science fiction. The president's plan was for U.S. missiles to intercept incoming missiles and destroy them above the atmosphere before they could strike American soil. SDI is discussed in more detail in document 17.2.

SOURCE: *Public Papers of the Presidents: Ronald Reagan, 1985* (Washington, D.C.: USGPO, 1986), 135.

I come before you to report on the state of our Union, and I'm pleased to report that after four years of united effort, the American people have brought forth a nation renewed, stronger, freer, and more secure than before.

Four years ago we began to change, forever I hope, our assumptions about government and its place in our lives. Out of that change has come great and robust growth—in our confidence, our economy, and our role in the world. . . .

Tonight we can take pride in twenty-five straight months of economic growth, the strongest in thirty-four years; a three-year inflation average of 3.9 percent, the lowest in seventeen years; and 7.3 million new jobs in two years, with more of our citizens working than ever before. . . .

We're here to speak for millions in our inner cities who long for real jobs, safe neighborhoods, and schools that truly teach. We're here to speak for the American farmer, the entrepreneur, and every worker in industries fighting to modernize and compete. And, yes, we're here to stand, and proudly so, for all who struggle to break free from totalitarianism, for all who know in their hearts that freedom is the one true path to peace and human happiness. . . .

We honor the giants of our history not by going back but forward to the dreams their vision foresaw. My fellow citizens, this nation is poised for greatness. The time has come to proceed toward a great new challenge—a second American Revolution of hope and opportunity; a revolution carrying us to new heights of progress by pushing back frontiers of knowledge and space; a revolution of spirit that taps the soul of America, enabling us to summon greater strength than we've ever known; and a revolution that carries beyond our shores the golden promise of human freedom in a world of peace.

Let us begin by challenging our conventional wisdom. There are no constraints on the human mind, no walls around the human spirit, no barriers to our progress except those we ourselves erect. Already, pushing down tax rates has freed our economy to vault forward to record growth.

In Europe, they're calling it "the American Miracle." Day by day, we're shattering accepted notions of what is possible. When I was growing up, we failed to see how a new thing called radio would transform our marketplace. Well, today, many have not yet seen how advances in technology are transforming our lives. . . .

We stand on the threshold of a great ability to produce more, do more, be more. Our economy is not getting older and weaker; it's getting younger and stronger. It doesn't need rest and supervision; it needs new challenge, greater freedom. And that word "freedom" is the key to the second American Revolution that we need to bring about.

Let us move together with an historic reform of tax simplification for fairness and growth. Last year I asked Treasury Secretary—then—[Donald] Regan to develop a plan to simplify the tax code, so all taxpayers would be treated more fairly and personal tax rates could come further down.

We have cut tax rates by almost 25 percent, yet the tax system remains unfair and limits our potential for growth. Exclusions and exemptions cause similar incomes to be taxed at different levels. Low-income families face steep tax barriers that make hard lives even harder. The Treasury Department has produced an excellent reform plan, whose principles will guide the final proposal that we will ask you to enact. . . .

To encourage opportunity and jobs rather than dependency and welfare, we will propose that individuals living at or near the poverty line be totally exempt from Federal income tax. To restore fairness to families, we will propose increasing significantly the personal exemption.

And tonight, I am instructing Treasury Secretary James Baker to begin working with congressional authors and committees for bipartisan legislation conforming to these principles. We will call upon the American people for support, and upon every man and woman in this chamber. Together, we can pass, this year, a tax bill for fairness, simplicity, and growth, making this economy the engine of our dreams and America the investment capital of the world. So let us begin.

Tax simplification will be a giant step toward unleashing the tremendous pent-up power of our economy. But a second American Revolution must carry the promise of opportunity for all. It is time to liberate the spirit of enterprise in the most distressed areas of our country.

This government will meet its responsibility to help those in need. But policies that increase dependency, break up families, and destroy self-respect are not progressive; they're reactionary. Despite our strides in civil rights, blacks, Hispanics, and all minorities will not have full and equal power until they have full economic power. . . .

We'll continue to support the Job Training Partnership Act, which has a nearly two-thirds job placement rate. Credits in education and health care vouchers will help working families shop for services that they need.

Our administration is already encouraging certain low-income public housing residents to own and manage their own dwellings. It's time that all public housing residents have that opportunity of ownership. . . .

To move steadily toward a balanced budget, we must also lighten government's claim on our total economy. We will not do this by raising taxes. We must make sure that our economy grows faster than the growth in spending by the federal government. In our fiscal year 1986 budget, overall government program spending will be frozen at the current level. It must not be one dime higher than fiscal year 1985, and three points are key.

First, the social safety net for the elderly, the needy, the disabled, and unemployed will be left intact. Growth of our major health care programs, Medicare and Medicaid, will be slowed, but protections for the elderly and needy will be preserved.

Second, we must not relax our efforts to restore military strength just as we near our goal of a fully equipped, trained, and ready professional corps. National security is government's first responsibility; so in past years defense spending took about half the Federal budget. Today it takes less than a third. We've already reduced our planned defense expenditures by nearly a hundred billion dollars over the past four years and reduced projected spending again this year.

You know, we only have a military-industrial complex until a time of danger, and then it becomes the arsenal of democracy. Spending for defense is investing in things that are priceless—peace and freedom.

Third, we must reduce or eliminate costly government subsidies. For example, deregulation of the airline industry has led to cheaper airfares, but on Amtrak taxpayers pay about $35 per passenger every time an Amtrak train leaves the station. It's time we ended this huge federal subsidy.

Our farm program costs have quadrupled in recent years. Yet I know from visiting farmers, many in great financial distress, that we need an orderly transition to a market-oriented farm economy. We can help farmers best not by expanding federal payments but by making fundamental reforms, keeping interest rates heading down, and knocking down foreign trade barriers to American farm exports. . . .

Nearly fifty years of government living beyond its means has brought us to a time of reckoning. Ours is but a moment in history. But one moment of courage, idealism, and bipartisan unity can change American history forever. . . .

As we do all this, we'll continue to protect our natural resources. We will seek reauthorization and expanded funding for the Superfund program to continue cleaning up hazardous waste sites which threaten human health and the environment.

Now, there's another great heritage to speak of this evening. Of all the changes that have swept America the past four years, none brings greater promise than our rediscovery of the values of faith, freedom, family, work, and neighborhood.

We see signs of renewal in increased attendance in places of worship; renewed optimism and faith in our future; love of country rediscovered by our young, who are leading the way. We've rediscovered that work is good in and of itself, that it ennobles us to create and contribute no matter how seemingly humble our jobs. We've seen a powerful new current from an old and honorable tradition—American generosity.

From thousands answering Peace Corps appeals to help boost food production in Africa, to millions volunteering time, corporations adopting schools, and communities pulling together to help the neediest among us at home, we have re-found our values. Private sector initiatives are crucial to our future.

I thank the Congress for passing equal access legislation giving religious groups the same right to use classrooms after school that other groups enjoy. But no citizen need tremble, nor the world shudder, if a child stands in a classroom and breathes a prayer. We ask you again, give children back a right they had for a century and a half or more in this country.

The question of abortion grips our nation. Abortion is either the taking of a human life or it isn't. And if it is—and medical technology is increasingly showing it is—it must be stopped. It is a terrible irony that while some turn to abortion, so many others who cannot become parents cry out for children to adopt. We have room for these children. We can fill the cradles of those who want a child to love. And tonight I ask you in the Congress to move this year on legislation to protect the unborn. . . .

Of all the changes in the past twenty years, none has more threatened our sense of national well-being than the explosion of violent crime. One does not have to be attacked to be a victim. The woman who must run to her car after shopping at night is a victim. The couple draping their door with locks and chains are victims; as is the tired, decent cleaning woman who can't ride a subway home without being afraid.

We do not seek to violate the rights of defendants. But shouldn't we feel more compassion for the victims of crime than for those who commit crime? For the first time in twenty years, the crime index has fallen two years in a row. We've convicted over 7,400 drug offenders and put them, as well as leaders of organized crime, behind bars in record numbers.

But we must do more. I urge the House to follow the Senate and enact proposals permitting use of all reliable evidence that police officers acquire in good faith. These proposals would also reform the *habeas corpus* laws and allow, in keeping with the will of the overwhelming majority of Americans, the use of the death penalty where necessary. . . .

For the past twenty years we've believed that no war will be launched as long as each side knows it can retaliate with a deadly counterstrike. Well, I believe there's a better way of eliminating the threat of nuclear war. It is a Strategic Defense Initiative aimed ultimately at finding a non-nuclear defense against ballistic missiles. It's the most hopeful possibility of the nuclear age. But it's not very well understood.

Some say it will bring war to the heavens, but its purpose is to deter war in the heavens and on Earth. Now, some say the research would be expensive. Perhaps, but it could save millions of lives, indeed humanity itself. And some say if we build such a system, the Soviets will build a defense system of their own. Well, they already have strategic defenses that surpass ours; a civil defense system, where we have almost none; and a research program covering roughly the same areas of technology that we're now exploring. And finally some say the research will take a long time. Well, the answer to that is: "Let's get started." . . .

We must stand by all our democratic allies. And we must not break faith with those who are risking their lives—on every continent, from Afghanistan to Nicaragua—to defy Soviet-supported aggression and secure rights which have been ours from birth.

The Sandinista dictatorship of Nicaragua, with full Cuban–Soviet bloc support, not only persecutes its people, the church, and denies a free press, but arms and provides bases for Communist terrorists attacking neighboring states. Support for freedom fighters is self-defense and totally consistent with the OAS and U.N. Charters. It is essential that the Congress continue all facets of our assistance to Central America. I want to work with you to support the democratic forces whose struggle is tied to our own security.

And tonight, I've spoken of great plans and great dreams. They're dreams we can make come true. Two hundred years of American history should have taught us that nothing is impossible. . . .

Thank you, and God bless you.

BIOGRAPHICAL SKETCH
Patrick Buchanan

Patrick Buchanan is the leader of a vocal faction within the Republican Party that is, by its own admission, to the right of mainstream conservatives, to the right of the Bush family, and to the right of what Buchanan has always called the neoconservatives, or the neocons. He is, unfortunately, often defined by his critics, who tag him with being everything from an isolationist to a fascist. But for anyone who is interested in the far reaches of American politics, Pat Buchanan is always interesting, provocative, and passionate about his opinions.

Buchanan was born in 1938 in Washington, D.C., into a strict Catholic family. He attended Georgetown University and the Columbia University School of Journalism. His first job was as an editorial writer for the *St. Louis Globe Democrat*, where his editorials established him as a right-wing conservative who was a master at stirring up controversy. As his reputation expanded, he came to the attention of Republican Party regulars, and in 1966 he was tapped to become an advisor to Richard Nixon, who was then at a low point in his political career. Buchanan is often credited, at least in part, with orchestrating Nixon's resurrection from his sixties political defeats to a strong Republican candidate in 1968. He followed Nixon to the White House, and served there until 1974 as an advisor and speech writer. He was with Nixon in China, and attended Nixon's final Soviet summit in Yalta in 1974.

In 1985, Buchanan joined Ronald Reagan's administration as the Director of White House Communications. Reagan's brand of conservatism became Buchanan's brand of conservatism, and Reagan became Buchanan's political touchstone.

Following Reagan's tenure, Buchanan mined his celebrity to return to television appearances as a regular on *The McLaughlin Group* and *The Capitol Gang*, and as co-host on CNN's *Crossfire*. He acquired a following as a leader of the Republican Right, the keeper of the flame (as many saw it) of Reagan conservatism. With the nationwide support of conservative radio talk show commentators like Rush Limbaugh, Buchanan entered the 1992 Republican presidential primary against President George H.W. Bush. He charged that Bush was a moderate who had taken the Republican Party away from Reagan conservatism. His challenge attracted some three million votes in the various Republican primaries, enough to give him recognition as the leader of a legitimate wing within his party. Buchanan made his strongest appeal to working people who believed they were being hurt by job losses due to globalization of the national economy. And he attacked Bush for repudiating his "no new taxes" pledge by supporting the 1990 tax bill to raise federal taxes.

Buchanan's respectable showing in the primary run won him a primetime spot at the 1992 Republican convention in Houston. His speech rocked the convention—but it also hurt the party. He hit at Hillary Clinton, the wife of the Democratic Party's nominee, as a "radical feminist," and called the coming campaign a religious and cultural war. Moderates in the party winced at the stridency of his speech; others were apprehensive about his divisive politics, which focused squarely on racial and cultural differences in the nation.

In 1996, Buchanan again made a stab at the Republican nomination and put the nation on notice with a surprising victory in New Hampshire over party frontrunner Bob Dole. His brand of conservative populism continued to appeal to blue-collar workers who were losing their jobs to low-wage overseas workers. Although his campaign faded quickly, he continued to be the darling of the Republican Right.

In 1999, Buchanan decided to leave the Republican Party and join the Reform Party. His 2000 campaign made barely a ripple in the greater scheme, prompting Buchanan to announce that he would no longer be a candidate for president.

Buchanan is usually described as a strict isolationist who believes that U.S. military interventions (including World War II) were generally unnecessary and did little to further U.S. national interests. As a cultural warrior, he opposes feminism, multiculturalism, and immigration. His critics see him as the last gasp of a social order that time has left behind.

Buchanan continues to appear as a regular on political talk shows where he espouses a conservatism that, he argues, has been abandoned by the two Bush administrations. He remains one of the most fascinating figures on the political Right.

STUDY QUESTIONS

1. In what ways did Reagan exude optimism? Why was that important in 1981?
2. How was Reagan's second administration a "new American revolution?" What was so revolutionary about it?
3. Why did T. Boone Pickens support Reagan?
4. What impact has Pat Buchanan had on the political process?

FURTHER READINGS

William C. Berman, *America's Right Turn: From Nixon to Bush* (1994).
Louis Cannon, *President Reagan: The Role of a Lifetime* (1991).
Godfrey Hodgson, *The World Turned Right Side Up* (1997).
William Pemberton, *Exit with Honor: The Life and Presidency of Ronald Reagan* (1998).
Ronald Reagan, *An American Life* (1990).
David Stockman, *Triumph of Politics: Why the Reagan Revolution Failed* (1986).

17 • The Reagan Foreign Policy and a New Soviet Confrontation

INTRODUCTION

In 1980, while he was running for the White House, candidate Ronald Reagan told a reporter that he was certain that he would succeed as president "for one simple reason. . . . The American people want somebody in command." The Carter administration's foreign policy had often appeared weak and passive. The nation's woes, however, were born more from an aversion to world affairs than from any Carter administration policy. The Vietnam experience, still fresh in the American mind, had made the nation unsure of itself, of its ability to work its will in the world. Reagan seemed to understand that. But his strong leadership and outspoken patriotism—as refreshing and inspirational as it was—led to a new aggressiveness that threatened to open old cold war wounds, bring an end to détente, and begin another dangerous phase in the cold war.

Reagan's strident language in the early 1980s did a lot to sour détente, but the Soviet invasion of Afghanistan in 1979 was the real beginning of the deterioration of U.S.-Soviet relations, a deterioration that lasted through the Reagan years. The Soviets finally withdrew from Afghanistan in 1989, generally beaten. In that conflict the United States had aided the anti-Soviet forces, or Mujahideen, mostly with Stinger anti-aircraft weapons that were devastating to Soviet helicopters. The effort to occupy and control Afghanistan was destructive to the Soviet economy, further aiding in the collapse of the Soviet Union. It also fostered the emergence of a radical Islamic state in Afghanistan that openly harbored anti-Western terrorists—including Osama bin Laden and his al-Qaeda organization.

In early 1982, Reagan sent a peacekeeping force into Lebanon to stop a civil war there between forces supported by Israel and Syria. In October, a terrorist blast in Beirut killed 241 Marines. Reagan reacted by cutting his losses and withdrawing the troops. The incident seemed to show the world that the United States was easily stung, and would not hesitate to withdraw when the going got tough.

The American people's sense of insecurity in the post-Vietnam era became abundantly clear when President Reagan tried to involve U.S. forces in a situation in Central America that reminded many of Vietnam. Reagan was determined to overthrow the left-leaning Sandinista government of Nicaragua using a U.S.-supplied Central American force that he called the Contras. As the situation heated up, Congress in 1982 voted to prohibit the administration from spending money to overthrow the Sandinistas, and in 1984 banned all aid to the Contras. The Reagan administration, however, continued to funnel private money to the Contras, first through right-wing organizations, and then with funds from the sale of weapons to Iran, which was then at war with Iraq. This strategem eventually erupted in the "Iran-Contra" scandal. Finally, in 1988, Congress banned all military aid to the Contras from all sources.

The world order changed considerably in the summer of 1989 when communism in Eastern Europe and the USSR collapsed under the weight of a rapidly weakening economy and a disintegrating society. Then in 1991, the Soviet Union itself broke up and the cold war came to an end—an end so abrupt that the CIA missed the signals. Reagan's evil empire was gone, and there was a new world order.

DOCUMENT 17.1
President Ronald Reagan's "Evil Empire" Speech (March 1983)

When Ronald Reagan came to office in 1981, most of America was content with the idea of détente. It did not solve any cold war conflicts, but, for the populations on both sides, détente reduced the fears of a nuclear holocaust. But on March 8, 1983, President Reagan seemed prepared to cast all that aside. On that date, speaking to his political base at the Annual Convention of the National Association of Evangelicals in Orlando, Florida, Reagan charged that the Soviet Union continued to act with the "aggressive impulse of an evil empire." He argued that the United States should not enter into any agreements with the Soviets that would freeze nuclear stockpiles at their current levels and that peace would be attained only through strength. This "evil empire speech," as it became known, characterized Reagan's view of the Soviet Union, and threatened to bring an end to détente. The speech reflected Reagan's long-held belief that the Soviet Union would eventually collapse, and set the tone for U.S.-Soviet relations for the next six years.

SOURCE: *Public Papers of the Presidents: Ronald Reagan, 1983* (Washington, D.C.: USGPO, 1984), 362–64.

During my first press conference as president, in answer to a direct question, I pointed out that, as good Marxist-Leninists, the Soviet leaders have openly and publicly declared that the only morality they recognize is that which will further their cause, which is world revolution. I think I should point out I was only quoting Lenin, their guiding spirit, who said in 1920 that they repudiate all morality that proceeds from supernatural ideas—that's their name for religion—or ideas that are outside class conceptions. Morality is entirely subordinate to the interests of class war. And everything is moral that is necessary for the annihilation of the old, exploiting social order and for uniting the proletariat.

Well, I think the refusal of many influential people to accept this elementary fact of Soviet doctrine illustrates a historical reluctance to see totalitarian powers for what they are. We saw this phenomenon in the 1930s. We see it too often today.

This doesn't mean we should isolate ourselves and refuse to seek an understanding with them. I intend to do everything I can to persuade them of our peaceful intent, to remind them that it was the West that refused to use its nuclear monopoly in the forties and fifties for territorial gain and which now proposes a 50 percent cut in strategic ballistic missiles and the elimination of an entire class of land-based, intermediate-range nuclear missiles.

At the same time, however, they must be made to understand we will never compromise our principles and standards. We will never give away our freedom. We will never abandon our belief in God. And we will never stop searching for a genuine peace. But we can assure none of these things America stands for through the so-called nuclear freeze solutions proposed by some.

The truth is that a freeze now would be a very dangerous fraud, for that is merely the illusion of peace. The reality is that we must find peace through strength.

I would agree to freeze if only we could freeze the Soviets' global desires. A freeze at current levels of weapons would remove any incentive for the Soviets to negotiate seriously in Geneva and virtually end our chances to achieve the major arms reductions which we have proposed. Instead, they would achieve their objectives through the freeze.

A freeze would reward the Soviet Union for its enormous and unparalleled military buildup. It would prevent the essential and long overdue modernization of United States and allied defenses and would leave our aging forces increasingly vulnerable. And an honest freeze would require extensive prior negotiations on the systems and numbers to be limited and on the measures to ensure effective verification and compliance. And the kind of a freeze that has been suggested would be virtually impossible to verify. Such a major effort would divert us completely from our current negotiations on achieving substantial reductions. . . .

Yes, let us pray for the salvation of all of those who live in that totalitarian darkness—pray they will discover the joy of knowing God. But until they do, let us be aware that while they preach the supremacy of the state, declare its omnipotence over individual man, and predict its eventual domination of all peoples on the earth, they are the focus of evil in the modern world. . . .

So, I urge you to speak out against those who would place the United States in a position of military and moral inferiority. . . . So, in your discussions of the nuclear freeze proposals, I urge you to beware the temptation of pride—the temptation of blithely declaring yourselves above it all and label both sides equally at fault, to ignore the facts of history and the aggressive impulses of an evil empire, to simply call the arms race a giant misunderstanding and thereby remove yourself from the struggle between right and wrong and good and evil.

I ask you to resist the attempts of those who would have you withhold your support for our efforts, this administration's efforts, to keep America strong and free, while we negotiate real and verifiable reductions in the world's nuclear arsenals and one day, with God's help, their total elimination.

While America's military strength is important, let me add here that I've always maintained that the struggle now going on for the world will never be decided by bombs or rockets, by armies or military might. The real crisis we face today is a spiritual one. At root, it is a test of moral will and faith. . . .

I believe we shall rise to the challenge. I believe that communism is another sad, bizarre chapter in human history whose last pages even now are being written. I believe this because the source of our strength in the quest for human freedom is not material, but spiritual. And because it knows no limitation, it must terrify and ultimately triumph over those who would enslave their fellow man. For in the words of Isaiah: "He giveth power to the faint; and to them that have no might He increased strength. . . . But they that wait upon the Lord shall renew their strength; they shall mount up with wings as eagles; they shall run, and not be weary. . . ."

Yes, change your world. One of our Founding Fathers, Thomas Paine, said, "We have it within our power to begin the world over again." We can do it, doing together what no one church could do by itself.

God bless you, and thank you very much.

DOCUMENT 17.2
President Ronald Reagan's "Star Wars" Speech (March 1983)

In the same month as his "evil empire" speech, President Reagan spoke to the nation again. This time he defended a massive increase in the military budget, and then, near the end of the speech, he explained his plan to develop a new system for a missile defense shield that would reduce the threat of nuclear attack and thus end the strategy of nuclear deterrence. This Strategic Defense Initiative, or SDI, became more popularly known as "Star Wars," after the science-fiction movie, because it was meant to destroy missiles from space. Any successes that ultimately came out of the program and the billions of dollars invested in it are debatable. Many experts consider it to be questionable science that produced very few results.

Almost immediately after Reagan's SDI speech, Soviet premier Yuri Andropov began calling the president "irresponsible" and "insane." The Soviets feared that such a system would increase the risk that the United States might launch a first-strike attack against the Soviet Union with no fear of a Soviet retaliation. It also forced the Soviets to begin research on their own missile defense system, a massive investment of resources that their already-weak economy could ill afford. Whatever its scientific merits, Reagan's Star Wars plan undoubtedly contributed to the collapse of the Soviet Union.

SOURCE: *Public Papers of the Presidents: Ronald Reagan, 1983*, 437–43.

Tonight, I want to explain to you what the defense debate is all about and why I'm convinced that the budget now before the Congress is necessary, responsible, and deserving of your support. And I want to offer hope for the future.

But first, let me say what the defense debate is not about. It is not about spending arithmetic. I know that in the last few weeks you've been bombarded with numbers and percentages. . . .

The defense policy of the United States is based on a simple premise: The United States does not start fights. We will never be an aggressor. We maintain our strength in order to deter and defend against aggression—to preserve freedom and peace.

Since the dawn of the atomic age, we've sought to reduce the risk of war by maintaining a strong deterrent and by seeking genuine arms control. "Deterrence" means simply this: making sure any adversary who thinks about attacking the United States, or our allies, or our vital interest, concludes that the risks to him outweigh any potential gains. Once he understands that, he won't attack. We maintain the peace through our strength; weakness only invites aggression.

This strategy of deterrence has not changed. It still works. But what it takes to maintain deterrence has changed. It took one kind of military force to deter an attack when we had far more nuclear weapons than any other power; it takes another kind now that the Soviets, for example, have enough accurate and powerful nuclear weapons to destroy virtually all of our missiles on the ground. Now, this is not to say that the Soviet Union is planning to make war on us. Nor do I believe a war is inevitable—quite the contrary. But what must be recognized is that our security is based on being prepared to meet all threats. . . .

For twenty years the Soviet Union has been accumulating enormous military might. They didn't stop when their forces exceeded all requirements of a legitimate defensive capability. And they haven't stopped now. During the past decade and a half, the Soviets have built up a massive arsenal of new strategic nuclear weapons—weapons that can strike directly at the United States.

As an example, the United States introduced its last new intercontinental ballistic missile, the Minute Man III, in 1969, and we're now dismantling our even older Titan missiles. But what has the Soviet Union done in these intervening years? Well, since 1969 the Soviet Union has built five new classes of ICBM's, and upgraded these eight times. As a result, their missiles are much more powerful and accurate than they were several years ago, and they continue to develop more, while ours are increasingly obsolete. . . .

There was a time when we were able to offset superior Soviet numbers with higher quality, but today they are building weapons as sophisticated and as modern as our own.

As the Soviets have increased their military power, they've been emboldened to extend that power. They're spreading their military influence in ways that can directly challenge our vital interests and those of our allies. . . .

Some people may still ask: Would the Soviets ever use their formidable military power? Well, again, can we afford to believe they won't? There is Afghanistan. And in Poland, the Soviets denied the will of the people and in so doing demonstrated to the world how their military power could also be used to intimidate. . . .

The Soviet Union is acquiring what can only be considered an offensive military force. They have continued to build far more intercontinental ballistic missiles than they could possibly need simply to deter an attack. Their conventional forces are trained and equipped not so much to defend against an attack as they are to permit sudden, surprise offensives of their own.

Our NATO allies have assumed a great defense burden, including the military draft in most countries. We're working with them and our other friends around the world to do more. Our defensive strategy means we need military forces that can move very quickly, forces that are trained and ready to respond to any emergency. . . .

I know that all of you want peace, and so do I. I know too that many of you seriously believe that a nuclear freeze would further the cause of peace. But a freeze now would make us less, not more, secure and would raise, not reduce, the risk of war. It would be largely unverifiable and would seriously undercut our negotiations on arms reduction. It would reward the Soviets for their massive military build up while preventing us from modernizing our aging and increasingly vulnerable forces. With their present margin of superiority, why should they agree to arms reductions knowing that we were prohibited from catching up? . . .

The solution is well within our grasp. But to reach it, there is simply no alternative but to continue this year, in this budget, to provide the resources we need to preserve the peace and guarantee our freedom.

Now, thus far tonight I've shared with you my thoughts on the problems of national security we must face together. My predecessors in the Oval Office have appeared before you on other occasions to describe the threat posed by Soviet power and have proposed steps to address that threat. But since the advent of nuclear weapons, those steps have been increasingly directed toward deterrence of aggression through the promise of retaliation. . . .

One of the most important contributions we can make is, of course, to lower the level of all arms, and particularly nuclear arms. We're engaged right now in several negotiations with the Soviet Union to bring about a mutual reduction of weapons. I will report to you a week from tomorrow my thoughts on that score. But let me just say, I'm totally committed to this course.

If the Soviet Union will join with us in our effort to achieve major arms reduction, we will have succeeded in stabilizing the nuclear balance. Nevertheless, it will still be necessary to rely on the specter of retaliation, on mutual threat. And that's a sad commentary on the human condition. Wouldn't it be better to save lives than to avenge them? Are we not capable of demonstrating our peaceful intentions by applying all our abilities and our ingenuity to achieving a truly lasting stability? I think we are indeed. Indeed, we must.

After careful consultation with my advisers, including the Joint Chiefs of Staff, I believe there is a way. Let me share with you a vision of the future which offers hope. It is that we embark on a program to counter the awesome Soviet missile threat with measures that are defensive. Let us turn to the very strengths in technology that spawned our great industrial base and that have given us the quality of life we enjoy today.

What if free people could live secure in the knowledge that their security did not rest upon the threat of instant U.S. retaliation to deter a Soviet attack, that we could intercept and destroy strategic ballistic missiles before they reached our own soil or that of our allies?

I know this is a formidable, technical task, one that may not be accomplished before the end of the century. Yet, current technology has attained a level of sophistication where it's reasonable for us to begin this effort. It will take years, probably decades of efforts on many fronts. There will be failures and setbacks, just as there will be successes and breakthroughs. And as we proceed, we must remain constant in preserving the nuclear deterrent and maintaining a solid capability for flexible response. But isn't it worth every investment necessary to free the world from the threat of nuclear war? We know it is. . . .

I clearly recognize that defensive systems have limitations and raise certain problems and ambiguities. If paired with offensive systems, they can be viewed as fostering an aggressive policy, and no one wants that. But with these considerations firmly in mind, I call upon the scientific community in our country, those who gave us nuclear weapons, to turn their great talents now to the cause of mankind and world peace, to give us the means of rendering these nuclear weapons impotent and obsolete.

Tonight, consistent with our obligations of the ABM treaty and recognizing the need for closer consultation with our allies, I'm taking an important first step. I am directing a comprehensive and intensive effort to define a long-term research and development program to begin to achieve our ultimate goal of eliminating the threat posed by strategic nuclear missiles. This could pave the way for arms control measures to eliminate the weapons themselves. We seek neither military superiority nor political advantage. Our only purpose—one all people share—is to search for ways to reduce the danger of nuclear war.

My fellow Americans, tonight we're launching an effort which holds the promise of changing the course of human history. There will be risks, and results take time. But I believe we can do it. As we cross this threshold, I ask for your prayers and your support.

Thank you, good night, and God bless you.

DOCUMENT 17.3
Ronald Reagan Recalls His Frustrations over Central America (1990)

When President Reagan proposed to involve U.S. forces in Central America, many Americans thought immediately of the experience in Vietnam. Reagan, however, saw the situation in terms of Cuba and the threat of new Marxist regimes coming to power in the Western Hemisphere. He was determined to overthrow the Sandinista government in Nicaragua and defeat a leftist insurgency in El Salvador. The force in opposition to this insurgency was the U.S.-supplied Contras. Reagan called El Salvador the "last domino."

Reagan left office with the Sandinistas still in power. In 1990 the anti-Sandinista candidate Violeta Barrios de Chamorro defeated the Sandinista candidate Daniel Ortega Saavedra in an election monitored closely by international observers. What follows is an excerpt from Reagan's 1990 memoir, An American Life.

SOURCE: Ronald Reagan, *An American Life* (New York, 1990).

In 1984, 1985, and 1986, as [Democratic Speaker of the House] Tip O'Neill and his allies intensified their campaign to abandon the Contras, the Nicaraguan freedom fighters began to face shortages of guns and ammunition, sometimes even of food and medical supplies. It didn't help matters when Tip, declaring he was going to retire in 1986, asked fellow Democrats to vote against the Contras as a farewell gift. Now we had the emotional sentiment surrounding a very popular Speaker of the House involved in setting foreign policy.

While I battled with Congress to get support for the Contras reinstated, I felt we had to do everything we legally could to keep the force in existence. I told the staff: We can't break the law, but, within the law, we have to do whatever we can to help the Contras survive.

I knew that there must be among our allies other countries that shared our concern about the threat to democracy in Latin America, and I believed we should communicate to them our strong convictions regarding the importance of tangible international support for the Contras. Several countries responded and extended help—a case of friendly nations believing we all had a stake in fighting for democracy.

I believed, then and now, that the president has the absolute constitutional right and obligation to share such thoughts and goals with leaders of other nations.

At about the same time, churches and various groups around our country began forming committees with the intention of helping the freedom fighters and refugees from the Sandinistas. They were made up of private citizens worried about the threat of Communism in Latin America and about things they had read in papers concerning the misguided actions of Congress. . . .

While I continued trying to educate the American people and seek their support in persuading Congress to provide badly needed aid to the freedom fighters, dedicated Americans began contributing money and supplies—one woman contributed enough to buy a helicopter—and helped buy advertising to counter the Sandinistas' Madison Avenue disinformation campaign. I regarded them as patriots, people from the grass roots of America who were voluntarily trying to bring to our neighbors in Central America the same kind of freedom we enjoyed in the United States.

It was only later, when the Tower Board and Congress completed their investigations, that I learned that some on the NSC [National Security Council] staff had gone farther to help the Contras than I was aware of.

Let me be clear. I wanted the Contras maintained as a force, to the fullest extent that was legal, until I could convince Congress to appropriate new funds for the freedom fighters; but I was distressed by the investigations' conclusions that the NSC staff had been so heavily involved in the Contra operation. Press reports appeared suggesting that the NSC and the CIA had gone beyond limits set by the Boland Amendment, and were conducting what some members of Congress claimed was an illegal war in Nicaragua. When I inquired about this, I was told the reports were inaccurate. I later repeated some of these assurances to the American people, and assured them we had been abiding by the law. . . .

I knew Oliver North only slightly when he worked for the National Security Council. What impressions I did have of him were favorable. My main recollection of Ollie North, before the Iran-Contra affair erupted, was that he had a good record as a marine officer in Vietnam. Although press reports claimed that he told others that we met together privately many times, I knew little about him personally and never saw very much of him at the White House. I never met with him privately and never had a one-on-one conversation with him until I called him on his last day at the NSC to wish him well. I don't believe he attended more than a handful of meetings where I was present, and then he was always part of a group, in the role of a junior staff member under Bud McFarlane or John Poindexter.

McFarlane, Poindexter, Casey, and, I presume, North knew how deeply I felt about the need for the Contras' survival as a democratic resistance force in Nicaragua. They also knew how frustrated I was over many battles with Congress. Perhaps that knowledge, along with their own belief in the importance of the Contras' survival, their adherence to the code that absolute secrecy is necessary in intelligence operations, and a belief that the NSC was exempt from the Boland Amendment, led them to support the Contras secretly and saw no reason to report this to me.

As president, I was at the helm, so I am the one who is ultimately responsible. But to those who question why I wasn't more aware of what was going on, I would say this: Central America was only one of many things that occupied me at the time. Besides trying to end the recession, we were working on modernization of our military forces, trying to get a new nuclear arms reduction initiative off the ground, trying to cut federal spending, trying to end the fighting in Lebanon and the Middle East—and many other things were on my plate as well. A president simply cannot monitor the day-to-day conduct of all of his subordinates. He must concentrate as much as possible on setting the tone and direction of the administration, establishing broad policies, and selecting good people to implement these policies. Unfortunately, there will occasionally be transgressions; but had I attempted to involve myself in the details of the activities of the NSC staff, I would have been unable to attend to the other wide-ranging issues before me at the time.

DOCUMENT 17.4
NATO's "London Declaration" and the End of the Cold War (July 1990)

Interestingly, the end of the cold war was not greeted by any special fanfare in the United States. There was nothing like a V-E Day or Armistice Day celebration. The destruction of the Berlin Wall in November 1989, and the celebrations in Europe that accompanied that event, were the images that captured the end of the cold war. But, although most Americans have never heard of the London Declaration, it was probably that document, more than any other, that proclaimed the official end to the cold war.

In the summer of 1990 the North Atlantic Treaty Organization (NATO) issued a statement in response to the events unfolding in Eastern Europe. It was NATO, of course, that was the West's chief rampart against Soviet military action in Europe, and thus the primary cold war instrument of the United States.

The declaration refers to the CSCE, the Commission for Security and Cooperation in Europe. This commission was designed to foster cooperation among the European nations. The United States and Canada were included as members. The CSCE's Final Act is the Commission's organizational agreement, signed in Helsinki in 1975.

Before 1995 the commission was made up of the major Western European nations. After 1995 the commission was renamed the Organization for Security and Cooperation in Europe (OSCE). It has expanded to include nearly all the nations of Europe and many in Central Asia. The organization fosters cooperation among member nations on the economic, cultural, environmental, technical, and scientific level, and monitors the protection of human rights.

The document also refers to "Open Skies." This policy (first introduced by President Eisenhower but always rejected by the Soviets) would allow for military flyovers by signatories for the purpose of monitoring military buildups. The purpose was always to diffuse suspicions. By 1990, however, the need for a policy of Open Skies had been satisfied instead by means of improvements in satellite image photography.

SOURCE: www.nato.int/docu.

Europe has entered a new, promising era. Central and Eastern Europe is liberating itself. The Soviet Union has embarked on the long journey towards a free society. The walls that once confined people and ideas are collapsing. Europeans are determining their own destiny. They are choosing freedom. They are choosing economic liberty. They are choosing peace. They are choosing a Europe whole and free. As a consequence, this Alliance must and will adapt.

The North Atlantic Alliance [NATO] has been the most successful defensive alliance in history. As our Alliance enters its fifth decade and looks ahead to a new century, it must continue to provide for the common defense. This Alliance has done much to bring about the new Europe. No one, however, can be certain of the future. We need to keep standing together, to extend the long peace we have enjoyed these past four decades. Yet our Alliance must be even more an agent of change. It can help build the structures of a more united continent, supporting security and stability with the strength of our shared faith in democracy, the rights of the individual, and the peaceful resolution of disputes. We reaffirm that security and stability do not lie solely in the military dimension, and we intend to enhance the political component of our Alliance. . . .

The unification of Germany means that the division of Europe is also being overcome. A united Germany in the Atlantic Alliance of free democracies and part of the growing political and economic integration of the European Community will be an indispensable factor of stability, which is needed in the heart of Europe. The move within the European Community towards political union, including the development of a European identity in the domain of security, will also contribute to Atlantic solidarity and to the establishment of a just and lasting order of peace throughout the whole of Europe.

We recognize that, in the new Europe, the security of every state is inseparably linked to the security of its neighbors. NATO must become an institution where Europeans, Canadians and Americans work together not only for the common defense, but to build new partnerships with all the nations of Europe. The Atlantic Community must reach out to the countries of the East which were our adversaries in the Cold War, and extend to them the hand of friendship.

We will remain a defensive alliance and will continue to defend all the territory of all our members. We have no aggressive intentions and we commit ourselves to the peaceful resolution of all disputes. We will never in any circumstance be the first to use force.

The member states of the North Atlantic Alliance propose to the member states of the Warsaw Treaty Organization a joint declaration in which we solemnly state that we are no longer adversaries and reaffirm our intention to refrain from the threat or use of force against the territorial integrity or political independence of any state, or from acting in any other manner inconsistent with the purposes and principles of the United Nations Charter and with the CSCE [Commission on Security and Cooperation in Europe] Final Act. We invite all other CSCE member states to join us in this commitment to non-aggression.

In that spirit, and to reflect the changing political role of the Alliance, we today invite [Soviet] President [Mikhail] Gorbachev on behalf of the Soviet Union, and representatives of the other Central and Eastern European countries to come to Brussels and address the North Atlantic Council. We today also invite the governments of the Union of Soviet Socialist Republics, the Czech and Slovak Federal Republic, the Hungarian Republic, the Republic of Poland, the People's Republic of Bulgaria and Romania to come to NATO, not just to visit, but to establish regular diplomatic liaison with NATO. This will make it possible for us to share with them our thinking and deliberations in this historic period of change. . . .

The significant presence of North American conventional and U.S. nuclear forces in Europe demonstrates the underlying political compact that binds North America's fate to Europe's democracies. But, as Europe changes, we must profoundly alter the way we think about defense. . . .

As Soviet troops leave Eastern Europe and a treaty limiting conventional armed forces is implemented, the Alliance's integrated force structure and its strategy will change fundamentally to include the following elements:

- NATO will field smaller and restructured active forces. These forces will be highly mobile and versatile so that Allied leaders will have maximum flexibility in deciding how to respond to a crisis. It will rely increasingly on multinational corps made up of national units.
- NATO will scale back the readiness of its active units, reducing training requirements and the number of exercises.
- NATO will rely more heavily on the ability to build up larger forces if and when they might be needed.

To keep the peace, the Alliance must maintain for the foreseeable future an appropriate mix of nuclear and conventional forces, based in Europe, and kept up to date where necessary. But, as a defensive Alliance, NATO has always stressed that none of its weapons will ever be used except in self-defense and that we seek the lowest and most stable level of nuclear forces needed to secure the prevention of war.

The political and military changes in Europe, and the prospects of further changes, now allow [those] Allies concerned to go further. They will thus modify the size and adapt the tasks of their nuclear deterrent forces. They have concluded that, as a result of the new political and military conditions in Europe, there will be a significantly reduced role for sub-strategic nuclear systems of the shortest range. They have decided specifically that, once negotiations begin on short-range nuclear forces, the Alliance will propose, in return for reciprocal action by the Soviet Union, the elimination of all its nuclear artillery shells from Europe.

New negotiations between the United States and the Soviet Union on the reduction of short-range forces should begin shortly after a CFE agreement is signed. The Allies concerned will develop an arms control framework for these negotiations which takes into account our requirements for far fewer nuclear weapons, and the diminished need for sub-strategic nuclear systems of the shortest range.

Finally, with the total withdrawal of Soviet stationed forces and the implementation of a CFE agreement, the Allies concerned can reduce their reliance on nuclear weapons. These will continue to fulfill an essential role in the overall strategy of the Alliance to prevent war by ensuring that there are no circumstances in which nuclear retaliation in response to military action might be discounted. However, in the transformed Europe, they will be able to adopt a new NATO strategy making nuclear forces truly weapons of last resort. . . .

In the context of these revised plans for defense and arms control, and with the advice of NATO Military Authorities and all member states concerned, NATO will prepare a new Allied military strategy moving away from "forward defense" where appropriate, towards a reduced forward presence and modifying "flexible response" to reflect a reduced reliance on nuclear weapons. In that connection NATO will elaborate new force plans consistent with the revolutionary changes in Europe. NATO will also provide a forum for Allied consultation on the upcoming negotiations on short-range nuclear forces.

Today, our Alliance begins a major transformation. Working with all the countries of Europe, we are determined to create enduring peace on this continent.

BIOGRAPHICAL SKETCH
Oliver North

The Reagan administration's man on the ground was Oliver North. A Marine lieutenant colonel, decorated Vietnam veteran, and aide to National Security Advisor Admiral John Poindexter, North was involved in planning the attacks on Grenada and Libya, and carrying out the administration's policy of funding aid to the Nicaraguan Contra movement through the sale of weapons to Iran.

North emerged from the shadows in 1987 when he was called to testify before Congress in what became known as the Iran-Contra Affair. He admitted (after receiving limited immunity for his testimony) that he had lied to Congress and destroyed evidence. "I am not," he said, "at all ashamed of any of the things that I did. I was given a mission and I tried to carry it out." It was clear that the administration attempted to set up North as the scapegoat for the entire operation (insisting that he was a "loose cannon"). North took much of the heat for the operation, and emerged as a champion of the political Right.

The Iran-Contra scandal, and Oliver North's complicity in it, began in 1981 when President Reagan ordered CIA Director William Casey to organize and train a group of anti-communist insurgents in Central America for the purpose of overthrowing Nicaragua's Sandinista government, which was widely perceived to be communist, or at least communist-inspired. But as the Central American jungle war began to look more and more like Vietnam, public opinion polls showed that a majority of Americans opposed U.S. involvement or aid to anti-Sandinista forces. In December 1982, Congress passed the Boland Amendment, forbidding the use of U.S. funds for the purpose of overthrowing the Sandinista government.

Reagan responded by working to circumvent the will of Congress. He instructed Director Casey, National Security Advisor Robert McFarlane, and North to pressure U.S. allies to contribute money to aid the anti-Sandinista rebels, known as the Contras. The contributing nations included South Africa, Israel, Taiwan, South Korea, and Saudi Arabia. North solicited additional funds from wealthy private contributors in the United States.

At around the same time, the administration became involved in an attempt to free American hostages being held by pro-Iranian terrorists in Lebanon. Iran was involved in a bloody war with Iraq and desperately needed U.S.-built advanced weapons. In July 1985 the Reagan administration made a deal with several Iranian arms dealers to sell one hundred TOW missiles to Iran in exchange for the release of the hostages in Lebanon. But Iran held out for more. Finally, in December, a deal was struck between North and the Iranians. The hostages would be released in exchange for some 3,500 TOW missiles and two hundred HAWK surface-to-air missiles. For all this, only one American hostage was released, while two more hostages were taken. After two additional shipments of arms to Iran, a second hostage was released.

It was North who came up with the plan (he later called it a "neat idea") to divert the money (ultimately some $48 million) from the sale of these weapons to the Contras in Central America.

In October 1986, a plane hauling weapons to the Contras was shot down over Nicaragua and the pilot confessed to his captors that he was a part of the Reagan administration's plan to continue support for the Contras. In mid-November, Attorney-General Edwin Meese announced that profits from the Iranian arms sales had, in fact, been sent to the Contras, but he implied that it was done without the administration's knowledge. Reagan immediately called a press conference and insisted that he knew nothing of the deal, and put the blame squarely on North and Poindexter for undertaking the operation without approval from the White House.

In March 1987, Reagan spoke to the nation on Iran-Contra and acknowledged responsibility for the affair, but said that he knew nothing of North's plan to use the money to buy arms for the Contras.

Reagan appointed a commission to investigate the entire affair. Headed by retired Senator John Tower, the commission held televised hearings through the summer of 1987. Major General Richard Secord and former National Security Advisor Robert McFarlane insisted that they had continually briefed Reagan about the arms-for-hostages deals with Iran. North and Poindexter testified that they both intentionally withheld from Reagan information about the plan to use the money from the weapons sales to support the Contras, and that they had intentionally misinformed Congress about the plan. North passionately defended his actions before the commission (and on television) as moral, patriotic, and in the national interest.

The reaction from the American public was mixed. People felt sympathy for Reagan's efforts to free the hostages in Lebanon. Most deplored the sale of weapons to Iran, but they were basically apathetic about the use of the money to further the war in Central America. The Tower Commission, without much public support to press the issue and no real mandate to push the investigation all the way to the White House, let the matter pass with only a report that criticized the president as having the ultimate responsibility for the affair and for the wrongdoing of North and his other aides.

In March 1988 North was convicted on three of sixteen felony counts and was given a three-year suspended sentence, two years of probation, and a $150,000 fine. In September 1991, the case was dismissed. Poindexter, at his trial in 1990, admitted that Reagan had ordered all aspects of the operations. Reagan was then called to testify. His responses were convoluted and confusing, and finally he said that he could not remember whether he had authorized the diversion of the cash to the Contras. For Reagan's supporters, his lack of memory was the first sign of the Alzheimer's disease that would finally take his life in 2004; to his critics, it was "plausible deniability."

North emerged from the scandal as an unapologetic spokesman for the Republican Right. His autobiography, *Under Fire: An American Story* (1991), was a bestseller. He ran for the Senate from Virginia in 1994 and lost, but his campaign won him additional notoriety. He hosts *Common Sense*, a radio talk show, and *War Stories with Oliver North* on Fox News.

In the view of his supporters, Ollie North is an American patriot who carried out the Reagan administration's fight against the communist movement in Central America, despite the resistance of Congress. In the view of his critics, he is the man who sold weapons to an outlaw regime to raise money for illegal purposes.

STUDY QUESTIONS

1. How did Reagan explain Iran-Contra? Did he take any responsibility? What is the meaning of "plausible deniability?"
2. How did the actions of Oliver North and the Reagan administration in the Iran-Contra dealings damage U.S. foreign policy? Consider a comparison to actions by the Eisenhower administration in the 1950s.
3. What sort of Europe did the London Declaration envision in the post–cold war era? In what ways is the Declaration optimistic?
4. Discuss Reagan's perception of the Soviet Union. How did that change from earlier foreign policies, particularly that of Henry Kissinger?

FURTHER READINGS

Theodore Draper, *A Very Thin Line: The Iran-Contra Affair* (1991).
Roy Gutman, *Banana Diplomacy* (1988).
Michael Mandelbaum, *Reagan and Gorbachev* (1987).
Ronald Reagan, *An American Life* (1990).
Seth Tillman, *The United States and the Middle East: Interests and Obstacles* (1982).

18 • More Culture Wars

INTRODUCTION

From the late 1970s on into the 1990s, more and more Americans began to push back against what they perceived as the cultural radicalism and permissiveness of the 1960s and 1970s. They worried that the nation had moved too far from its cultural roots that revolved around family and the values of the home and church. It was not that they wanted to restore the past; rather, they feared the impact of a new permissiveness that they believed had invaded society. These people saw a nation wracked with crime, racial conflict, pornography, atheism, and a general slippery slope of immorality.

They were sometimes accused of racism, but it is unfair to tag all cultural traditionalists with that harsh label. They often opposed affirmative action plans, arguing that such initiatives gave African Americans an unfair advantage in a system that should be conducted on a level playing field. In the same vein, they opposed (sometimes violently) bussing as a means of integrating the nation's schools, arguing instead for strong neighborhood schools that parents could control. From the standpoint of African Americans, however, it was not difficult to see these attitudes as indicative of white America trying to maintain a hold on the nation's jobs and institutions.

The cultural traditionalists became ever more vocal in the early 1970s, and then their strategies folded into politics during the Nixon administration. Although Nixon's "silent majority" strategy focused initially on those who supported the president's Vietnam policy, it included numerous outreach efforts seeking to build a new political base of Americans who identified as patriotic, culturally conservative, and (increasingly) "born-again Christians." Their political impact was clear in the next several elections: by the mid-1980s their moralism had become a basic component of a new American conservatism, and politically they settled in as a major voting bloc within the Republican Party, which aggressively courted their support. Thus it would be the Republicans (as it had been the Democrats in the early decades of the century) who carried the banner of cultural reform and moral righteousness into the next century.

DOCUMENT 18.1
Regents of the University of California v. Bakke (1978)

In 1973 and again in 1974 Allan Bakke, a thirty-five-year-old white male, applied for admission to the University of California at Davis Medical School. He was rejected both times. The school had a policy of reserving sixteen places in each year's class of one hundred for what it called "qualified" minorities. This affirmative action program was designed—as the school explained—"to redress longstanding, unfair minority exclusions from the medical profession." Bakke's qualifications (based mostly on his college GPA and MCAT test scores) exceeded those of any of the minority students admitted in the two years in which his applications were rejected. He argued, first in the California courts, then in the Supreme Court, that he was excluded from admission solely on the basis of race.

In the final analysis, four of the Supreme Court justices argued that the university's quota system was based solely on race and thus violated the Civil Rights Act of 1964. Justice Lewis F. Powell, Jr., agreed, casting the deciding vote ordering the medical school to admit Bakke. However, in his opinion, Powell argued that racial quotas as employed at UC Davis also violated the equal protection clause of the Fourteenth Amendment to the Constitution.

The case brought into question all affirmative action policies. Those who supported affirmative action argued that these policies gave minorities opportunities in a system that had historically excluded them. Those in opposition called the programs reverse discrimination.

Below is the case abstract along with a summation of the opinions in the case.

SOURCE: *Regents of the University of California v. Bakke,* 438 U.S. 265 (1978).

Argued October 12, 1977
Decided June 28, 1978

The Medical School of the University of California at Davis had two admissions programs for the entering class of one hundred students—the regular admissions program and the special admissions program. Under the regular procedure, candidates whose overall undergraduate grade point averages fell below 2.5 on a scale of 4.0 were summarily rejected. About one out of six applicants was then given an interview, following which he was rated on a scale of one to one hundred by each of the committee members, his rating being based on the interviewers' summaries, his overall grade point average, his science courses grade point average, his Medical College Admissions Test (MCAT) scores, letters of recommendation, extracurricular activities, and other biographical data, all of which resulted in a total "benchmark score." The full admissions committee then made offers of admission on the basis of their review of the applicant's file and his score, considering and acting upon applications as they were received.

A separate committee, a majority of whom were members of minority groups, operated the special admissions program. The 1973 and 1974 application forms, respectively, asked candidates whether they wished to be considered as "economically and/or educationally disadvantaged" applicants and members of a "minority group" (blacks, Chicanos, Asians, American Indians). If an applicant of a minority group was found to be "disadvantaged," he would be rated in a manner similar to the one employed by the general admissions committee. Special candidates, however, did not have to meet the 2.5 grade point cutoff and were not ranked against candidates in the general admissions process. About one-fifth of the special applicants were invited for interviews in 1973 and 1974, following which they were given benchmark scores, and the top choices were then given to the general admissions committee, which could reject special candidates for failure to meet course requirements or other specific deficiencies. The special committee continued to recommend candidates until sixteen special admission selections had been made.

During a four-year period sixty-three minority students were admitted to Davis under the special program and forty-four under the general program. No disadvantaged whites were admitted under the special program, though many applied. Respondent [Allan Bakke], a white male, applied to Davis in 1973 and 1974, in both years being considered only under the general admissions program. Though he had a 468 out of 500 score in 1973, he was rejected since no general applicants with scores less than 470 were being accepted after respondent's application, which was filed late in the year, had been processed and completed. At that time four special admission slots were still unfilled.

In 1974 respondent applied early, and though he had a total score of 549 out of 600, he was again rejected. In neither year was his name placed on the discretionary waiting list. In both years special applicants were admitted with significantly lower scores than respondent's. After his second rejection, respondent filed this action in state court . . . to compel his admission to Davis, alleging that the special admissions program operated to exclude him on the basis of his race in violation of the Equal Protection Clause of the Fourteenth Amendment, a provision of the California Constitution, and 601 of Title VI of the Civil Rights Act of 1964, which provides . . . that no person shall on the ground of race or color be excluded from participating in any program receiving federal financial assistance. Petitioner [University of California, Davis] cross-claimed for a declaration that its special admissions program was lawful. . . .

MR. JUSTICE POWELL, concluded:

Racial and ethnic classifications of any sort are inherently suspect and call for the most exacting judicial scrutiny. While the goal of achieving a diverse student body is sufficiently compelling to justify consideration of race in admissions decisions under some circumstances, petitioner's special admissions program, which forecloses consideration to persons like respondent, is unnecessary to the achievement of this compelling goal and therefore invalid under the Equal Protection Clause. Since petitioner could not satisfy its burden of proving that respondent would not have been admitted even if there had been no special admissions program, he must be admitted.

MR. JUSTICE BRENNAN, MR. JUSTICE WHITE, MR. JUSTICE MARSHALL, and MR. JUSTICE BLACKMUN concluded:

Racial classifications call for strict judicial scrutiny. Nonetheless, the purpose of overcoming substantial, chronic minority underrepresentation in the medical profession is sufficiently important to justify petitioner's remedial use of race. Thus, the judgment below must be reversed in that it prohibits race from being used as a factor in university admissions.

MR. JUSTICE STEVENS, joined by THE CHIEF JUSTICE, MR. JUSTICE STEWART, and MR. JUSTICE REHNQUIST, being of the view that whether race can ever be a factor in an admissions policy is not an issue here; that Title VI applies; and that respondent was excluded from Davis in violation of Title VI, concurs in the Court's judgment insofar as it affirms the judgment of the court below ordering respondent admitted to Davis. . . .

MR. JUSTICE POWELL announced the judgment of the Court.

This case presents a challenge to the special admissions program of the petitioner, the Medical School of the University of California at Davis, which is designed to assure the admission of a specified number of students from certain minority groups. The Superior Court of California sustained respondent's challenge, holding that petitioner's program violated the California Constitution, Title VI of the Civil Rights Act of 1964 . . . and the Equal Protection Clause of the Fourteenth Amendment. The court enjoined petitioner from considering respondent's race or the race of any other applicant in making admissions decisions. It refused, however, to order respondent's admission to the Medical School, holding that he had not carried his burden of proving that he would have been admitted but for the constitutional and statutory violations. The Supreme Court of California affirmed those portions of the trial court's judgment declaring the special admissions program unlawful and enjoining petitioner from considering the race of any applicant. It modified that portion of the judgment denying respondent's requested injunction and directed the trial court to order his admission.

For the reasons stated in the following opinion, I believe that so much of the judgment of the California court as holds petitioner's special admissions program unlawful and directs that respondent be admitted to the Medical School must be affirmed. For the reasons expressed in a separate opinion, my Brothers THE CHIEF JUSTICE, MR. JUSTICE STEWART, MR. JUSTICE REHNQUIST, and MR. JUSTICE STEVENS concur in this judgment.

I also conclude for the reasons stated in the following opinion that the portion of the court's judgment enjoining petitioner from according any consideration to race in its admissions process must be reversed. For reasons expressed in separate opinions, my Brothers MR. JUSTICE BRENNAN, MR. JUSTICE WHITE, MR. JUSTICE MARSHALL, and MR. JUSTICE BLACKMUN concur in this judgment.

DOCUMENT 18.2
Jerry Falwell, *Listen America* (1980)

Jerry Falwell is one of the most prominent leaders of the evangelical Christian movement, which became a dominant force within the Republican Party in the 1980s. On his nationally televised program, Falwell has attacked all things liberal, including abortion rights and tolerance of homosexuality, while supporting school prayer, school vouchers, and federal money for church-based social services. His agenda and his personal popularity brought thousands of conservative churchgoers into the electoral process—and into the Republican Party. Their numbers remain significant. In 1980, Falwell took aim at the Equal Rights Amendment.

SOURCE: From *Listen America* by Jerry Falwell, copyright © 1980 by Jerry Falwell. Used by permission of Doubleday, a division of Random House, Inc.

I believe that at the foundation of the women's liberation movement there is a minority core of women who were once bored with life, whose real problems are spiritual problems. Many women have never accepted their God-given roles. They live in disobedience to God's laws and have promoted their godless philosophy throughout our society. God Almighty created men and women biologically different and with differing needs and roles. He made men and women to complement each other and to love each other.

Not all the women involved in the feminist movement are radicals. Some are misinformed, and some are lonely women who like being housewives and helpmates and mothers, but whose husbands spend little time at home and who take no interest in their wives and children.

Sometimes the full load of rearing a family becomes a great burden to a woman who is not supported by a man. Women who work should be respected and accorded dignity and equal rewards for equal work. But this is not what the present feminist movement and equal rights movement are all about. The Equal Rights Amendment is a delusion. I believe that women deserve more than equal rights. And, in families and in nations where the Bible is believed, Christian women are honored above men. Only in places where the Bible is believed and practiced do women receive more than equal rights.

Men and women have differing strengths. The Equal Rights Amendment can never do for women what needs to be done for them. Women need to know Jesus Christ as their Lord and Savior and be under His Lordship. They need a man who knows Jesus Christ as his Lord and Savior, and they need to be part of a home where their husband is a godly leader and where there is a Christian family.

The Equal Rights Amendment strikes at the foundation of our entire social structure. If passed, this amendment would accomplish exactly the opposite of its outward claims. By mandating an absolute equality under the law, it will actually take away many of the special rights women now enjoy.

ERA is not merely a political issue, but a moral issue as well. A definite violation of Holy Scripture, ERA defies the mandate that "the husband is the head of the wife, even as Christ is the head of the church" (Ep. 5:23). In Peter 3:7 we read that husbands are to give their wives honor as unto the weaker vessel, that they are both heirs together of the grace of life. Because a woman is weaker does not mean that she is less important.

DOCUMENT 18.3
Kandy Stroud: "Stop Pornographic Rock" (*Newsweek* Op-ed, May 1985); Frank Zappa Responds: "Cultural Terrorism" (ca. 1985)

In the mid-1980s many baby-boomer parents of young children began to listen more critically to the lyrics in popular rock music. Never mind that sixties and seventies rock was loaded with sexual innuendo and double meanings. In the document below, Kandy Stroud, writing in the "My Turn" section of

Newsweek, *makes the point that there is a significant difference between suggestiveness and the explicit sexual references that she cites.*

That same year, members of the Parents Music Resource Center (PMRC) testified before the Senate Commerce, Technology and Transportation Committee. The PMRC recommended that the recording industry voluntarily place warning labels on its packaging. One leader of the PMRC who gave testimony was "Tipper" Gore, the wife of Tennessee Senator Al Gore, a member of the committee. Stroud's "My Turn" article was published along with the committee'a proceedings.

In the second part of this document, rock singer Frank Zappa (of the group The Mothers of Invention) responds to the PMRC's testimony. Zappa also testified before the Commerce Committee, and the document below was posted on his web site following the committee meeting. Also testifying before the committee were Dee Snyder of shock-rock group Twisted Sister, and folk-rocker John Denver.

SOURCE: *Newsweek* (May 6, 1985).

Kandy Stroud, "Stop Pornographic Rock"

My fifteen-year-old daughter unwittingly alerted me to the increasingly explicit nature of rock music. "You've got to hear this, Mom!" she insisted one afternoon, fast-forwarding Prince's "Purple Rain" to the song "Darling Nikki." "But don't listen to the words," she added, an instant tip-off to pay attention. The beat was hard and pulsating, the music burlesque in feeling, as Prince, who has sold more than nine million copies of "Purple Rain," began:

> I knew a girl named Nikki
> I guess you could say she was a sex fiend
> I met her in a hotel lobby
> Masturbating with a magazine

Unabashedly sexual lyrics like these, augmented by orgasmic moans and howls, compose the musical diet millions of children are now being fed at concerts, on albums, on radio and MTV. Rock stations may play Sheena Easton's latest hit, "Sugar Walls," as many as a dozen times a day. "I hate this song," my thirteen-year-old, rock-crazed son muttered on the way from school one day as he inadvertently tuned in Easton's lewd and crude song about genital arousal. My own Mr. Cool was visibly embarrassed. Embarrassed? I almost drove off the road.

I confess to being something of a rock freak. I may be a singer of sacred music, but I've collected rock since its birth in the '50s. I've danced to it, and now I do aerobics to it; I love the beat and the sound. But as both parent and musician I am concerned about the number of hit tunes that can only be called porn rock, and about the tasteless, graphic and gratuitous sexuality saturating the air waves and filtering into our homes. . . .

"Feels so good inside," squeals Madonna on her triple-platinum album, "Like a Virgin." Rock's latest "it" girl hardly touts virginal innocence, as one can gather from her gyrations and undulations on Friday-night video shows.

"Relax when you want to come," the English group Frankie Goes to Hollywood wails on "Relax," now the fourth-best-selling record in British history, a lofty position that being banned by the BBC did much to ensure. On the album "Defenders of Faith," the group Judas Priest sings "Eat Me Alive," which deals with a girl being forced to commit oral sex at gunpoint. In "Ten Seconds to Love," Motley Crue croons about intercourse on an elevator. In concert, W.A.S.P.'s lead singer, Blackie Lawless, has appeared onstage wearing a codpiece with a buzz-saw blade between his thighs. During "The Torture Never Stops," Lawless pretends to pummel a woman dressed in a G-string and black hood, and, as fake blood cascades from the hood, he attacks her with the blade.

Aristotle said music has the power to form character. The Bach B-Minor Mass can be a link with the eternal. But while music can ennoble and inspire, it can also degrade. Some drug programs forbid teenage patients to attend rock concerts or even to sport a T-shirt of rock groups. Some schools where smoking and drinking are prohibited have added rock music to the list of taboos. "At the very least," says Father James Conner, the pastor of Holy Trinity Church in Washington, D.C., "rock is turning sex into something casual. It's as if society is encouraging its youngsters to get sexually involved." . . .

Surprisingly, the majority of parents I've spoken to have expressed partial or total ignorance of the music their children are dancing to, doing homework to, falling asleep to. Most claim they don't listen to rock or can't understand the words if they do. They also admit that they don't want to add another item to the laundry list of things they already monitor—movies, books, magazines, parties, friends, homework.

Dollars: Legislative action may be needed, or better yet, a measure of self-restraint. If distillers can voluntarily keep their products off the public airwaves, then the record industry can also curb porn rock—or, at the very least, make sure that kids under seventeen are not allowed into sexually explicit concerts.

And what about the musicians themselves? If forty-six pop superstars can cooperate to raise millions of dollars for African famine relief with their hit,

"We Are the World," why can't musicians also ensure that America's own youth will be fed a diet of rock music that is not only good to dance to but healthy for their hearts and minds and souls as well?

SOURCE: Frank Zappa, "Zappa's Z-Pack," Intercontinental Absurdities, LTD., otse.com

Frank Zappa Responds: "Cultural Terrorism" (ca. 1985)

These cultural terrorists are attempting to create a hostage situation. . . .

The PMRC's [Parent's Music Resource Center] case is totally without merit, based on a hodge-podge of fundamentalist frogwash and illogical conclusions. Shrieking in terror at the thought of someone hearing references to masturbation on a Prince record, the PMRC's members put on their "guardian of the people" costumes and the media comes running. It is an unfortunate trend of the '80's that the slightest murmur from a special interest group . . . causes a knee-jerk reaction of appeasement from a wide range of industries that ought to know better.

If you are an artist reading this, think for a moment, did anyone ask you if you wanted to have the stigma of "potential filth" plopped onto your next release via this "appeasement sticker?" If you are a songwriter, did anyone ask you if you wanted to spend the rest of your career modifying your lyric content to suit the spiritual needs of an imaginary eleven-year-old?

The answer is, obviously, NO. In all of this, the main concern has been the business agenda of the major labels versus the egos and sexual neuroses of these vigilant ladies.

A record company has the right to conduct its business and to make a profit, but not at the expense of the people who make the product possible, someone still has to write and perform THE MUSIC. . . . The "voluntary sticker" will not appease these creatures. . . . There are no promises or guarantees here, only threats and insinuations from PMRC. . . .

I do not deny anyone the right to their opinions on any matter, but when certain people's opinions have the potential to influence my life, and the lives of my children because of their special access to legislative machinery, I think it raises important questions of law.

Ronald Reagan came to office with the proclaimed intention of getting the federal government off our backs. The secret agenda seems to be not to remove it, but to force certain people to wear it like a lampshade at a [Washington] D.C. Tupperware party. . . .

These creatures can hurt you. Their ignorance is like a virus. Get mad. Fight back. Use the phone. Use the telex. . . . Demand fairness for the record industry's legislation in the Thurmond Committee. Remind them that they have a duty to the people who elected them that takes priority over their domestic relationships.

DOCUMENT 18.4
Dan Quayle Attacks *Murphy Brown* (May 1992)

In the spring of 1992, riots broke out in South Central Los Angeles after four white police officers who had beaten an African American motorist, Rodney King, were acquitted by a mostly white jury. King's beating a year earlier had been videotaped by a witness and then televised. More than fifty people died in the riots, which also caused significant property damage and destruction to part of the city.

Just three weeks after the Los Angeles riots, Vice President Dan Quayle spoke at the Commonwealth Club in San Francisco. The focus of his speech was to try to explain the causes of the riots. What in American society caused such a breakdown in law and order and social structure? The answer he offered was that a large segment of American society (and he made it clear that he was directing his criticisms at the African American community) had lost its moral compass, and that greater attention to basic moral values would go a long way toward solving the nation's social problems.

As the Republicans approached the 1992 election, Dan Quayle's "moral values" merged into "family values" as the answer to many of the nation's ills. Family values were usually defined in terms of the traditional two-parent family, traditional religious convictions, and patriotism. At the Republican Party convention later in the summer of 1992, family values emerged as a major party theme—and then a political issue—along with the clear implication that Democrats lacked traditional family values. Democrats responded, with some effect, that the Republicans' standard for family values left out the vast majority of American society. The Republicans lost the 1992 election, but family values continued to be a primary theme of the Republican appeal through the remainder of the decade.

Dan Quayle's speech remained the classic statement of the issue, and many have continued to sum up the debate with the judgment "Dan Quayle was right." But the substance of the Commonwealth Club speech itself was overshadowed at the time by Quayle's criticism of Murphy Brown, a television character (played by Candice Bergen) who had unapologetically borne a child out of wedlock.

SOURCE: Office of the Vice President, Prepared Remarks by the Vice President, Commonwealth Club of California, San Francisco, CA, May 19, 1992.

Ladies and gentlemen, it's great to be back with you and, as you may know, I've just returned from a weeklong trip to Japan. . . . From the perspective of many Japanese, the ethnic diversity of our culture is a weakness compared to their homogeneous society. I begged to differ with my host. I explained that our diversity is our strength and I explained that the immigrants who come to our shores have made and continue to make vast contributions to our culture and to our economy. It is wrong to imply that the Los Angeles riots were an inevitable outcome of our diversified society. But the question that I tried to answer in Japan is one that needs answering here. What happened? Why? And most importantly, how can we prevent it in the future?

One response has been predictable. Instead of denouncing wrongdoing, some have shown tolerance for rioters. Some have enjoyed saying "I told you so." And some have simply made excuses for what happened. All of this has been accompanied by pleas for more money. I'll readily accept that we need to understand what happened, but I reject the idea that we should tolerate or excuse it.

When I have been asked during these last weeks who caused the riots and the killings in L.A., my answer has been direct and simple. Who is to blame for the riots? The rioters are to blame. Who is to blame for the killings? The killers are to blame. Yes, I can understand how people were shocked and outraged by the verdict in the Rodney King trial. But, my friends, there is simply no excuse for the mayhem that followed. To apologize or in any way to excuse what happened is wrong. It is a betrayal of all those people equally outraged and equally disadvantaged who did not loot, who did not riot, and who were, in many cases, victims of the rioting. No matter how much you may disagree with the verdict, the riots were wrong. If we as a society don't condemn what is wrong, how can we teach our children what is right? But after condemning the riots, we do need to try to understand the underlying situation.

In a nutshell, I believe the lawless social anarchy that we saw is directly related to the breakdown of the family structure, personal responsibility and social order in too many areas of our society. For the poor, the situation is compounded by a welfare ethos that impedes individual efforts to move ahead in society and hampers their ability to take advantage of the opportunities America offers. If we don't succeed in addressing these fundamental problems and in restoring basic values, any attempt to fix what's broken will fail. One reason I believe we won't fail is that we have come so far in the last twenty-five years. There's no question that this country has had a terrible problem with race and racism. The evil of slavery has left a long and ugly legacy.

But we have faced racism squarely and we have made progress in the past quarter of a century. With landmark civil rights bills of the 1960s, we removed legal barriers to allow full participation by blacks in the economic, social and political life of the nation. By any measure, the America of 1992 is more egalitarian, more integrated and offers more opportunities to black Americans and all other minority members than the America of 1964. There is more to be done, but I think that all of us can be proud of our progress. And let's be specific about one aspect of this progress. The country now has a black middle class that barely existed a quarter-century ago. Since 1967, the median income of black two-parent families has risen by 60 percent in real terms. The number of black college graduates has skyrocketed. Black men and women have achieved real political power. Black mayors head forty-eight of our largest cities, including Los Angeles. These are real achievements, but as we all know, there's another side to that bright landscape.

During this period of progress, we have also developed a culture of poverty. Some call it the underclass that is far more violent and harder to escape than it was a generation ago. The poor you always have with you, scripture tells us, and in America we have always had poor people. But in this dynamic, prosperous nation, poverty has traditionally been a stage through which people pass on their way to joining the great middle class. And if one generation didn't get very far up the ladder, their ambitious, better-educated children would. But the underclass seems to be a new phenomenon. It is a group whose members are dependent on welfare for very long stretches and whose young men are often drawn into lives of crime. There is far too little upward mobility, because the underclass is disconnected from the rules of American society. And these problems have, unfortunately, been particularly acute for black Americans.

Let me share with you a few statistics on the difference between black poverty in the 1960s and now. In 1967, 68 percent of black families were headed by married couples. In 1991, only 48 percent of black families were headed by both a husband and a wife. In 1965, the illegitimacy rate among black families was 28 percent. In 1989, 65 percent, two-thirds of all black children were born with never-married mothers. In 1951, 9 percent of black youths between sixteen and nineteen were unemployed. In 1965, it was 23 percent. In 1980, it was 35 percent. By 1989, the number had declined slightly, but it was still 32 percent. The leading cause of death of young black males today is homicide. . . .

I was born in 1947, so I'm considered one of those baby boomers that we keep reading about. But let's look at one unfortunate legacy of the so-called boomer generation. When we were young, it was fashionable to declare war against traditional values. Indulgence and self-gratification seemed to have no consequences. Many of our generation glamorized casual sex and drug use, evaded responsibility and trashed authority. Today, the boomers are middle-aged and middle class. The responsibility of having families has helped many recover traditional values. And, of course, the great majority of those in the middle class survived the turbulent legacy of the '60s and '70s. But many of the poor, with less to fall back on, did not. The inter-generational poverty that troubles us so much today is predominantly a poverty of values.

Our inner cities are filled with children having children, with people who have not been able to take advantage of educational opportunities, with people who are dependent on drugs or the narcotic of welfare. To be sure, many people in the ghetto struggle very hard against these tides and sometimes win. But too many people feel they have no hope and nothing to lose. This poverty is, again, fundamentally a poverty of values. Unless we change the basic rules of society in our inner cities, we cannot expect anything else to change. We will simply get more of what we saw three weeks ago. New thinking, new ideas, new strategies are needed. For the government, transforming underclass culture means that our policies and our programs must create a different incentive system. Our policy must be premised on and must reinforce values such as family, hard work, integrity, personal responsibility. I think we can all agree the government's first obligation is to maintain order. We are a nation of laws, not looting. It has become clear that the riots were fueled by the vicious gangs that terrorize the inner cities. We are committed to breaking those gangs and restoring law and order. . . .

Empowering the poor will strengthen families, and right now the failure of our families is hurting America deeply. When family fails, society fails. The anarchy and lack of structure in our inner cities are a testament to how quickly civilization falls apart when the family foundation crashes. Children need love and discipline; they need mothers and fathers. A welfare check is not a husband; the state is not a father. It is from parents that children learn how to behave in society. It is from parents, above all, that children come to understand values and themselves as men and women, mothers and fathers. And for those who are concerned about children growing up in poverty, we should know this—marriage is probably the best anti-poverty program of all.

Among families headed by married couples today, there is a poverty rate of 5.7 percent. But 33.4 percent of the families headed by a single mother are in poverty. Nature abhors a vacuum. Where there are no mature, responsible men around to teach boys how to be good men, gangs serve in their place. In fact, gangs have become a surrogate family for much of a generation of inner-city boys. . . .

The system perpetuates itself as these young men father children whom they have no intention of caring for, by women whose welfare checks support them. Teenage girls mired in the same hopelessness lack sufficient motive to say no to this trap. Answers to our problems won't be easy, my friends. We can start by dismantling a welfare system that encourages dependency and subsidizes broken families. We can attach conditions such as school attendance or work to welfare. We can limit the time a recipient gets benefits. We can stop penalizing marriage for welfare mothers. We can enforce child-support payments. Ultimately, however, marriage is a moral issue that requires cultural consensus and the use of social sanctions.

Bearing babies irresponsibly is simply wrong. Failing to support children one has fathered is wrong and we must be unequivocal about this. It doesn't help matters when primetime TV has Murphy Brown, a character who supposedly epitomizes today's intelligent, highly paid professional woman, mocking the importance of fathers by bearing a child alone and calling it just another lifestyle choice. I know it's not fashionable to talk about moral values, but we need to do it. Even though our cultural leaders in Hollywood, network TV and the national newspapers routinely jeer at them, I think most of us in this room know that some things are good and other things are wrong. And now, it's time to make the discussion public. It's time to talk again about the family, hard work, integrity and personal responsibility. We cannot be embarrassed out of our belief that two parents married to each other are better, in most cases, for children than one. That honest work is better than handouts or crime, that we are our brother's keepers. That is worth making an effort, even when the rewards aren't immediate. . . .

Though our hearts have been pained by the events in Los Angeles, we should take this tragedy as an opportunity for self-examination and progress. So let the national debate roar on. I, for one, will join it. The president will lead it; the American people will participate in it, and as a result, we will become an even stronger nation. Thank you very much and God bless you.

BIOGRAPHICAL SKETCH
Jerry Falwell

The conservative revolution of the 1980s had many sides and many faces, but it was the evangelical Christians who may have had the greatest impact. That movement brought into the political process—mainly to the benefit of the Republican Party—large numbers of voters who had not been part of the political process on any level before. They changed the nature of the national political landscape. Their numbers were apparent in the 1980 election of Ronald Reagan, and by the time George W. Bush ran for the presidency in 2000, evangelical Christians were a core component of the Republican Party coalition. In 2003, President Bush spoke to a group of evangelicals and let them know their significance. He greeted them with: "You are my base."

The mobilization of this new political force owed a lot to Jerry Falwell, an obscure Baptist minister who turned a thirty-five-member congregation in

Lynchburg, Virginia, into a media empire. By the mid-1970s he was convincing conservative-thinking churchgoers throughout the nation to vote. As he put it, he wanted to "get them saved, baptized, and registered."

Falwell made himself the standard bearer for a number of issues that appealed to his followers, particularly the maintenance of conservative family values, voluntary prayer in the public schools, and opposition to abortion, pornography, homosexuality, and even rock music. Collectively, these issues and values struck a chord among the conservative, white, churchgoing public. Falwell's initial successes were in the South, but his popularity spread across the country.

The evangelicals of today were once called fundamentalists, from the basic belief that the Bible, as Falwell once said, "is the inerrant word of God, and totally accuate in all respects." This was, of course, in direct opposition to those in what Falwell called the "liberal church," who saw the Bible as the central focus of the Judeo-Christian teachings and beliefs, but generally filled with legends, lessons and parables.

Falwell began his modest ministry in the mid-1950s. A half-hour radio broadcast, called *The Old Time Gospel Hour*, grew into a popular Sunday morning television program that went national in 1971, and by mid-decade reached a national audience of millions.

In 1979, Falwell took his first steps into the world of politics by founding the Moral Majority, an organization dedicated to promoting conservative and religious causes, intent on supporting like-minded political candidates. "If a [candidate] stands by this book," Falwell said, speaking of the Bible, "vote for him. If he doesn't, don't." When Ronald Reagan won in 1980, pulling in large numbers of evangelical supporters, Falwell took a great deal of credit.

In 1983, *Hustler* magazine printed a phony interview with Falwell in which he supposedly admitted to having an incestuous relationship with his mother. Falwell sued the magazine and its flamboyant editor, Larry Flynt, for libel and incurred emotional distress. In *Hustler Magazine v. Jerry Falwell*, the Supreme Court ruled in February 1988 that public figures could not recover damages suffered from the publication or broadcast of parodies. In 1996 these events became the basis of a feature film, directed by Oliver Stone, *The People vs. Larry Flynt*, in which Falwell was portrayed in an extremely unflattering light.

In 1989 Falwell announced that he was dissolving the Moral Majority because, he said, its goals had been met. He focused his efforts on Liberty University, a full-fledged educational institution he had founded in Lynchburg with a focus on teaching fundamentalism as interpreted by Falwell, the university chancellor. Through the late 1980s, the school engaged in an ambitious building campaign, but by 1990 the university was still incomplete and some $110 million in debt. Falwell's pleadings to his followers for more money seemed to cause donations to drop off rather than increase, and his financial troubles multiplied.

During the 1990s Falwell devoted a lot of attention to attacking President Bill Clinton. He sold an infomercial video exposing what he called the crimes of the Clinton administration, and he called Clinton an "ungodly liar." In 1996, Falwell was invited to give the benediction at the Republican National Convention, but he later complained that during the 1996 and 2000 presidential campaigns he had been pushed into the background by the Republican Party leaders. He later said that George W. Bush was the closest thing to true Republicanism since Reagan left the White House, a statement that was widely interpreted as a swipe at party leaders, like George H.W. Bush and Bob Dole, who had kept him at arm's length. As the 2004 presidential campaign approached, Falwell promised he would do everything possible to assure the reelection of George W. Bush because, he said, the nation needed "eight years to begin recovering from the radical programs of the Clintons."

Falwell is occasionally back in the news when one of his statements stimulates the wrath of the press and the jokes of late night comedians. In 1999 he charged that Tinky Winky, the purple Teletubby on a popular children's program, carried a subliminal homosexual message for children. That same year he said to fellow ministers that the anti-Christ was a Jewish male living today. Following the September 11 attacks, Falwell insisted that the events had been caused by abortionists, gays, and lesbians, and by groups like the American Civil Liberties Union and People for the American Way—those who had "thrown God out." "I point a finger in their face," he continued, "and say, 'you helped this happen.'"

Falwell continues to preach Sunday services at the Thomas Road Baptist Church in Lynchburg, Virginia, the church where he began his ministry in the mid-1950s.

STUDY QUESTIONS

1. Discuss the *Bakke* decision. How did it change the race laws in the nation?
2. How were family values defined? Who did they include? Who did they exclude?
3. Why did Dan Quayle focus on Murphy Brown? What did she represent in the early 1990s culture wars?
4. Why did the evangelical religious agenda appeal to the Republicans? If it is true that this group of potential voters was up for grabs in the early-to-mid 1970s, why did the Democrats not adopt the issues that were of concern to them?

5. If the movie industry can self-censor its product, why cannot the recording industry? Censorship necessarily dilutes and homogenizes rock music. Discuss.

FURTHER READINGS

Howard Ball, *The Bakke Case: Race, Education and Affirmative Action* (2000).

Peter Blecha, *Taboo Tunes: A History of Banned Bands and Censored Songs* (2004).

Frances Fitzgerald, "A Disciplined, Charging Army," *New Yorker* (May 18, 1981).

19 • Bill Clinton's America and the Impeachment of a President

INTRODUCTION

In March 1991, just after the end of the Gulf War, President George H.W. Bush's approval rating reached an astounding 91 percent. Nearly everyone in the country seemed to think the president was doing a good job.

When World War II ended in 1945, Winston Churchill, England's dynamic wartime prime minister, was summarily voted out of office. It was said at the time that Churchill had won the war, but lost the peace. George H.W. Bush suffered the same problem. As the American economy sagged and the longest economic recession since World War II set in, Bush's poll numbers began to sag proportionately. The explanation from economists was that consumers, who had gone deeply into debt during the go-go eighties, now settled down to pay off their loans, causing consumer spending to drop drastically. Then Bush made a huge political blunder by telling the nation that the recession would be a short one, and that his administration should not step in to deal with the problem. He cited a need to balance the budget, instead of cutting taxes to stimulate the economy or arranging for relief to those hurt by the economic downturn. He seemed insensitive to the hardships of many ordinary Americans. Between October and November 1991, Bush's job performance rating crashed sixteen points to 51 percent. He was vulnerable.

The Democrats turned to a moderate southern governor, Bill Clinton of Arkansas, as their candidate in the 1992 presidential race. Clinton came from working-class origins, attended Georgetown University, and then, in 1968, won a prestigious Rhodes Scholarship to Oxford University in England. That good fortune, along with some dubious maneuvering, enabled Clinton to avoid service in Vietnam—something that he later owned up to with surprising candor in a speech before the 2004 Democratic National Convention. Following his time in England, he attended Yale Law School where he met his future first lady, Hillary Rodham. He served five terms as governor of Arkansas before running for president.

In the summer of 1992, Clinton won his party's nomination and chose Tennessee senator Al Gore as his running mate. As Clinton and Gore pulled their party to the center, the Republicans appeared to be shifting the other way when Bush allowed the Republican convention to be dominated by his party's right wing. Political columnist Pat Buchanan, who had challenged the incumbent President Bush by making a run for the Republican nomination from the right, spoke to the convention (and the nation) in strident terms, proclaiming a religious and cultural war in the coming campaign. The tone of the convention offended many moderates and made Bush appear to be a captive of his party's right wing—which he really was not. Some wondered aloud whether the Republicans had declared war over culture issues simply to distract attention from the sluggish economy.

Bush also had to withstand another attack from the Right when self-made Texas billionaire H. Ross Perot announced that he would run as an independent. The feisty Perot talked of running the nation like a business, balancing the budget, cutting taxes, and taking the government out of the hands of professional politicians. His simple, direct approach to the issues was appealing to many people who distrusted (or did not understand) government, and by May Perot was outpolling both Clinton and Bush. Just before the Republican convention, however, Perot unexpectedly dropped out of the race and, just as surprisingly, threw his support to Clinton.

One of the primary themes of the 1992 race was Clinton's moral character. Early in the campaign a former nightclub singer named Gennifer Flowers told a supermarket tabloid that she and Clinton had been romantically linked for some twelve years. In an interview on the television program *60 Minutes,* Clinton, without mentioning Flowers's name, admitted past failings as a husband and reaffirmed his relationship with his wife. The event seemed to contain the issue, but it would not be the last time that Clinton's indiscretions would threaten to derail his career.

Bush, meanwhile, could not get out from under the issue of a weak economy and the image of being a president who would not or could not seek to solve the problem. He tried to characterize Clinton as an old-style tax-and-spend liberal who would cause runaway deficits, and he accused Clinton of being unpatriotic by avoiding the Vietnam-era draft and visiting the Soviet Union when he was a student in England. Clinton, however, was able to sell his message to the nation on the need for affordable health care and a promise to tax the rich and cut taxes on the middle class. In the general election, Clinton took thirty-two states and 370 electoral votes.

Bush carried only eighteen states and received 168 electoral votes. Perot, who had jumped back into the race, pulled 19 percent of the popular vote but failed to carry a single state. Most analysts concluded that Perot hurt Bush more than Clinton.

Clinton's moderation pulled together much of the old Democratic Party coalition. African Americans voted for Clinton, and he chipped away at the Republican-dominated South. By appealing to industrial workers hard hit by the recession, he took Ohio, Pennsylvania, Michigan, and Illinois—midwestern states that were bastions of social conservatism and had been part of Reagan's electoral base. Clinton also won the youth vote and a majority of women voters.

DOCUMENT 19.1
The Republican "Contract with America" (September 1994)

Below is a synopsis of the Republican Party's book-length Contract with America. *Published in September 1994, just before the midterm elections, it was designed as a sort of promise to the nation that the Republicans would achieve a series of proposed objectives if they gained a majority in Congress. The election did bring in a Republican Congress. It was the first time Republicans had controlled both houses since Eisenhower's generous coattails in 1952.*

The man behind the Contract *was Newt Gingrich, congressman from Georgia, and, after the election, Speaker of the House of Representatives. Gingrich considered himself a disciple of Ronald Reagan and a leader of the Republican Right, locked in mortal combat with the Democrats and the Clinton White House. Within two years the constant head butting between the two political parties had resulted in a stalemate, with Congress and the White House unable to come to any compromise on an operating budget—leading to a short-term shutdown of the federal government.*

SOURCE: Republican National Committee, *Contract With America: The Bold Plan by Representative Newt Gingrich, Representative Dick Armey and the House Republicans to Change the Nation* (New York, 1994).

This year's election offers the chance, after four decades of one-party control, to bring to the House a new majority that will transform the way Congress works. That historic change would be the end of government that is too big, too intrusive, and too easy with the public's money. It can be the beginning of a Congress that respects the values and shares the faith of the American family.

Like Lincoln, our first Republican president, we intend to act "with firmness in the right, as God gives us to see the right." To restore accountability to Congress. To end its cycle of scandal and disgrace. To make us all proud again of the way free people govern themselves.

On the first day of the 104th Congress, the new Republican majority will immediately pass the following major reforms, aimed at restoring the faith and trust of the American people in their government:

First: require all laws that apply to the rest of the country also apply equally to the Congress;

Second: select a major, independent auditing firm to conduct a comprehensive audit of Congress for waste, fraud or abuse;

Third: cut the number of House committees, and cut committee staff by one-third;

Fourth: limit the terms of all committee chairs;

Fifth: ban the casting of proxy votes in committee;

Sixth: require committee meetings to be open to the public;

Seventh: require a three-fifths majority vote to pass a tax increase;

Eighth: guarantee an honest accounting of our Federal Budget by implementing zero base-line budgeting.

Thereafter, within the first one hundred days of the 104th Congress, we shall bring to the House floor the following bills, each to be given full and open debate, each to be given a clear and fair vote and each to be immediately available this day for public inspection and scrutiny.

1. The Fiscal Responsibility Act: A balanced budget/tax limitation amendment and a legislative line-item veto to restore fiscal responsibility to an out-of-control Congress, requiring them to live under the same budget constraints as families and businesses.

2. The Taking Back Our Streets Act: An anti-crime package including stronger truth-in-sentencing, "good faith" exclusionary rule exemptions, effective death penalty provisions, and cuts in social spending from this summer's "crime" bill to fund prison construction and additional law enforcement to keep people secure in their neighborhoods and kids safe in their schools.

3. The Personal Responsibility Act: Discourage illegitimacy and teen pregnancy by prohibiting welfare to minor mothers and denying increased AFDC [Aid to families with Dependent Children] for additional children while on welfare, cut spending for welfare programs, and enact a tough two-years-and-out provision with work requirements to promote individual responsibility.

4. The Family Reinforcement Act: Child support enforcement, tax incentives for adoption, strengthening rights of parents in their children's education, stronger child pornography laws, and an elderly dependent care tax credit to reinforce the central role of families in American society.

5. The American Dream Restoration Act: A $500 per child tax credit, begin repeal of the marriage tax penalty, and creation of American Dream Savings Accounts to provide middle class tax relief.

6. The National Security Restoration Act: No U.S. troops under U.N. command and restoration of the essential parts of our national security funding to strengthen our national defense and maintain our credibility around the world.

7. The Senior Citizens Fairness Act: Raise the Social Security earnings limit which currently forces seniors out of the work force, repeal the 1993 tax hikes on Social Security benefits and provide tax incentives for private long-term care insurance to let older Americans keep more of what they have earned over the years.

8. The Job Creation and Wage Enhancement Act: Small business incentives, capital gains cut and indexation, neutral cost recovery, risk assessment/cost-benefit analysis, strengthening the Regulatory Flexibility Act and unfunded mandate reform to create jobs and raise worker wages.

9. The Common Sense Legal Reform Act: "Loser pays" laws, reasonable limits on punitive damages and reform of product liability laws to stem the endless tide of litigation.

10. The Citizen Legislature Act: A first-ever vote on term limits to replace career politicians with citizen legislators.

Further, we will instruct the House Budget Committee to report to the floor and we will work to enact additional budget savings, beyond the budget cuts specifically included in the legislation described above, to ensure that the federal budget deficit will be less than it would have been without the enactment of these bills.

Respecting the judgment of our fellow citizens as we seek their mandate for reform, we hereby pledge our names to this Contract with America.

DOCUMENT 19.2
"The New Covenant." President Bill Clinton's State of the Union Address (January 1995)

President Bill Clinton's "New Covenant," which he explains below in his 1995 State of the Union message, was clearly intended to be a direct response (and a Democratic alternative) to the Republican Party's "Contract with America." In fact, Clinton addresses directly several of the Contract's primary points. Following Clinton's speech, the Republican reformers lost their momentum and produced very little.

The gridlock between the Republican-dominated Congress and the president continued on, and in fact became more debilitating as Clinton began his second term. Not surprisingly, the result was that very little was accomplished. There was one bright spot. In May 1997, the White House and Congress reached an agreement to balance the budget, and in the 1998 fiscal year the federal government produced its first balanced budget in thirty years.

SOURCE: *Public Papers of the Presidents: William J. Clinton, 1995,* 75–86.

Over two hundred years ago, our founders changed the entire course of human history by joining together to create a new country based on a single powerful idea: "We hold these truths to be self-evident, that all men are created equal, endowed by their Creator with certain inalienable rights, and among these are life, liberty and the pursuit of happiness."

It has fallen to every generation since then to preserve that idea—the American idea—and to deepen and expand its meaning to new and different times: To Lincoln and his Congress, to preserve the Union and to end slavery. To Theodore Roosevelt and Woodrow Wilson, to restrain the abuses and excesses of the Industrial Revolution, and to assert our leadership in the world. To Franklin Roosevelt, to fight the failure and pain of the Great Depression, and to win our country's great struggle against fascism. And to all our presidents since, to fight the Cold War. . . .

Record numbers of Americans are succeeding in the new global economy. We are at peace and we are a force for peace and freedom throughout the world. We have created almost six million new jobs since I became president, and we have the lowest combined rate of unemployment and inflation in twenty-five years. Our businesses are more productive, and we have worked to bring the deficit down, to expand trade, to put more police on our streets, to give our citizens more of the tools they need to get an education and to rebuild their own communities.

But the rising tide is not lifting all boats. While our nation is enjoying peace and prosperity, too many of our people are still working harder and harder for less and less. While our businesses are restructuring and growing more productive and competitive, too many of our people still can't be sure of having a job next year or even next month. And far more than our material riches are threatened, things far more precious too us—our children, our families, our values. . . .

More than sixty years ago, at the dawn of another new era, President Roosevelt told our nation: "New conditions impose new requirements on government and those who conduct government." And from that simple proposition, he shaped the New Deal, which helped to restore our nation to prosperity and define the relationship between our people and their government for half a century.

That approach worked in its time. But today, we face a very different time and very different conditions. We are moving from an Industrial Age built on gears and sweat to an Information Age, demanding skills and learning and flexibility. Our government, once a champion of national purpose, is now seen by many as simply a captive of narrow interests, putting more burdens on our citizens rather than equipping them to get ahead. The values that used to hold us all together seem to be coming apart.

So tonight, we must forge a new social compact to meet the challenges of this time. As we enter a new era, we need a new set of understandings, not just with government, but even more important, with one another as Americans.

That's what I want to talk with you about tonight. I call it the New Covenant. But it's grounded in a very, very old idea—that all Americans have not just a right, but a solid responsibility to rise as far as their God-given talents and determination can take them; and to give something back to their communities and their country in return. Opportunity and responsibility: They go hand in hand. We can't have one without the other. And our national community can't hold together without both.

Our New Covenant is a new set of understandings for how we can equip our people to meet the challenges of a new economy, how we can change the way our government works to fit a different time, and, above all, how we can repair the damaged bonds in our society and come together behind our common purpose. We must have dramatic change in our economy, our government and ourselves. . . .

I hope very much that as we debate these specific and exciting matters, we can go beyond the sterile discussion between the illusion that there is somehow a program for every problem on the one hand, and the other illusion that the government is a source of every problem we have. Our job is to get rid of yesterday's government so that our own people can meet today's and tomorrow's needs. And we ought to do it together.

You know, for years before I became president, I heard others say they would cut government and how bad it was. But not much happened. We actually did it. We cut over a quarter of a trillion dollars in spending, more than three hundred domestic programs, more than 100,000 positions from the federal bureaucracy in the last two years alone. Based on decisions already made, we will have cut a total of more than a quarter of a million positions from the federal government, making it the smallest it has been since John Kennedy was president. . . .

Under the leadership of Vice President Gore, our initiatives have already saved taxpayers $63 billion. The age of the $500 hammer and the ashtray you can break on David Letterman is gone. Deadwood programs like mohair subsidies are gone. We've streamlined the Agriculture Department by reducing it by more than 1,200 offices. We've slashed the small business loan form from an inch thick to a single page. We've thrown away the government's 10,000-page personnel manual. And the government is working better in important ways: FEMA, the Federal Emergency Management Agency, has gone from being a disaster to helping people in disasters. . . .

Previous government programs gather dust. The reinventing government report is getting results. And we're not through. There's going to be a second round of reinventing government. We propose to cut $130 billion in spending by shrinking departments, extending our freeze on domestic spending, cutting sixty public housing programs down to three, getting rid of over one hundred programs we do not need, like the Interstate Commerce Commission and the Helium Reserve Program. And we're working on getting rid of unnecessary regulations and making them more sensible. The programs and regulations that have outlived their usefulness should go. We have to cut yesterday's government to help solve tomorrow's problems. . . .

Now, my budget cuts a lot. But it protects education, veterans, Social Security, and Medicare, and I hope you will do the same thing. You should, and I hope you will.

And when we give more flexibility to the states, let us remember that there are certain fundamental national needs that should be addressed in every state, north and south, east and west—immunization against childhood disease, school lunches in all our schools, Head Start, medical care and nutrition for pregnant women and infants. All these things are in the national interest.

I applaud your desire to get rid of costly and unnecessary regulations. But when we deregulate, let's remember what national action in the national interest has given us: safer foods for our families, safer toys for our children, safer nursing homes for our parents, safer cars and highways, and safer workplaces, clean air and cleaner water. Do we need common sense and fairness in our regulations? You bet we do. But we can have common sense and still provide for safe drinking water. We can have fairness and still clean up toxic dumps, and we ought to do it.

Should we cut the deficit more? Well, of course, we should. But we can bring it down in a way that still protects our economic recovery and does not unduly punish people who should not be punished, but instead should be helped. . . .

Nothing has done more to undermine our sense of common responsibility than our failed welfare system. This is one of the problems we have to face here in Washington in our New Covenant. It rewards welfare over work. It undermines family values. It lets millions of parents get away without paying their child support. It keeps a minority, but a significant minority of the people on welfare trapped on it for a very long time. . . .

Last year I introduced the most sweeping welfare reform plan ever presented by an administration. We have to make welfare what it was meant to be—a second chance, not a way of life. We have to help those on welfare move to work as quickly as possible, to provide child care and teach them skills if that's what they need for up to two years. And after that, there ought to be a simple hard rule: anyone who can work must go to work. If a parent isn't paying child support, they should be forced to pay. We should suspend drivers' licenses, track them across state lines, make them work off what they owe. That is what we should do. Governments do not raise children, people do. And the parents must take responsibility for the children they bring into this world.

I want to work with you, with all of you, to pass welfare reform. But our goal must be to liberate people and lift them up, from dependence to independence, from welfare to work, from mere childbearing to responsible parenting. Our goal should not be to punish them because they happen to be poor. . . .

I know the members of this Congress are concerned about crime, as are all the citizens of our country. And I remind you that last year, we passed a very tough crime bill—longer sentences, three strikes and you're out, almost sixty new capital punishment offenses, more prisons, more prevention, 100,000 more police. And we paid for it all by reducing the size of the federal bureaucracy and giving the money back to local communities to lower the crime rate. . . .

America is once again the world's strongest economic power, almost six million new jobs in the last two years, exports [are] booming, inflation [is] down, high-wage jobs are coming back. A record number of American entrepreneurs are living the American Dream. If we want it to stay that way, those who work and lift our nation must have more of its benefits.

Today, too many of those people are being left out. They're working harder for less. They have less security, less income, less certainty that they can even afford a vacation, much less college for their kids or retirement for themselves. We cannot let this continue.

If we don't act, our economy will probably keep doing what it's been doing since about 1978, when the income growth began to go to those at the very top of our economic scale and the people in the vast middle got very little growth, and people who worked like crazy but were on the bottom then fell even further and further behind in the years afterward—no matter how hard they worked.

We've got to have a government that can be a real partner in making this new economy work for all of our people; a government that helps each and every one of us to get an education, and to have the opportunity to renew our skills. That's why we worked so hard to increase educational opportunities in the last two years—from Head Start to public schools, to apprenticeships for young people who don't go to college, to making college loans more available and more affordable. That's the first thing we have to do. We've got to do something to empower people to improve their skills.

The second thing we ought to do is to help people raise their incomes immediately by lowering their taxes. We took the first step in 1993 with a working family tax cut for fifteen million families with incomes under $27,000; a tax cut that this year will average about $1,000 a family. And we also gave tax reductions to most small and new businesses.

Before we could do more than that, we first had to bring down the deficit we inherited, and we had to get economic growth up. Now we've done both. And now we can cut taxes in a more comprehensive way. But tax cuts should reinforce and promote our first obligation—to empower our citizens through education and training to make the most of their own lives.

The spotlight should shine on those who make the right choices for themselves, their families and their communities. I have proposed the Middle Class Bill of Rights, which should properly be called the Bill of Rights and Responsibilities because its provisions only benefit those who are working to educate and raise their children and to educate themselves. It will, therefore, give needed tax relief and raise incomes in both the short run and the long run in a way that benefits all of us.

There are four provisions:

First, a tax deduction for all education and training after high school. If you think about it, we permit businesses to deduct their investment, we permit individuals to deduct interest on their home mortgages, but today an education is even more important to the economic well-being of our whole country than even those things are. We should do everything we can to encourage it. And I hope you will support it.

Second, we ought to cut taxes, $500 for families with children under thirteen.

Third, we ought to foster more savings and personal responsibility by permitting people to establish an Individual Retirement Account and withdraw from it tax free for the cost of education, health care, first-time home-buying or the care of a parent.

And fourth, we should pass a G.I. Bill for America's workers. We propose to collapse nearly seventy federal programs and not give the money to the states, but give the money directly to the American people; offer vouchers to them so that they, if they're laid off or if they're working for a very low wage, can get a voucher worth $2,600 a year for up to two years to go to their local community colleges or wherever else they want to get the skills they need to improve their lives. Let's empower people in this way. Move it from the government directly to the workers of America.

Now, any one of us can call for a tax cut, but I won't accept one that explodes the deficit or puts our recovery at risk. We ought to pay for our tax cuts fully and honestly.

Just two years ago, it was an open question whether we would find the strength to cut the deficit. Thanks to the courage of the people who were here then, many of whom didn't return, we did cut the deficit. We began to do what others said could not be done. We cut the deficit by over $600 billion, about $10,000 for every family in this country. It's coming down three years in a row for the first time since Mr. Truman was president, and I don't think anybody in America wants us to let it explode again. . . .

From the day I took the oath of office, I pledged that our nation would maintain the best-equipped, best-trained and best-prepared military on Earth. We have, and they are. They have managed the dramatic downsizing of our forces after the Cold War with remarkable skill and spirit. But to make sure our military is ready for action, and to provide the pay and the quality of life the military and their families deserve, I'm asking the Congress to add $25 billion in defense spending over the next six years. . . .

Well, my fellow Americans, that's my agenda for America's future: Expanding opportunity, not bureaucracy; enhancing security at home and abroad; empowering our people to make the most of their own lives. It's ambitious and achievable, but it's not enough. We even need more than new ideas for changing the world or equipping Americans to compete in the new economy; more than a government that's smaller, smarter and wiser; more than all the changes we can make in government and in the private sector from the outside in. . . .

I believe every person in this country still believes that we are created equal, and given by our Creator, the right to life, liberty and the pursuit of happiness. This is a very, very great country. And our best days are still to come.

Thank you, and God bless you all.

DOCUMENT 19.3
Scandal Engulfs President Bill Clinton (1998)

In 1995, Independent Counsel Kenneth Starr was appointed to investigate possible illegal activities by Bill and Hillary Clinton in an obscure Arkansas land deal some twenty years before, known as Whitewater. By 1998, Starr had uncovered nothing on the Clintons and was being criticized by Democrats for harassing the president and wasting public funds. In January 1998, a story broke in the press that Clinton had been sexually involved for some eighteen months with a young White House intern named Monica Lewinsky. Starr im-

mediately changed his focus, and on January 27 he convened a grand jury to investigate the Clinton-Lewinsky affair.

A week before the grand jury convened, Clinton went on Newshour with Jim Lehrer *and insisted that he did not have an improper relationship with Lewinsky. Clinton had also been accused in the press of telling Lewinsky to lie before a grand jury—or of asking his friend Vernon Jordan to convince Lewinsky to lie. He denied both charges. Following several other public denials that week, Clinton refused to answer questions or discuss the matter further.*

Despite all the mudslinging, the economy remained strong and President Clinton's approval ratings remained high. The same polls showed that Starr and his work were unpopular with a majority of Americans.

On July 17, Starr subpoenaed the president to testify before the grand jury. Clinton agreed to testify from the White House and the subpoena was withdrawn. On August 6, Lewinsky testified, admitting in excruciating detail her relationship with the president. Clinton then testified on August 17. Later that evening he spoke to the American people and admitted to having had an improper relationship with Lewinsky. The speech hurt Clinton badly because it was apparent that the president had deceived the nation for over seven months. Starr's report, delivered on September 7, showed that Clinton may have committed perjury, obstructed justice, tampered with witnesses, and abused the power of the presidency. The charges immediately led to an impeachment inquiry.

Clinton was always concerned about his legacy as president—what the nation and the world would think about him after he left office. It would be Clinton's legacy that he was an effective president who helped facilitate a strong economy in a time of general peace. However, he will also be remembered as a man who degraded the office.

Clinton later wrote in his autobiography that the only reason he became involved with Lewinsky was "because I could." For most Americans that was a decidedly weak explanation.

SOURCE: pbs.org/newshour.

Clinton Interview on *Newshour with Jim Lehrer* (January 21, 1998)

Jim Lehrer: Mr. President, welcome.
President Clinton: Thank you, Jim.
Lehrer: The news of this day is that Kenneth Starr, the independent counsel, is investigating allegations that you suborned perjury by encouraging a

twenty-four-year-old woman, a former White House intern, to lie under oath in a civil deposition about her having had an affair with you. Mr. President, is that true?

Clinton: That is not true. That is not true. I did not ask anyone to tell anything other than the truth. There is no improper relationship. And I intend to cooperate with this inquiry. But that is not true.

Lehrer: No improper relationship. Define what you mean by that.

Clinton: Well, I think you know what it means. It means that there is not a sexual relationship, an improper sexual relationship, or any other kind of improper relationship.

Lehrer: You had no sexual relationship with this young woman?

Clinton: There is not a sexual relationship. That is accurate.

We are doing our best to cooperate here, but we don't know much yet. And that's all I can say now.

What I'm trying to do is to contain my natural impulses and get back to work. I think it's important that we cooperate. I will cooperate. But I want to focus on the work at hand.

Lehrer: Just for the record, to make sure I understand what you're answer means, so there's no ambiguity about it. . . . You had no conversations with this young woman, Monica Lewinsky, about her testimony or possible testimony before in giving a deposition?

Clinton: I did not urge—I did not urge anyone to say anything that was untrue. I did not urge anyone to say anything that was untrue. That's my statement to you.

Lehrer: Did you talk to her?

Clinton: And beyond that . . . I think it's very important that we let the investigation take its course. But I want you to know that that is my clear position. I didn't ask anyone to go in there and say something that's not true.

Lehrer: What about your having had—another one of the allegations is that you may have asked, or the allegation that's being investigated is, that you asked your friend Vernon Jordan . . .

Clinton: To do that?

Lehrer: To do that.

Clinton: I absolutely did not do that. I can tell you I did not do that. I did not do that. He is in no ways involved in trying to get anybody to say anything that's not true at my request.

I didn't do that.

Now, I don't know what else to tell you. I don't even know—all I know what is what I have read here. But I'm going to cooperate. I didn't ask anybody not to tell the truth. There is no improper relationship. The allegations I have read are not true. I do not know what the basis of them is other than just what you know. We'll just have to wait and see. And I will be vigorous about it. But I have got to get back to the work of the country. . . .

SOURCE: cnn.com/ALLPOLITICS/1998/08/17.

President Bill Clinton's Speech to the Nation (August 17, 1998)

Good evening.

This afternoon in this room, from this chair, I testified before the Office of Independent Counsel and the grand jury.

I answered their questions truthfully, including questions about my private life, questions no American citizen would ever want to answer.

Still, I must take complete responsibility for all my actions, both public and private. And that is why I am speaking to you tonight.

As you know, in a deposition in January, I was asked questions about my relationship with Monica Lewinsky. While my answers were legally accurate, I did not volunteer information.

Indeed, I did have a relationship with Ms. Lewinsky that was not appropriate. In fact, it was wrong. It constituted a critical lapse in judgment and a personal failure on my part for which I am solely and completely responsible.

But I told the grand jury today and I say to you now that at no time did I ask anyone to lie, to hide or destroy evidence or to take any other unlawful action.

I know that my public comments and my silence about this matter gave a false impression. I misled people, including even my wife. I deeply regret that.

I can only tell you I was motivated by many factors. First, by a desire to protect myself from the embarrassment of my own conduct.

I was also very concerned about protecting my family. The fact that these questions were being asked in a politically inspired lawsuit, which has since been dismissed, was a consideration, too. . . .

The independent counsel investigation moved on to my staff and friends, then into my private life. And now the investigation itself is under investigation.

This has gone on too long, cost too much and hurt too many innocent people.

Now, this matter is between me, the two people I love most—my wife and our daughter—and our God. I must put it right, and I am prepared to do whatever it takes to do so.

Nothing is more important to me personally. But it is private, and I intend to reclaim my family life for my family. It's nobody's business but ours.

Even presidents have private lives. It is time to stop the pursuit of personal destruction and the prying into private lives and get on with our national life.

Our country has been distracted by this matter for too long, and I take my responsibility for my part in all of this. That is all I can do. . . .

Thank you for watching. And good night.

DOCUMENT 19.4
Articles of Impeachment (December 16, 1998)

In December 1998 the House Judiciary Committee sent four articles of impeachment to the full House. The House adopted two of the four—one count of perjury and one count of obstruction of justice.

The final vote in the Senate was anticlimactic. With a two-thirds vote necessary to find the president guilty and remove him from office, the Republicans were unable to muster even a majority, with forty-five in favor and fifty-five opposed. The president was acquitted of all charges.

Clinton survived the event, and the American people seemed to want to forgive him for his personal failings, but the affair damaged his presidency badly.

SOURCE: House of Representatives, "Impeachment of William Jefferson Clinton, President of the United States," 105 Cong., 2nd sess. (Dec. 16, 1998), Rept. 105.

Resolution Impeaching William Jefferson Clinton, President of the United States, for High Crimes and Misdemeanors

Resolved, That William Jefferson Clinton, President of the United States, is impeached for high crimes and misdemeanors and that the following articles of impeachment be exhibited to the United States Senate:

Articles of impeachment exhibited by the House of Representatives of the United States of America in the name of itself and of the people of the United States of America, against William Jefferson Clinton, President of the United States of America, in maintenance and support of its impeachment against him for high crimes and misdemeanors.

Article I

In his conduct while President of the United States, William Jefferson Clinton, in violation of his constitutional oath faithfully to execute the office of President of the United States and, to the best of his ability, preserve, protect and defend the Constitution of the United States, and in violation of his constitutional duty to take care that the laws be faithfully executed, has willfully corrupted and manipulated the judicial process of the United States for his personal gain and exoneration, impeding the administration of justice, in that:

On August 17, 1998, William Jefferson Clinton swore to tell the truth, the whole truth and nothing but the truth before a Federal grand jury of the United States. Contrary to that oath, William Jefferson Clinton willfully provided perjurious, false and misleading testimony to the grand jury concerning one or more of the following:

(1) The nature and details of his relationship with a subordinate Government employee;
(2) Prior perjurious, false and misleading testimony he gave in a Federal civil rights action brought against him;
(3) Prior false and misleading statements he allowed his attorney to make to a Federal judge in that civil rights action; and
(4) His corrupt efforts to influence the testimony of witnesses and to impede the discovery of evidence in that civil rights action.

In doing this, William Jefferson Clinton has undermined the integrity of his office, has brought disrepute on the Presidency, has betrayed his trust as President and has acted in a manner subversive of the rule of law and justice, to the manifest injury of the people of the United States.

Wherefore, William Jefferson Clinton, by such conduct, warrants impeachment and trial, and removal from office and disqualification to hold and enjoy any office of honor, trust or profit under the United States. . . .

Article III

In his conduct while President of the United States, William Jefferson Clinton, in violation of his constitutional oath faithfully to execute the office of President of the United States and, to the best of his ability, preserve, protect and defend the Constitution of the United States, and in violation of his constitutional duty to take care that the laws be faithfully executed, has prevented, obstructed and impeded the administration of justice, and has to that end engaged personally, and through his subordinates and agents, in a course of conduct or scheme designed to delay, impede, cover up and conceal the existence of evidence and testimony related to a Federal civil rights action brought against him in a duly instituted judicial proceeding.

The means used to implement this course of conduct or scheme included one or more of the following acts:

(1) On or about December 17, 1997, William Jefferson Clinton corruptly encouraged a witness in a Federal civil rights action brought against him to execute a sworn affidavit in that proceeding that he knew to be perjurious, false and misleading.

(2) On or about December 17, 1997, William Jefferson Clinton corruptly encouraged a witness in a Federal civil rights action brought against him to give perjurious, false and misleading testimony if and when called to testify personally in that proceeding.

(3) On or about December 28, 1997, William Jefferson Clinton corruptly engaged in, encouraged or supported a scheme to conceal evidence that had been subpoenaed in a Federal civil rights action brought against him.

(4) Beginning on or about December 7, 1997, and continuing through and including January 14, 1998, William Jefferson Clinton intensified and succeeded in an effort to secure job assistance to a witness in a Federal civil rights action brought against him in order to corruptly prevent the truthful testimony of that witness in that proceeding at a time when the truthful testimony of that witness would have been harmful to him.

(5) On January 17, 1998, at his deposition in a Federal civil rights action brought against him, William Jefferson Clinton corruptly allowed his attorney to make false and misleading statements to a Federal judge characterizing an affidavit, in order to prevent questioning deemed relevant by the judge. Such false and misleading statements were subsequently acknowledged by his attorney in a communication to that judge.

(6) On or about January 18 and January 20–21, 1998, William Jefferson Clinton related a false and misleading account of events relevant to a Federal civil rights action brought against him to a potential witness in that proceeding, in order to corruptly influence the testimony of that witness.

(7) On or about January 21, 23 and 26, 1998, William Jefferson Clinton made false and misleading statements to potential witnesses in a Federal grand jury proceeding in order to corruptly influence the testimony of those witnesses. The false and misleading statements made by William Jefferson Clinton were repeated by the witnesses to the grand jury, causing the grand jury to receive false and misleading information.

In all of this, William Jefferson Clinton has undermined the integrity of his office, has brought disrepute on the Presidency, has betrayed his trust as President and has acted in a manner subversive of the rule of law and justice, to the manifest injury of the people of the United States.

Wherefore, William Jefferson Clinton, by such conduct, warrants impeachment and trial, and removal from office and disqualification to hold and enjoy any office of honor, trust or profit under the United States.

BIOGRAPHICAL SKETCH
Madeleine Albright

In late 1996 President Bill Clinton nominated Madeleine Albright to become secretary of state. She was unanimously confirmed by the Senate, and took the oath of office in January 1997. She was the first woman to hold that position, and as such was the highest ranking woman (either elected or appointed to office) in American history until Condoleezza Rice became President George W. Bush's secretary of state in 2005.

Madeleine Albright was born Maria Jana Korbelova in Prague, Czechoslovakia, in 1937. Her father was a high-ranking diplomat. When the Nazis rolled into Czechoslovakia, the Korbel family fled to London. They returned home after the war, but when the communists seized power in Czechoslovakia, the family again fled, this time to the United States. Her father took a teaching post at the University of Denver and established the university's School of International Studies.

Madeleine Korbel received a scholarship to Wellesley College in Massachusetts and later studied at the School of Advanced International Studies at Johns Hopkins University. She continued her education at Columbia University where she received a Master's degree and a PhD in international relations and went on to teach at Georgetown University. She also served as president of the Center for National Policy and was a legislative assistant to Senator Edmund Muskie.

In 1993, Madeleine Albright was named U.S. ambassador to the United Nations. It was on Albright's watch that the situation in the Balkans heated up. The breakup of the Yugoslav Federation had sparked brutal warfare between Serbs, Croatians, and Muslims in the multiethnic republic of Bosnia. In December 1995, a ceasefire was brokered, but the area exploded again when Kosovo, a province with about 1.8 million ethnic Albanian Muslims within the borders of Serbia, attempted to create an autonomous government. The Serbs, under the leadership of Slobodan Milosevic, who vowed that Kosovo would always remain part of Serbia, retaliated with a brutal attack against the

Kosovars. The Clinton administration, along with the European NATO allies, demanded that Milosevic pull back and end the attacks. When he refused, NATO, under the command of U.S. Army general Wesley Clark, began an aerial bombing campaign against the Serb government in March 1999. Milosevic responded by escalating his drive to "ethnically cleanse" Kosovo by expelling the Muslim population.

Within a few weeks, Milosevic's ethnic cleansing campaign forced some 800,000 Kosovars over the borders and into surrounding countries. An additional 600,000 were forced from their homes, but continued to hide out inside Kosovo. Thousands of Kosovars were captured and murdered by the Serbs, and another 100,000 are still missing and presumed dead. As the NATO attacks increased, the Serbian infrastructure nearly collapsed, but the ethnic cleansing continued.

Under pressure from Republicans in Congress, Clinton and Albright considered the idea of sending in troops to complete the job that the air war, it seemed, could not. But the war was becoming increasingly unpopular with the American public. Finally, after seventy-eight days of bombing, Milosevic signed an agreement. NATO sent in 7,500 U.S. soldiers, deployed as peacekeepers, and the Serbian army withdrew from Kosovo. It was not in the plan, however, that Kosovo would formally become independent.

For Clinton and Albright, the Kosovo intervention was a success, if only as a humanitarian venture. But the cost was high, and the war itself was not popular at home.

STUDY QUESTIONS

1. Compare the "Contract with America" with Bill Clinton's "New Covenant." How are they different? How are they the same?
2. Polls showed that Bill Clinton's "apology" to the nation did not sit well with the American people. Why?
3. Bill Clinton spent much of his second term obsessed with his "legacy." How do you think Bill Clinton will be remembered? Will history focus on eight years of peace and prosperity, or will his personal failings overshadow his accomplishments in the long run?

FURTHER READINGS

Robert Busby, *Defending the American Presidency: Clinton and the Lewinsky Scandal* (2001).
Bill Clinton, *My Life* (2004).
Hillary Clinton, *Living History* (2001).
Kosovo Report: Conflict, International Response, Lessons Learned (2000).

20 • The Election of George W. Bush, Terrorism, and the Crisis in the Gulf

INTRODUCTION

As the 2000 election approached, Vice President Al Gore, the Democratic Party candidate, had a small (and shrinking) lead over the Republican nominee, Texas governor George W. Bush. Those who bothered to go to the polls on election day produced an almost unimaginably close race. Gore won the popular vote: 50.99 million to Bush's 50.45 million. Gore was also ahead in the Electoral College, not counting Florida, by 266 to 249; he needed only four votes to give him a majority of the electoral votes, while Bush needed eleven. So it was Florida that would decide.

But Florida refused to cooperate. After several embarrassing flip-flops, the television networks finally classified Florida as "too close to call." Immediately, accusations began to fly. Civil rights leaders charged that large groups of black voters had been systematically kept from voting in several Florida counties. The state's antiquated voting machines made things worse when it became apparent that large numbers of voters in Palm Beach County had been confused by the "butterfly" format of the ballot. Professional "counters" were brought in to determine the validity of certain ballots in which the chad (the bit of cardboard punched from a hole on the ballot) was not punched all the way through. As Gore fell behind in the balloting, he called for a recount in those counties where there had been irregularities. The Republicans argued that there should be no recount. Florida governor Jeb Bush, the Republican candidate's brother, called a halt to the recount. The Florida Supreme Court, in a unanimous decision, ruled that the recount should continue.

On December 12, 2000, the U.S. Supreme Court, in a five-to-four decision, overturned the unanimous decision of the Florida Supreme Court and stopped the ballot count, arguing that there was not enough time to complete a recount. At that point in the counting, George Bush had a 537-vote lead. The Supreme Court awarded Florida's twenty-five electoral votes to Bush. In a strongly worded dissenting opinion, Justice Stephen Breyer wrote that the Court's decision "runs the risk of undermining the public's confidence in the Court itself." It was the closest election in U.S. history, and many Americans, when it was over, wondered whether we would ever know what the vote count really was. Some also speculated about the "spoiler" role of the two main third-party candidates, Ralph Nader on the Left, who polled 2.89 million votes for the Green Party, and Pat Buchanan on the Right.

Ten months later, on the morning of September 11, 2001, at 8:45 eastern time, the United States was irrevocably changed (and much of the world was forced to change with it) when a passenger jet struck the North Tower of the World Trade Center in New York City. Twenty minutes later the second tower was struck. Within ninety minutes both towers had collapsed, killing some 2,800 people. A third airliner hit the Pentagon, and a fourth, probably diverted from Washington by a group of courageous passengers, crashed into a field not far from Pittsburgh. It was one of the most horrific days in American history. As Americans searched for historical parallels, they could only come up with the Japanese attack on Pearl Harbor, sixty years before.

The evening of the next day, President George W. Bush spoke to the nation and called the attacks an act of war against the United States by the terrorist group al Qaeda. He ordered the Taliban government of Afghanistan, where the terrorists trained and were protected, to turn over all members of al Qaeda, including their leader Osama bin Laden, or face military attack. He then added that any state that harbored terrorists could expect to suffer severe consequences. With one dissenting vote, Congress voted to give the president the power to take the actions he determined necessary to deal with terrorism.

When the Afghan government refused to cooperate with U.S. demands, Bush quickly cobbled together a disparate coalition and launched an attack against the Taliban leadership and the al Qaeda terrorist organization in Afghanistan. The air war began on October 7, 2001, and by mid-November, the Islamic fundamentalist Taliban regime had collapsed, as troops from the Northern Alliance (an anti-Taliban coalition) entered the capital of Kabul. Resistance continued and Osama bin Laden remained at large, but by early January 2002, the forces of the Taliban were defeated and a primary training ground for anti-Western terrorism was eliminated.

In his State of the Union address delivered that same month, President Bush startled listeners when he identified Iraq, Iran, and North Korea as what he called an "axis of evil." Through the spring and summer of 2002 there was a great deal of verbal sparring between the United States and Iraq over Iraq's refusal to allow UN weapons inspections on its territory. In

September, Bush, in a speech at the United Nations, told the world organization to confront the "grave and gathering danger in Iraq" or stand aside. He insisted that Iraq was building weapons of mass destruction—chemical and biological weapons, and possibly even nuclear weapons—for use against the West. In November, the UN sent weapons inspectors into Iraq backed by a strongly worded resolution that threatened "serious consequences" if Iraq refused to cooperate.

The response from Iraqi president Saddam Hussein was evasive. In February 2003, Bush announced: "Iraq is building and hiding weapons that could enable [Saddam] to dominate the Middle East and intimidate the civilized world—and we will not allow it." The next month, chief weapons inspector Hans Blix reported that Saddam was cooperating and that his group needed more time to verify Iraqi compliance and to continue weapons inspections.

For George Bush, however, the diplomatic process was at an end. On March 17, 2003, he gave Saddam and his sons forty-eight hours to leave Iraq or face war. Three days later, U.S. Tomahawk cruise missiles began hitting targets in Baghdad. In the following days, U.S. and British ground troops entered Iraq from the south. They faced minimal resistance, and on April 9, sooner than anyone expected, U.S. forces entered central Baghdad. Saddam had fled. On May 2, in a celebratory appearance aboard the U.S.S. *Abraham Lincoln,* President Bush declared "mission accomplished." It was a premature statement.

In 1991, after weighing the possible consequences of occupying Iraq, President George H.W. Bush had backed off from invading Baghdad and toppling Saddam. In 2003, his son, George W. Bush, found himself in control of Iraq, essentially a military occupier, with very few allies aside from British prime minister Tony Blair. Although most Iraqis welcomed the fall of Saddam, many did not welcome a military occupation, and by the late summer of 2003 the situation on the ground in Iraq began to grow increasingly violent.

A primary argument President Bush had made for the preemptive strike against Iraq was the urgent need to end Saddam's production of weapons of mass destruction. By late 2003, it was clear that Iraq had no such weapons. Bush had also repeatedly suggested that there was a direct relationship between Iraq and al Qaeda terrorists. In the summer of 2004 a lengthy report by the Senate-appointed 9/11 Commission concluded that there were no significant connections between Saddam Hussein and al Qaeda. Yet Bush administration officials continued to imply that such connections did exist, and that Saddam had had the "capability" of producing weapons of mass destruction. Questions and doubts about the justification for an increasingly costly "war of choice" disquieted the American public.

As the 2004 presidential campaign approached, the nation was once again divided, even polarized. A documentary by Michael Moore, *Fahrenheit 911*, showed a Bush administration detached from the human consequences of the September 11 attacks and the wars in Afghanistan and Iraq. Conservative talk show hosts railed against liberals, whom they accused of being unpatriotic in their lack of fervor for the war. Seeking the Democratic presidential nomination, former Vermont governor Howard Dean received enthusiastic support for his strong stance against the war in Iraq. The Democratic nominee, John Kerry, took a more balanced stance, but in the process failed to offer a clearly defined alternative to the Bush administration's policies. In November 2004, George W. Bush won a second close election to begin his second term in office.

In the early spring of 2005 Iraq held its first national election and a year later formed its first elected government, but the insurgency continued, as did the threat of civil war.

DOCUMENT 20.1
The 2000 Presidential Election: A Contested Outcome

In the 2000 presidential race, Texas governor George W. Bush defeated Vice President Al Gore in a hotly contested election that was tainted—or at least questionable—in the minds of many participants. The first of two texts below is an excerpt from the U.S. Supreme Court decision Bush v. Gore (issued December 12, 2000). The court concluded, for a variety of reasons, that the decision by the Florida Supreme Court to continue the recounting of votes should be overturned and the recount should be ended. The second text is George W. Bush's victory speech, delivered the next day at the Texas State House in Austin.

SOURCE: 531 U.S. (2000) No. 00–949.

Bush v. Gore (December 12, 2000)

The right to vote is protected in more than the initial allocation of the franchise. Equal protection applies as well to the manner of its exercise. Having once granted the right to vote on equal terms, the State may not, by later arbitrary and disparate treatment, value one person's vote over that of another. It must be remembered that "the right of suffrage can be denied by a debasement or dilution of the weight of a citizen's vote just as effectively as by wholly prohibiting the free exercise of the franchise." *Reynolds* v. *Sims,* 377 U.S. 533, 555 (1964).

There is no difference between the two sides of the present controversy on these basic propositions. Respondents say that the very purpose of vindicating the right to vote justifies the recount procedures now at issue. The question before us, however, is whether the recount procedures the Florida Supreme Court has adopted are consistent with its obligation to avoid arbitrary and disparate treatment of the members of its electorate.

Much of the controversy seems to revolve around ballot cards designed to be perforated by a stylus but which, either through error or deliberate omission, have not been perforated with sufficient precision for a machine to count them. In some cases a piece of the card—a chad—is hanging, say by two corners. In other cases there is no separation at all, just an indentation.

The Florida Supreme Court has ordered that the intent of the voter be discerned from such ballots. For purposes of resolving the equal protection challenge, it is not necessary to decide whether the Florida Supreme Court had the authority under the legislative scheme for resolving election disputes to define what a legal vote is and to mandate a manual recount implementing that definition. The recount mechanisms implemented in response to the decisions of the Florida Supreme Court do not satisfy the minimum requirement for non-arbitrary treatment of voters necessary to secure the fundamental right. Florida's basic command for the count of legally cast votes is to consider the "intent of the voter." This is unobjectionable as an abstract proposition and a starting principle. The problem inheres in the absence of specific standards to ensure its equal application. The formulation of uniform rules to determine intent based on these recurring circumstances is practicable and, we conclude, necessary.

The law does not refrain from searching for the intent of the actor in a multitude of circumstances; and in some cases the general command to ascertain intent is not susceptible to much further refinement. In this instance, however, the question is not whether to believe a witness but how to interpret the marks or holes or scratches on an inanimate object, a piece of cardboard or paper which, it is said, might not have registered as a vote during the machine count. The factfinder confronts a thing, not a person. The search for intent can be confined by specific rules designed to ensure uniform treatment.

The want of those rules here has led to unequal evaluation of ballots in various respects. See *Gore* v. *Harris* ("Should a county canvassing board count or not count a 'dimpled chad' where the voter is able to successfully dislodge the chad in every other contest on that ballot? Here, the county canvassing boards disagree"). As seems to have been acknowledged at oral argument, the standards for accepting or rejecting contested ballots might vary not only from county to county but indeed within a single county from one recount team to another.

The record provides some examples. A monitor in Miami-Dade County testified at trial that he observed that three members of the county canvassing board applied different standards in defining a legal vote. And testimony at trial also revealed that at least one county changed its evaluative standards during the counting process. Palm Beach County, for example, began the process with a 1990 guideline which precluded counting completely attached chads, switched to a rule that considered a vote to be legal if any light could be seen through a chad, changed back to the 1990 rule, and then abandoned any pretense of a *per se* rule, only to have a court order that the county consider dimpled chads legal. This is not a process with sufficient guarantees of equal treatment.

The State Supreme Court ratified this uneven treatment. It mandated that the recount totals from two counties, Miami-Dade and Palm Beach, be included in the certified total. The court also appeared to hold *sub silentio* that the recount totals from Broward County, which were not completed until after the original November 14 certification by the Secretary of State, were to be considered part of the new certified vote totals even though the county certification was not contested by Vice President Gore. Yet each of the counties used varying standards to determine what was a legal vote. Broward County used a more forgiving standard than Palm Beach County, and uncovered almost three times as many new votes, a result markedly disproportionate to the difference in population between the counties.

In addition, the recounts in these three counties were not limited to so-called undervotes but extended to all of the ballots. The distinction has real consequences. A manual recount of all ballots identifies not only those ballots which show no vote but also those which contain more than one, the so-called overvotes. Neither category will be counted by the machine. This is not a trivial concern. At oral argument, respondents estimated there are as many as 110,000 overvotes statewide. As a result, the citizen whose ballot was not read by a machine because he failed to vote for a candidate in a way readable by a machine may still have his vote counted in a manual recount; on the other hand, the citizen who marks two candidates in a way discernable by the machine will not have the same opportunity to have his vote count, even if a manual examination of the ballot would reveal the requisite indicia of intent. Furthermore, the citizen who marks two candidates, only one of which is discernable by the machine, will have his vote counted even though it should have been read as an invalid ballot. The State Supreme Court's inclusion of vote counts based on these variant standards exemplifies concerns with the remedial processes that were under way. . . .

The question before the Court is not whether local entities, in the exercise of their expertise, may develop different systems for implementing elections. Instead, we are presented with a situation where a state court with the power to assure uniformity has ordered a statewide recount with minimal procedural safeguards. When a court orders a statewide remedy, there must be at least some assurance that the rudimentary requirements of equal treatment and fundamental fairness are satisfied.

Given the Court's assessment that the recount process underway was probably being conducted in an unconstitutional manner, the Court stayed the order directing the recount so it could hear this case and render an expedited decision. The contest provision, as it was mandated by the State Supreme Court, is not well calculated to sustain the confidence that all citizens must have in the outcome of elections. The State has not shown that its procedures include the necessary safeguards. The problem, for instance, of the estimated 110,000 overvotes has not been addressed. . . .

Upon due consideration of the difficulties identified to this point, it is obvious that the recount cannot be conducted in compliance with the requirements of equal protection and due process without substantial additional work. It would require not only the adoption (after opportunity for argument) of adequate statewide standards for determining what is a legal vote, and practicable procedures to implement them, but also orderly judicial review of any disputed matters that might arise. In addition, the [Florida] Secretary of State has advised that the recount of only a portion of the ballots requires that the vote tabulation equipment be used to screen out undervotes, a function for which the machines were not designed. If a recount of overvotes were also required, perhaps even a second screening would be necessary. Use of the equipment for this purpose, and any new software developed for it, would have to be evaluated for accuracy by the [Florida] Secretary of State. . . .

The Supreme Court of Florida has said that the legislature intended the State's electors to "participat[e] fully in the federal electoral process." . . . That statute, in turn, requires that any controversy or contest that is designed to lead to a conclusive selection of electors be completed by December 12. That date is upon us, and there is no recount procedure in place under the State Supreme Court's order that comports with minimal constitutional standards. Because it is evident that any recount seeking to meet the December 12 date will be unconstitutional for the reasons we have discussed, we reverse the judgment of the Supreme Court of Florida ordering a recount to proceed. . . .

None are more conscious of the vital limits on judicial authority than are the members of this Court, and none stand more in admiration of the Constitution's design to leave the selection of the President to the people, through their legislatures, and to the political sphere. When contending parties invoke the process of the courts, however, it becomes our unsought responsibility to resolve the federal and constitutional issues the judicial system has been forced to confront.

The judgment of the Supreme Court of Florida is reversed, and the case is remanded for further proceedings not inconsistent with this opinion.

Pursuant to this Court's Rule 45.2, the Clerk is directed to issue the mandate in this case forthwith.

It is so ordered.

SOURCE: CNN.com/ELECTION/2000

George W. Bush Declares Victory (December 13, 2000)

Thank you very much.

Good evening, my fellow Americans. I appreciate so very much the opportunity to speak with you tonight.

Mr. Speaker, Lieutenant Governor, friends, distinguished guests, our country has been through a long and trying period, with the outcome of the presidential election not finalized for longer than any of us could ever imagine.

Vice President Gore and I put our hearts and hopes into our campaigns. We both gave it our all. We shared similar emotions, so I understand how difficult this moment must be for Vice President Gore and his family. He has a distinguished record of service to our country as a congressman, a senator and a vice president.

This evening I received a gracious call from the vice president. We agreed to meet early next week in Washington and we agreed to do our best to heal our country after this hard-fought contest.

Tonight I want to thank all the thousands of volunteers and campaign workers who worked so hard on my behalf. I also salute the vice president and his supporters for waging a spirited campaign. And I thank him for a call that I know was difficult for him to make. Laura and I wish the vice president and Senator Lieberman and their families the very best. . . .

Tonight I chose to speak from the chamber of the Texas House of Representatives because it has been a home to bipartisan cooperation. Here, in a place where Democrats have the majority, Republicans and Democrats have worked together to do what is right for the people we represent. We've had spirited disagreements. And in the end, we found constructive consensus. It is an experience I will always carry with me; an example I will always follow. . . .

Across the hall in our Texas capitol is the state Senate. And I cannot help but think of our mutual friend, the former Democrat lieutenant governor, Bob Bullock. His love for Texas and his ability to work in a bipartisan way continue to be a model for all of us.

The spirit of cooperation I have seen in this hall is what is needed in Washington, D.C. It is the challenge of our moment. After a difficult election, we must put politics behind us and work together to make the promise of America available for every one of our citizens. I am optimistic that we can change the tone in Washington, D.C.

I believe things happen for a reason, and I hope the long wait of the last five weeks will heighten a desire to move beyond the bitterness and partisanship of the recent past. Our nation must rise above a house divided. Americans share hopes and goals and values far more important than any political disagreements.

Republicans want the best for our nation, and so do Democrats. Our votes may differ, but not our hopes. I know America wants reconciliation and unity. I know Americans want progress. And we must seize this moment and deliver. Together, guided by a spirit of common sense, common courtesy and common goals, we can unite and inspire the American citizens.

Together, we will work to make all our public schools excellent, teaching every student of every background and every accent, so that no child is left behind.

Together, we will save Social Security and renew its promise of a secure retirement for generations to come.

Together, we will strengthen Medicare and offer prescription drug coverage to all our seniors.

Together, we will give Americans the broad, fair and fiscally responsible tax relief they deserve.

Together, we will have a bipartisan foreign policy true to our values and true to our friends, and we will have a military equal to every challenge and superior to every adversary.

Together we will address some of society's deepest problems one person at a time, by encouraging and empowering the good hearts and good works of the American people.

This is the essence of compassionate conservatism and it will be a foundation of my administration.

During the fall campaign, we differed about the details of these proposals, but there was remarkable consensus about the important issues before us: excellent schools, retirement and health security, tax relief, a strong military, a more civil society. We have discussed our differences. Now it is time to find common ground and build consensus to make America a beacon of opportunity in the 21st century.

I'm optimistic this can happen. Our future demands it and our history proves it. Two hundred years ago, in the election of 1800, America faced another close presidential election. A tie in the Electoral College put the outcome into the hands of Congress. After six days of voting and 36 ballots, the House of Representatives elected Thomas Jefferson the third president of the United States. That election brought the first transfer of power from one party to another in our democracy.

Shortly after the election, Jefferson, in a letter titled "Reconciliation and Reform," wrote this: "The steady character of our countrymen is a rock to which we may safely moor; unequivocal in principle, responsible in manner. We should be able to hope to do a great deal of good to the cause of freedom and harmony."

Two hundred years have only strengthened the steady character of America. And so as we begin the work of healing our nation, tonight I call upon that character: respect for each other, respect for our differences, generosity of spirit, and a willingness to work hard and work together to solve any problem.

I have something else to ask you, to ask every American. I ask for you to pray for this great nation. I ask for your prayers for leaders of both parties. I thank you for your prayers for me and my family, and I ask you to pray for Vice President Gore and his family.

I have faith that with God's help we as a nation will move forward together as one nation, indivisible. And together we will create an America that is open, so every citizen has access to the American dream; an America that is educated, so every child has the keys to realize that dream; and an America that is united in our diversity and our shared American values that are larger than race or party.

I was not elected to serve one party, but to serve one nation. The President of the United States is the president of every single American, of every race and every background. Whether you voted for me or not, I will do my best to serve your interests and I will work to earn your respect.

I will be guided by President Jefferson's sense of purpose, to stand for principle, to be reasonable in manner, and above all, to do great good for the cause of freedom and harmony. The presidency is more than an honor. It is more than an office. It is a charge to keep, and I will give it my all.

Thank you very much, and God bless America.

DOCUMENT 20.2
"Our Very Freedom Came Under Attack."
President George W. Bush Addresses the Nation
on the Evening of September 11, 2001

The events of September 11, 2001, were devastating to Americans. The tragedy awakened a great wave of patriotism. Flags waved everywhere. Money poured into New York to aid the victims' families. "Ground Zero" became a sacred site. Polls showed that the public wanted quick and decisive action against the perpetrators of those awful murders.

On the night of the events, President Bush addressed a stunned nation. His voice was tense as he told the American people that the nation may have taken a blow from a ruthless enemy, but it was still strong.

SOURCE: whitehouse.gov/news/releases/20010911.

Good evening. Today, our fellow citizens, our way of life, our very freedom came under attack in a series of deliberate and deadly terrorist acts. The victims were in airplanes or in their offices: secretaries, businessmen and women, military and federal workers, moms and dads, friends and neighbors.

Thousands of lives were suddenly ended by evil, despicable acts of terror. The pictures of airplanes flying into buildings, fires burning, huge structures collapsing have filled us with disbelief, terrible sadness and a quiet, unyielding anger.

These acts of mass murder were intended to frighten our nation into chaos and retreat. But they have failed. Our country is strong. A great people has been moved to defend a great nation.

Terrorist attacks can shake the foundations of our biggest buildings, but they cannot touch the foundation of America. These acts shatter steel, but they cannot dent the steel of American resolve.

America was targeted for attack because we're the brightest beacon for freedom and opportunity in the world. And no one will keep that light from shining.

Today, our nation saw evil, the very worst of human nature, and we responded with the best of America, with the daring of our rescue workers, with the caring for strangers and neighbors who came to give blood and help in any way they could.

Immediately following the first attack, I implemented our government's emergency response plans. Our military is powerful, and it's prepared. Our emergency teams are working in New York City and Washington, D.C., to help with local rescue efforts.

Our first priority is to get help to those who have been injured and to take every precaution to protect our citizens at home and around the world from further attacks.

The functions of our government continue without interruption. Federal agencies in Washington which had to be evacuated today are reopening for essential personnel tonight and will be open for business tomorrow.

Our financial institutions remain strong, and the American economy will be open for business as well.

The search is underway for those who are behind these evil acts. I've directed the full resources for our intelligence and law enforcement communities to find those responsible and bring them to justice. We will make no distinction between the terrorists who committed these acts and those who harbor them.

I appreciate so very much the members of Congress who have joined me in strongly condemning these attacks. And on behalf of the American people, I thank the many world leaders who have called to offer their condolences and assistance.

America and our friends and allies join with all those who want peace and security in the world and we stand together to win the war against terrorism.

Tonight I ask for your prayers for all those who grieve, for the children whose worlds have been shattered, for all whose sense of safety and security has been threatened. And I pray they will be comforted by a power greater than any of us spoken through the ages in Psalm 23: "Even though I walk through the valley of the shadow of death, I fear no evil for you are with me."

This is a day when all Americans from every walk of life unite in our resolve for justice and peace. America has stood down enemies before, and we will do so this time. None of us will ever forget this day, yet we go forward to defend freedom and all that is good and just in our world.

Thank you. Good night and God bless America.

DOCUMENT 20.3
"States Like These . . . Constitute an Axis of Evil."
President George W. Bush's State of the Union Address (January 2002)

As the American people were taking satisfaction from the success of the drive to topple the Taliban regime in Afghanistan, President George W. Bush, in his 2002 State of the Union message, told his listeners that there was an "axis of evil" in the world. He was referring to Iraq, Iran, and North Korea, "rogue nations," as they were being called, and he appeared to have them in the crosshairs. Would the United States try to overthrow these governments? Not long after his State of the Union speech, the president and his advisors began talking of "regime change" in Iraq. By the beginning of 2003, it was clear that Bush was determined to take the country to war against his father's old enemy.

SOURCE: whitehouse.gove/news/releases/20020129.

As we gather tonight, our nation is at war, our economy is in recession, and the civilized world faces unprecedented dangers. Yet the state of our Union has never been stronger.

We last met in an hour of shock and suffering. In four short months, our nation has comforted the victims, begun to rebuild New York and the Pentagon, rallied a great coalition, captured, arrested, and rid the world of thousands of terrorists, destroyed Afghanistan's terrorist training camps, saved a people from starvation, and freed a country from brutal oppression.

The American flag flies again over our embassy in Kabul. Terrorists who once occupied Afghanistan now occupy cells at Guantanamo Bay. And terrorist leaders who urged followers to sacrifice their lives are running for their own.

America and Afghanistan are now allies against terror. We will be partners in rebuilding that country, and this evening we welcome the distinguished interim leader of a liberated Afghanistan: Chairman Hamid Karzai.

The last time we met in this chamber, the mothers and daughters of Afghanistan were captives in their own homes, forbidden from working or going to school. Today, women are free, and are part of Afghanistan's new government. . . .

Our progress is a tribute to the spirit of the Afghan people, to the resolve of our coalition, and to the might of the United States military. When I called our troops into action, I did so with complete confidence in their courage and skill, and tonight, thanks to them, we are winning the war against terror. The men and women of our armed forces have delivered a message, now clear to every enemy of the United States: Even seven thousand miles away, across oceans and continents, on mountaintops and in caves, you will not escape the justice of this nation. . . .

Our cause is just, and it continues. Our discoveries in Afghanistan confirmed our worst fears, and show us the true scope of the task ahead. We have seen the depth of our enemies' hatred in videos where they laugh about the loss of innocent life. And the depth of their hatred is equaled by the madness of the destruction they design. We have found diagrams of American nuclear power plants and public water facilities, detailed instructions for making chemical weapons, surveillance maps of American cities, and thorough descriptions of landmarks in America and throughout the world.

What we have found in Afghanistan confirms that—far from ending there—our war against terror is only beginning. Most of the nineteen men who hijacked planes on September 11th were trained in Afghanistan's camps—and so were tens of thousands of others. Thousands of dangerous killers, schooled in the methods of murder, often supported by outlaw regimes, are now spread throughout the world like ticking time bombs—set to go off without warning.

Thanks to the work of our law enforcement officials and coalition partners, hundreds of terrorists have been arrested—yet tens of thousands of trained terrorists are still at large. These enemies view the entire world as a battlefield, and we must pursue them wherever they are. So long as training camps operate, so long as nations harbor terrorists, freedom is at risk—and America and our allies must not, and will not, allow it.

Our nation will continue to be steadfast, and patient, and persistent in the pursuit of two great objectives. First, we will shut down terrorist camps, disrupt terrorist plans, and bring terrorists to justice. Second, we must prevent the terrorists and regimes who seek chemical, biological, or nuclear weapons from threatening the United States and the world.

Our military has put the terror training camps of Afghanistan out of business, yet camps still exist in at least a dozen countries. A terrorist underworld—including groups like Hamas, Hezbollah, Islamic Jihad, and Jaish-i-Mohammed—operates in remote jungles and deserts, and hides in the centers of large cities. . . .

Our second goal is to prevent regimes that sponsor terror from threatening America or our friends and allies with weapons of mass destruction. Some of these regimes have been pretty quiet since September 11th. But we know their true nature. North Korea is a regime arming with missiles and weapons of mass destruction, while starving its citizens.

Iran aggressively pursues these weapons and exports terror, while an unelected few repress the Iranian people's hope for freedom.

Iraq continues to flaunt its hostility toward America and to support terror. The Iraqi regime has plotted to develop anthrax, and nerve gas, and nuclear weapons for over a decade. This is a regime that has already used poison gas to murder thousands of its own citizens—leaving the bodies of mothers huddled over their dead children. This is a regime that agreed to international inspections—then kicked out the inspectors. This is a regime that has something to hide from the civilized world.

States like these, and their terrorist allies, constitute an axis of evil, arming to threaten the peace of the world. By seeking weapons of mass destruction, these regimes pose a grave and growing danger. They could provide these arms to terrorists, giving them the means to match their hatred. They could attack our allies or attempt to blackmail the United States. In any of these cases, the price of indifference would be catastrophic.

We will work closely with our coalition to deny terrorists and their state sponsors the materials, technology, and expertise to make and deliver weapons of mass destruction. We will develop and deploy effective missile defenses to protect America and our allies from sudden attack. And all nations should know, America will do what is necessary to ensure our nation's security.

We will be deliberate, yet time is not on our side. I will not wait on events, while dangers gather. I will not stand by, as peril draws closer and closer. The United States of America will not permit the world's most dangerous regimes to threaten us with the world's most destructive weapons.

Our war on terror is well begun, but it is only begun. This campaign may not be finished on our watch—yet it must be and it will be waged on our watch.

We cannot stop short. If we stopped now—leaving terror camps intact and terror states unchecked—our sense of security would be false and temporary. History has called America and our allies to action, and it is both our responsibility and our privilege to fight freedom's fight. . . .

September 11th brought out the best in America, and the best in this Congress, and I join the American people in applauding your unity and resolve. Now Americans deserve to have this same spirit directed toward addressing problems here at home. I am a proud member of my Party—yet as we act to win the war, protect our people, and create jobs in America, we must act first and foremost not as Republicans, not as Democrats, but as Americans. . . .

None of us would ever wish the evil that was done on September 11th, yet after America was attacked, it was as if our entire country looked into a mirror and saw our better selves. We were reminded that we are citizens, with obligations to each other, to our country, and to history. We began to think less of the goods we can accumulate, and more about the good we can do.

For too long our culture has said, "If it feels good, do it." Now America is embracing a new ethic and a new creed: "Let's roll." In the sacrifice of soldiers, the fierce brotherhood of firefighters, and the bravery and generosity of ordinary citizens, we have glimpsed what a new culture of responsibility could look like. We want to be a nation that serves goals larger than self. We have been offered a unique opportunity, and we must not let this moment pass. . . .

America will lead by defending liberty and justice because they are right and true and unchanging for all people everywhere. No nation owns these aspirations, and no nation is exempt from them. We have no intention of imposing our culture—but America will always stand firm for the non-negotiable demands of human dignity: the rule of law, limits on the power of the state, respect for women, private property, free speech, equal justice, and religious tolerance.

America will take the side of brave men and women who advocate these values around the world—including the Islamic world—because we have a greater objective than eliminating threats and containing resentment. We seek a just and peaceful world beyond the war on terror.

In this moment of opportunity, a common danger is erasing old rivalries. America is working with Russia, China, and India in ways we never have before to achieve peace and prosperity. In every region, free markets and free trade and free societies are proving their power to lift lives. Together with friends and allies from Europe to Asia, from Africa to Latin America, we will demonstrate that the forces of terror cannot stop the momentum of freedom.

The last time I spoke here, I expressed the hope that life would return to normal. In some ways, it has. In others, it never will. Those of us who have lived through these challenging times have been changed by them. We've come to know truths that we will never question. Evil is real, and it must be opposed. Beyond all differences of race or creed, we are one country, mourning together and facing danger together. Deep in the American character, there is honor, and it is stronger than cynicism. Many have discovered again that even in tragedy—especially in tragedy—God is near. . . .

Steadfast in our purpose, we now press on. We have known freedom's price. We have shown freedom's power. And in this great conflict, my fellow Americans, we will see freedom's victory.

Thank you, and may God bless the United States of America.

DOCUMENT 20.4
The 9/11 Commission Report (2004)

The 9/11 Commission was established by Congress to pull together all relevant material concerning the terrorist attacks of September 11, 2001. The result was the 9/11 Commission Report, *published in 2004. Its primary directive, as stated in the report's preface, was to answer two questions: How did this happen and how can we avoid such tragedy again? The 567-page report was published commercially and immediately hit the* New York Times *bestseller list. As promised, it covered every conceivable aspect of the attacks. Also as promised, the report made recommendations on how to stop future terrorist acts. One such recommendation was the establishment of a National Intelligence Director to oversee an ever-widening and diverse intelligence network.*

When the report was published, there was a great deal of pressure on the president and Congress to get behind the commission's recommendations. But President Bush and several members of Congress balked at the proposal to place an independent director above the CIA and other intelligence agencies. This hesitation on the part of the president soon created an impression he was rejecting the committee's recommendations and in the end, he reluctantly supported the plan.

Below is the controversial section of the commission's report recommending the appointment of a National Intelligence Director. In the spring of 2005, President Bush named John Negroponte to the post.

SOURCE: Thomas H. Kean, Lee H. Hamilton, et al., *The 9/11 Commission Report: Final Report of the National Commission on Terrorist Attacks Upon the United States* (New York, 2004).

Recommendation: The current position of Director of Central Intelligence should be replaced by a National Intelligence Director with two main areas of responsibility: (1) to oversee national intelligence centers on specific subjects of interest across the U.S. government and (2) to manage the national intelligence program and oversee the agencies that contribute to it.

First, the National Intelligence Director should oversee national intelligence centers to provide all-source analysis and plan intelligence operations for the whole government on major problems.

One such problem is counterterrorism. In this case, we believe that the center should be the intelligence entity (formerly TTIC) inside the National Counterterrorism Center [NCTC] we have proposed. It would sit there alongside the operations management unit we described earlier, with both making up the NCTC, in the Executive Office of the President. Other national intelligence centers—for instance, on counterproliferation, crime and narcotics, and China—would be housed in whatever department or agency is best suited for them.

The National Intelligence Director would retain the present DCI's [Director of Central Intelligence] role as the principal intelligence adviser to the president. We hope the president will come to look directly to the directors of the national intelligence centers to provide all-source analysis in their areas of responsibility, balancing the advice of these intelligence chiefs against the contrasting viewpoints that may be offered by department heads at State, Defense, Homeland Security, Justice, and other agencies.

Second, the National Intelligence Director should manage the national intelligence program and oversee the component agencies of the intelligence community.

The National Intelligence Director would submit a unified budget for national intelligence that reflects priorities chosen by the National Security Council, an appropriate balance among the varieties of technical and human intelligence collection, and analysis. He or she would receive an appropriation for national intelligence and apportion the funds to the appropriate agencies, in line with that budget, and with authority to reprogram funds among the national intelligence agencies to meet any new priority (as counterterrorism was in the 1990s). The National Intelligence Director should approve and submit nominations to the president of the individuals who would lead the CIA, DIA [Defense Intelligence Agency], FBI Intelligence Office, NSA [National Security Agency], NGA [National Geospatial-Intelligence Agency], NRO [National Reconnaissance Office], Information Analysis and Infrastructure Protection Directorate of the Department of Homeland Security, and other national intelligence capabilities.

The National Intelligence Director would manage this national effort with the help of three deputies, each of whom would also hold a key position in one of the component agencies.

> Foreign intelligence (the head of the CIA)
> Defense intelligence (the under secretary of defense for intelligence)
> Homeland intelligence (the FBI's executive assistant director for intel-
> ligence or the under secretary of homeland security information
> analysis and infrastructure protection)

Other agencies in the intelligence community would coordinate their work within each of these three areas, largely staying housed in the same departments or agencies that support them now.

Returning to the analogy of the Defense Department's organization, these three deputies—like the leaders of the Army, Navy, Air Force, or Marines—would have the job of acquiring the systems, training the people, and executing the operations planned by the national intelligence centers.

And, just as the combatant commanders also report to the secretary of defense, the directors of the national intelligence centers—e.g., for counterproliferation, crime and narcotics, and the rest—also would report to the National Intelligence Director.

The Defense Department's military intelligence programs—the joint military intelligence program (JMIP) and the tactical intelligence and related activities program (TIARA)—would remain part of that department's responsibility.

The National Intelligence Director would set personnel policies to establish standards for education and training and facilitate assignments at the national intelligence centers and across agency lines. The National Intelligence Director also would set information sharing and information technology policies to maximize data sharing, as well as policies to protect the security of information.

Too many agencies now have an opportunity to say no to change. The National Intelligence Director should participate in an NSC executive committee that can resolve differences in priorities among the agencies and bring the major disputes to the president for decision.

The National Intelligence Director should be located in the Executive Office of the President. This official, who would be confirmed by the Senate and would testify before Congress, would have a relatively small staff of several hundred people, taking the place of the existing community management offices housed at the CIA. . . .

We are wary of too easily equating government management problems with those of the private sector. But we have noticed that some very large private firms rely on a powerful CEO who has significant control over how money is spent and can hire or fire leaders of the major divisions, assisted by a relatively modest staff, while leaving responsibility for execution in the operating divisions.

There are disadvantages to separating the position of National Intelligence Director from the job of heading the CIA. For example, the National Intelligence Director will not head a major agency of his or her own and may have a weaker base of support. But we believe that these disadvantages are outweighed by several other considerations:

The National Intelligence Director must be able to directly oversee intelligence collection inside the United States. Yet law and custom has counseled against giving such a plain domestic role to the head of the CIA.

The CIA will be one among several claimants for funds in setting national priorities. The National Intelligence Director should not be both one of the advocates and the judge of them all.

Covert operations tend to be highly tactical, requiring close attention. The National Intelligence Director should rely on the relevant joint mission center to oversee these details, helping to coordinate closely with the White House.

The CIA will be able to concentrate on building the capabilities to carry out such operations and on providing the personnel who will be directing and executing such operations in the field.

Rebuilding the analytic and human intelligence collection capabilities of the CIA should be a full-time effort, and the director of the CIA should focus on extending its comparative advantages.

BIOGRAPHICAL SKETCH
Condoleezza Rice

The position of the national security advisor is almost always low-profile, generally out of the public eye. But that figure serves as the chief advisor to the president on national security issues and foreign policy matters.

The National Security Council (NSC) was created in the Truman administration as part of Truman's governmental reorganization of the national security apparatus. The function of the NSC, as outlined in the 1947 act, is to advise the president on foreign and military policies relating to national security. The National Security Council is chaired by the president, and its regular attendees include the vice president, the secretaries of state, defense, and the treasury; and the national security advisor, known officially as the Assistant to the President for National Security Affairs. The chairman of the

Joint Chiefs of Staff also sits on the NSC, as does the director of national intelligence (prior to the reorganization of the intelligence hierarchy, the CIA director attended the NSC meetings). At the president's pleasure, others may sit on the council, including the attorney general, the president's chief of staff, and others.

Most national security advisors have served quietly behind the scenes, but at various times the national security advisor (NSA) has become high profile. Possibly the most visible was Henry Kissinger, who served as Nixon's national security advisor from 1969 until 1975, after which he became secretary of state. Other national security advisors of note include McGeorge Bundy, who served under Kennedy and then into the Johnson administration as the war in Vietnam was escalating. Zbigniew Brzezinski served Jimmy Carter. Colin Powell was NSA at the end of the Reagan administration. Sandy Berger served during Clinton's second term.

President George W. Bush's first national security advisor, Condoleezza Rice, was extremely popular with the American public. She cultivated a nonpartisan image and seemed to smooth the edges of the administration's hard-line positions on many issues. Candidate Bush notoriously lacked depth in foreign policy and national security affairs, and Rice was initially recruited to conduct "seminars" designed to school him on these issues. Their working partnership continued throughout the first Bush term. In January 2005, Rice was named secretary of state in George W. Bush's second administration.

Rice's life is one of those great American stories of overcoming almost impossible odds. She was born in Birmingham, Alabama, in 1954, at a time when African Americans in the South could not sit at lunch counters, let alone rise to the highest positions in government. Her parents believed that education—far more than anything else—would allow their talented daughter to rise above the racism and segregation of that place and time. The young Ms. Rice evidently took that to heart; she was able to enroll at the University of Denver at age fifteen. In an interesting confluence of historical events, it was Denver professor Josef Korbel, the father of Clinton's secretary of state Madeleine Albright, who inspired Rice to study international relations and, more specifically, the Soviet Union.

By age twenty-six, Rice had earned her doctorate from the Denver School of International Studies (the school founded by Korbel) and became a fellow at Stanford University's Center for International Security and Arms Control. After serving as the Soviet affairs advisor on the National Security Council in the administration of George H.W. Bush, she returned to Stanford to become the first female, the first African American, and the youngest provost in the university's history. Her books include *Germany Unified and Europe Transformed* (1995) with Philip Zelikow; *The Gorbachev Era* (1986), edited with Alexander Dallin; and *Uncertain Allegiance: The Soviet Union and the Czechoslovak Army* (1984).

STUDY QUESTIONS

1. Americans sometimes compare the September 11 attacks to the Japanese attack on Pearl Harbor. How, in fact, do these two events compare?
2. The Supreme Court had voted strongly for states' rights on nearly every issue before it for almost eight years. Why, do you think, in 2000, it was willing to overturn a unanimous state supreme court decision?
3. Why do you think George W. Bush focused his 2000 victory speech on the topic of national and political unity?
4. What were George W. Bush's reasons for invading Iraq? How did his reasoning differ from his father's reasons for invading Kuwait and Iraq in 1991?
5. How does President George W. Bush perceive tyranny? What, according to his State of the Union message, does he plan to do about it?

FURTHER READINGS

Douglas Brinkley, Kenneth Starr, et al., *36 Days: The Complete Chronicle of the 2000 Presidential Election Crisis* (2001).
John Miller and Michael Stone, *The Cell: Inside the 9/11 Plot and Why the FBI and CIA Failed to Stop It* (2002).
Kenneth Pollack, *The Threatening Storm: The Case for Invading Iraq* (2002).
Bob Woodward, *Bush at War* (2003).

About the Editor

Gary A. Donaldson is Professor of History at Xavier University in New Orleans where he specializes in twentieth century U.S. history and teaches courses on modern America, historiography and research, U.S. history survey, and world civilizations. His publications include *The Second Reconstruction: A History of the Modern Civil Rights Movement; America at War Since 1945: Politics and Diplomacy in Korea, Vietnam, and the Gulf War; American Foreign Policy: The Twentieth Century in Documents; The History of African Americans in the Military; Truman Defeats Dewey; The First Modern Campaign: Kennedy-Nixon and the Election of 1960;* and *Liberalism's Last Hurrah: The Presidential Campaign of 1964.*